SERVICE MANUAL

FOR

Viper, Venom, MSS, 'Clubman' 'Scrambler' Models and Thruxton Supplement

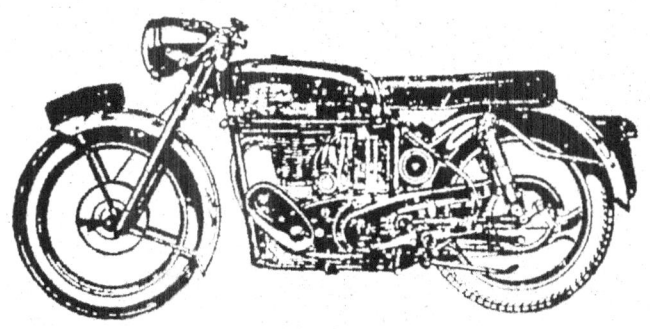

PAGE NUMBERS

The total number of pages in this manual is 204. However, the Service Manual and the Parts Manual have their own individual page numbers. The Parts Manual begins immediately after page 124 of the Service Manual.

INTRODUCTION

Welcome to the world of digital publishing ~ the book you now hold in your hand was printed using the latest state of the art digital technology. The advent of print-on-demand has forever changed the publishing process, never has information been so accessible and it is our hope that this book serves your informational needs for years to come. If this is your first exposure to digital publishing, we hope that you are pleased with the results. Many more titles of interest to the classic automobile and motorcycle enthusiast, collector and restorer are available via our website at www.VelocePress.com. We hope that you find this title as interesting as we do.

NOTE FROM THE PUBLISHER

The information presented is true and complete to the best of our knowledge. All recommendations are made without any guarantees on the part of the author or the publisher, who also disclaim all liability incurred with the use of this information.

TRADEMARKS

We recognize that some words, model names and designations, for example, mentioned herein are the property of the trademark holder. We use them for identification purposes only. This is not an official publication.

INFORMATION ON THE USE OF THIS PUBLICATION

This manual is an invaluable resource for those interested in performing their own maintenance. However, in today's information age we are constantly subject to changes in common practice, new technology, availability of improved materials and increased awareness of chemical toxicity. As such, it is advised that the user consult with an experienced professional prior to undertaking any procedure described herein. While every care has been taken to ensure correctness of information, it is obviously not possible to guarantee complete freedom from errors or omissions or to accept liability arising from such errors or omissions. Therefore, any individual that uses the information contained within, or elects to perform or participate in do-it-yourself repairs or modifications acknowledges that there is a risk factor involved and that the publisher or its associates cannot be held responsible for personal injury or property damage resulting from the use of the information or the outcome of such procedures.

WARNING!

One final word of advice, this publication is intended to be used as a reference guide, and when in doubt the reader should consult with a qualified technician.

FOREWORD

This Service Manual is issued as a guide to the complete servicing and repair of the Viper, Venom, MSS, Clubman, and Scrambler models and is intended primarily for the use of Agents and Repairers.

Intentionally omitted are some of the various routine maintenance jobs and adjustments already covered by the Owners' Handbook for the same model as these are usually undertaken by the rider.

References are made in places to special Service Tools which are essential for certain operations. It is earnestly hoped that Agents and Repairers will equip their workshops with them. They avoid the risk of damaging components and save so much labour that their acquisition is well justified.

It is possible that some private owners who are in the habit of doing most of their own repairs will obtain copies of this book. To any of these we suggest that in their own interest they entrust any repairs, which are likely to prove beyond their capacity, to their local Agent and not "bite off more than they can chew."

If you are in any doubt as to the correct method to adopt in carrying out any of the instructions given in this Manual, ask our Technical Staff for help.

The Supplement deals exclusively with the THRUXTON and details the variations to and in substitution of, the instructions given for the Venom Clubman.

MARCH 1971   2½M.

Publication No. F484/11R.

WHEN MAKING ANY ENQUIRY RELATING TO THE MACHINE AND WHEN ORDERING SPARES FOR IT

ALWAYS BE SURE TO QUOTE

THE ENGINE PREFIX LETTERS AS WELL AS THE SERIAL NUMBER (AND SUFFIX IF ANY). THE VARIOUS MODELS ARE NUMBERED FROM ZERO ONWARDS SO THAT THE NUMERALS ALONE DO NOT IDENTIFY THE TYPE AND THUS ARE INSUFFICIENT ALONE FOR INDICATING THE MODEL REFERRED TO.

CONTENTS

A.
	Page
Air cleaner. Maintenance of	71
Ammeter. Testing	73
Automatic timing unit. Removal of	39
Automatic timing unit. (Illustration)	40
Automatic voltage regulator	80

B.
Ball valve assembly	20
Ball valve assembly. (Illustration)	18
Ballrace retaining ring tool. (Illustration)	53
Battery. Filling and charging	83
Battery. Maintenance and storage of	84
Big-end bearing. Overhauling	45
Big-end rollers. Oversizes of	45
Brake assembly. Front	11
Brake assembly. Rear	55
Brake adjustment. Rear. (Illustration)	88
Brakes. Relining	56

C.
Carburetter. (Illustration)	70
Carburetter. Sectional view	63, 64
Carburetter, Description of	62
Carburetter. Dismantling, etc.	62
Carburetter. Setting and adjusting	71
Chain adjustment. (Primary)	88
Chain adjustment. (Primary) (Illustration)	37
Chain adjustment. (Rear)	89
Chain adjustment. (Rear) (Illustration)	88
Cleaning the machine	91
Clutch. Description of working	29
Clutch. Diagram of operating mechanism	28
Clutch. Dismantling	50
Clutch. Reassembling	50
Clutch. Adjustment of	29
Clutch adjustment. (Illustration)	30
Clutch thrust bearing	50
Commutator. Cleaning	77
Commutator connections. (Illustration)	76

	Page
Compression Plates	39
Coil Ignition	49, 113
Coil Ignition System	115
Crankcase. Separating	43
Crankcase. Main bearings	43
Crankcase suction filter	21
Crankcase suction filter. (Illustration)	21
Crankshaft timing-pinion. Removal of	43
Crankshaft-pinion extractor. (Illustration)	43
Cut-out. Adjustment of	83
Cut-out. (Illustration)	81
Cylinder. Removal of	39
Cylinder. Refitting	46
Cylinder bore diameter	39
Cylinder head. Removal of	24
Cylinder head. Refitting	26

D.
Decarbonising and grinding in valves	23
Dynamo belt adjustment	80
Dynamo belt adjustment (Illustration)	22
Dynamo belt cover. Removal of	33
Dynamo. Dismantling and reassembling	77
Dynamo. Exploded view	78
Dynamo. Removal of	33
Dynamo. Testing	74
Dynamo. Special spanner	79

E.
Engine bearings	43
Engine lubrication system	18
Engine. Overhauling	39
Engine. Removal from frame	38
Engine shaft shock absorber	23

F.
Fabric oil filter	21
Fabric oil filter. (Illustration)	18
Flywheel assembly. Lining up	46
Flywheel assembly. Overhauling	45
Flywheel assembly. Refitting	44
Fork. Description of working	13
Fork. Dismantling	16
Fork. Maintenance of	16
Fork. Reassembling	17
Fork. (Sectional illustration)	14

G.

	Page.
Gearbox bearings	52
Gearbox. Dismantling	51
Gearbox end cover. (Illustration).	37
Gearbox Reassembling	54
Gearbox. Removal from frame	38
Gearbox. Separating from engine	38
Gear operating mechanism	52

H.

Headlamp. (Illustration)	75
Hub (Front). (Sectional illustration)	10
Hub. (Rear). (Sectional illustration)	56
Hub bearings. (Front). Dismantling	11
Hub bearings. (Rear). Dismantling	56

I.

Intermediate timing gear adjustment	48
Intermediate timing gear. (Illustration)	48
Index to Illustrations	5

K.

Kickstart mechanism. (Illustration)	37
Kickstart mechanism. Dismantling	35
Kickstart mechanism. Reassembling	38
Kickstart return spring. Replacing	36

L.

Lamps	73
Lamp bulbs	73
Lighting set	73
Lubrication of chains	87
Lubrication of engine	18
Lubrication of fork	16
Lubrication of gearbox	6
Lubrication of magneto	86
Lubrication of wheel bearings	11 & 57

M.

Main bearings. Removal	43
Main bearings. Refitting	44
Maintenance. Periodical	101
Magneto. Maintenance	88
Magneto. Removal	89
Magneto. Refitting	89
Magneto. Testing	88
Magneto. Timing	49
Magneto. (Illustration)	87

O.

	Page.
Oil circulation system	18
Oil filter (Suction)	21
Oil filter (Suction). (Illustration)	21
Oil filter (Fabric)	18
Oil filter (Fabric). (Illustration)	18
Oil-pump. Priming	19
Oil-pump. Overhaul	40
Oil-pump. Removal	40
Oil-pump. Removal. (Illustration)	41
Oil-pump alignment tool. (Illustration)	41,42
Oil. Recommended grades	6

P.

Phases of throttle opening. (Illustration)	66
Petrol tap and strainer. (Illustration)	72
Piston. Removal	39
Piston. Refitting	46
Piston ring gaps	7
Primary chain. Removal	33
Primary chain. Refitting	34
Primary chain adjustment. (Illustration)	37
Primary chain case. Removal	33
Primary chain case. Refitting	35

R.

Rear suspension. Adjustment	58
Rear suspension adjustment. (Illustration)	58
Rear suspension. Maintenance	58
Rear suspension units	58
Rocker box. Removal	23
Rocker box. Refitting	26
Retiming ignition	49

S.

Scrambler models	94
Shock absorber. Removal	23
Sleeve gear nut. Refitting	34
Sleeve gear nut adaptor. (Illustration)	35,36
Sleeve gear nut and spanner. (Illustration)	35,36
Sparking plug. Maintenance	73
Steering head bearing. Adjustment	12

	Page.
Steering head. (Illustration)	12
Steering head bearing tool. (Illustration)	15

T.

	Page.
Tappet adjustment. (Illustration)	25
Tappet clearances	7
Technical data	7
Theoretical wiring diagram	82
Timing gear	47
Timing gear markings. (Illustration)	48
Timing-pinion. Removal	43
Timing cover. Removal	39
Torque arms. Removal	60
Torque arms. Realignment	61
Torque arm clamp tool. (Illustration)	60
Transfers. Instructions for fixing	90
Trunnion shaft. Removal	60
Trunnion shaft. Refitting	61
Tyres. Maintenance	91
Tyre pressures	19

V.

	Page.
Valves. Refacing and grinding in	24
Valves. Removal. (Illustration)	24
Valve guide. Renewal	27
Valve guide location. (Illustration)	27
Voltage regulator. Testing and adjusting	80

W.

	Page.
Wheel bearings (Front). Removal	11
Wheel bearing (Rear). Removal	55
Wheel bearings	11 & 56

Thruxton 500 Supplement 103/115

Index to Illustrations

		Page
Fig.	1—Front hub—Sectional View	10
,,	2—The steering head	12
,,	3—The Velocette telescopic fork	14
,,	4—Draw bolt for fitting head bearing cups	15
,,	5—Oil tank, ball valve, and filter	18
,,	6—Crankcase suction filter	21
,,	7—Dynamo belt adjustment, etc.	22
,,	8—Adjustment of tappets	25
,,	9—Setting of valve guides	27
,,	10—Diagram of clutch operating mechanism	28
,,	11—Adjustment of clutch	30
,,	12—Sleeve gear nut and peg spanner	34
,,	13—Sleeve gear nut adapter X2959	35 & 36
,,	14—Kickstart ratchet and springs	37
,,	15—The gearbox end cover, etc.	37
,,	16—Lucas automatic timing unit	40
,,	17—Removal of oil-pump and crankshaft pinion	41
,,	18—Pump alignment tool X2719	41, 42
,,	19—Crankshaft pinion extractor X2721	43
,,	19a—Crankpin extractor and assembly tool	45
,,	20—Positions of timing marks	48
,,	21—Ballrace retaining ring tool X2725	53
,,	22—Positions of selector forks	54
,,	23—Rear hub assembly. Sectional view	56
,,	24—Rear suspension adjustment	58
,,	25—Assembly tool X2992	59
,,	26—Torque tube clamp tool X2938	60
,,	27—The Amal carburetter (Section)	63, 64
,,	28—Section through pilot passages	64, 65
,,	29—Phases of throttle openings	66
,,	30—The Carburetter	69, 70
,,	31—Fuel tap and strainer	72
,,	33—Miller type 79 CV headlamp	75
,,	34—Miller dynamo. Commutator end	76
,,	35—Miller dynamo. Exploded view	78
,,	36—Miller bearing lock ring spanner	79
,,	37—Miller cut-out	81
,,	39—Theoretical diagram. (Miller dynamo and Regulator)	82
,,	40—Lucas type KIF magneto	85
,,	41—Rear brake and rear chain adjustment	88

THRUXTON SUPPLEMENT

Fig.	43—Amal G.P.2 Carburetter	106
,,	44—Front Hub and Brake	104
,,	45—Wiring Diagram (Lucas Lighting Set)	109
,,	—Lucas Diagram	110
,,	—Contact Breaker	110
,,	8—Lucas Contact Breaker, dismantled	112
,,	9—Lucas adjustment of Contact Breaker	112
,,	1—6ca—Contact Breaker Assembly	117
,,	—Lucas Stop Tail Lamp	122

RECOMMENDED LUBRICANTS

	B.P.	DUCKHAMS	MOBILOIL	SHELL	CASTROL	FILTRATE
ENGINE: Summer Ambient temperatures above 60° Fahrenheit	Visco-Static* or Energol SAE 40	Q20/50*	Special* or 'BB'	Shell Super* Motor Oil or X100-40	GTX	Plus 20/50 Oil
ENGINE: Winter Ambient temperatures below 60° Fahrenheit	Visco-Static* or Energol SAE 30	Q20/50*	Special* or 'A'	Shell Super* Motor Oil or X100 '30'	GTX	Plus 10/30 Oil
GEARBOX	Energol SAE 40	Q20/50	'BB' or Mobilube GX90	X100 '40'	GTX	Plus 20/50 Oil
FRONT FORK	En. SAE '20' W	NOL 'Ten'	Arctic	X100 20W	Castrolite	Zero 20/20W
WHEEL HUB BEARINGS	Energrease L2	LB10	Mobilgrease MP or Mobilgrease Spl.	Retinax 'A'	Castrolease LM	Super Lithium Grease
PRIMARY CHAIN	Energol SAE 40	Q20/50	'BB'	X100 '40'	GTX	Plus 20/50 Oil
REAR CHAIN	Energrease L2	LB10	Mobilgrease MP or Mobilgrease Spl.	Retinax 'A'	Castrolease Graphited	Linklyfe or Super Lithium Grease
FOR GREASE GUN	Energrease L2	LB10	Mobilgrease MP or Mobilgrease Spl.	Retinax 'A'	Castrolease LM	Super Lithium Grease
FOR OIL CAN	Visco-Static	NOL 'Ten' or NOL 'Twenty'	Mobil Handy Oil	Shell Super Motor Oil	Everymans Oil	Polyoil

Do not use Additives in Oil or Fuel *Indicates Multi-Grade Oil*

Technical Data

Identification Markings.
(To be quoted when ordering spares or requesting Service information)
Engine Number *(Prefix VR, VM or MSS). Stamped on crankcase at left-hand side below cylinder base. (Scramblers have suffix 'S'.)
Frame Number *(Prefix RS). Stamped on right-hand side of seat front mounting lug. (Scramblers have suffix 'S' or /35.)
Gearbox Number *(Prefix 12- or 14-). Stamped on top of gearbox housing on right-hand side. (T.T. close ratio boxes have suffix 'R'.)
* The prefix letters or numbers identify the type and must always be quoted. The serial number alone is insufficient.

Engine Dimensions.

	Thruxton, Venom, Scrambler and MSS		Viper	350 Scrambler
Cylinder capacity (swept volume) :	499 c.c.	30.45 cu. in.	349 c.c.	31.39 cu. in.
Cylinder bore :	86 mm.	3.3878-in.	72 mm.	2.8362-in.
Stroke :	86 mm.	3.385-in.	86 mm.	3.3858-in.

Tappet Clearances.† (Set cold).
Running clearance* .. .. Inlet .006-in. Exhaust .008-in.
For checking timing .. Inlet .053-in. Exhaust .052-in.
†See page 25 before checking or adjusting.
*For Scrambler clearances see page 96. Thruxton model see supplement

Valve Timing. When checked with tappet clearances of .053° inlet, and .052° exhaust.
Cam M17/8, Venom and Viper from En. No. VR1262 and Scrambler.
Inlet opens .. .. .. 45° before top dead centre.
Inlet closes .. .. .. 55° after bottom dead centre.
Exhaust opens .. .. .. 65° before bottom dead centre.
Exhaust closes .. .. .. 35° after top dead centre.
Cam M17/7, MSS and Viper to En. No. VR1261—
Inlet opens .. .. .. 19° before top dead centre.
Inlet closes .. .. .. 49° after bottom dead centre.
Exhaust opens .. .. .. 49° before bottom dead centre.
Exhaust closes .. .. .. 19° after top dead centre.

Compression Ratios. MSS 6.8 to one (86 to 88 c.c.). Venom 8 to one (68 to 69 c.c.). Viper 8.5 to one (47 to 48 c.c.). 350 Scrambler and Viper Clubman 9.3 to 1 (42 c.c.). 500 Scrambler and Venom Clubman 8.75 to 1 (64-65 c.c.).

Sparking Plug. 14 m.m. dia. 18 m.m. (extra long) reach.
Suitable types for MSS : Champion NA8; KLG FE80; Lodge HLN.
For Venom and Viper : Champion NA10 : KLG FE100 : Lodge 3HLN. See also page 71.

Piston Rings.

	MSS.	Venom.	Viper.	Scrambler 500. & Venon Clubman.
Compression rings :	.015-in.	.010-in.	.010-in.	.020-in.
Oil control ring :	.015-in.	.010-in.	.012-in.	.020-in.

Side clearances are : Compression rings .001-in. to .003-in.
Oil control ring .0027-in. to .0047-in.
Details for the 350 c.c. Scrambler and Viper Clubman are as for the Viper.

Valves. Seat angle 45°
Gudgeon Pin. .8235-in. diameter. (+.0001-in.) (−.0001-in.)
Small end Bush. .8245-in. diameter. (+.0005-in.) (−.0002-ins.)

Big End. Crankpin roller track diameter, 1.499-in.
Crankpin rollers, $\frac{3}{16}$-in. + $\frac{9}{16}$-in. 18 off, caged, single row.
Rollers stocked .0002-in. and .0004-in. oversize.

Carburetters. Monobloc or Concentric type 8° downdraught. Early Clubman and Scrambler models were fitted with the Amal 10TT9 type.

Clubman models and Scramblers use Amal 10.TT.9.

Model.	MSS.	Viper.	Viper.	Venom.	Venom.	Venom
Type	376/49	376/56	376/61	389/14	389/15	R930/29
Size	1$\frac{1}{16}$-in.	1-in.	1$\frac{1}{16}$-in.	1$\frac{1}{8}$-in.	1$\frac{3}{16}$-in.	1$\frac{3}{16}$-in
Main jet	240	230	270	260	330	270
Needle jet	105	106	106	106	106	106
Needle position	3	2	3	2	4	3
Throttle valve	3$\frac{1}{2}$	3$\frac{1}{2}$	3$\frac{1}{2}$	3$\frac{1}{2}$	3$\frac{1}{2}$	3
Pilot jet	25	25	30	30	30	622/107

Earlier Venom models were fitted with the Concentric type carburetter Type R930/15, which had the following settings: Main Jet 270 Needle Jet 107 Pilot Jet 30 Throttle Valve 4 Needle Set in bottom groove position.

Ignition Timing. Fully advanced before top dead centre:

MSS.	Viper.	Venom.	500 Scrambler.	350 Scrambler.
36°	38°	38°	38°	38°

Magneto. Lucas type K1F. Fixed ignition, anti-clockwise rotation. Fitted with Lucas type JY16A Automatic timing unit.
B.T.H. Type BKH1 (Hand controller on Clubman and Scrambler models).

Coil Ignition. Lucas type.

Lighting Equipment.

Dynamo. Miller. Type DVR 6-volt. Belt driven anti-clockwise rotation with Automatic Voltage regulator unit.

Head Lamp. Miller Type 79CV, incorporating switch and ammeter. (1955 to Mid 1956).
Miller Type 180CV on Viper, Venom and MSS.
Lucas type SS700P.

Lighting Bulbs. Headlamp main bulb. 6-volt, 30 × 24W. Bifocal prefocussed.
Headlamp parking bulb. 6-volt, 3W. M.E.S. Cap.
Rear lamp. 6-volt, 6W. S.C.C. Cap on MSS.
Rear and stop lamp bulb. 6-volt, 18 × 6W. (Offset pin.), Viper and Venom.
Speedometer bulb. 6-volt, .18W. M.B.C. Cap.

Battery. 6-volt 13 ampere hour. Varley, Lucas, or Exide.

Gearbox. Four speed, constant mesh, foot controlled. Oil lubricated.

Gear Ratios.

Gearboxes, Prefix No. 14 : (MSS.)
With solo sprocket (18T): First, 12.4; Second, 8.57; Third, 6.52; Fourth, 4.9 to one.
With s/car sprocket (16T): First, 13.91; Second, 9.625; Third, 7.32; Fourth, 5.5 to one.

Gearboxes Prefix No. 12. (Viper and Venom.)
Venom. With solo sprocket (18T): First, 11.24; Second, 7.78; Third, 5.91; Fourth, 4.9 to one.
Venom. With s/car sprocket (16T): First, 12.62; Second, 8.73; Third, 6.64; Fourth, 5.5 to one.
Viper. With solo sprocket (21T): First, 12.62; Second, 8.73; Third, 6.64; Fourth, 5.5 to one.

Gearboxes Prefix 12 : Suffix R. (Clubman models).
  Venom. With solo sprocket (18T) : First, 9.25; Second, 7.03; Third, 5.35; Top, 4.9.
  Viper. With solo sprocket (21) : First, 10.45; Second, 7.94; Third, 6.03; Top, 5.5.

Chains and Sprockets.
  Primary Chain : .5-in. pitch; .305-in. wide; .335-in. roller dia.;
    MSS and Venom 68 pitches; Viper 67 pitches.
  Rear Chain : MSS and Venom : .625-in. pitch; .380-in. wide;
    .4-in. roller dia.; .101 pitches.
    .100 Pitches when 16T driving sprocket is fitted.
  Viper. .5-in. pitch; .305-in. wide; 124 pitches.

Sprockets.
  MSS and Venom : Engine. 23T. Clutch, 44T.
    Gearbox (Solo) 18T. Gearbox (S/car) 16T.
    Rear Wheel, 46 T.
  Viper. Engine. 21T. Clutch, 44T.
    Gearbox. 21T. Rear wheel, 55T.

Wheels and Tyres.
  Rims : WM2×19-in. front. WM2×19-in. rear.

Viper Special
Viper Sports
Viper Clubman
Venom Special   } 3.25×19   18-lb. p.s.i. front
Venom Sports   24-lb. p.s.i. rear
Venom Clubman
M.S.S.
Endurance

Viper Veeline .. .. ..
Viper Veeline Clubman   } 3.25×19   19-lb. p.s.i. front
Venom Veeline .. ..   25-lb. p.s.i. rear
Venom Clubman Veeline

350 c.c. Scrambler } 3.00×21 21-lb. p.s.i. front
500 c.c. Scrambler } 4.00×19 16-lb. p.s.i. rear

Thruxton .. 3.00×19 22-lb. p.s.i. front
              3.25×19 24-lb. p.s.i. rear

See page 91 for further information.

Fuel and Oil Capacities.
  Fuel Tank : 4¼ imperial gallons. 19.3 litres. 5.1 U.S. gallons.
  Oil Tank : .5 imperial gallons. 2.27 litres. .6 U.S. gallons.
  Gearbox : 1 imperial pint. .56 litres. 1.2 U.S. Pint.
  Front Fork : (per strut) .125 imperial pint. 71 cubic cm. .15 U.S. Pint.
  Chain Case : ⅛-pint. 71c.c. .15 U.S. pint.

Principle Dimensions.
  Wheel base : (in normal loaded position) 53.75-ins. 136.5 cms
  Ground clearance : (,, ,, ,,) 5.5-ins. 14 cms.
  Seat height : (,, ,, ,,) 30.5-ins. 77.5 cms.

Overall Width. 27.5-ins. 70 cms.

Overall Length. 7-feet. 213 cms.

Unladen Weight. M.S.S. & Venom 385-lbs. 174 kilograms.
                    Viper.   380-lbs. 172 kilogram.

THE FRONT HUB—SECTIONAL VIEW

The arrangement of the bearings etc. in the full-width type hub is identical.

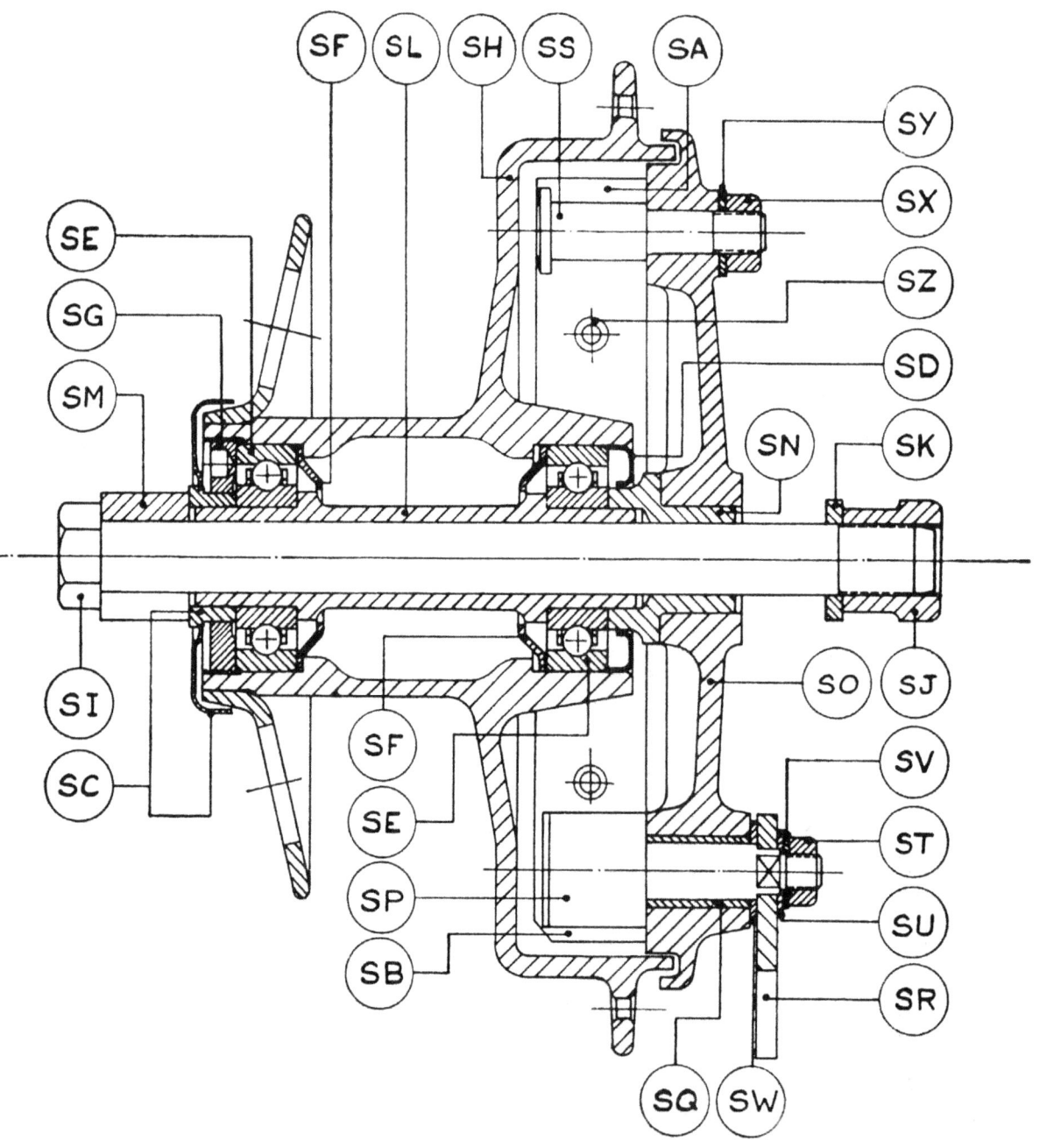

FIG. 1

SA. Brake Shoes	SJ. Nut for Detachable Spindle	SR. Lever or Brake Cam.
SB. Brake Shoe Slipper.		SS. Fulcrum Pin.
SC. Outer Dust Cap and Sleeve.	SK Washer for Spindle Nut.	ST. Nut for Cam.
SD. Inner Dust Cap.	L. Hollow Spindle.	SU. Square Hole Washer for Cam.
SE. Ballraces.	SM. Split Sleeve for Spindle.	SV. Lock Washer
SF. Grease Retainers.	SN. Bearing Clamping Sleeve	SW. Felt Washer for Cam
SG. Ballrace Retaining Ring.	SO. Brake Plate.	SX. Nut for Fulcrum Pin
SH. Front Hub Shell.	SP. Brake Cam.	SY. Plain Washer for Fulcrum Pin.
S.I. Detachable Spindle.	Q. Bush for Brake Cam	SZ Brake Shoe Spring.

THE FRONT HUB, BEARINGS AND BRAKE. (Fig. 1.)

The front hub is supported on a hollow spindle (SL) by two non-adjustable Journal ball bearings (SE) which are a parallel-press fit in the hub (SH) and on the spindle. They are packed during initial assembly with high melting point grease which is sufficient for at least 20,000 miles running without attention, in normal circumstances.

Dismantling.

Dismantling the bearings for renewal or for repacking with grease is carried out as follows : Remove the front wheel assembly from the fork. On removal of the wheel the fork sliders will tend to spring over to the right. They are set in this way intentionally to keep the springs secured in their mountings when the wheel is in place.

Pull out the brake plate and brake shoe assembly from the drum. The bearing clamping sleeve (SN) will probably come away with the brake plate.

Enter a brass or aluminium punch in the opposite end (left-hand side) of the hollow spindle and drive the spindle and the brake side ball bearing out towards the brake drum. A punch about 9-in. long by just under $\frac{7}{8}$-in. diameter reduced to just under $\frac{5}{8}$-in. diameter for about $\frac{1}{2}$-in. at one end will be needed. (The same punch also suits the rear hub.) The dust caps (SC and SD) from both sides, will be removable now, together with the grease retainer (SF) from the brake side. The left hand ballrace and retaining ring (SG) will remain.

Unscrew the ballrace retaining ring and drive out the bearing (SE) towards the left, using a punch about 9-in. long $\times 1\frac{3}{16}$-in. diameter, reduced at one end to just under $\frac{7}{8}$-in. for about $\frac{1}{2}$-in. The other grease retainer (SF) will now be free.

Reassembling Front Hub Bearings.

Place one grease retainer (SF) convex side inwards into the ballrace housing in the left side of the hub and enter the ballrace into position. Press or drive the ballrace home in the housing, applying the pressure to the outer race only. Pack firmly with high melting point grease. Refit and tighten the ballrace retaining ring. Replace the other grease retainer in the brake side ballrace housing, convex side inwards, and pack the housing with grease. Take the hollow spindle with ballrace fitted to it and enter the spindle through the grease retainer and hub, locating the end in the left-hand ballrace, and the brake side ball-race in its housing. Press the spindle and ballrace home. Note that if the brake side ball bearing was removed from the spindle that it is fitted to the shorter ground end of the spindle. Incorrect mounting (on the longer end of the hollow spindle) will make it impossible to assemble the hub correctly.

Pack the bearing with grease and press the inner dust cap (SD) into the hub. On the opposite side, press the outer dust cap and sleeve assembly (SC) on to the protruding end of the hollow spindle.

Refitting the Brake Plate and Shoe Assembly.

Verify the condition of the brake liners and renew them, or fit a pair of re-lined brake shoes, if the liners are worn flush with the rivet heads. See that the cam works freely and ease off if tight. See that the bearing clamping sleeve (SN) is in place in the brake-plate and fit the brake plate and shoe assembly in the drum, locating the sleeve over the protruding end of the hollow spindle. Refit the front wheel, and check fork for freedom of working. See page 17.

THE STEERING HEAD AND BEARINGS.

Adjustment. (Fig 2.) (MSS, Venom, Viper).

There is no adjustment on Scramblers. See page 95.

Slack off the steering damper fully before checking.

Final adjustment must leave the column quite free without trace of play. To take up play, slacken the top cross member clamp bolt (No. 2., Fig. 2) and the two nuts (39, Fig. 3), Tighten down the steering column lock nut (No. 1, Fig. 2) until the column begins to bind when checked with the front of the machine supported so that the front tyre clears the ground. Gradually slacken the lock nut until the column is just free in all positions with no trace of play or roughness in working. When correctly adjusted, tighten the three clamp bolt nuts securely.

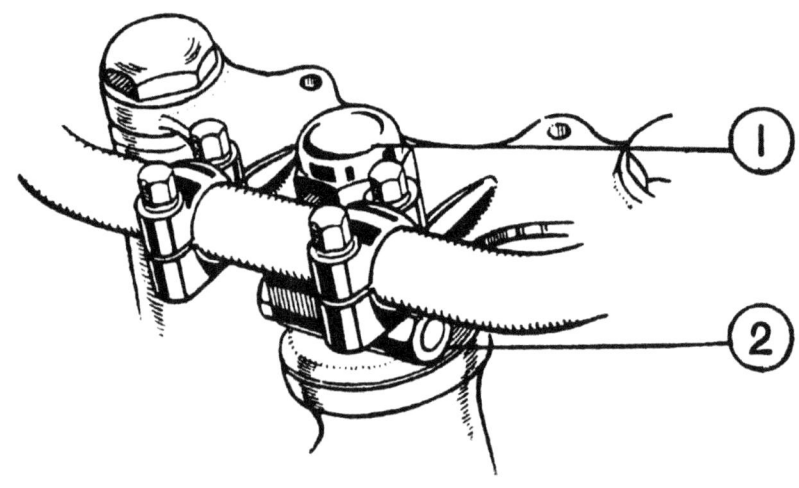

THE STEERING HEAD

(1) Steering Column Nut

(2) Clamping Bolt Nut

Should the column turn jerkily or roughly suspect that the head race cups and cones are pitted, and dismantle the column from the steering head for inspection and if necessary renew the bearings.

Removal of Steering Column. (Fig. 3.)

Note.—Procedure is different on Scramblers, see page 94.

This will involve removal of the front fork assembly from the steering head, and is easier if the front wheel is removed first, together with the front mudguard and stays.

Disconnect the leads from the battery+terminal. Disconnect the speedometer driving flex from the instrument. Unscrew the steering damper knob and rod right out, and remove them. Take off the lower nut from the stud below the steering head lug and remove the $\frac{1}{4}$-in. B.S.F. bolt (62). Take away the damper plate (58) and friction disc (57) etc. Remove the handlebar clip bolts and caps and lay the handlebar across the tank top after putting a covering of rag or corrugated paper to protect the tank enamel. Replace the handlebar caps and bolts in the positions from which they were taken. The headlamp may be taken right off after removing the front and reflector and disconnecting all wiring from the switch and lamp, or it may be left connected to the wiring and laid back on the tank, after the front fork crossmember (41) has been removed.

Unscrew and lift up both fork damper piston rod adaptors (32) and attach to each rod a length of wire, say 22 S.W.G., and about 18-in. long. These wires are essential to pull up the damper piston rods (27) on reassembling, and unless secured in this way they will drop down into the fork tubes on removal of the adaptors and will be difficult to retrieve.

Loosen the adaptor lock nuts (33) and screw the adaptors right off the rods. Loosen the clamp bolt nut (43) and remove the column lock nut (40). Support the fork underneath and tap the top cross member (41) up and off the column and fork tubes (1). If the headlamp has not been detached from the wiring, remove it from the brackets (16 and 17) and lay it on the tank. See that it is protected from damage.

Take off the dust cover from the top steering head bearing, and lower the fork gently through the steering head of the frame, meanwhile catching any bearing balls which fall out of the races. The upper bearing cone will be left in the top bearing. Store the fork upright to prevent loss of oil.

Renewal of Steering Head Bearings.

Remove the top cone and all the bearing balls and wipe the parts clean. Inspect them carefully for wear or pitting of the ball tracks. To remove the bearing cups from the steering head lug they must be driven out using a suitable steel punch passed through the head and engaged with the edges of the cups. Work from below to remove the top one and from above for the bottom one.

New cups have to be drawn into place quite square with the housings and a convenient way of doing this is to use a $\frac{3}{4}$-in. bolt $8\frac{1}{2}$-in. long, threaded B.S.F. for about $2\frac{1}{2}$-in., and two stout washers to locate in the cups.

The washers should be not less than $\frac{3}{16}$-in. (.1875-in.) thick and must be $1\frac{31}{32}$-in. (1.968-in.) diameter recessed on one edge to 1.860-in. diameter to a depth of about $\frac{1}{16}$-in. (.0625-in.) to locate in the cups. (Fig. 4.)

Enter the cups lightly into the housings and with one washer over the bolt, spigot upwards, thread the bolt up through the steering head, fit the other washer, spigot downwards, and thread the nut on to the bolt to hold all parts in place. See that the washers are located in the cups, and the latter quite square, and tighten down the nut until the cups are fully home.

Reassembling the Steering Column.

The bottom steering head cone can be tapped off the column if in need of renewal, and a new one pressed on. Note that the top and bottom cones differ. The top cone is deeper than the bottom one and its inside diameter is smaller.

Stick the bearing balls into the cups with grease, nineteen $\frac{1}{4}$-in. diameter balls in each cup. Push the steering column up into place through the steering head and hold it up firmly into the bearing. Push the top cone down over the column followed by the dust cap. See that the top locating cups (18), the buffers (20), and their housings (21), are all in place on the lamp bracket assemblies. Bring the headlamp forward, leading the wiring down between the lamp bracket tubes and the frame head lug and place the top cross member in position, threading the wires from the damper piston rods through the holes. Fit the column lock nut and screw the adaptors on to the damper piston rods, and tighten the locknuts. Remove the wires and tighten down the adaptors.

See section dealing with Scrambler models, page 94.

Readjust the head bearing as previously described and refit the handlebar, tightening the clip bolts evenly.

THE FRONT FORK. (Fig. 3.)
Description of Working.

Suspension is by coil springs (13), oil damped. The oil for damping, and lubrication is carried in the fork struts.

The working is as follows : On extension of the fork, that is on recoil after a shock, the damper tubes (23) attached to the unsprung sliders

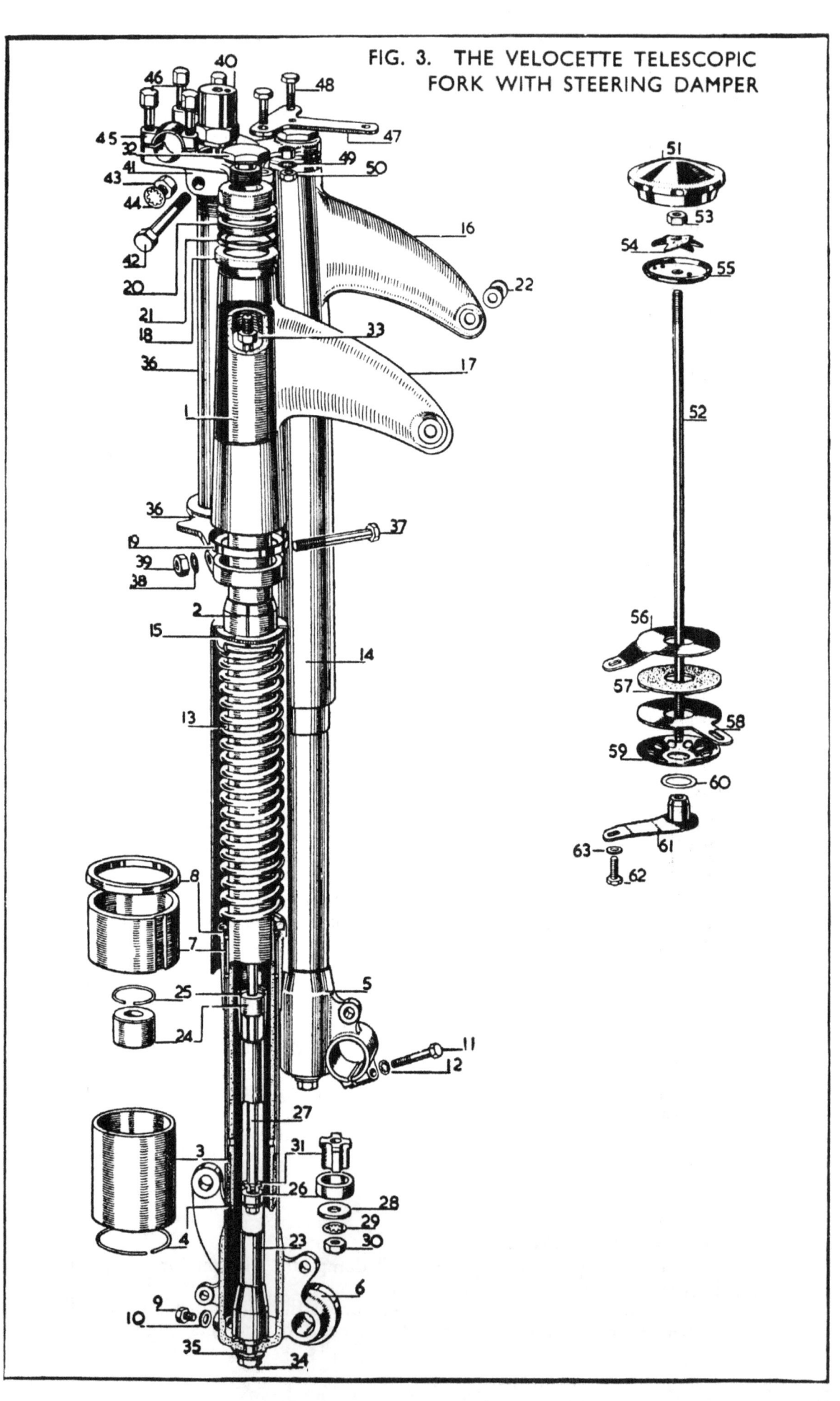

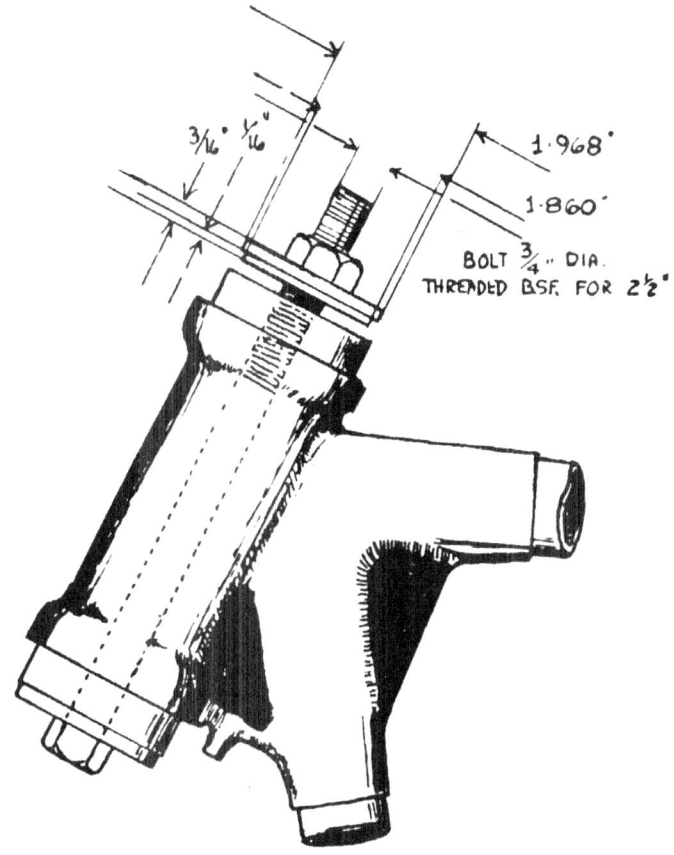

FIG. 4.
STEERING HEAD BEARING CUP TOOL.

move downwards away from the damper piston rods (27) which are fixed at the top to the adaptors (32) on the sprung part of the fork. The damper pistons (26) move into contact with the damper piston rod washers (28) closing the valves. The upward movement of the pistons relative to the damper tubes causes oil from the sliders (5 and 6) to be forced through radial holes in the damper tubes to fill the spaces below the pistons.

On compression of the fork the movement is reversed and the damper tubes move upwards relative to the piston rods, and the pistons lift off the piston rod washers, allowing oil to pass freely from below the pistons through the damper valves (31) into the upper parts of the damper tubes.

Again on recoil the damper tubes below the pistons are replenished, but the oil above the pistons is trapped and can get out only through restricted openings at the top ends of the damper tubes, providing the resistance necessary to give the desired degree of damping

Oil from the upper ends of the damper tubes drains down into the sliders and is available for use again.

The outer lower ends of the damper tubes are shaped to form cones, and any impact sufficient to force the sliders up almost to their limit brings the open ends of the fork tubes (1) over the cones, and a hydraulic lock is formed which prevents metallic contact and " bottoming " in severe conditions.

Scramblers are also damped on compression.

During the whole time the machine is running over rough surfaces the above cycle of operations is going on, and the more irregular the surface the greater is the degree of damping. It has been found that over almost smooth surfaces the fork works almost undamped and moves freely over slight inequalities in the road, thus overcoming the objection usually found with most damping systems that they prevent movement of the fork altogether under slight impact.

Fitting a sidecar will necessitate heavier springs being fitted to the fork. These are obtainable from us—for details see Spare Parts List.

Maintenance.

Apart from external cleaning, the fork needs no attention. The oil supply lasts almost indefinitely and topping up is unnecessary. Should an owner wish to do so the oil can be drained out and fresh oil put in after 10,000 miles running.

Drain plugs (9) are fitted into the bottom of the sliders at the rear. After refitting the drain plugs, unscrew the two adaptors (32) from the top of the fork tubes. They can then be lifted far enough to get oil in quite easily. ⅛ pint (71 c.c.) or 2.5 fluid ozs will be needed in each side (120 c.c. on Scramblers).

The Fork Spring Dust Covers. (Fig. 3.)

Occasionally a slight rattle may develop due to a loose dust cover. This must be rectified at once otherwise the rubber washers (15) between the inside of the dust covers and the split sleeves (2) will be damaged and will have to be replaced.

To eliminate rattle the split sleeve on the side needing attention has to be moved up the fork tube to "nip" the buffer. To do this first drain out all oil from *both* fork sliders, except on Scramblers (see page 94). Slightly loosen the clamp bolt (37) on the side required. Do not slack it right off.

Bounce the front wheel sharply several times on the ground until the cover is prevented from rattling and retighten the clamp bolt. The dust covers will never be held so firmly that they cannot be turned by hand, but they must be secure and unable to rattle.

Complete draining of the fork is essential to avoid forming a hydraulic lock which otherwise will prevent the full closure of the fork springs, and the split sleeve will not move. Only partial slackening of the clamp bolt is required. If it is loosened too much the sleeve will move down again when the spring extends.

Refit drain plugs, refill fork with oil, and tighten clamp bolts fully after the work is done.

Dismantling the Fork. (Fig. 3.)

Drain the oil from the struts. If dealing with a Scrambler fork see page 94.

After removal from the machine—described previously—hold the steering column in a vice so that the fork is horizontal. Cover the jaws to prevent damaging the column. The procedure deals with only one strut, but it applies equally to both. Only the sliders (5 and 6) and the lamp bracket assemblies (16 and 17) are "handed" and their positions must be noted for correct reassembly.

Pull off the two buffer housings (21) and the locating cup from the top of the lamp bracket assembly. Remove the lamp bracket assembly and the cup (19) in which it is located at the bottom. Slacken off the clamp bolt (37) fully and pull the split sleeve (2) with the main tube, spring, dust cover, and slider, etc., through the bottom cross member of the column assembly away from the column. Twist the assembly when pulling which will make it come away easier.

Remove the column and the other assembly from the vice. Pull off the spring dust cover (14) and the rubber buffer (15) from the split sleeve. Hold the top end of the main tube (1) horizontally in the vice, hold the spring, and tap the split sleeve round until it comes free of the spring. Take the tube out of the vice and remove the split sleeve from it. Hold the slider in the vice and by grasping the spring firmly, twist it out of the mounting on the slider

Take the slider in one hand and the main tube in the other and after pushing the slider up the tube as far as it will go, draw them apart as sharply as possible to dislodge the oil seal (8) and the slider bush (7) from the top of the slider. The main tube with the fork tube bush (3)

will then come away. To remove the fork tube bush first prise the circlip (4) from its groove in the end of the tube and tap the bush carefully off the tube.

The Fork Damper Assembly is removable from the slider after removing the nut (34) and washer (35) from the end of the slider, and will tap out of place. To dismantle remove the damper bush circlip (25) from the damper tube and remove the bush by a similar process to that adopted to remove the slider bush and oil seal from the slider. The damper piston rod (27) with the piston and valve, etc., will then pull out. If the piston (26) or damper valve (31) are removed note the correct order of replacement and see that the shiny face of the piston is set facing the bottom (next to the washer (28). Also when replacing the damper bush (24) note that the end with the chamfer fits uppermost, otherwise the circlip will not go into place.

Reconditioning—a Warning. The slider assemblies will be seriously damaged if stoved at temperatures exceeding 212° Fahrenheit after re-enamelling.

Reassembling the Fork. (Fig. 3.)

If dealing with a Scrambler, see page 94.

Fit the assembled damper to the slider being careful to locate the damper tube spigot properly in the hole in the slider. Fit the washer and nut and tighten. See that the fork tube bush and circlip are properly fitted to the main tube, slide the upper bush (7) over the tube and towards the bottom, noting that the groove across the end face must be facing the bottom bush.

Hold the tube horizontally in the vice and after lubricating the bushes fit the slider over it, entering the damper piston rod through the tube and the bottom bush (on the tube) in the slider. Twist the slider bush (7) to bring the groove, which is cut down the outside, to the top. Hold the slider so that the wheel spindle mounting lug points downwards. Enter the slider bush into the slider and drive it firmly into place using Service Tool Let 796, which consists of a specially shaped split collar which can be fitted over the tube. Remove the tube from the vice and fit the oil seal (8) over it and slide it down to the top of the slider into which it must be fitted by using Service Tool LET 796 once more. Slide the spring down into position and by holding the slider in the vice twist the spring firmly into its mounting. Extend the slider along the tube as far as it will go.

Push the split sleeve (2) down the tube until the upper edge of its taper section is set exactly 7.187-in. (7 $\frac{3}{16}$-in.) from the top of the tube. Hold it firmly in this position and push the slider and spring towards it, engaging the spring in its mounting on the split sleeve and twisting it firmly into place. Invert the assembly until the damper piston rod protrudes from the tube and attach a piece of wire to it as described on page 13. Fit the rubber buffer (15) and dust cover (14) over the sleeve, thread the wire, and the tube through the bottom cross member, and partly tighten the clamp bolt. See that the assembled tube, spring and slider are fitted on the correct side. The slider which carries the wheel spindle clamp is always on the left (remote from the brake drum).

When assembling the fork—prior to refitting it to the machine—always set the struts so that the fork ends of the sliders point over to the right at about 20° off the centre line. This ensures that when the wheel is fitted after the clamp bolts (37) are tightened the sliders tend to hold the springs firmly into their mountings.

Reassembly of the lamp brackets only calls for care in fitting them to their respective sides and seeing that they are located properly in their top and bottom collars and that the top buffers are fitted between the hollow (concave) sides of the buffer housings.

The wires attached to the damper piston rods enable these to be drawn up for the attachment of the adaptors (32).

Before refilling with oil verify that the dust covers do not rattle, and after fitting the wheel make certain that the fork works freely before finally tightening the spindle clamp bolt. If the dust covers are loose see page 16.

Setting the Front Mudguard Stays.

As a fork is seldom removed and dismantled unless the machine is accidentally damaged, care should be taken when fitting the front mudguard stays, whether new or repaired ones, that they go into place without having to be forced. Before fitting them therefore they must be set to the correct widths between the ends as follow : Front stay 6⅝-in. (6.625-in.) ; Central stay, 6¾-in. (6.75-in.); Bottom (rear) stay fitted outside the centre stay, 6½-in. (6.5-in.).

In any instance where the fork does not work freely, and this is not due to the wheel mounting, remove the stays and reset them.

ENGINE LUBRICATION SYSTEM.
Description of Working.

From the oil tank oil is taken to the feed side of a double gear pump in the crankcase, through a non-return ball valve fitted between the oil tank and the oil feed pipe. The oil feed pipe is primed with oil during original assembly—in this connection refer to page 19.

The oil pump body carries two pairs of gears, one pair form the feed pump and the other pair which are much wider, form the return pump and return oil to the oil tank after it has circulated through the engine. Due to the greater width of the return gears the feed cannot overtake the supply and cause the crankcase sump to become flooded. The pump is driven from a worm on the timing side mainshaft.

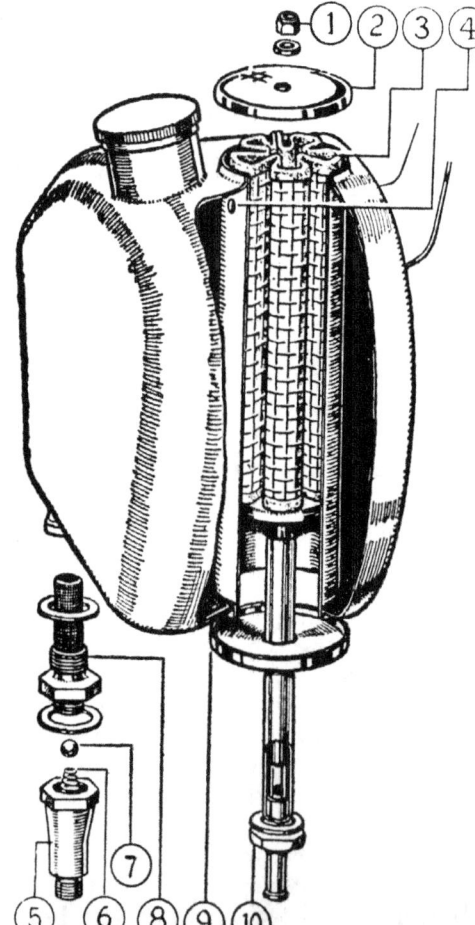

FIG. 5

OIL TANK, BALL VALVE AND FILTER

(1) Oil Tank Filter Stud Nut
(2) Oil Tank Filter Cap—Top
(3) Oil Filter Element
(4) Outlet to Tank
(5) Ball Valve Body
(6) Ball Valve Spring
(7) Ball Valve Ball
(8) Oil Strainer Assembly
(9) Oil Tank Filter Cap—Bottom
(10) Oil Tank Filter Tube Assembly

From the feed pump gears the oil is forced through a drilling in the crankcase to the timing cover in the face of which is a hole which matches

ENGINE LUBRICATION SYSTEM (*continued*).

with the outlet of the drilling in the crankcase. The timing cover acts as a distributor for the oil supply and carries feeds to the big end bearing through the crankshaft oil jet, to the cams, bottom rockers, and to the overhead rocker gear.

The feed to the cams and bottom rockers is through the cam oil jet, one end of which locates in a hole in the cover. The rocker oil feed pipe leading to the rocker box is attached to a union at the top of the timing cover. By the removal of the oil pipe from this union it is possible to check whether the pump is working and it is essential that this check is made should the oil feed pipe or oil tank have been removed, or the oil-pipe emptied of oil. A fourth outlet from the cover feeds the cam wheel bush.

Through drillings in the rocker box oil is directed into the bearings for the overhead rockers, and from here lubricates the valve stems, guides, and the ball cups at the top ends of the push rods. The surplus drains down to the timing case through the push rod cover tubes, lubricating the push rod ball cups formed in the bottom rockers, and falls on to the timing gears.

The surplus oil from the cam wheel bush and the cam oil jet drains into the timing case, from which it goes back into the crankcase through a hole in the wall between the crankcase and timing case.

The piston, cylinder, and small end are lubricated by oil dissipated by the rapidly revolving big-end, and oil draining down the crankcase wall on the timing side is caught in a drilling leading to the intermediate gear bush. Both main bearings are kept constantly supplied.

From the bottom of the crankcase the oil is taken up to the return half of the pump, but before reaching the pump has to pass the Suction Filter (Fig. 6). The filter is formed by a plug screwed into the oil return passage at the bottom right hand rear corner of the crankcase. The diametric clearance between the filter and the passage is too small to pass anything which might damage the pump.

The oil from the crankcase is piped to a connection under the oil tank, and passes up a tube inside the oil filter chamber in the tank, and after passing through a fabric filter element enters the main oil tank through a hole at the upper end of the filter chamber below the filler cap opening.

The fabric filter is easily removed for replacement and should be discarded and replaced by a new one every 10,000 miles.

Oil in circulation can be observed issuing from the opening in the filter chamber when the engine is running.

Checking the Oil Circulation.

Owing to the use of a spring loaded non-return ball valve between the oil tank and the pump, **the pump will not feed oil to the engine unless the feed-pipe is full of oil.** After a normal spell of running this pipe will always be left full and priming is only needed during initial assembly, after a full engine overhaul, or if for any reason the oil feed pipe has been disturbed and emptied of oil.

After priming the oil pump, and before starting the engine it is essential to disconnect, temporarily, the union at the lower end of the overhead rocker oil feed pipe. A moment after starting the engine oil should be forced out of the union on the cover. Allow the engine to run for about two minutes at slow speed to make certain that the flow is continuous before stopping the engine and refitting the union nut.

ENGINE LUBRICATION SYSTEM (continued).

In normal circumstances the flow can be checked occasionally by noting the oil returned to the tank through the hole in the filter chamber.

Bear in mind that this flow will usually be somewhat intermittent and irregular. It may be constant and greater than normal after starting an engine which has been stationary for some time, because an accumulation of oil which has had time to drain to the bottom of the crankcase off all the internal parts will be cleared. After this, and if the throttle is opened and the engine speed increased the flow may be observed to cease temporarily, only to resume again at a greater rate on the engine slowing down. This is due to the time taken for the suddenly increased amount from the pump, to get round the system and to find its way back to the oil sump.

These symptoms are quite normal, but it should be noted that if the oil filter chamber in the tank is not refilled with oil after cleaning the tank, or replacing the filter element, no return into the tank will be seen until the chamber has filled up to the outlet hole with oil pumped back from the engine. Also the level of oil in the main tank will be reduced by the amount trapped in the filter chamber. It is, therefore, advisable to refill the filter chamber as well as the tank if it has been drained.

The Ball Valve Assembly (Fig. 5.)

This is composed of a threaded union carrying a gauze strainer (8) screwed into the oil tank and formed to act as a seating for the ball (7), which is kept into contact with it when the engine is stationary by the spring (6) carried below the ball in the Ball-valve Body (5).

The purpose of the ball valve is to prevent oil from the tank draining, into the engine by gravity through the pump when the engine is standing as this would eventually flood the crankcase and make starting very difficult.

In the ordinary way the ball valve will seldom need attention, but if there are indications that the valve is leaking, such as excessive and prolonged smoking at the exhaust after starting up, or if the crankshaft is felt to be very sluggish to rotate on starting (provided that this is not due to excessive cold or the use of summer viscosity oil in cold weather) the ball valve assembly should be dismantled for attention. Excess oil can be drained from the crankcase before attempting to start if the ball valve has been leaking.

After detaching the oil feed-pipe union nut from the Ball-Valve Body (5) the Ball-Valve Assembly can be unscrewed from the tank using a spanner on the upper hexagon formed on the Oil-strainer assembly (8). Unless the tank has previously been drained a tin must be provided to catch the oil as the Oil-strainer assembly is removed.

By holding the Ball-valve Body upright in the vice the strainer assembly can be unscrewed out of it leaving the ball and spring exposed.

Note that a gasket is used between the strainer assembly and the body and do not remove the spring needlessly. The body can be cleaned out with the spring in place.

The seating for the ball in the strainer assembly can be inspected, but if leaking, the strainer assembly should be replaced. The expedient sometimes adopted of tapping the ball sharply against the seating to bed it in is deprecated because it widens the seating, and consequently reduces the unit pressure of the ball upon it, making subsequent leakage more likely, and should only be used as a temporary measure.

When reassembling the strainer to the body see that the gasket is in place, and the ball resting on top of the spring. The ball *must be above the spring as illustrated*, otherwise the flow of oil will be cut off effectively with disastrous results to the engine. If the spring is taken out see that when it is refitted it seats right down into the ball valve body otherwise the pressure upon the ball will be too great and this may fail to open when the engine starts.

ENGINE LUBRICATION SYSTEM (continued).

Refit the Ball-valve assembly to the tank not omitting the gasket, and if the oil pipe is full of oil re-attach it to the Ball-valve body and tighten the union nut. If the oil pipe has been disturbed, or is empty, prime it by filling with oil. See that the drain plug is in place and tighten. Refill the tank.

Before starting the engine undo the union nut of the Rocker oil pipe and free the nipple. Start up and check the oil flow (see page 19). If there is no flow stop the engine at once, reprime the oil-feed-pipe and test again.

The oil pipe can be filled more easily if the banjo union hollow bolt is loosened to relieve air locks. Tighten up as soon as the pipe is full.

When all is in order refit and tighten the rocker-oil pipe union nut.

The Suction Filter. (Fig. 6.)

The Filter Plug (Fig. 6) should be unscrewed and removed for cleaning at intervals of 2,000 miles, or if at any time continuous and excessive smoking at the exhaust indicates that the crankcase is not being cleared satisfactorily of oil. Wash the plug in clean petrol, dry off and replace. Note that a gasket is fitted between the head of the plug and the crankcase. Make certain that this is in good condition and replace if faulty. Tighten the plug fully to eliminate air leakage.

On some models the crankcase suction filter plug is not used, this being replaced by a small hexagon headed plug.

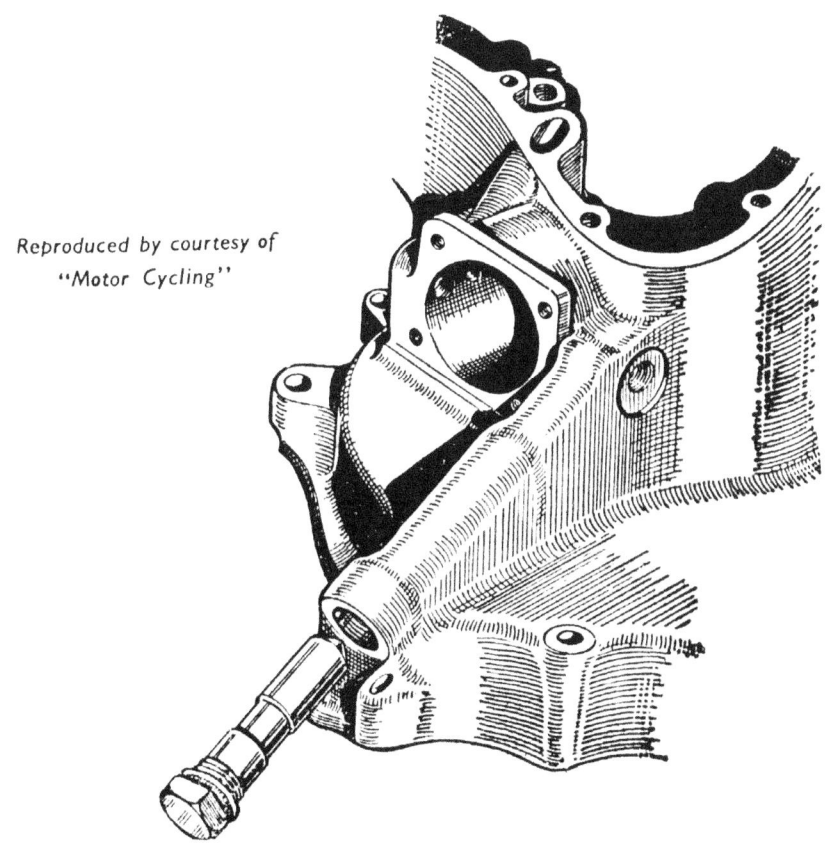

Reproduced by courtesy of "Motor Cycling"

FIG. 6. THE CRANKCASE SUCTION FILTER

Fabric Oil Filter (Fig. 5).

The filter element should be renewed every 10,000 miles or less and the old one discarded. To replace the element it is not necessary to remove the oil tank, although if it is desired to wash out the tank this is easier if it is taken off.

ENGINE LUBRICATION SYSTEM (continued).

Drain out all oil, by removing the oil tank drain plug. Drain the filter chamber by loosening the filter stud nut (1) sufficiently to permit the bottom cap (9) to pull away a little from the bottom of the tank, and catch the oil from the filter chamber in a tin.

When all oil has drained away, remove the nut and top cap and pull down the stud and bottom cap clear of the tank and take them away. Pull the old filter element out from the top.

Wash the filter chamber, filter tube assembly (10) and both caps in clean petrol and dry off. Fit the replacement filter element setting it so that a recess is opposite to oil outlet hole, and put back the bottom cap with its gasket and thread the filter tube assembly up through the filter chamber. Have the top cap, with its gasket, nut, and washer handy for refitting. Hold the filter tube assembly firmly up to the cap and the cap against the bottom of the tank and fill the filter chamber with clean oil up to the level of the outlet hole (4). Refit the top cap with its gasket and the washer and nut, and tighten up the nut. The gaskets must be properly centralized to prevent leakage.

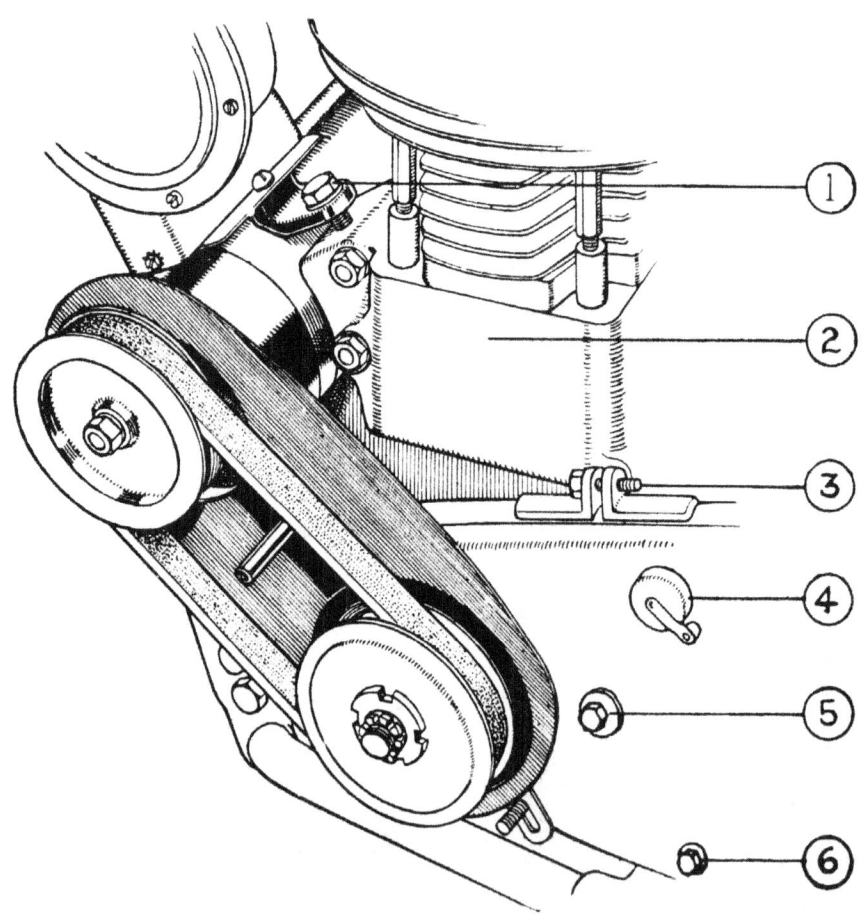

FIG. 7. DYNAMO BELT ADJUSTMENT

(1) Dynamo Clamp Bolt
(2) Location of Engine Serial Number and Prefix
(3) Chain Case Strap Fixing Pin
(4) Chain Case Inspection Cap
(5) Chain Case Bolt
(6) Chain Case Drain Plug

Replace the tank drain-plug and refill the tank with oil.

Additives are unnecessary and should not be used.

If the oil feed pipe has been disturbed fill it with oil and check the circulation. See page 19.

The main oil feed pipe must be airtight. If chafed or deteriorated in any way check under pressure for possible leakages.

ENGINE SHAFT SHOCK ABSORBER. (Fig. 7.)

The shock absorber spring, and the splined shock absorber clutch can be removed for inspection or replacement without removing the front half of the primary chaincase and are accessible after removal of the front of the dynamo belt cover, the belt, and the mainshaft nut or shock absorber spring collar.

Dismantle the cover as shown, take off the belt and withdraw the split cotter from the mainshaft. Engage top gear and hold the rear brake on whilst the nut is loosened and removed. The spanner A229 is required. A hammer will be needed on the spanner to start the nut.

As the collar unscrews, the dynamo pulley flange and pulley, which locate on the collar, will come off with it. The spring and shock absorber clutch will then pull off.

When refitting, grease the splines and shock absorber cam-faces liberally and note that the projection on the pulley must engage the slot in the pulley flange, and the projection on the pulley flange must be engaged with one of the slots in the edge of the collar.

Replace the plain washer on the end of the shaft, and fit the collar. Tighten fully, and fit a new split cotter, afterwards spreading out the ends of the cotter.

DECARBONISING THE ENGINE AND GRINDING IN VALVES.

The mileage that an engine will run efficiently without being decarbonised depends to a great extent upon driving conditions. A new engine is the better for receiving this attention after the first 2,000 to 3,000 miles have been covered. Afterwards it will probably be found to run perfectly satisfactorily for very much greater distances without similar attention. Whilst it is impossible to lay down any hard and fast rule it may be said that generally the average private owner does the work too often rather than too seldom.

If the engine is running well, and there is no noticeable loss of power, or other evidence such as a tendency to " pink " excessively it is best not to disturb it.

During the operation do not remove the cylinder barrel, unless there is good reason to do so. Removal means disturbing the piston rings, which can never be replaced in exactly the positions in which they have settled and bedded in to the cylinder and piston, and their frequent removal and reassembly may cause an increase in oil consumption.

Removal of Fuel Tank.

Turn off the fuel. Remove the pipe; holding the taps whilst undoing the unions to prevent it twisting. Remove the carburetter. Take off the bracing strap from underneath the front of the tank. Slacken the rear holding bolt and take out both the front ones. Lift off the tank.

Removal of Rocker Box Assembly.

Remove the sparking plug. Take off the rocker oil feed pipe assembly by disconnecting it from the rocker box and timing cover. Detach the rocker cover at the right hand side, and remove the two nuts and washers from the top push rod cover flange stud.

Turn the crankshaft by means of the kickstart and observe the movement of the rockers. Turn until the inlet rocker and push rod are seen to rise and then fall. The piston will now be rising on the compression stroke. Note its position through the sparking plug hole and stop turning as it reaches the top. Both valves will now be closed. This is essential before the rocker box bolts are loosened.

Slacken off all nine rocker box bolts in sequence and each a little at a time until quite free. Do not slack off one or two fully, leaving the rest tight. When all are clear of the threads raise the rocker box assembly until the flange studs are pulled out clear of the holes in the cylinder head.

Work from the right hand side of the machine and hold the rocker box assembly clear of the head. Swivel it round with the push rods as centre, in a clockwise direction towards the front until it is across the machine—at right angles to its original position. Lift it up further to clear the push rods and remove it.

Removal of Cylinder Head Assembly.

Lift out the push rods, being careful not to drop out and lose the loose cups, and mark them so that they are not interchanged when reassembling. Wet indelible pencil will do.

Unscrew and remove the hollow bolts securing the rocker box oil drain pipe assembly to the head and push rod cover. Remove the gaskets and take away the pipe. Telescope the upper push rod cover into the lower section and take away the two top flange gaskets and the guide plate which is between them.

Slacken off the cylinder head nuts each a little at a time in sequence until clear of the head, and then screw them right off. If any of the studs screw out with them they can be separated later and before reassembling. Unscrew any studs left in place by applying a screwdriver to their top ends.

Lift the cylinder head assembly off the cylinder barrel; preserving the joint gasket.

It is best to leave the cylinder in place so do not disturb it.

Decarbonising.

Before removing the valves scrape the combustion head clear of carbon using a brass or aluminium scraper to avoid scratching the surface. This, will prevent the valve seatings being marked. It will be possible also to clean most of the carbon from the exhaust port, but final cleaning of the port and head will be necessary after removing the valves. The port can be cleaned and polished with emery cloth.

Never use emery cloth or other abrasive to clean the piston crown, but scrape off the carbon with the brass or aluminium scraper. After cleaning thoroughly, lower the piston a little in the cylinder and wipe all traces of carbon dust off the cylinder wall. Bring the piston back to the top after wiping clean.

Removal of Valves and Springs.

The Service Tool KA.163/2 will be required to compress the valve springs. Fit this over the side of the cylinder head across the top face locating the forked end on the valve spring collar and the screw in the centre of the valve head. Tighten the screw until the split cotter is exposed and pick out the two halves. Release the compresser and take it off. Lift off the valve collar, spring collars and the valve springs. Push the valve out of the guide. Both valves are dealt with in the same manner, but the valves and split cotters are not interchangeable.

Although interchangeable the springs, collars, and washers should not be interchanged after being in use and should be set aside in separate boxes marked for identification when reassembling.

Refacing and Grinding in Valves.

To avoid needless wearing of the seatings in the head by lengthy grinding-in it is recommended that the valves be polished and refaced valve on a refacing machine. The seat angle is 45°.

Remove any hard scale by using a piece of Carborundum; polishing up the surface afterwards. Do not in any circumstances polish the bearing surfaces of the stems.

To hold the valves for grinding-in, use special tools.

Using fine grade compound; grind in each valve with a semi-rotary motion. Lift the valve frequently from the seating and bring it down in another position to distribute the grinding compound evenly and to prevent forming concentric rings and ridges on the seats. A light coil spring threaded over the valve stem between the head and the guide will help by raising the valve off the seat when pressure is removed from the holding tool.

Aim at an even grey matt surface on the seating—not a polish.

ADJUSTMENT OF TAPPET CLEARANCES

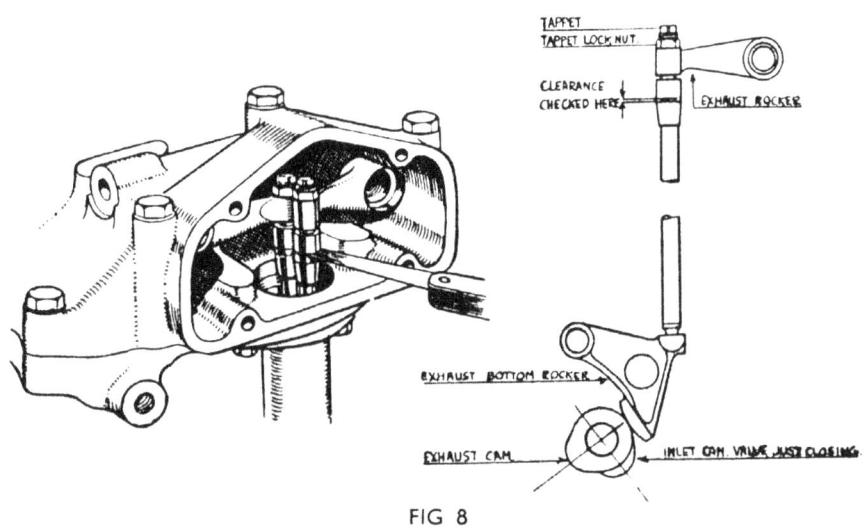

FIG 8

Refacing the Cylinder Head Valve Seats.

This will only be needed after very long service. Ordinary valve seating cutters will not be satisfactory and the seatings will need attention from a standard 45° valve refacing stone.

Refitting the Valves and Springs.

See that all traces of grinding compound and carbon dust, etc., are cleaned from the combustion head, seatings, and valve ports. Preferably blow all parts clean with a compressed-air jet after washing down the head. Be particularly careful to clean the valve guides thoroughly. A little clean rag rolled into a "pencil" and pushed or drawn through the guides is recommended.

Assemble the hairpin valve springs into the bottom collar and fit the collar and springs over the appropriate valve guide. The closed ends of the springs overlap each other.

Smear a little clean oil or graphite grease over the valve and insert the stem into the guide. Place the valve spring collar and inner rotating collar over the end of the valve stem.

Compress the springs with service tool KA.163/2 until there is room to allow the cotter to be fitted. Smear a little grease inside the halves of the cotter and fit them into place, small ends facing the valve guide, and the lips engaged in the groove on the valve stem. Press them together and release the compresser until the valve collar holds them firmly in place.

Remove the compresser and fit the other valve and springs in the same manner.

Refitting Cylinder Head Assembly.

Clean the piston crown, and the top of the cylinder barrel. See that no carbon dust is left in the cylinder bore or in the sparking plug thread. If the joint gasket is in good order refit it to the cylinder. If deteriorated fit a new one. Clean the cylinder head joint face carefully, and screw in the sparking plug. Wipe off any particles of dust, etc., dislodged by the sparking plug. Centralise the gasket and fit the head assembly into position lining it up so that the stud holes register with those in the cylinder barrel.

Thread the four long cylinder studs down through the cylinder head and barrel and screw them into the cylinder crankcase studs; using a screwdriver in the screwdriver slots at the top ends of the studs.

Fit the stud washers and the special cylinder head nuts. Note that these are special nuts and ordinary nuts are unsuitable as replacements.

Tighten down carefully, a little at a time in sequence. That is : do not tighten one nut fully before the others, but work on each in turn working round until all are tight. Do not force the nuts. A good gastight joint is obtainable without excessive tightening. The tension increases as the engine parts get hot so that overtightening initially may cause damage later.

Refitting Rocker Box Assembly.

Fit the push rod guide plate between the two gaskets on the flange of the top push rod cover. Locate the flange and gaskets, etc., approximately with the stud holes. Fit the push rods, guiding them down through the guide plate and engage the bottom ball ends in the sockets formed in the bottom rockers.

During dismantling, the push rods should have been marked to prevent interchanging them. The inlet push rod is the one nearer the cylinder.

Carefully wipe clean the joint face on the cylinder head and the corresponding face on the rocker box. Fit a new gasket; sticking this to the rocker box face with a light smear of grease, or Gasket Goo jointing compound. (Makers : The Wilcot Parent Co., Fishponds, Bristol).

Set the piston at the top of the compression stroke. If the engine was turned whilst dismantled find this position by rotating the crankshaft forward slowly whilst the finger is rested on the inlet push rod. Turn, and note the inlet push rod rise and then fall. As it falls the piston will be rising on the compression stroke. Stop turning when the piston reaches the top. See that the two loose ends are fitted into the tops of the push rods, and refit the rocker box. This is done by holding it at right angles to its fitted position with the rocker cover opening facing the rear. Lift it into place so that the round opening for the push rods is located centrally over the push rod ends. Pivot the rocker box assembly about this point anti-clockwise into its normal position and lower it on to the head, engaging the tips of the adjustable tappets in the push rod cups meanwhile, and entering the flange studs through the holes in the cylinder head and push rod cover flange.

Fit the rocker box bolts and tighten down evenly, a little at a time in sequence. Do not tighten one bolt fully before the others, but work on each in turn until all are tight. Fit and tighten the top push rod flange stud nuts. Attach the rocker oil drainpipe to the cylinder head and push rod cover and tighten the hollow bolts, being careful not to shear them off.

Re-adjustment of Tappet Clearances. (Fig. 8).

The running clearances must be set when the engine is cold, and must be checked and set with the bearing face of the bottom rocker resting on the base of the cam. See page 105 for Thruxton settings.

The cams are ground with quietening ramps so that the essential clearance allowed is taken up and restored gradually and there is consequently only a very limited part of each cam at which the full clearance can be checked or set correctly. The crankshaft therefore has to be turned to bring each cam into the right position before the clearance on the corresponding valve tappet is checked or set.

To obtain the two positions necessary rotate the crankshaft and observe the movement of the rockers through the opening in the rocker box.

Note the inlet rocker—the one nearer the cylinder—rise, and as it begins to fall—as the valve is closing—turn very slowly until the rocker and push rod just reach the lowest point; then stop. This position; that is with the inlet valve on the point of closing brings the correct part of the base of the exhaust cam below the exhaust bottom rocker. Set the exhaust tappet clearance when the cam is in this position.

Before attending to the inlet tappet turn the crankshaft forward for about two thirds of a revolution (240°) until the exhaust valve rocker is seen to be on the point of rising. This will bring the base of the inlet cam below the inlet bottom rocker which is the only position at which the inlet valve clearance can be set correctly.

The adjustable tappets are accessible for checking and adjustment through the opening in the rocker box, and the feeler gauge is used by inserting it between the top of the push rod end (fixed) and the loose push rod cup above.

Slacken the locknut above the rocker and turn the tappet by applying the small tappet adjusting spanner to the square end. Turn clockwise to decrease clearance. A full turn will alter the clearance about .038-in. When correctly set tighten the locknut. Always re-check after locking, in case the tappet has been moved a little in the process.

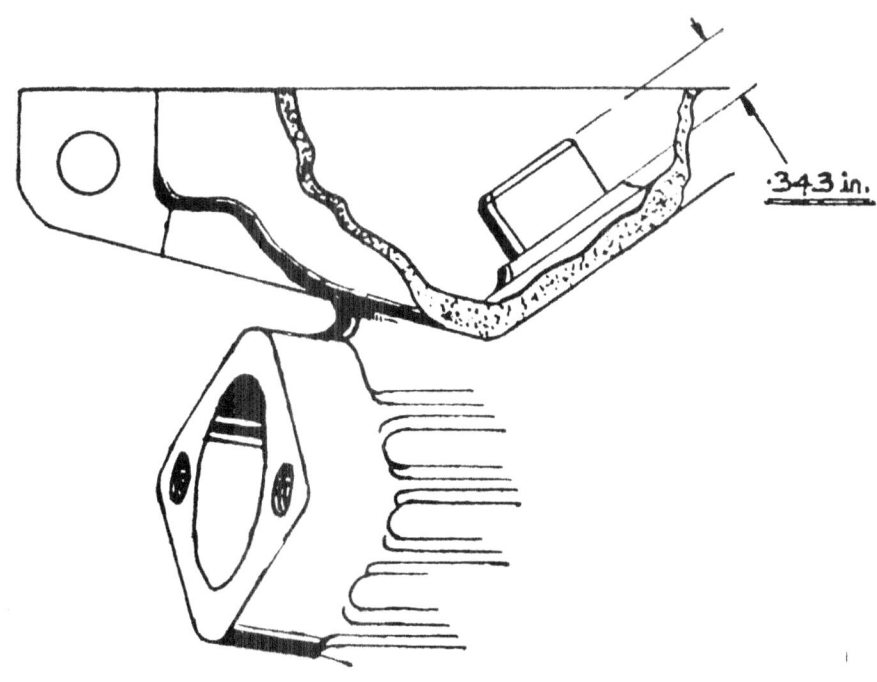

FIG. 9.
RENEWAL OF VALVE GUIDES.

Renewal of Valve Guides. (Fig. 9.)

The valve guides are bored to allow diametrical clearances from the valve stems of .00125-in. to .0025-in. inlet, and .00225-in. to .0035-in. exhaust. The cylinder head is heated during manufacture when the guides are fitted. Do not attempt to press out a valve guide unless the metal around it is heated. The temperature should not exceed about 100 centigrade (boiling point of water). Immersion in boiling water is a suitable method of heating. Alternatively the metal surrounding the guide can be heated with a blowlamp provided that the flame is not concentrated and allowed to play too long on one spot.

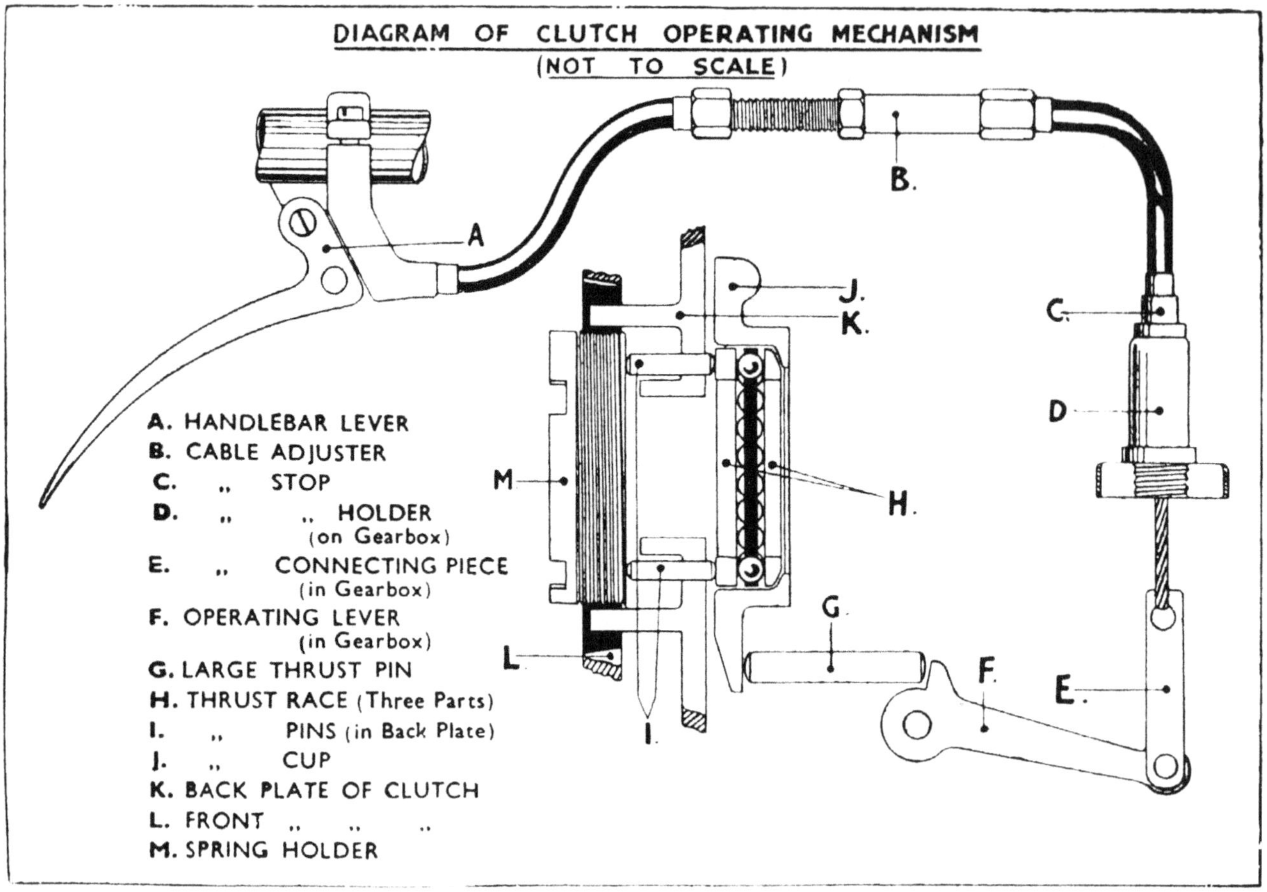

DIAGRAM OF CLUTCH OPERATING MECHANISM
(NOT TO SCALE)
A. HANDLEBAR LEVER
B. CABLE ADJUSTER
C. ,, STOP
D. ,, ,, HOLDER (on Gearbox)
E. ,, CONNECTING PIECE (in Gearbox)
F. OPERATING LEVER (in Gearbox)
G. LARGE THRUST PIN
H. THRUST RACE (Three Parts)
I. ,, PINS (in Back Plate)
J. ,, CUP
K. BACK PLATE OF CLUTCH
L. FRONT ,, ,, ,,
M. SPRING HOLDER
A
B.
C
D
E.
F
G.
H.
I.
J.
K.
L
M

FIG. 10

CABLE ADJUSTER
CLUTCH THRUST RING
3 CLUTCH BACK-PLATE THRUST PINS
CLUTCH SPRING HOLDER

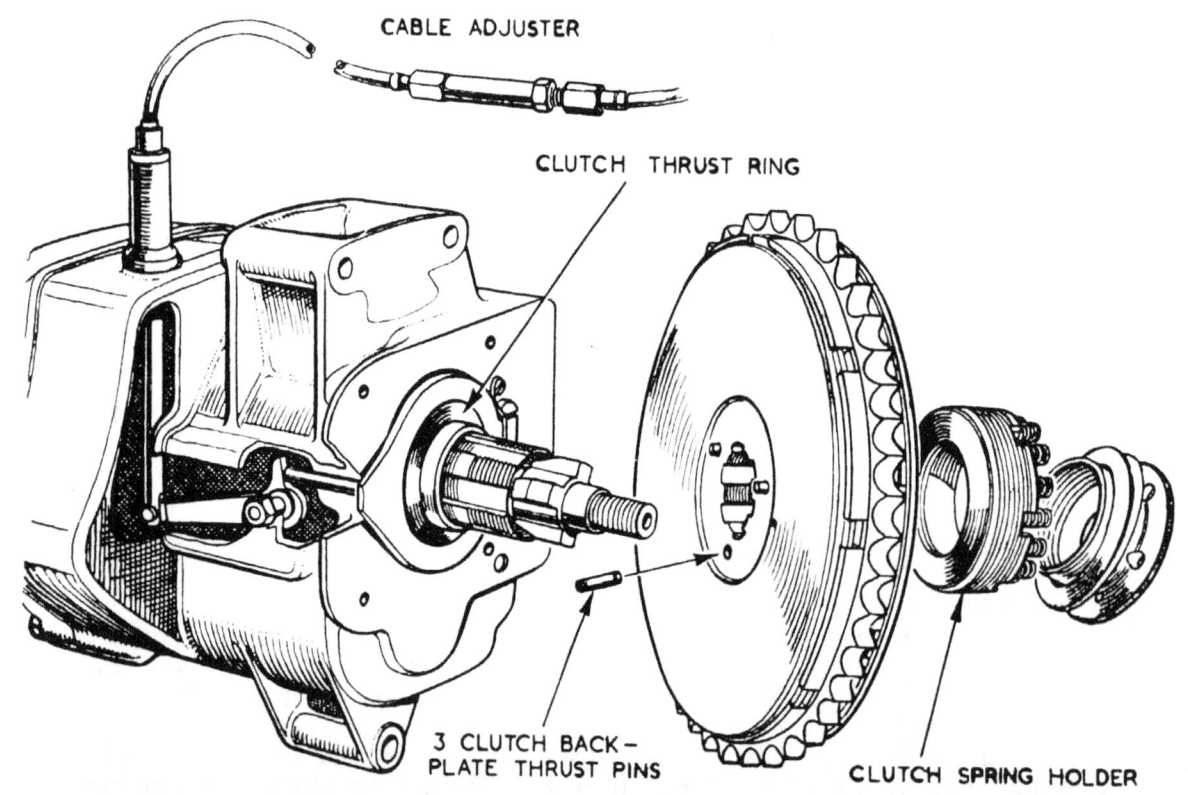

By courtesy of "The Motor Cycle."

THE CLUTCH OPERATING MECHANISM SHOWING INTERNAL LEVER AND THRUST PIN

The head must also be heated before fitting new guides which are pressed in leaving $\frac{11}{32}$-in. protruding from the machined face around the valve guide hole.

True up the seats concentric with the guide bores after fitting, and grind in the valves.

THE CLUTCH.
Description of Working. (Fig. 10).

The clutch is operated by a thrust cup carrying a thrust bearing instead of by the more usual single thrust rod operating through a hollow gear shaft as on the L.E. Model, the Valiant, and most other makes. The adjustment which becomes necessary periodically to allow for settling and wear on the friction linings is made by means of the screwed clutch spring holder threaded into the front plate of the clutch, and not by alteration to the cable adjustment. A cable adjuster is fitted, but this is used for controlling the cable adjustment only and must not be used as a "first-aid" remedy for a slipping clutch.

Before attempting any adjustment to the clutch it is important that the operation of the clutch is properly understood and the following explanation should be studied by anyone unfamiliar with the design.

The operating mechanism is shown diagrammatically below.

The movement of the handlebar lever (A) raises the operating lever (F) in the gearbox and the raised tip of the lever forces the large thrust pin (G) against the projecting lip of the thrust cup (J), causing the thrust cup to hinge outwards with the opposite side acting as the fulcrum.

If the outer clutch plate is observed whilst the handlebar lever is operated, with the clutch stationary, the plate will be seen to tilt outwards, as only that part of the plate nearest the thrust pin side of the clutch is freed from contact with the friction linings.

For the clutch to become fully disengaged the plates have to complete one revolution, after which the spherically seated, self-aligning ball thrust bearing (H) seated in the thrust cup levels the plates and frees them from the friction linings.

The disengagement of the front plate is arranged by the transmission of the outward movement of the thrust through the bearing (H) and three thrust pins (I) against the adjustable clutch spring holder (M) screwed into the front plate (L).

The thrust pins (I) are fitted freely in holes in the back plate (K).

Because of the tilting of the front plate the plates are "peeled off" from contact with each other so that when correctly adjusted and maintained this type of clutch does not cause the unpleasant grating of the gears on starting away which is often noticeable with other makes.

It will be understood that in normal use and a condition of correct adjustment the thrust pins and thrust bearing are free of all thrust loading. It will also be noted that settling or wear of the friction linings will allow the outer plate (L) to close slightly towards the backplate (K) due to the reduction in friction lining thickness. As the thrust cup (J), when not in operation, is held against its seating and the face of the gearbox by a spring clip (not shown), it follows that the initial freedom in the thrust bearing and thrust pins will gradually be reduced, until a stage is reached in which, if adjustment is not carried out the thrust pins and bearings will be carrying part of the pressure of the clutch springs. The result will be clutch slip and premature wearing of the thrust bearing.

In such circumstances adjustment has to be made to the clutch spring holder (M) which must be turned forward (anti-clockwise) in relation to the front plate (L) to restore free movement in the thrust mechanism.

Adjustment of Clutch. (Fig. 11.)

Only in special circumstances, as described later, is adjustment of the clutch cable midway adjuster required.

In the ordinary way the adjustment is made by turning the clutch spring holder in the clutch front plate by engaging the flat end of the adjusting

FIG. 11. ADJUSTMENT OF CLUTCH.

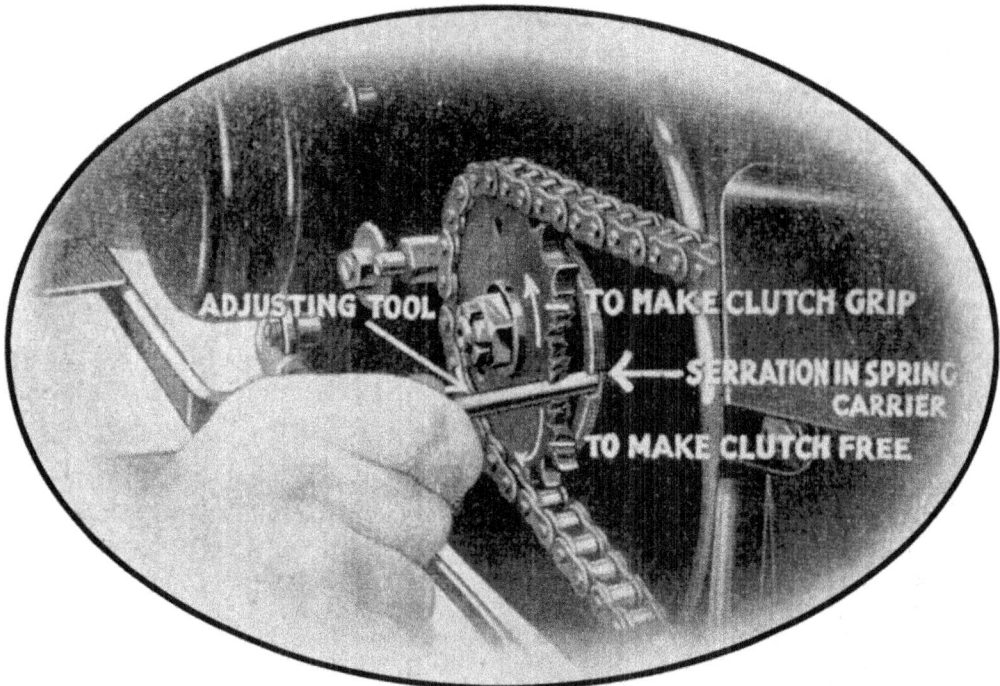

For clarity the sprocket is shown "broken away" to show the adjusting tool engaged in the clutch spring holder. (The movement is reversed if a gear is engaged whilst adjusting. See page 32).

tool KA62/2 with one of the notches in the edge of the clutch spring holder through the ¼-in hole in the final drive sprocket and moving the rear wheel in the direction required.

To use the adjusting peg in the sprocket the front section of the rear chain guard has to be detached from the primary chain case. The chain guard is marked to indicate the need for its removal.

The adjustment is made normally with the gears in neutral, and only in an exceptional case is it made when an indirect gear is engaged. Such contingencies will be dealt with later.

To prevent clutch slip, i.e., to increase free movement in the operation, pull the rear wheel forward so that the final drive sprocket and adjusting tool will move the clutch spring holder forward in relation to the clutch front plate.

Should the clutch fail to free properly after this adjustment, the clutch cable adjustment may need a little correction: see next section.

Adjustment of Clutch on New Machines or after fitting New Cable Assembly.

The adjustment of the clutch is correct when a new machine is despatched from the factory, but the friction linings (clutch inserts) may settle during the first few hundred miles running, and readjustment may be needed fairly soon.

The clutch cable adjustment seldom needs attention after the initial compression and settling of the outer casings and ferrules of a new cable assembly has taken place. The control cable itself does not stretch, but very slight shortening of the total length of the casings may occur with new parts and has the same effect as a lengthened inner wire.

A careful watch should be kept on the clutch lever during the running in period of a new machine, if the clutch has been relined, or a new cable assembly has been fitted.

The settling down of the clutch inserts allows the clutch front plate to close in gradually towards the back plate and reduces the freedom allowed in the thrust bearing during assembly.

This in turn causes the control cable to lose some free movement. On the other hand any shortening of the control cable casings due to compression will tend to hide the fact that the inserts have settled and clutch slip is possible even whilst there is still some lost motion in the cable.

It is recommended, therefore, that during the service check normally carried out after the first 500 miles running, the clutch adjustment should be dealt with by carrying out a series of operations, each very simple, exactly as described later and in the order given.

With the clutch in correct adjustment it must be possible to pull back the clutch lever quite freely, and without operating the clutch at all, far enough to move the inner wire (or clutch cable) $\frac{1}{8}$-in. to $\frac{3}{16}$-in. Should this free movement be seen to have decreased, re-adjustment must be made at once.

The sequence of operations for adjusting as mentioned previously is as follows :

Operation 1.—Slacken off the midway cable adjuster fully to allow the nipple to be detached from the handlebar lever and slip it out of the hole in the lever.

Operation 2.—Open both throttle and air controls fully. Select neutral position of the gears, and depress the kickstart against compression and test for clutch slip. If the clutch is felt to slip omit Operation 3 and carry on with Operation 4.

If no slip can be felt carry on with Operation 3.

Operation 3.—Using the clutch adjusting peg as already described, pull the rear wheel backward a quarter of a turn at a time checking for clutch slip after each movement. This will involve taking out the adjusting peg from engagement with the clutch spring holder before each test. As soon as the clutch can be felt to slip (and only just slip), proceed with Operation 4.

Operation 4.—Refit the cable nipple to the handlebar lever. Re-adjust the midway adjuster until all lost motion is taken out of the cable and the lever is just drawn up against the lever bracket on the handlebar. Do not force the adjustment but *only just* remove all play. When correct tighten the cable adjuster locknut.

Finally, refit the adjusting peg to the sprocket, engage it with the clutch spring holder, and pull the rear wheel forward a little at a time until free movement begins to appear on the cable when the handlebar lever is checked.

Adjust until there is free travel on the cable of $\frac{1}{8}$-in. to $\frac{3}{16}$-in

The adjustment is now completed.

Although the foregoing may seem complicated at first sight the whole "drill" is both easily and quickly carried out, and after the initial settling of a new cable assembly has taken place is only likely to be needed in special circumstances, as for instance if it is not known whether adjustment is needed to the cable or the spring holder. The effect of the two adjustments is inter-related.

If in doubt as to whether the cable or spring holder should be adjusted the following should be referred to :—

Symptom :   Clutch slipping. No lost motion on control cable.
Remedy :   Readjust clutch spring holder forward.

Symptom :   Clutch slipping. Lost motion present on control cable.*
Remedy :   Carry out Operation 4 of Adjustment "drill."

Symptom :   Clutch not freeing. Normal or excess lost motion on cable.
Remedy :   Carry out full Adjustment "drill."

Symptom :   Clutch slipping and also not freeing.*
Remedy :   Carry out Operation 4 of Adjustment "drill."

It can be accepted that if clutch trouble is not eliminated by carrying out the "drill" exactly as described the clutch will have to be dismantled to attend to a mechanical fault, to rectify incorrect assembly, or to replace worn parts.

* See next section.

Adjusting a Tight Clutch Spring Holder.

If excessive slip through neglect of the adjustment, or a spring holder which is tight in the clutch front plate, causes the clutch front plate to turn with it when adjustment is attempted, the adjustment should be made in the following manner.

Engage either second or third gear, and after passing the adjusting peg through the sprocket, move the clutch by means of the kickstart until one of the notches in the spring holder is opposite the peg and engage the peg in the notch.

To make the clutch grip *move the rear wheel backwards*. This is the opposite direction to that used when adjusting with the gears in neutral.

By adjusting with an indirect gear engaged advantage is taken of the difference in the rates of movement of the clutch sleeve gear (to which the clutch driven plates are attached) and the final drive sprocket.

Oil in the Clutch.

The primary chain case is intended to carry enough oil to lubricate the chain, and the clutch will grip satisfactorily even if there is an excess of oil in the cover provided that from the outset the cover has had oil in it.

It has been found however, that a clutch which has been run completely free of oil over a period will be subject to slip if oil is subsequently introduced on to the friction surfaces. In such circumstances the clutch must be relined, and assembled with oil in the cover.

REMOVAL OF DYNAMO AND BELT COVER. (Fig. 7.)

Remove the outer half of the cover by unbolting it from the back half and taking off the nut holding it to the primary chain case.

Disconnect the positive (+) leads from the rear (red) terminal of the battery. This is most important.

Remove the dynamo clamp bolt (1) and turn the dynamo carcase in its mounting to loosen the belt. Take off the belt.

Pull out the single pin plug from the socket which protrudes through the commutator cover. The cover is marked +B at this point. (Fig. 34, page 76).

Take out the two screws holding the voltage regulator base to the dynamo strap.

Pull the dynamo and the back half of the belt cover out to the left side of the machine from under the strap, at the same time leading the two cables connecting the regulator to the dynamo out between the crankcase and strap.

To take the back half of the cover off the dynamo, remove the armature nut and draw the belt pulley off the taper. If a claw extractor is used be careful not to break the flange of the pulley.

It is usually possible to remove the pulley, after taking off the nut, by supporting it from the back and delivering a light sharp blow on the end of the armature. Always use a soft punch to avoid harming the thread if this method is used.

PRIMARY CHAIN COVER.

Removal of Front Half.

Proceed as described in the preceding section to remove the dynamo belt, but do not take out the dynamo clamp bolt. Remove the front part of the rear chain cover to expose the rear chain driving sprocket. Remove the split cotter from the shock absorber collar nut. Drain the primary cover.

With the rear brake held on; loosen and remove the sprocket nut and the shock absorber collar nut, using spanner A61/2AS for the former and A229 for the latter. Preserve the plain washers which are fitted behind these nuts. The driving pulley, and pulley flange will come off with the collar nut. Remove the shock absorber spring and shock absorber clutch from the engine shaft.

The rear half of the belt cover can be raised over the engine shaft and the cover swung round out of the way of the primary cover.

Unscrew the primary chain cover strap fixing pin (3), Fig. 7, page 22, from the lug on the strap. Free the strap from the cover all round and push it off and over the back half of the cover. Remove the chain case fixing bolt (5) and distance piece. Pull out the joint moulding.

Remove the cover. Preserve the distance tube fitted between the halves of the cover, and the felt oil seal.

Removal of Primary Chain.

Fix the sprockets to prevent them turning by mounting a sprag from the bottom of the engine sprocket to the top of the clutch chain wheel. Take off the sleeve gear nut locking plate, held to the sleeve gear nut by a $\frac{1}{8}$-in. Whit. screw, and unscrew the sleeve gear nut, using the pegged end of the spanner A61/2AS. It will have to be started by driving it round, using a mallet on the spanner (Fig. 12).

As the chain is endless the engine sprocket and clutch assembly have to be drawn off their respective shafts together. The clutch may have to be levered off to start it by using levers carefully between the clutch back plate and the chain case. If care is taken to hold the clutch front plate and back-plate firmly together the clutch can then be refitted afterwards without it having been separated, unless of course it needs attention. Preserve the three thrust pins from the clutch back plate.

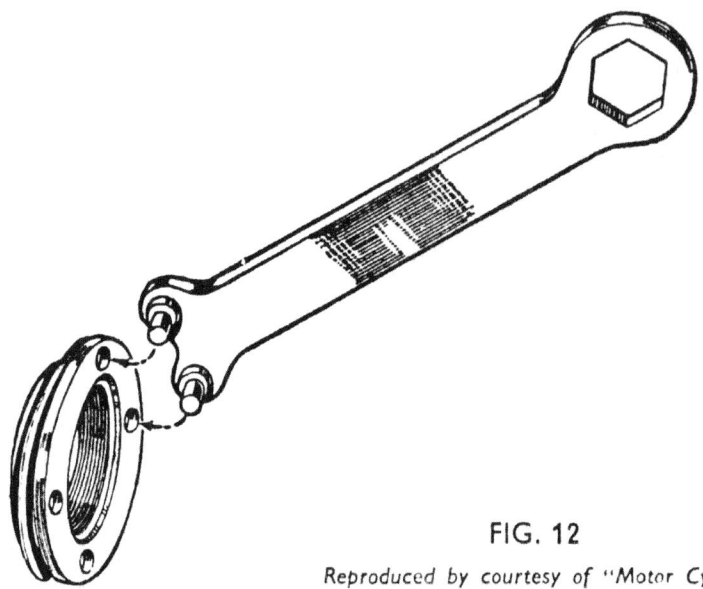

FIG. 12

Reproduced by courtesy of "Motor Cycling."

SPANNER A61/2AS AND SLEEVE GEAR NUT.

Removal of Rear Half of the Primary Chain Cover.

Having removed the clutch, the clutch thrust bearing is accessible, and the four screws securing the half cover to the gearbox can be taken out after cutting and drawing out the locking wires from the screw heads.

A gasket is fitted between the cover and the gearbox and an oil seal ring between the cover and crankcase.

Refitting the Rear Half.

Verify that the chain case oil seal is in good order and in place on the crankcase main bearing boss. Stick the gasket—or a new one if needed—to the face of the gearbox with grease. Mount the chain case back half in place. Insert the four fixing screws and tighten fully. Fit new locking wires and twist the ends round securely to lock them.

Use two lengths of wire passed through the screws horizontally. Do not wire upper to lower screws as this will interfere with the working of the thrust cup.

Refitting Primary Chain.

Engage top gear to prevent the sleeve gear slipping through its ballrace as the clutch is fitted. Verify the condition of the clutch thrust bearing, grease well, and replace, and see that the sleeve gear distance piece is in place on the sleeve gear and fitted through the thrust bearing.

Take up the clutch assembly, holding the back and front plates firmly together and stick the three thrust pins with grease into the holes in the clutch back plate. These pins are each $\frac{3}{16}$-in. dia. $\times$ .453-in., and must not be confused with the thrust pins used in the kickstart ratchet—so that if this also has been dismantled the point should be checked.

Hang the chain over the clutch chain wheel, and rest the engine sprocket in the loop. The clutch assembly and engine sprocket with the chain in place have now to be placed on their respective shafts. Care is necessary not to allow the clutch plates to separate, and assistance is desirable for this part of the work.

Refitting the Sleeve Gear Nut.

In order easily to refit the sleeve gear nut, which sometimes makes it necessary to compress the clutch springs slightly, the use of Service Tool X2959 sleeve gear nut adaptor (Fig. 13) is advisable. This is fitted over the gearshaft with the pegs engaged in the holes in the sleeve gear nut and the gear shaft nut used to compress the springs enough to start the sleeve gear nut on the thread. The four holes in the adaptor are to enable the peg spanner A61/2AS to be used to turn it.

After starting the sleeve gear nut on the threads, and having fitted the shock absorber clutch, spring, pulley, washer, and shock absorber collar nut sprag the chain and tighten both the sleeve gear nut and the shock absorber collar nut fully, finally driving the spanners round with a mallet. Fit the split-pin to the engine shaft. Readjust the clutch. See page 30.

Refitting Front Half of Primary Chain Cover. (Fig. 7.)

Put the chain case sealing strap in place over the back of the rear half of the primary chain cover. Fit the oil seal felt into its housing inside the cover around the opening for the clutch spring holder.* Fit the front half into place, setting it in line with the back half, locating the chain case bolt distance piece over the plunged in edges of the bolt holes in the covers, fit the bolt with its distance piece and washer (5) and tighten up.

Press the joint moulding into place round the edges of the two halves of the cover with the ends at the top, and see that the centre rib fits between the cover faces. Bring the sealing strap over from the back into place over the moulding and tighten the bolt (3).

The reassembly of the dynamo belt cover calls for no special mention.

Refill the chain case with oil, it needs about ⅛ pint of S.A.E.40 oil.

* A new felt should be stuck in place with Bostick and be soaked in oil or molten tallow.

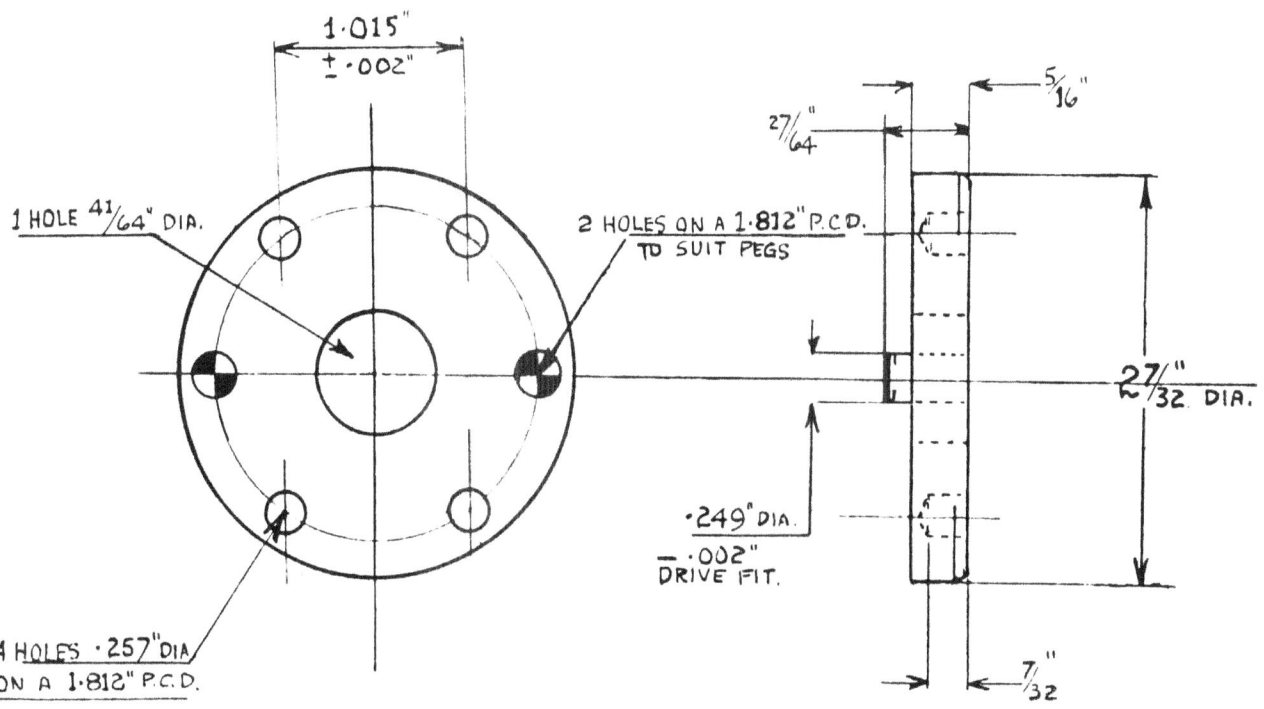

FIG. 13.
X2959. SLEEVE GEAR NUT ADAPTOR.

THE KICKSTART.

Dismantling Kickstart Ratchet and Spring. (Fig. 14).

Drain the oil from the gearbox by removing the plug from the end cover (Fig. 15). Take out the three ¼-in. bolts holding the kickstart bearing to the end cover and draw it out of position with the ratchet, and kickstart crank, etc. Preserve the layshaft thrust washer from inside the ratchet.

Should the spring be broken the kickstart crank cotter can be removed at once, but if not the bearing and ratchet have to be held against the tension of the spring whilst driving out the cotter.

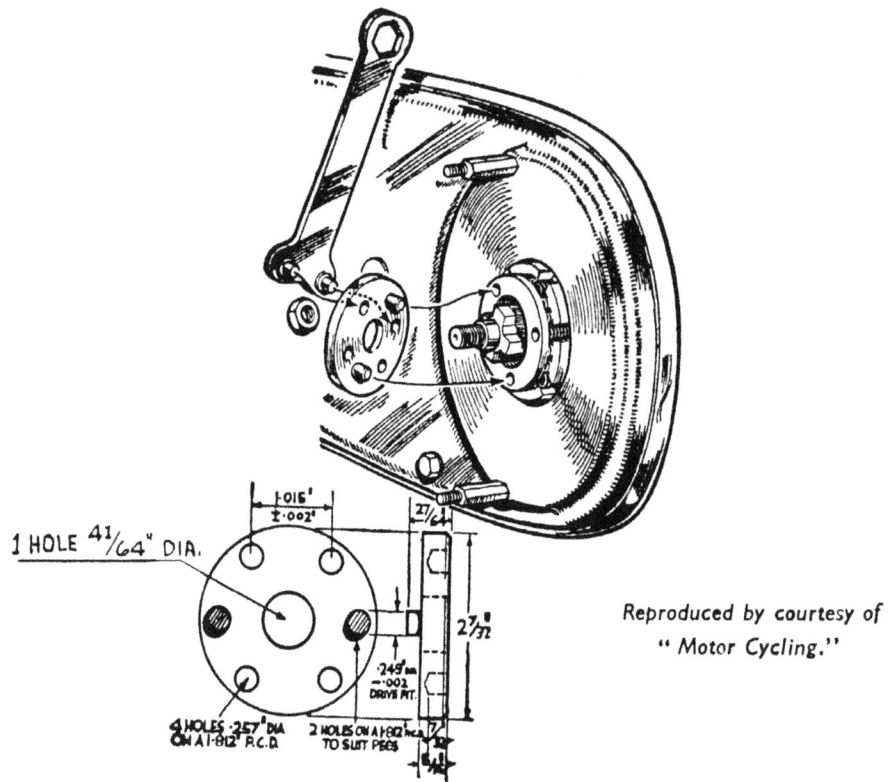

FIG. 13a. (SEE FIG. 13.)

Remove the cotter nut and washer. Obtain two 2-in. nails of small enough diameter to enter the breather holes in the ratchet. Knock these into the bench 1 19/32-in. (1.593-in.) apart, or into a piece of wood held in the vice. Cut off the heads leaving about ½-in. protruding from the surface of the wood.

Place the kick-start assembly, with the ratchet teeth downwards over the nails, entering the nails into the breather holes. Turn the kickstart bearing in a clockwise direction against the spring sufficiently to allow the head of the cotter to clear the disengaging ramp on the bearing. Drive out the cotter and gradually release the bearing.

If the spring is broken the ratchet will pull out of the bearing when the crank is tapped off. If unbroken tap the ratchet through far enough to expose the loop of the spring where this is fitted to the ratchet. Unhook the spring from its mounting and pull out the ratchet.

Note that the ratchet carries three thrust pins, $\frac{3}{16}$-in. dia. $\times$ $\frac{9}{16}$-in. long (.187-in. $\times$ .5625-in.) which must be preserved for refitting. These must not be confused with the three clutch thrust pins which are much shorter.

Take out the engaging spring which will be loose inside the kickstart bearing. Unscrew the kickstart spring anchor peg and remove the return spring—or the part of it if broken.

Replacement of Kick-start Spring. (Fig. 14.)

Push the end of the spring with the smaller loop (X) into the mouth of the kickstart bearing and by twisting the spring clockwise whilst holding the bearing firmly it will be found possible to work round the spring coil by coil and get it into place. In its free state the outside diameter of the spring is greater than the internal diameter of the kickstart bearing, but by twisting it round as described the coils will be compressed and will enter easily.

FIG. 14.

Reproduced by courtesy of " Motor Cycling."

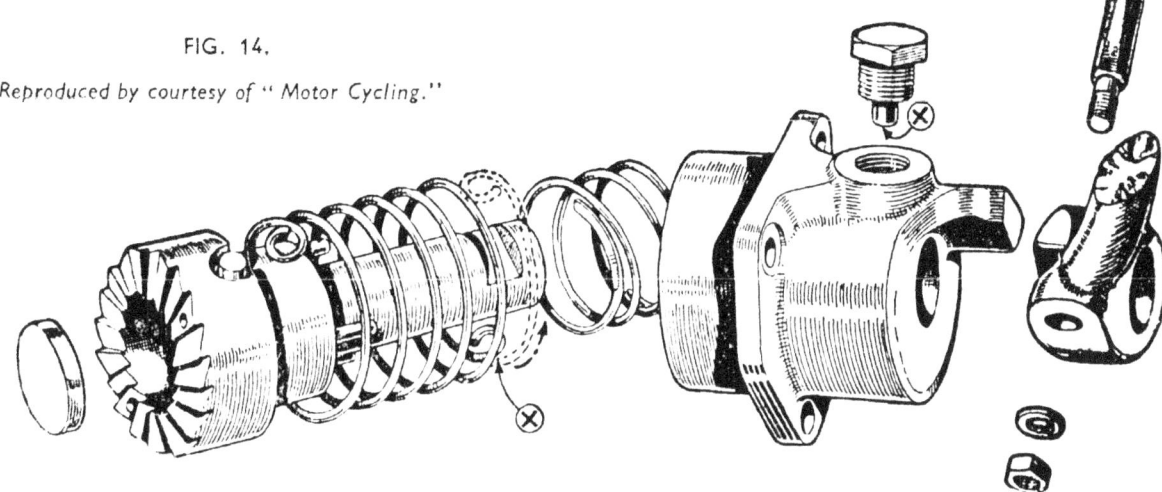

KICKSTART RATCHET AND SPRINGS.

Leave the end of the spring with the larger loop, and one coil protruding, and manoeuvre the smaller loop in the kickstart bearing under the hole which carries the anchor peg and screw the peg home with its tip (X) through the spring loop.

Fit the three thrust pins into the ratchet. There are six holes, but the three breather holes are slightly smaller than the others. **Note specially** that the correct thrust pins must be used. These are $\frac{3}{16}$-in. $\times \frac{9}{16}$-in. and are the same part as the big-end rollers. Discarded big-end rollers can be used as replacements. Do not, however, confuse them with the clutch thrust pins which are only .453-in. long. Stick them in place with a little grease.

FIG. 15.

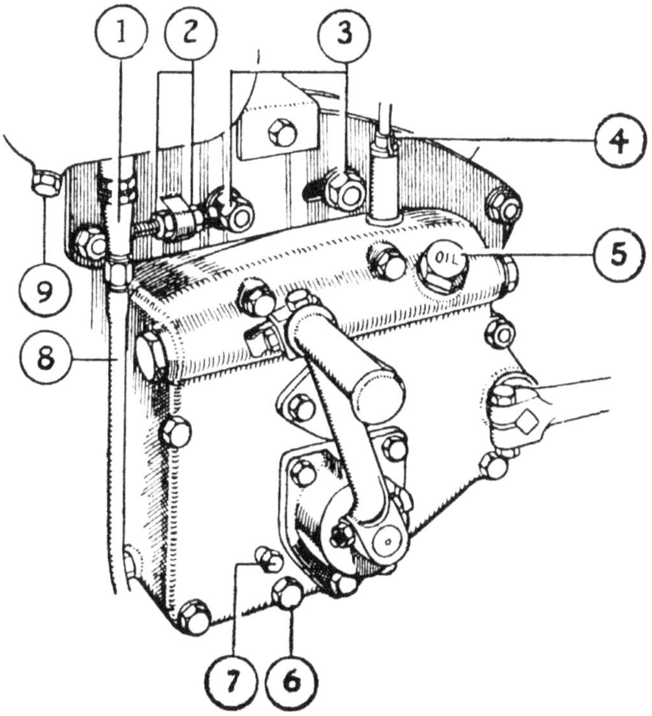

(1) Ball Valve Assembly
(2) Chain Adjuster Nuts
(3) Gearbox Mounting Bolt Nuts
(4) Clutch Cable Stop
(5) Gearbox Oil Filler Plug
(6) Gearbox Oil Drain Plug
(7) Gearbox Oil Level Plug
(8) Engine Oil Feed Pipe
(9) Oil Tank Drain Plug

Fit the engaging spring over the ratchet and push the ratchet into the kickstart bearing, engaging the loop of the spring (that was left protruding) over the anchor lug, that is formed on the ratchet. Twist the ratchet round clockwise and push it further into the bearing at the same time entering the spring.

Place the ratchet over the two nails that were used in dismantling and fit the kickstart crank over the end of the ratchet.

Turn the housing round clockwise just far enough to allow the cotter to go through the crank across the flat on the ratchet. It fits from front to back. Do not in any circumstances turn the housing further than is needed to fit the cotter. Any extra tensioning of the spring will permanently distort and damage it.

Refitting Kickstart Assembly. (Fig. 14.)

Before fitting the assembly to the gearbox see that the layshaft washer is in place against the ratchet gear, the kickstarter bearing bush on the end of the layshaft, and the kickstart layshaft thrust washer in the ratchet

Do not use a gasket between the face of the kickstart bearing and the gearbox end cover. Tighten the three bolts fully. Refill the gearbox.

REMOVAL OF ENGINE AND GEARBOX FROM FRAME.

The engine and gearbox are held together as a unit by the rear engine plates and any extensive overhaul of the engine that involves separating the crankcase will necessitate removing the engine and gearbox units together. The primary chain cover, etc., should also be left in place.

It is possible, however, to renew any of the gears or shafts in the gearbox without removing the housing from the frame, and only the replacement of the sleeve gear bearing, or lay-shaft ball-bearing that are both fitted to the housing would require its removal. The engine would then have to come out as well. The cylinder head steady, carburetter, and exhaust pipe must, of course, be removed.

The air cleaner assembly and oil tank are attached to the frame at the top and to the rear engine plates at the bottom, and have to be removed as a preliminary to reach the rear engine plates.

The oil tank need not necessarily be drained before removal.

Remove the dynamo; see page 33. Take off the front section of the rear chain guard, it is attached to the primary chain cover by two ¼-in. B.S.F. nuts.

Disconnect the clutch and exhaust lift cable assemblies at the handlebar levers and pull the cables clear from any clips on the frame.

Pull out the split cotter from the shock absorber collar. If the gearbox is to be dismantled it is a help if at this stage the gearbox end cover plate is removed from the gearbox end cover, and the gearbox mainshaft nut inside the opening loosened. The shaft can then be held from turning by applying the rear brake.

Also loosen the shock absorber collar. Next remove the gearbox sprocket nut and pull the final drive sprocket off the shaft with the chain. The chain need not be removed unless it is to be cleaned or replaced.

Take the weight of the unit on a block below the crankcase, and remove all bolts from the front engine plates and three from the rear plates. One at the top rear corner, one from the bottom rear corner, and one bolt passing through the frame lug, bottom front ends of the engine plates, and crankcase. On this last there is a distance piece between the frame lug and the engine plate on the right hand side.

The whole unit can now be levered forwards and lifted out of the frame.

Separation of Gearbox from Engine.

Remove the primary chain cover front half, the clutch, engine sprocket, and primary chain, and the rear half of the chain cover from the gearbox (see page 33). The bolt holding the engine plates to the crankcase is now accessible for removal after which the gearbox assembly and rear engine plates will pull away from the crankcase.

OVERHAULING THE ENGINE.

Removal of Cylinder and Piston.

The removal of the cylinder head is dealt with on page 24.

Remove the cylinder barrel. This will be made easier if the crankcase bolts and studs are freed off first. Note that if compression plates are fitted between the cylinder and crankcase they must be kept aside for refitting when rebuilding the engine.

The piston is removable after taking out one circlip and driving out the gudgeon pin. A slot will be found running into the circlip groove at one side of the piston for the purpose of allowing the use of a sharp bradawl or scriber to prise it out. Use a soft metal punch against the opposite end of the gudgeon pin, have an assistant support the piston against the force of the blows and drive out the gudgeon pin. Help is essential here otherwise there is a risk of bending the connecting rod. The pin is a light driving fit when the piston is cold.

Inspection of Cylinder, Piston and Rings.

Examine the bore for wear or scoring. The original bore diameters are on page 7. Reboring is generally considered necessary if wear in excess of .008-in. has taken place or the bore is damaged or scored. Cylinders do not wear uniformly, but the maximum wear will be found to have occurred towards the top of the bore at the back. To measure the wear therefore, take an accurate reading of the diameter from front to back, just below the ridge left at the top end of the ring travel. This reading may then easily be compared with a measurement taken below the part traversed by the rings which will usually be found almost unworn.

Piston rings should be examined for uneven bearing on the cylinder, excessive gap, or side play in the grooves. Any patches of discolouration on the bearing surfaces of the rings indicate that blow-by has been taking place and renewal may be necessary. The ring gaps of course increase with wear and may increase up to 50% before replacement.

New piston rings supplied by us are correctly gapped for unworn bores. Clearances are given on page 7.

Pistons and rings are obtainable in two oversizes +.020-in. and +.040-in. on diameter. Oversize piston rings cannot be fitted to a worn bore unless the bore is reground to the correct diameter of the replacement rings, in which case an oversize piston would be essential also.

Compression Plates

It will be noted that M.S.S. and Venom models produced from early 1969 onwards will be fitted with the Thruxton type cylinder (M22/18.) The two .062-in. thick plates present at the base of the cylinder **must not be removed** in efforts to increase the compression ratio. Compression plates .010-in. or .031-in. thick which may also be present are fitted as required when the engine is initially built.

Dismantling the Timing Cover and Timing Gears.

The timing cover is held to the crankcase by ten screws. Remove these and tap the cover gently at the edges with a mallet or soft hammer to free it from the joint face and pull it off. Do not insert wedges between the faces.

Remove four bolts (2; $\frac{5}{16}$-in., and 2; $\frac{1}{4}$-in.) holding the timing gear steady plate to the crankcase and the bottom rocker and intermediate gear spindles, also take off the nut from the end of the camwheel spindle. The second nut on the steady plate holds the cam oil jet and should be left in place. Remove the steady plate.

Undo the magneto armature nut in the centre of the timing unit. After loosening, the nut will tighten and begin to withdraw the timing unit from the armature.

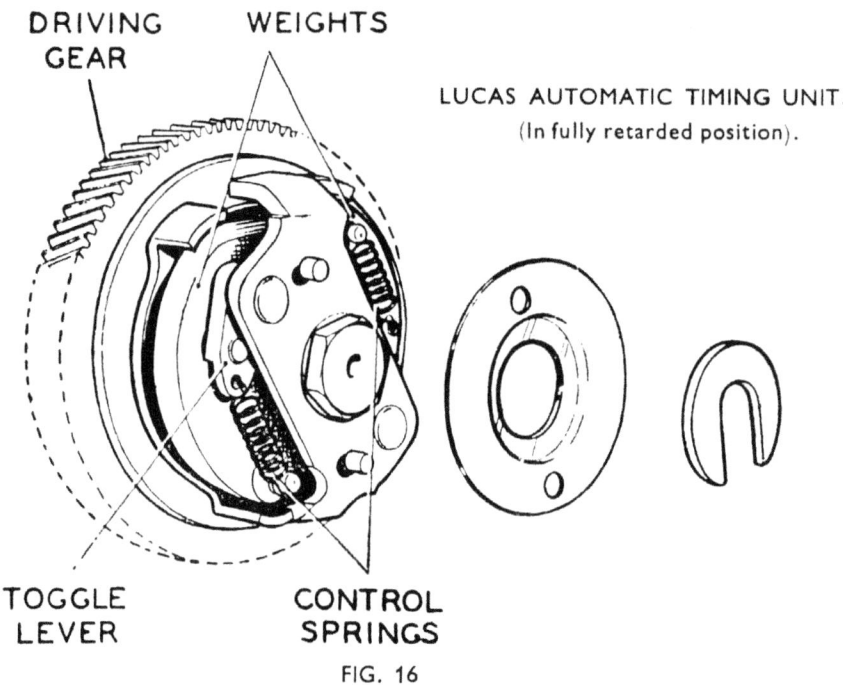

LUCAS AUTOMATIC TIMING UNIT.
(In fully retarded position).

FIG. 16

Pull the cam followers off the spindle, being careful to preserve the "Belleville" thrust washer that is fitted between the inlet cam follower and the crankcase. Draw from their respective spindles the camwheel assembly and intermediate gear assembly. The crankshaft pinion and oil-pump worm cannot be drawn off the shaft until the oil pump is out of the way, but the mainshaft nut (left-hand thread) can be removed at this stage. Preserve the timing shaft (tongued) washer which is behind it.

Removal of Oil Pump. (Fig. 17.)

It is important not to attempt to take out the oil pump assembly before heating the crankcase around the pump to expand the pump housing. If forced out cold the housing will be scored which may scrap the crankcase.

Take out the four oil pump fixing screws which hold the pump base plate to the crankcase. Three of the holes in the base plate and two of those in the crankcase are visible in the illustration. Note that the screw fitted to the inner front corner is longer than the other three.

Heat the crankcase around the oil pump housing. A blow lamp can be used if care is taken not to play the flame continuously on one point or overheat the metal. As the metal is warmed up tap the pump carefully on the top from inside the timing case until it comes clear. Do not tap on the end of the pump spindle. Do not take the oil pump apart unnecessarily. It is seldom that it needs any attention, and if working freely, and if there has been no lubrication trouble it is best left alone, as a special tool is needed to rebuild it.

Dismantling the Oil Pump.

Take out the four screws securing the pump body and its cover to the base plate. Removal of the plate exposes the two return gears and the cover will pull off the pump body bringing with it the pump spindle and the feed gear cut integral with it. The two return gears and the loose feed gear are then removable from the housing, but as they are taken out mark them with indelible pencil for replacement in the same positions, as it is possible for the two loose gears to be fitted inverted. This is not recommended once the gears have been working and have bedded in to the respective matching gears on the driving spindle.

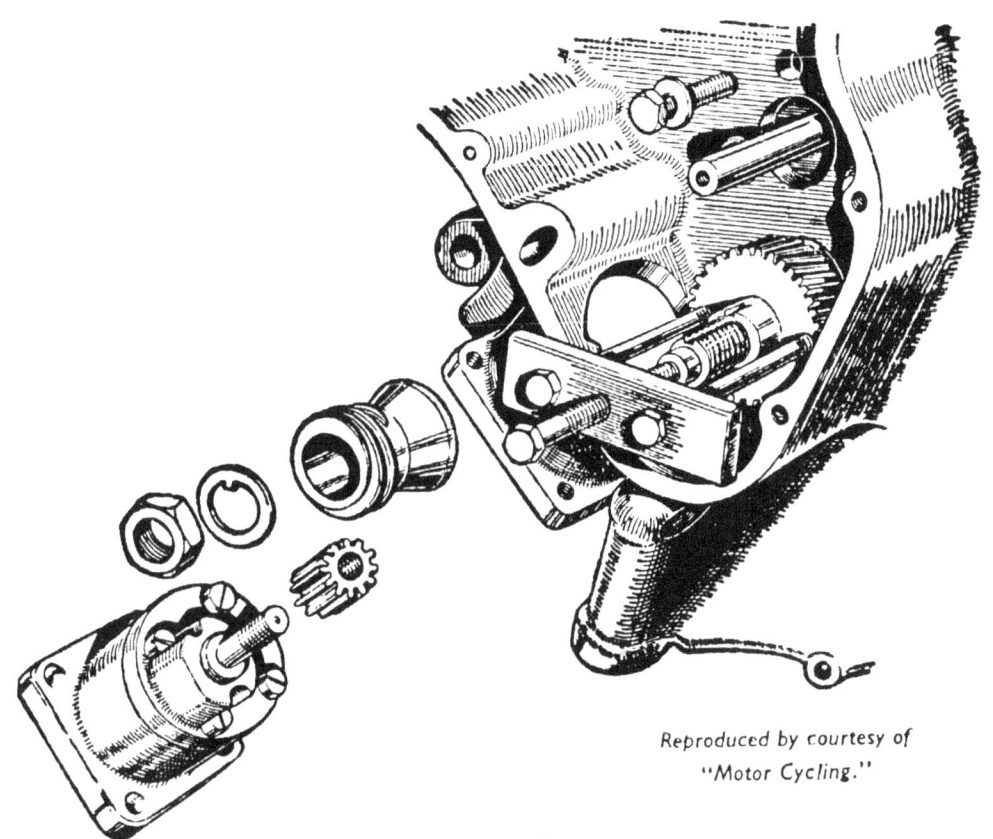

FIG. 17
REMOVAL OF OIL PUMP AND CRANKSHAFT PINION.

The Oil-pump is illustrated after removal, and with small driven pinion taken off. The Crankshaft Timing-pinion is about to be pulled off the shaft with the extractor. X2721.

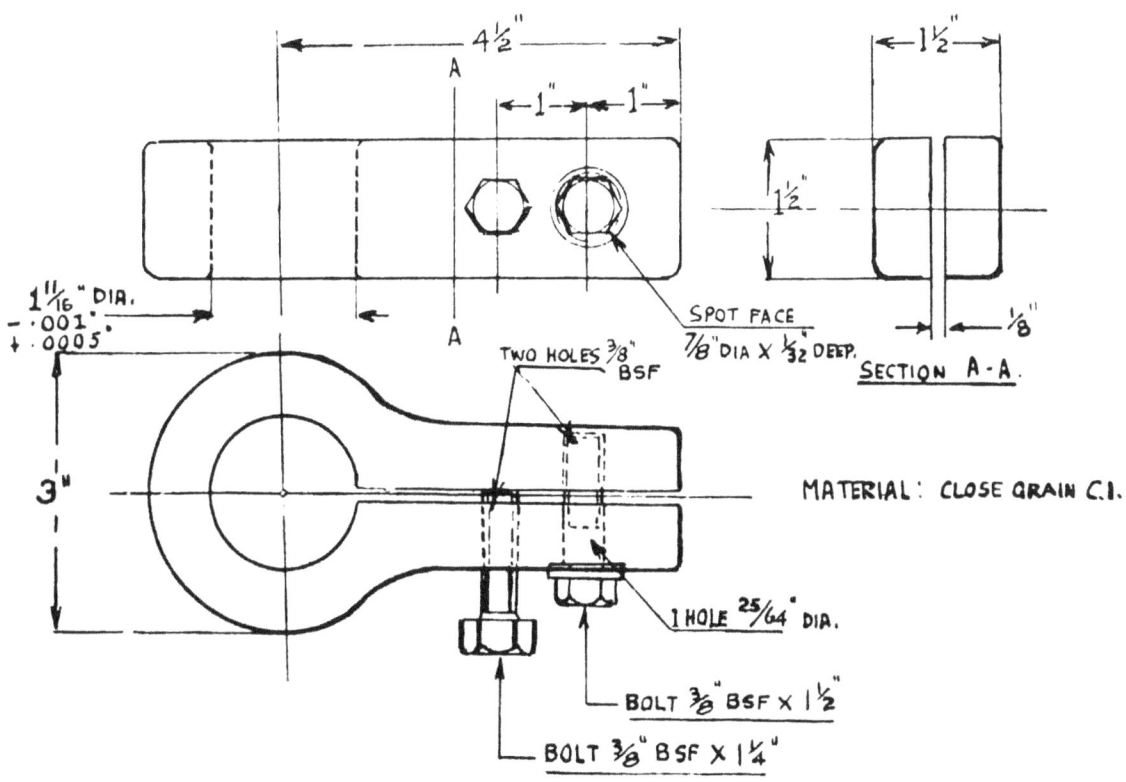

FIG. 18. X2719 OIL PUMP ALIGNMENT TOOL

Overhauling the Oil Pump.

When inspecting the pump, scrutinize the recesses in the pump body, in which the gears run, for any signs of scoring on the walls.

To work efficiently the pump gears must have the minimum clearance possible between the tops of the teeth and the body. They must also revolve freely with at little end float as possible when the pump body and cover are bolted to the base plate.

End float is removable by lapping down the appropriate end face of the pump body so that when in place the gear end faces are practically flush. Any lapping needed must be most carefully done using medium grade grinding compound and rubbing the pump face whilst held quite flat on a surface plate or sheet of plate glass.

Should new gears be fitted, carefully inspect them for any roughness or fraize around the edges and remove this very carefully indeed by polishing with a strip of superfine emery cloth (Grade OO) held on a small file. To take out the spindle from the oil pump cover remove the driving gear that meshes with the worm on the mainshaft. Hold the spindle firmly and unscrew the gear anti-clockwise. A convenient method of holding the spindle to avoid damage is to get a scrap splined return oil pump gear, file flats opposite to each other, and hold it in a vice. The splines of the spindle can then be held in the splines in the gear whilst unscrewing the driven gear.

Reassembling the Oil Pump.

After reassembling the gears and spindle to the pump the pump cover has to be accurately lined up to the body before tightening the four oil pump screws holding the pump to the base plate. For this work Service Tool X2719 oil-pump alignment tool is required (Fig. 18).

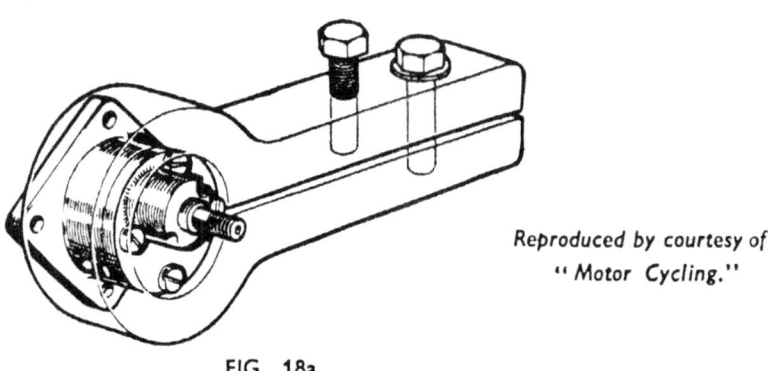

Reproduced by courtesy of "Motor Cycling."

FIG. 18a.

The pump body and cover, loosely mounted to the base plate, are clamped in the tool and the four screws tightened up. Test the pump for freedom of working by turning the spindle. If tight, try slackening off the four screws. If this frees the pump gears the trouble is lack of end play and the pump must be dismantled, the offending gear or gears located, and eased off by lapping down their end faces perfectly square to the bore.

Slight roughness or "lumpiness" can be cured by running a mixture of oil and Turkey stone powder through the pump whilst the pump spindle is rotated in a lathe or drilling machine. After this treatment complete dismantling and scrupulous cleaning in petrol are essential before putting the pump together again in the alignment tool, tightening the body to the base plate and refitting to the engine.

Refitting the Oil Pump to Crankcase.

Heat up the crankcase around the oil pump housing using a blow lamp, but taking care to keep the flame moving about and not concentrated on one spot. Make certain that the crankshaft timing pinion and oil pump drive worm are fitted as they cannot be got into place after fitting the pump. Fit a new base plate gasket over the pump.

Push the pump into the housing lining up the holes in the pump base plate with the screw holes in the crankcase and meshing the driven gear with the worm. The illustration (Fig. 17) shows how the pump is located with the spindle outermost. Tap the pump home and fit the four fixing screws. Note that the long screw fits into the inner front screw hole. This hole is just visible in the illustration in the right-hand bottom corner of the base plate.

Removal of Crankshaft Timing Pinion. (Fig. 19.)

After removal of the oil pump and the left-hand thread mainshaft nut (unscrewed by turning clockwise) pull off the tongue washer behind the nut, and draw the pinion off the shaft, using Service Tool X2721 (Fig. 19).

This is attached to the pinion as shown in Fig. 17 and the tightening of the centre bolt draws the pinion from the mainshaft.

Separating the Crankcase.

Removal of all crankcase bolts and studs enables the crankcase halves to be parted and the flywheel assembly removed. The bearing outer rings will remain in the crankcase and the inner rings with rollers and roller cages come away with the flywheels.

Condition of Main Bearings.

Any uneven wear or pitting of the rollers or roller tracks which would make the bearings run roughly and noisily must be taken as indication that new bearings are necessary. The condition of the outer rings is easily visible without removing them from the crankcase and usually gives some idea of the condition of the inner races, although generally they are less subject to wear than the inners. If the condition of the inner races is in doubt, an inspection can be made after prising out one of the rollers from the cage.

Removal of Main Bearings.

The outer rings are removable from the housings in the crankcase by jarring them out after heating up the housings and the surrounding metal of the crankcase. A blow lamp can be used or the case heated over a gas ring provided that care is taken not to concentrate the flame on one point or overheat the material. A safer method is to immerse the crankcase in boiling water until the housings are expanded to free the bearing rings.

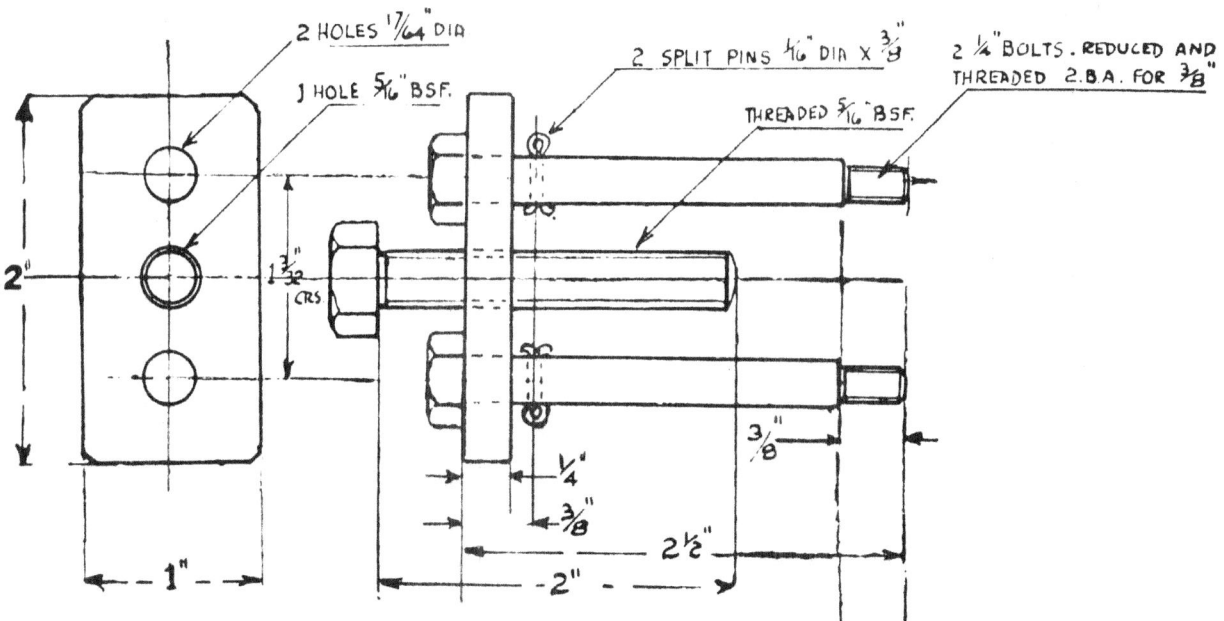

FIG. 19 X2721 CRANKSHAFT TIMING PINION EXTRACTOR.

To jarr out the rings take the crankcase half, protecting the hands with rag, and bring down the open side smartly and quite square on to the bench top or a large block of wood.

To control the end float on the flywheel assembly the lateral position of the bearing outer rings is set by packing shims inserted during assembly between them and their housing. Retain any shims that are fitted; keeping them so that they can be refitted to the housing from which they were taken. The mainshafts are tapered where the bearings seat.

To remove the inner rings, upon which the rollers are retained in cages, the cage must be cut away and the rollers removed. The inner rings must then be split to free them from the shafts. To do this grind through the ring with a small high speed grinding wheel. The operation calls for care and skill as in no circumstances must the grinding wheel be allowed to cut into, or mark the shaft.

Refitting Main Bearings.

Note.—*Do not fit bearings before reading paragraph marked * page 46.*
The taper roller bearings as supplied each consist of a centre ring, rollers, roller cage and outer ring. The centre ring with rollers and cage will separate from the outer ring, but the components of different bearings must not be interchanged.

To fit the outer rings the crankcase must be heated as described above for the dismantling process. When hot place the shims in the housing, or new shims of the same total thickness as those removed, and drop the outer ring squarely into place making sure that the smaller diameter inner end goes in first.

The inner rings each with rollers and cage, are then pressed squarely on to the mainshafts. In this connection be careful not to attempt to fit them on small end first. The taper rollers make it quite clear which way is correct as the larger ends of the rollers must be nearer the flywheel face.

Refitting the Flywheel Assembly.

It is assumed that the big end has not needed attention or has been overhauled as described on page 45, and is ready for refitting to the crankcase.

The intermediate gear spindle must be in place in the crankcase and the joint faces should have been carefully cleaned of all old jointing compound.

Place the timing side half on the bench resting on the timing case face. Oil the rollers of the timing side bearing and fit the flywheel assembly into position entering the timing shaft through the bearing housing and the rollers into the timing side outer ring.

Oil the driving side bearing rollers and fit the driving side half crankcase, setting this in alignment with the timing half. Fit the studs, nuts and bolts and tighten gradually so that the crankcase halves are brought together perfectly square. As the tightening proceeds check the flywheel assembly constantly for freedom of rotation. At the first sign of stiffness in the bearings stop tightening the nuts and bolts and check the extent of the gap left between the joint faces. If the tightening of the nuts, etc., has been done carefully the gap will be the same all round. A gap of .004-in. all round is correct, so that if the shimming behind the bearing outer rings has given this result, the crankcase may be separated for the application of a light smear of jointing compound on the joint faces and may then be reassembled and the studs and bolts finally tightened.

Should the crankcase halves meet, leaving the flywheel assembly free to rotate in the bearings extra shimming is needed to take up excess play.

First check the amount of end float—if any—and add shims behind the bearing outer rings (which must be removed for the purpose) of the thickness required to take out all float or end play **plus .004-in.** For example if the flywheel turns freely when the crankcase halves are pulled together tightly with no end play fit one .002-in. shim behind each bearing ring and reassemble.

If there is some end play additional shims will be needed; for instance end float of .005 will call for two .002-in. shims on one side and one .005-in. on the other.

Overhauling the Flywheel Assembly and Big End.

The tapered shanks of the crankpin fit into correspondingly tapered holes in the flywheel, so that to inspect the big end one shank of the pin must be pressed out of the flywheel.

To separate the flywheels a heavy geared mandrel press or Service Tool X3391 is essential. The flywheel assembly must be placed so that the end of the crankpin is below the ram and the upper flywheel supported so as to allow the shank of the crankpin to be pressed down and out of the flywheel, taking the connecting rod assembly and lower flywheel with it.

The connecting rod is then removable leaving the rollers and roller cage on the crankpin which is still fixed in the lower flywheel. Before removal mark the rod for replacement the same way round. If renewal of the big end outer ring is necessary press out the old ring and press in a new one square to the bore and set it centrally with the rod.

Also check the fit of the gudgeon pin in the small end bush and if slack refer to page 46.

Pull the roller cage and rollers off the crankpin and inspect the roller track for wear and pitting, or breaking up of the hardened surface. Near the edges the pin will be polished, from contact with the cage and provided that any wear here does not leave the roller track unsupported can be disregarded. Such wear will often appear to be much greater than it is.

Replacement rollers, which are obtainable .0002-in. or .0004 oversize in diameter, as well as standard, may be used to take up slight play if the outer ring and crankpin are in good condition.

Final assembly of the big end must leave the connecting rod quite free to rotate. Barely perceptible vertical play is permissable without oil in the bearing; there will be about .008-in. in side play. Slight stiffness can be eased by careful lapping of the outer ring when in place in the rod, or by lightly polishing the crankpin.

CRANKPIN EXTRACTOR AND ASSEMBLY TOOL. X3391.

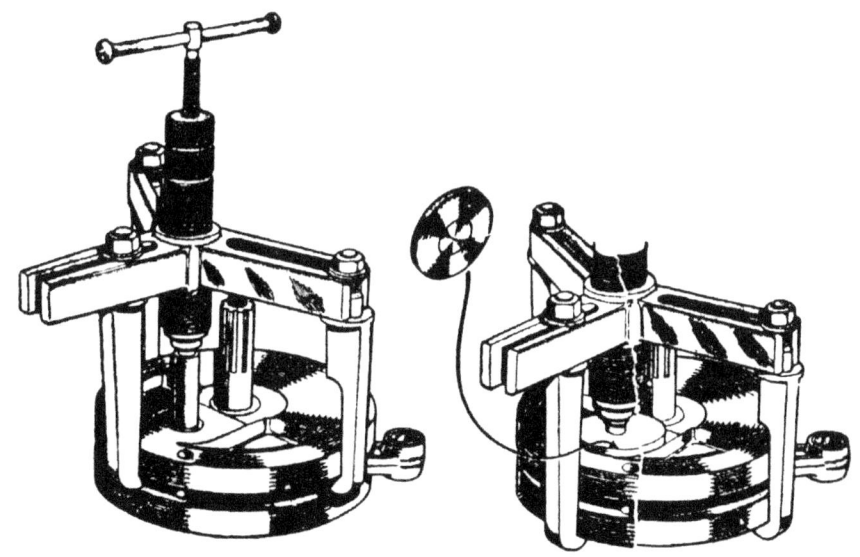

Reproduced by courtesy of " Motor Cycling."

FIG. 19a.

To renew the crankpin the old one must be removed from the flywheel in which it was left when dismantling, by supporting the flywheel on the press and pressing it out.

The crankpin is not drilled, so that it may be fitted either way round. See that the pin is quite clean and wipe out the hole in the flywheel. Push the pin into place and press until nearly flush with the outer face of the flywheel around the crankpin hole. Force oil through the oilways in the timing shaft, fit the roller cage and insert the rollers. These can be held in place with a little grease. Fit the connecting rod over the rollers observing that it fits according to the markings made when dismantling.

Place the other flywheel in position over the crankpin and line up the flywheel rims as closely as possible using a straight edge across the rims checking at several different points round the circumference. Press down the flywheel on to the crankpin right up to the shoulder. As the ends of the pin may protrude a little beyond the surrounding faces of the flywheels, the flywheel underneath should rest upon a stout bush or recessed block. The inner diameter of such a bush or recess must be more than the diameter of the small ends of the crankpin shanks. A diameter of 1.125 is suggested. A block is supplied with X3391.

* In order to mount the flywheel assembly finally for trueing up, some special equipment is needed. If the assembly is to be rotated in its own bearings in V-blocks two " slave " outer rings should be obtained, or the ones belonging to the engine taken from the crankcase for the purpose. Alternatively obtain two M.87 parallel double row roller races as used in the driving side crankcase on KSS and early MSS models and grind out the inner ring bores taper from 1.0056-in., at the large end to 1.0015-in.—.0005-in. at the small end.

If the taper roller bearings are used whilst trueing, the V-blocks must be adapted by fitting stops to them to prevent the bearing rings spreading across the blocks with the weight of the flywheel assembly.

The mainshaft must be " clocked " to run true to within .001-in. of complete accuracy. The trueing is done by striking the flywheel rims where necessary with a lead block to correct any innacuracy left from the initial setting. A heavy lead hammer will be needed to move them.

Replacement of Small End Bush.

Any vertical play on the gudgeon pin in the small end bush calls for replacement of the gudgeon pin or bush, or both. If the pin is worn it is worth trying a new pin in the original bush before deciding to renew the bush.

Whilst it is possible to draw out a small end bush and draw a new one into the rod with a suitable bolt and collars, etc., we do not recommend attempting to renew it unless the engine is dismantled and the connecting rod removed.

All connecting rods are checked and trued in production after the bushes are fitted and finished to size, ensuring perfect alignment between the small end and big end bearings, and this cannot be assured when other methods of fitting are employed. Further, as the replacement bush has to be drilled in position to match up with the oil hole in the connecting rod there is a serious risk of drillings getting into the crankcase. Connecting rods sent to us for rebushing will be lined up, before return, on a special fixture.

Refitting the Piston and Cylinder.

If the magneto has been removed refit it before fitting the cylinder. It is essential after reassembling the flywheels and crankcase, particularly if a new small end bush has been fitted other than at the factory, to check that the bore of the small end is in line with and parallel to the big end.

To test; obtain an accurately ground mandrel of .8235-in. diameter to fit closely and without play in the small end bush. Set the flywheels so that the lower edges of the small end bush are nearly flush with the cylinder face on the crankcase. Push the mandrel through the bush and check that it lies flat on the face at both sides of the small end. Should it touch at one side, but not on the other, the connecting rod must be reset.

The small end eye must also lie centrally in the mouth of the crankcase to avoid side thrust on the piston and this point should be checked, making due allowance for side play on the big end.

Fit the piston in place and push the gudgeon pin through the bush, finally driving it home up to the circlip, which will have been fitted to the piston. It is a help when fitting if the pin is first pushed into one boss so that it just protrudes inside the piston. The protruding end is then easily entered into the small end bush. Get help to support the piston from the opposite side when tapping the pin home. Note that the split in the piston skirt must be at the front. Finally fit the second circlip verifying that it seats properly in its groove, and see that the ends do not touch.

New circlips are occasionally found to need a small amount removing from one end to prevent the ends touching, which would prevent proper seating in the circlip groove.

Smear the cylinder bore with clean oil, fit a new gasket over the cylinder base, sticking it in place with a little grease, and if any compression plates were fitted originally fit these in place on the crankcase. Set the ring gaps 120° apart.

Support the piston and lower the cylinder over it compressing the rings one at a time to enter them in the bore. Lower the cylinder into place and push it firmly into the crankcase.

The reassembly of the cylinder head and overhead valve gear is dealt with from page 26

The Timing Gears.

The timing gear bushes in the camwheel and intermediate gear wheel assemblies seldom need replacement, but if renewed must be bored to suit the spindles and not reamed. Boring is essential to ensure the bearing being concentric with the gear teeth. The camwheel bush must be bored to .001-in. above the spindle diameter, and the intermediate gear bush to .0015-in. larger than its spindle. End float on the gears must not exceed .0015-in.

End float must be checked after bolting the steady plate firmly in place.

The gears are marked for refitting (Fig. 20). To fit, turn the crankshaft to bring the mark on the crankshaft pinion to the top. Fit the camwheel to its spindle setting the timing mark as illustrated and the cams pointing rearwards. Slide the intermediate gear into place and mesh its teeth with the camwheel and crankshaft pinion so that the marks register. There are two marks on the intermediate gear, but as they are not diametrically opposite the gear can only be fitted in one way to register the marks properly, i.e., with the longer section between the marks facing the front.

Note specially that owing to the intermediate gear having one more tooth than the camwheel it changes its position in relation to the other gears and lags behind the camwheel one tooth in every two turns of the crankshaft.

The result is that after resetting the timing gears with all marks coinciding, and then turning the crankshaft two complete turns, the marks on the intermediate gear will be out of register with the crankshaft, and cam gears which will be back in their original positions.

POSITIONS OF TIMING MARKS.

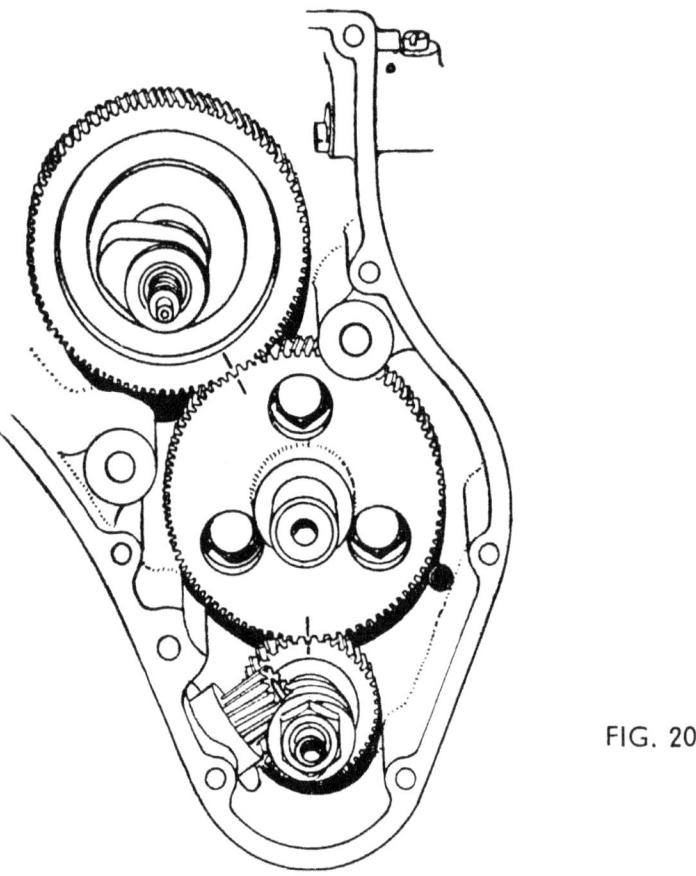

FIG. 20

The Intermediate Gear Spindle Bolt Heads are also visible through the holes in the gear.

This sometimes leads to the assumption that an engine is incorrectly timed as obviously the chance of the engine stopping so that the marks are in register or even nearly so is exceedingly remote. The marks will all coincide only once every 93 turns of the crankshaft. This feature of the design avoids loading the same teeth at each revolution and evens out any wear that takes place.

The Adjustable Intermediate Gear Spindle.

Mainly for purposes of original assembly the spindle carrying the intermediate gear is made adjustable, so that the backlash between the teeth of the gears may be varied. The adjustment normally does not need any alteration, and the spindle is set when new to give freedom in the gears at all positions with minimum clearances between the teeth.

The flange of the spindle is secured to the inner wall of the crankcase by three $\frac{1}{4}$-in. B.S.F. bolts which pass through clearance holes in the crankcase thus permitting a certain degree of movement. The flange which is machined with a flat is located by this flat portion fitting against a corresponding flat machined on the crankcase, thus allowing the spindle lateral movement only.

The heads of the spindle holding bolts are accessible through the three holes in the intermediate gear and are shown in Fig. 20, above.

Should excess backlash develop between the gears the adjustment can be made by removing the steady plate, slightly slacking off the three bolts and pushing the intermediate gear closer into mesh towards the rear (toward the left of the illustration).

It **is** important not to set the gear too close as this will cause gear whine

Retiming the Ignition.

Check and if necessary adjust the contact point gap. Refit the automatic timing unit loosely to the magneto armature. Attach a timing disc to the driving side mainshaft and fix a pointer made of stiff wire to some convenient fixed point, i.e., one of the engine or crankcase bolts. Bring the piston to top dead centre with both valves closed and bend the pointer to indicate zero on the timing disc. Turn the crankshaft backwards 36° as indicated by the pointer. With finger and thumb turn the front plate of the timing unit backwards to its limit, to advance it fully. The plate referred to carries the toggle levers and is shown in Fig. 16. The illustration shows the unit fully retarded. Holding the timing unit fully advanced set the contact breaker points just opening (apart by .0015-in.) Tighten the centre bolt to fix the timing unit to the taper on the armature. Check the timing before fitting the timing cover as follows:

Turn the crankshaft backwards and see that the contact points close. Open the points with the fingers and place between them a piece of cigarette paper, allowing the points to close on it. Obtain assistance to hold the timing unit fully advanced or insert a small block between the projections of the front plate and the back plate on the gear to wedge them apart. Very slowly move the crankshaft forward maintaining a light pull on the cigarette paper meanwhile. As soon as the paper will withdraw from between the points stop moving the crankshaft and check the position of the timing disc. The reading must be 36° on MSS, 36° on Viper or Venom engines.

Remove the wedge from the timing unit, if one was used, and check the tightness of the timing unit bolt.

Refitting the Timing Gear Cover.

It is advisable always to use a new gasket which can be stuck to the cover with Gasket Goo before fitting. Check that the crankshaft oil feed jet is clear and entered in the bore in the timing side mainshaft. Also engage the holes in the cover over the projecting tip of the cam-wheel spindle and cam oil jet. Tighten the cover screws firmly and evenly. The rocker oil pipe should be left disconnected at the bottom end for the time being so that the oil feed may be checked before finally connecting it and tightening the union (see page 19).

COIL IGNITION
Engine Timing

Ensure that the 6CA is in the fully advanced position by:—

(i) Removing the cam securing screw. Insert a washer ($\frac{7}{16}$-in. internal diameter) between the exisiting washer and the cam.

(ii) Holding the auto advance mechanism in the fully advanced position and re-tightening the securing screw. See diagram page 111.

Contact Breaker Timing

(iii) Slacken the two screws which secure the base plate to the engine.

(iv) Turn the engine to the correct timing position, 38° before top dead centre, this being determined, as described above, by the attachment of a timing disc to the driving side mainshaft.

(v) Rotate the base plate until the contacts are just opening. (A low wattage bulb, of appropriate voltage, connected between the contact breaker spring terminal and earth, will be illuminated instantly the contacts separate). Tighten the screws.

(vi) To obtain fine adjustment slacken the two screws (D) securing the C.B. plate and rotate the eccentric cam screw (E), adjusting the position of the C.B. heel until the contacts are just opening. Re-tighten the two securing screws.

Note—On completion of engine timing, remove the $\frac{7}{16}$-in. i.d. washer from the auto advance cam securing screw and re-tighten the screw.

Adjusting the Contact Breaker Gap

(i) Turn the engine until the contact breaker gap is open to its widest extent.

(ii) Slacken the screw (B) which secures the angle plate (fixed contact). See diagram page 110.

(iii) Turn the eccentric cam screw (C) and adjust the contact point gap between the limits 0.014-in. to 0.016-in. (0.35 to 0.40 m.m.).

(iv) Tighten the securing screw (B) and re-check the gap.
For further details see page 000.

See page 110 for wiring diagram.

THE CLUTCH.
Dismantling.

If the gearbox has not been removed with the engine from the frame the preliminary work of taking off the dynamo belt cover, belt and primary chain, etc. (see page 31) must be carried out. Unless attention is needed to the sleeve gear ballrace the inner half of the chain case can be left attached to the gearbox.

Draw the clutch assembly off the sleeve gear and push out the three thrust pins from the back plate. With the clutch assembly resting on the back plate lift off the component parts one by one beginning with the front plate. The ballrace is a sliding fit on the centre of the back plate and tight in the chainwheel.

One clutch plate with inserts, and one steel spacing plate fit between the front plate and the chainwheel. Between the chainwheel and the back plate there are two clutch plates and two spacing plates fitted alternately-steel to friction lining.

The inserts will continue to work satisfactorily until worn flush with the metal surrounding them. They must be firm in the plates and chainwheel. The ballrace must be quite free.

Relining the Clutch.

Worn inserts can be pushed out of place and renewed if necessary. Press in new inserts leaving them projecting an equal distance each side and make certain that the working surfaces are all level. Pressing them up against a truly flat surface will ensure this.

Reassembling the Clutch.

The back plate must be held firmly from rotating during re-assembly otherwise the spacing plates cannot be engaged with the front plate. The best thing to hold the plate is a disused sleeve gear from any single cylinder model Velocette. This is gripped in the vice by the gear teeth or driving dogs, and the clutch back plate fitted loosely over the splines.

Fit the first clutch plate in position followed by a spacing plate, second clutch plate, and the second spacing plate. Note that the external tongues on the clutch plates and internal tongues on the spacing plates must all point away from the chainwheel, i.e., downwards.

Centralize the four plates with the back plate, bring the tongues on each pair of plates into line and engage the internal tongues of the spacing plates in the slots machined in the back plate just inside the ground friction surface.

Hold the chainwheel with the deeper slotted rim underneath and fit it into position with the ballrace over the boss of the back plate. Enter the tongues of the clutch plates in the chainwheel and see that all friction surfaces come into contact. With the chainwheel fitted, put on the third spacing plate and clutch plate in that order and with their tongues pointing upwards, those of the clutch plate being engaged in the slots in the rim of the chainwheel. Centre the spacing plate carefully as its internal tongues must engage in slots on the clutch front plate.

Fit the front plate over the tongues of the back plate and move the chainwheel backwards and forwards maintaining light pressure on the front plate until it is felt to go into place and lie flat on the friction linings as the tongues on the spacing plate enter the slots.

See that the spring holder is screwed into place in the front plate, and fit the three thrust pins into the holes in the back plate sticking them in with a little grease.

The clutch assembly is now ready for refitting.

The Clutch Thrust Bearing.

This is a ball thrust bearing seated spherically in the clutch thrust cup and located centrally upon the sleeve gear by a distance-piece pushed over the sleeve gear behind the clutch back plate. There are three parts to the bearing; a hardened steel thrust ring flat on both sides, a cage carrying the bearing balls, and a spherical thrust washer. This has a spherical face to fit the thrust cup and a flat face providing a bearing for the balls during the operation of the clutch. (Fig. 10).

The thrust bearing should be inspected for wear. If pitted the parts affected should be replaced. The plain thrust ring if pitted on one side only often can be reversed to give it a new lease of life. Inspect the distance piece for grooving due to wear and replace if worn. If a new caged ballrace is fitted see that there are no rough edges on the cage that would prevent it sliding freely on the distance-piece. Coat all parts with grease before refitting.

The clutch thrust bearing is not intended to carry a constant thrust load, and when the clutch is correctly adjusted is loaded only when the clutch lever is operated, and the clutch is disengaged. It is therefore important at all times to keep the adjustment correct and when driving to avoid keeping the machine standing in gear with the engine running for longer than is necessary. In circumstances where the engine cannot be stopped, i.e., in traffic blocks, always select neutral.

THE GEARBOX.

Dismantling.

It is possible to remove all the shafts and gears from the gearbox without dismounting the housing from the frame, but if the layshaft ballrace and sleeve gear ballrace need renewal the housing must be taken out. The gearbox and engine are removed, together as a unit. See page 38.

Drain out all oil by removing the drain plug from the end cover, (Fig. 15). Take out the two a-in. B.S.F. bolts from the gearbox cover (above the kickstart bearing) and remove the cover. Hold the gearshaft from turning and unscrew the gearshaft nut that is exposed by the removal of the small cover.

Unless the kickstart spring or ratchet need attention the kickstart bearing should be left in place attached to the gearbox end cover. (For attention to kickstart see page 35.) Tap the gearshaft into the gearbox a little way clear of the ballrace, remove the seven ¼-in. B.S.F. cover bolts and pull the cover off the housing. Note the two dowels which may be left in the face of the housing or come away with the cover, and preserve these for refitting. The gear control pedal can be left attached to its spindle.

The layshaft is supported in the kickstart ratchet by a floating bush and this may be left on the end of the layshaft or come away in the ratchet. The hardened steel disc in the ratchet (Fig. 14), must be carefully retained for refitting. Also remove from the layshaft the layshaft washer fitted up against the ratchet gear.

Pull the gearshaft first gear wheel off the gearshaft.

Draw out the two selector fork rods—these are grooved near the ends to provide a means of gripping them. Pull the gearshaft right out towards the clutch side of the machine and lift out the double sliding gear and upper fork.

Removal of Layshaft Assembly and Sleeve Gear.

Note that close ratio, and " T.T." close ratio gearboxes having the prefix 12/ to the serial number have seventeen and eighteen tooth sleeve gears respectively. The layshaft assemblies on these gearboxes will withdraw in one position only due to the top gear pick-up teeth, of which there are sixteen on all models, masking the gear teeth in all but one place.

The layshaft must be turned therefore until the " clear " position is found when it will pull out bringing the selector fork with it.

If the clutch has been removed the sleeve gear will tap through its ballrace into the gearbox and can then be removed. Only the layshaft ballrace and the sleeve gear ballrace, together with the camplate and its attendant mechanism remain in position.

The Operating Mechanism.

Experience has shown that attention is seldom required to this part of the gearbox mechanism and it should not be disturbed needlessly.

Should the camplate be taken off its spindle note that it is mounted on a loose centre-piece—the camplate ratchet plate—and must be set correctly in relation to this part. Accordingly the two parts are marked and if removed from the ratchet plate the camplate must be fitted with the V mark on it facing the corresponding mark on the ratchet plate.

After very long use indeed some wear may be found on the steel pegs in the selector forks that engage the operating slots in the camplate. These are renewable separately by driving them out of position and pressing in new ones. No attention whatever is likely to be required to the gear change lever shaft and bearing in the end cover, the rocker shaft bushes, or connecting linkage.

The Gearbox Bearings.

The gearshaft bearing in the end cover will jar out of place after removal of its locating circlip if the cover is heated, and the gearbox housing should be heated in order to free the layshaft ballrace which also will jar out of its housing. To refit or replace heat the housing and cover and tap the bearings into place.

The sleeve gear ballrace which is fitted between two thin steel oil retaining shims is held by a retaining ring threaded into the housing. To reach this ring the back half of the primary chain cover must be removed, and the thrust cup taken away. The thrust cup is held into its seating by a small wire clip retained by two $\frac{1}{8}$-in. screws.

The metal surrounding the edge of the ballrace retaining ring is punched into the notches in the ring for locking purposes. The overlapping metal must be chiselled off carefully to clear the ring.

To unscrew the retaining ring use Service Tool X2725 (Fig. 21), which will avoid damaging the ring. The oil retaining shim outside the ballrace will lift out and the ballrace can be tapped out after heating the housing around the bearing. The second shim will now come away.

Examine the shims carefully and if in the slightest degree worn or showing any signs of splitting replace them. When refitting the shims and the ballrace—or renewing them—great care must be taken to centralise the shims accurately, otherwise the sleeve gear oil thrower and the distance piece will rub against them and cause wear, eventual failure, and oil leakages.

The ring when finally tightened should be in such a position that one of the grooves at the back of the ring, is at, or near the bottom so that any oil passing the shims and collecting in the recess behind the retaining ring can drain away back into the gearbox through the drilling in the housing. Preferably the ring should tighten up fully with one of the outer slots at or near the top which will ensure that one groove at the back will be near the bottom.

Refit the sleeve gear; noting that the oil thrower is in place with its concave side next to the gear teeth.

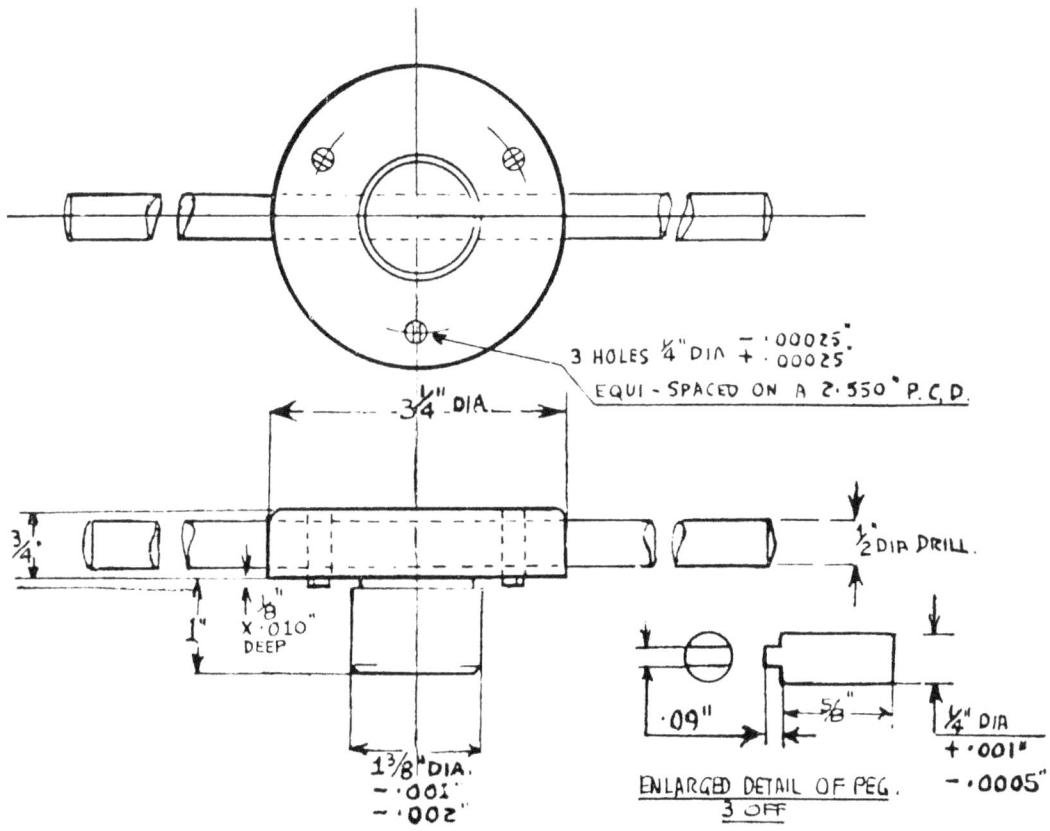

FIG. 21
X2725 BALLRACE RETAINING RING TOOL.

The bushes in the second and third speed layshaft gears and the low gear bush are easily replaced, but to renew the former the layshaft assembly must be dismantled as described in the next section.

The sleeve gear bush is pegged in position and before attempting to press it out, the peg which passes through the plain ground part of the sleeve gear, must be drilled out. A new sleeve gear bush must be located before pressing in so that the oil holes in the bush will come directly below the oil holes drilled through the gear between the teeth, and after fitting, must be drilled and pegged, and bored out to .001-in. above the gearshaft diameter. Bore to ensure concentricity with the ground part of the sleeve gear. Reaming is unsatisfactory.

It is unlikely that the bushes in the low gear, and in the second and third speed layshaft gears will need renewal, but if so they can be pressed out and new ones pressed in.

After fitting, the low gear bush must be finished bored to .625-in., and the layshaft gear bushes to .8125-in. The limits are plus .0007, minus 0005-in. in both cases.

Current models have two bushes in the low gear. These are pressed in from opposite sides so as to provide bearing flanges at both sides of the gear.

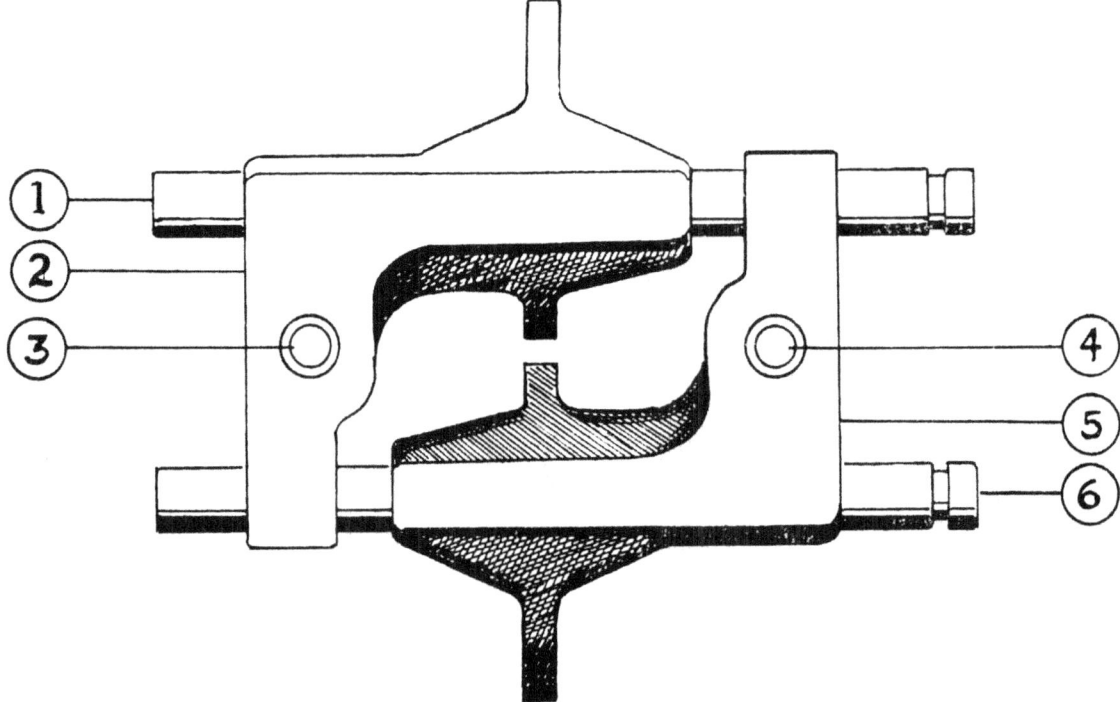

FIG. 22. POSITION OF SELECTOR FORKS FOR REFITTING. (Viewed from rear.)

(1) Selector Fork Rod   (1st and Top Gears).
(2) Selector Fork.   (1st and Top Gears).
(3)
(4) } Selector Fork Pegs.
(5) Selector Fork.   (2nd and 3rd Gears).
(6) Selector Fork Rod.   (2nd and 3rd Gears).

The Layshaft Assembly.

Whilst the layshaft assembly is removed inspect the teeth of the sliding dog, and the corresponding pick up teeth on the second and third gears for wear on the edges. The edges must be clean and sharp and if broken away, chipped, or rounded the part must be replaced.

A worn sliding dog can be replaced after removal of either of the end gears—these are splined to the shaft. They can be pressed or levered off the layshaft and will then allow the second and third speed layshaft gears to come off.

When reassembling note that the third gear—the larger one—fits next to the ratchet gear, and when pressing them back into place, press them on far enough to leave the loose gears no excess end float, but perfectly free to rotate. End float must not exceed .015-in. and is best left at about .005-in.

Refitting the Gears to the Housing.

The layshaft assembly should be held in one hand and the double sliding gear rested in position on the second and third speed sliding gears, noting that the larger gear of the double gear (the one with the internal pick up teeth) faces towards the largest gear on the layshaft (i.e., remote from the ratchet gear).

Engage the selector forks in the grooves of the double gear and sliding dog with the forks set so that in the case of the top one the lug carrying the selector fork peg is downwards and the peg between the actual fork and the clutch side of the gearbox (Fig. 22) and the bottom one the other way round.

Place the layshaft assembly, double gear, and forks into the housing, manoeuvring the end of the layshaft into the layshaft ballrace and meshing the layshaft gear with the sleeve gear. Note that in gear boxes Prefix No. 12/ with seventeen tooth sleeve gear and twenty-seven tooth layshaft gear engagement is only possible with the sleeve gear in one position (see page 52). Engage the selector fork pegs in the cam tracks in the camplate, and push the fork rods through the selector forks entering their plain ends in the holes in the gearbox housing. **Note.**—The lower selector fork rod is now $\frac{1}{16}$-in. longer overall than originally, so that if the rods are seen to be of different lengths always fit the longer one through the lower fork. The grooved ends fit into the end cover.

Push the gearshaft through the sleeve gear from the clutch side and enter the splines through the splines in the double gear. Refit the gearshaft first gear wheel over the end of the gearshaft, meshing it with the ratchet low gear.

Refitting the End Cover.

Should the kickstart bearing, and kickstart be attached to the cover, make sure before fitting that the kickstart layshaft thrust washer is in place in the kickstart ratchet. If the kickstart bearing is not attached to the cover it can be left for the time being and fitted after the end cover is in place.

Place the layshaft washer over the splines protruding beyond the ratchet low gear, place the kickstart bearing (floating) bush on the layshaft. After checking that the end cover ball bearing is in place, with the circlip fitted, put the cover in position using a new gasket on the face joint, and the dowels in position. It will be necessary, as the cover is pushed home to enter the ends of the selector fork rods in their holes in the cover, and the gearshaft through the end cover ballrace. Also the gear control lever must be held up so that the peg at the rear end of the gear change rocker shaft is engaged in the slot in the striking plate assembly. Tighten the holding bolts. Fit and tighten the gearshaft nut against the ballrace and refit the end cover-plate, using a new gasket. See that the drain plug is fitted.

Refit the kickstart assembly as described on page 38. Note when doing so that the kickstart bearing bush, the layshaft washer, and the layshaft thrust washer are all in their places. *Do not use a gasket or paper joint washer between the kickstart bearing and the gearbox end cover.*

Refill gearbox with oil and refit the level and filler plugs.

THE REAR WHEEL AND BRAKE.

Removal of Rear Wheel and Brake.

If attention is needed to the brake it is easier to take out the wheel with the brake assembly attached as follows :

Remove the rear detachable section of the mudguard, and the rear chain guard from the left-hand torque tube assembly. Detach the rear brake torque arm, the rear end of the speedometer drive flex from the reduction gearbox, and remove the rear brake adjusting nut. Take out the rear chain connecting link and take off the chain.

Loosen the rear wheel spindle, and the nut on the brake-plate locking bolt on the left-hand side (Fig. 41). Pull the rear wheel, with brake assembly out rearwards from the fork ends. Complete removal of the nut from the brake plate locking bolt permits the withdrawal of the brake-plate assembly from the drum, and by taking out the wheel spindle and removing the three wheel nuts the drum is freed from the wheel hub.

Relining the Brake

Replacement brake liners and rivets are available. When fitting replacement shoes be careful to fit the steel slippers which protect the ends of the shoes from wear by the cam and see that the cam works freely in its bearing in the brake plate.

A limited amount of wear can be taken up by inserting thin steel packings between the brake shoe ends and the slippers, but the brake lining rivets must be below the surface of the liner and unable to rub the drum.

Dismantling the Rear Hub Bearings. (Fig. 23).

This may be necessary to repack the bearings with grease or to renew them. The barrel of the hub does not carry any grease and the amount needed for adequate lubrication is kept in the bearings by grease retainers fitted between the bearings and the hub.

REAR HUB ASSEMBLY (Sectional View).

NOTE: The arrangement of the bearings etc. in the full width type hub is identical.

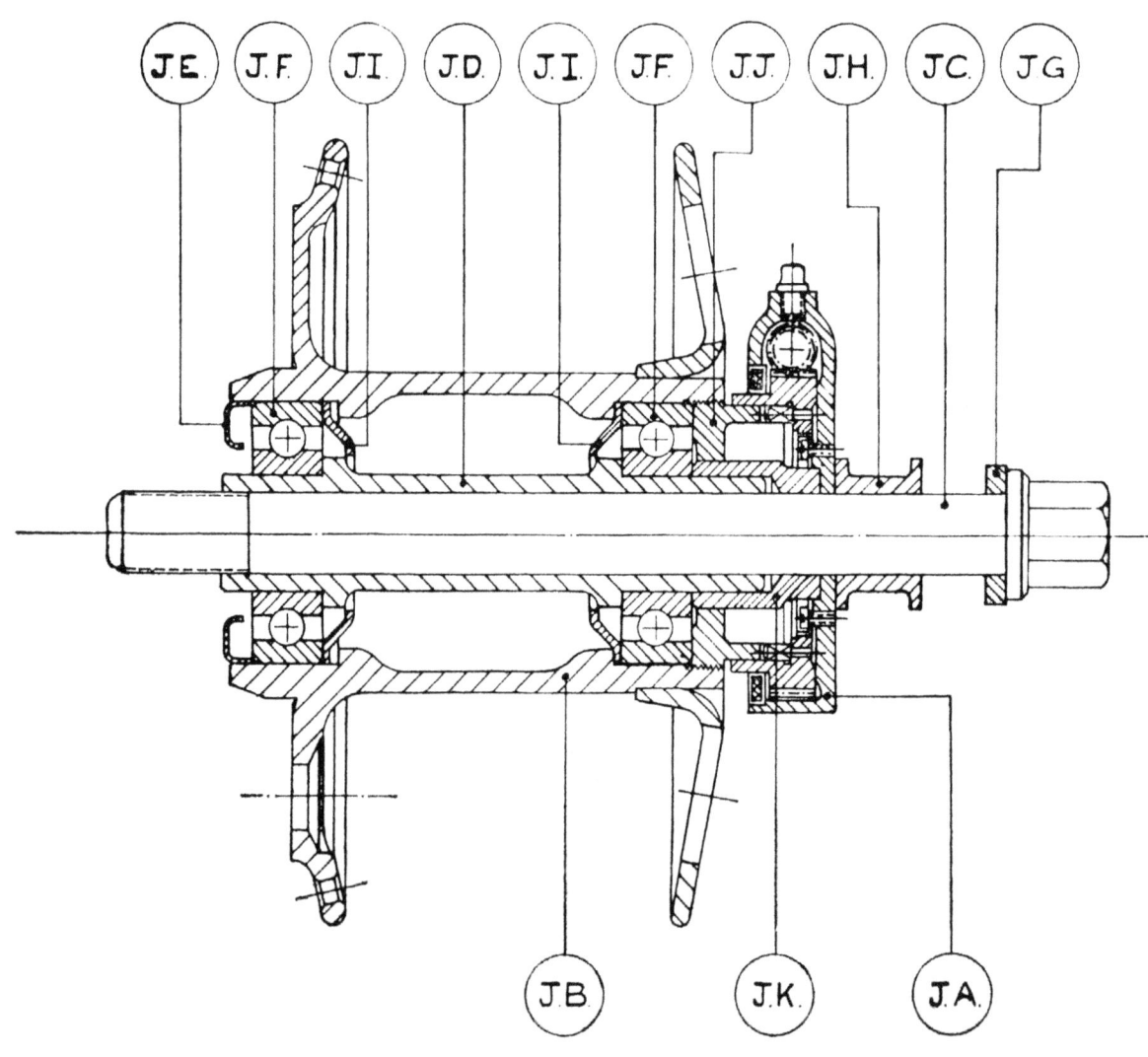

FIG. 23.

JA. Reduction Gearbox for Speedometer Drive.
JB. Hub Shell.
JC. Detachable Spindle.
JD. Hollow Spindle.
JE. Dust Cap (Brake Side).
JF. Ballraces.
JG. Spindle Washer.
JH. Distance Piece.
JI. Grease Retainers.
JJ. Ballrace Retaining Ring.
JK. Ballrace Clamping Sleeve.

To dismantle drive out the hollow spindle (JD) after pulling off the speedometer reduction gearbox (JA), and the ballrace clamping sleeve (JK). The spindle is driven out from the right-hand side of the machine towards the left and will take with it the left-hand side ballrace (JF) and dust cap (JE). A punch, 9-in. long, slightly less than $\frac{7}{8}$-in. diameter, and reduced at one end to just under $\frac{3}{8}$-in. for a distance of $\frac{1}{2}$-in., will be needed. The same punch is used for dealing with the front hub.

Unscrew and remove the **left-hand thread** ballrace retaining ring (JJ). The edge of this is slotted in four places. The wider slots will take a bar for undoing the ring. If the ballrace is in good condition and only needs repacking with grease, this can be done without removing it. If removal is needed drive the bearing out towards the right-hand side using a suitable punch inserted through the hub or insert one end of the hollow spindle into the bearing after removing the left-hand side ballrace, inserting the punch (previously described) into the other end of the hollow spindle.

Reassembling the Rear Hub. (Fig. 23.)

Place the right-hand side grease retainer (JI) in position, hollow (concave) side outwards as illustrated and press the ballrace into its housing. Pack it well with high melting point grease. Fit and tighten the retaining ring (JJ) using a bar across the two wide slots. Press the other ballrace on to the hollow spindle taking care to fit it to the shorter parallel ground end —refer to illustration. Place the left-hand side grease retainer in the housing hollow (concave) side outwards—pack the housing with grease and fit the hollow spindle through the hub entering the longer parallel ground end in the right-hand side ballrace, and the outer ring of the left-hand side ballrace in the hub. Press the ballrace home. Pack a little more grease into the ballrace and press in the dust cap (JE) hollow side towards the ballrace.

Push the ballrace clamping sleeve (JK) on to the hollow spindle, and fit the reduction gearbox—engaging its driving dogs with the two narrow slots in the ballrace retaining ring. The hub is then ready for refitting.

Reassembling the Brake Plate Assembly.

Push the brake plate support bolt through the brake-drum and grease shield. Fit the brake plate washer in place over the support bolt and fit the brake plate assembly, at the same time entering the brake shoes in the drum and the end of the support bolt through the hole in the brake cam steady. If desired the hub can now be attached to the brake drum and the wheel with brake assembly fitted to the machine.

THE REAR SUSPENSION. (Fig. 24.)

Description.

The rear suspension is by two self-contained suspension units containing the springs, the damper mechanism, and the oil necessary for damping and lubrication.

The objection to most rear springing systems is that they are unable to cope equally well with both solo and pillion riding conditions. Thus, if the springing is arranged for the heavier load it hardly works at all with a solo rider; and if arranged for solo use tends to bottom when a passenger is carried.

The Velocette rear suspension is easily and quickly adjustable for load in a manner which makes it unique in motor-cycle practice by means of a patented adjustment. Proper working and consequently reasonable comfort are obtainable by a light rider solo, or by two heavy persons, and at all intermediate loadings.

By altering the positions of the top mountings of the spring suspension units along the slots in the support lugs on the frame the springing can be adjusted from " light "—furthest forward as illustrated—to " heavy "—

right back. Any intermediate setting can be used, provided that the suspension units are in line, with the upper mounting bolts the same distance along the slots at each side.

Maintenance—Suspension Units.

Apart from external cleaning no attention is necessary. Should it be required to replace the dust covers or springs these are removable after taking the units off the machine. Removal of the covers discloses the springs.

To remove a cover for access to the spring or felt washer first remove the suspension unit from the machine by detaching it at the upper and lower pivots.

Hold the unit vertically in a vice gripping the bottom fixing lug between protected vice jaws.

REAR SUSPENSION-ADJUSTMENT FOR LOAD.

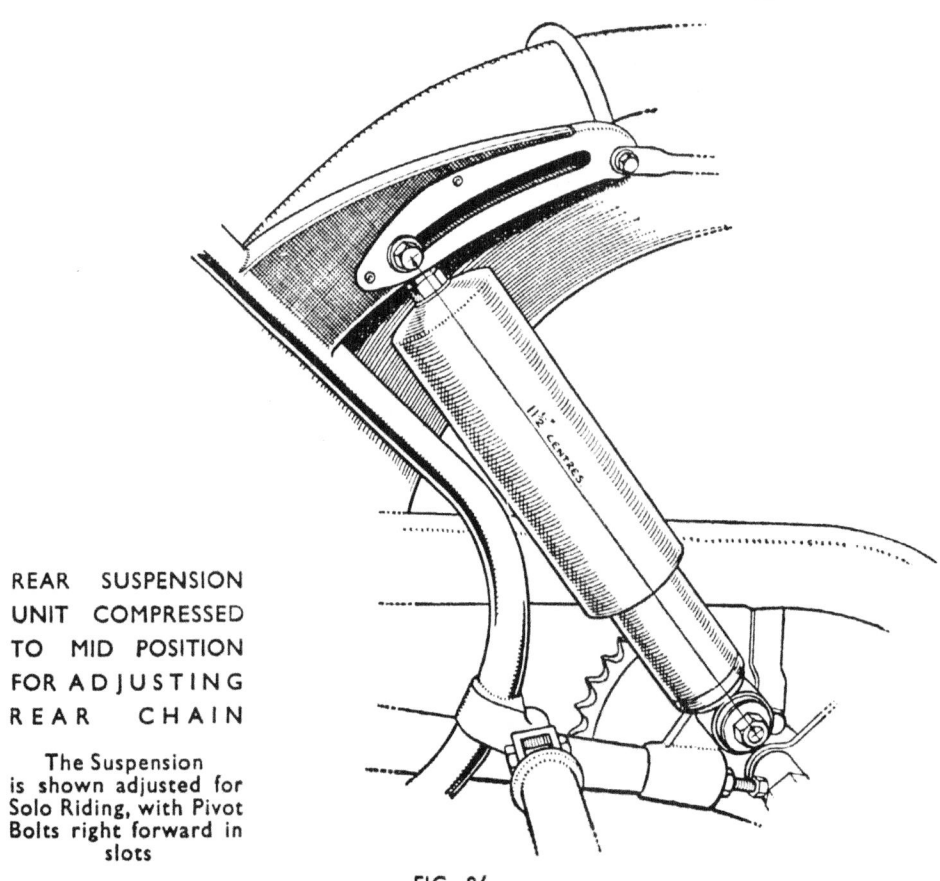

REAR SUSPENSION UNIT COMPRESSED TO MID POSITION FOR ADJUSTING REAR CHAIN

The Suspension is shown adjusted for Solo Riding, with Pivot Bolts right forward in slots

FIG. 24.

With both hands press down the dust cover against the spring far enough to allow the removal of the two halves of the split dust cover retainer. Help will be needed to pull them out whilst the spring is held compressed (a valve cotter is removed in the same way).

The dust cover, washer and spring will then come away over the top lug.

The remainder of the unit consisting of the lower part containing the damper mechanism cannot be taken apart, and will be found to function indefinitely

Rebushing the Suspension Unit Eyes.

Occasionally the eye bushes may need renewing. Those at the bottom are easily fitted by pushing them into place in the lower eyes, but the top ones call for the use of a special pressing tool—Service Tool No. X2992 (Fig. 25.)

This tool is used by first pressing the rubber sleeve into the eye, resting the fixing lug on the tool with the shoulder bush (1) entered in the sleeve. Before attempting to fit the sleeves lubricate them with soapy water.

Remove the shouldered bush (1). Rest the eye, with rubber sleeve fitted, on top of the tool. Fit the distance piece over the Opening Bush

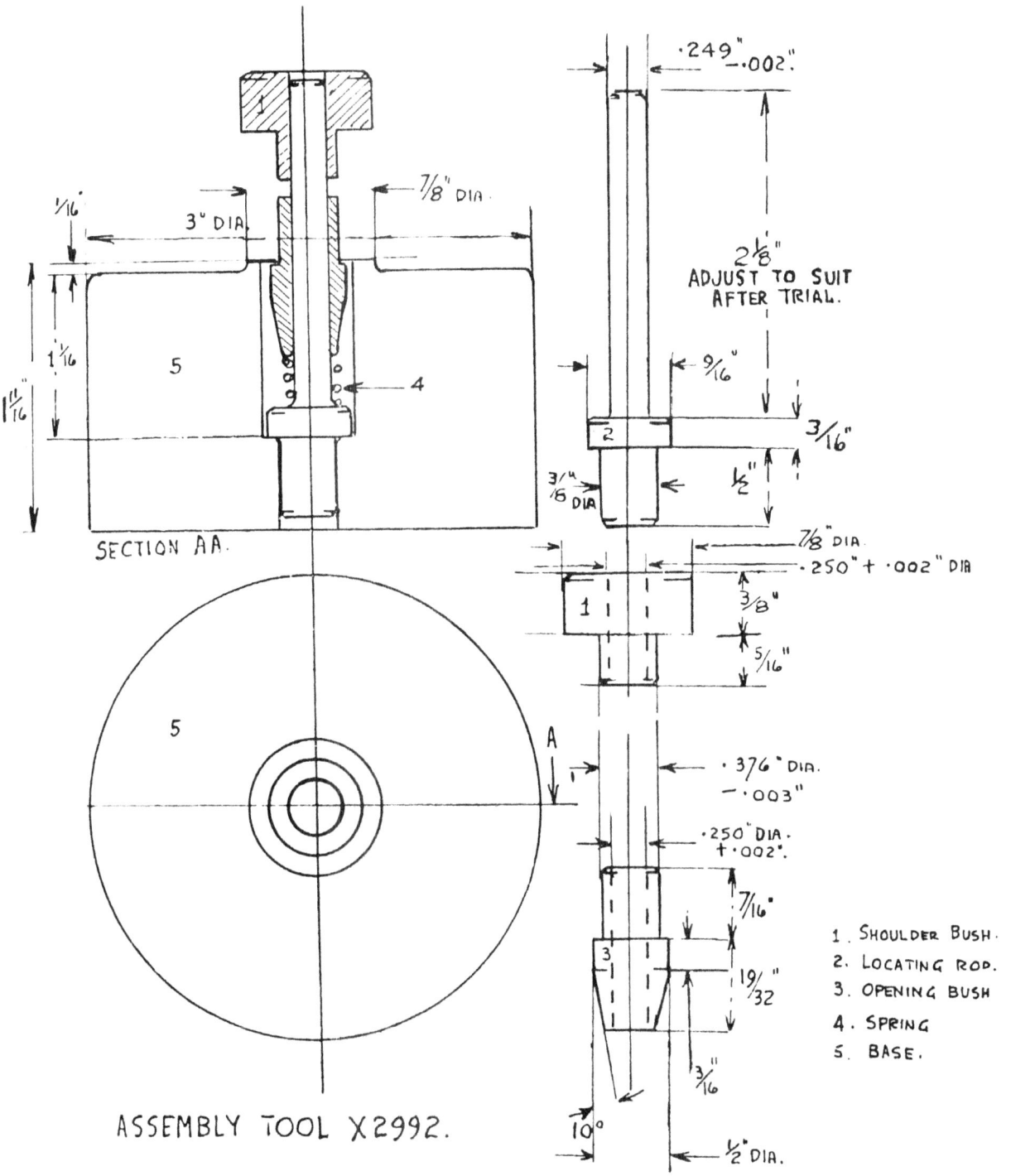

FIG. 25.

(3) and Shouldered bush (1) and fit the Opening Bush over the locating rod. Press down the Shoulder bush until the distance piece is fully home in the rubber sleeve.

Maintenance—Rear Swinging Fork.

Periodical lubrication of the trunnion shaft bearings through the grease nipples at each side of the trunnion lug on the frame is all that is needed. The greasers are on the underside of the lug.

Do not in any circumstances dismantle the swinging fork assembly needlessly.

The torque arm assemblies are very carefully and accurately lined up with each other during assembly at the factory with special equipment, while the clamping bolts are tightened up and the torque tube ends clamped to the trunnion shaft.

In the event of accidental damage or if it is essential for the assembly to be taken apart for any other reason the frame with the rear swinging fork assembly should be returned to the factory.

As this may be impractical in the case of Overseas Agents the method of dismantling, and reassembling the trunnion shaft and torque tube assemblies is detailed in the next section.

Dismantling the Trunnion Shaft.

As stated previously the torque arm assemblies should not be loosened or moved on the trunnion shaft, except in case of absolute necessity, such as to enable repairs to be carried out after accidental damage, or to renew the trunnion shaft bushes in the frame.

During initial assembly the two torque arm assemblies are lined up using a special torque tube-assembly Alignment Tool No. X2939, which ensures that when the rear wheel is in position the rear wheel spindle is parallel to the trunnion shaft. In addition, a clamp is needed to hold the

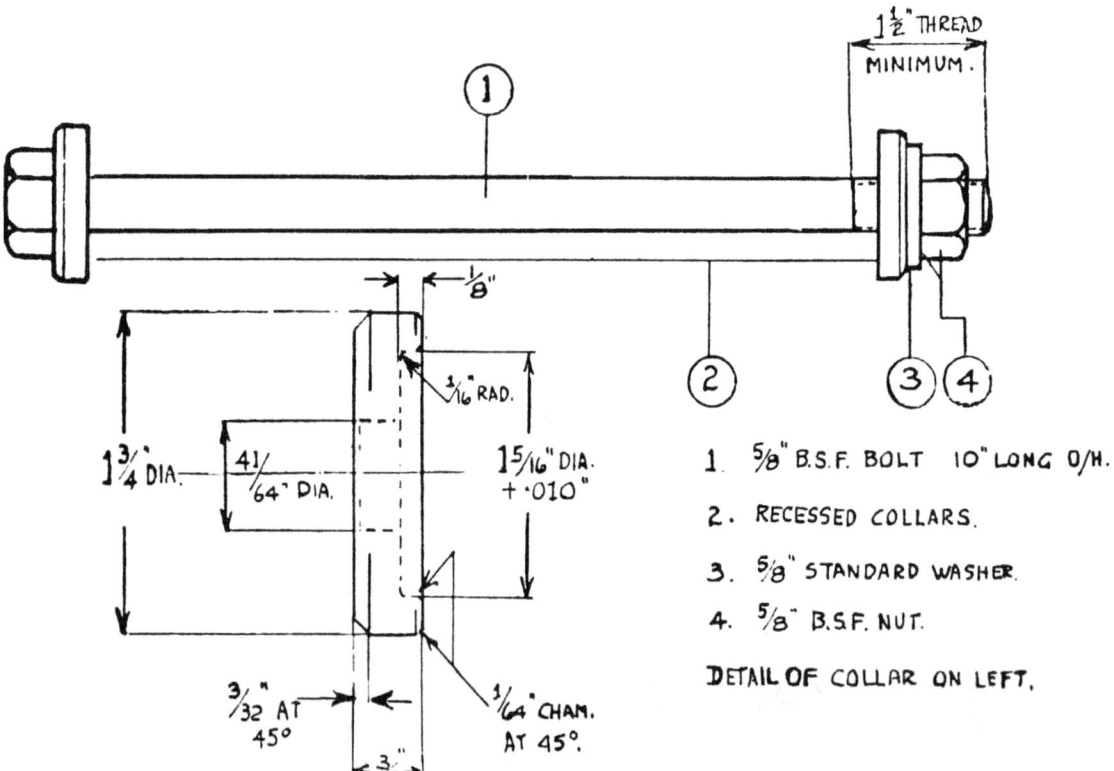

FIG. 26. X2938 TORQUE TUBE CLAMP TOOL.

torque arm assemblies compressed against the trunnion lug felt washers to take up all excess end float. This tool is the Torque Tube Clamp Tool X2938. (Fig. 26.)

The trunnion shaft is finished in three diameters, the offside (right-hand) end to take the offside torque arm assembly being .002-in. larger than the centre parallel portion which bears in the trunnion shaft bushes. The nearside (left-hand) end which carries the nearside torque arm assembly is .002-in. smaller than the centre section.

Before attempting to remove the shaft from a Scrambler model see page 95

To dismantle the shaft, therefore, it must be driven out towards the right or offside, after slacking off both trunnion lug clamp bolts and expanding the lugs from the shaft with suitable wedges driven into the slots in the lugs. The lugs must be expanded to avoid scratching the shaft. Care must be taken not to over-expand them and they must be opened only enough to free the shaft.

Before attempting to drive out the trunnion shaft (for which a soft metal spigoted punch is essential) remove the two rubber trunnion shaft end plugs.

After removal of the shaft the felts and felt housings will pull off the shoulders on the frame trunnion lug.

The Trunnion Shaft Bearing.

In the event of worn bushes these must be driven out of the trunnion lug, and new ones pressed in, after which they must be accurately bored or reamed out to 1.250-in. $+0.00075$-in.
$-.00025$-in.

Reassembling the Trunnion Shaft and Torque Arms.

Fit the trunnion shaft felt washers and felt housings to the machined shoulders on the trunnion shaft lug on the frame—The housings fit on first, with their flat faces against the lug, and the felts in their recessed faces.

See that the felts are well soaked in oil before fitting, particularly if they are new. Alternatively, soak them for a moment or two in molten tallow.

Set out the torque arm assemblies in the correct positions for replacement, noting that the offside (right-hand) one has an annular groove turned in the bore for identification purposes, and that there is a lug for carrying the rear chain guard on the upper part of the nearside (left-hand) torque tube.

Hold the right-hand torque arm assembly against the right-hand side of the trunnion lug, and having oiled the trunnion shaft push the smaller end through the torque arm assembly and into the bearings.

As the end comes out at the left-hand side, put the left-hand torque arm assembly (with the lug wedged open slightly) into position and push the trunnion shaft into it. Wedge open the right-hand lug slightly and press the shaft through. When the shaft has been pushed through until the chamfered end just protrudes beyond the face of the lug on the right, the wedges can be removed and the clamp bolts and nuts fitted. Tighten the bolt on the right-hand side fully, but for the time being leave that on the left loose.

The torque arms must now be drawn together towards the frame to compress the felts and to take up the side play. For this the torque tube clamp tool X2938 is required (Fig. 26). Clamp the torque arms to remove all side play, but leave the shaft free to turn in the bushes.

With the torque arms held with the clamping tool fix the Alignment Tool X2939 in position and locate it on the frame lugs with the two pegs. Bring the torque arms up into line with the holes in the rear ends of the alignment tool and pass the mandrel through the tool and the fork ends. With the torque arms thus held in alignment tighten the left-hand side clamp bolt.

As an alternative, but less satisfactory method of lining up the assembly before tightening the left-hand side clamp bolt, push two well-fitting $\frac{3}{8}$-in. bars through the two bolt holes for the rear engine plates. One hole is in the trunnion lug, and the other in the lug at the bottom of the seat tube. A third $\frac{1}{2}$-in. diameter mandrel is then placed through the fork ends and the assembly is then raised and a sight taken across this mandrel and the upper one at the front. When the torque arms have been adjusted on the trunnion shaft until the mandrels are seen to be parallel and the clamp bolt lightly tightened, the fork should be lowered and a similar test made by sighting across the bottom mandrel. If there is any variation set the fork by moving one of the torque arms on the trunnion shaft so that a mean between the two " sights" is obtained.

When correctly aligned tighten the clamp bolt fully and recheck.

It is emphasised that this method of setting the rear wheel spindle parallel to the trunnion shaft is for use only when the proper equipment is not available, and must be considered as a less satisfactory expedient. As its accuracy depends on the fit of the bars or mandrels in the frame and fork ends respectively and on the bars being perfectly straight it is necessary to get satisfactory materials for the job, and to be most careful when " sighting " across the mandrels.

THE CARBURETTER.

Description and Explanation of Working.

The illustrations should be referred to for explanation of the following sections. The purpose of the carburetter is to atomise the correct amount of fuel with the air that is induced into the engine, and thus supply a correctly-proportioned mixture at all speeds within the engine's range at all throttle settings.

This is achieved by the selection of the correct size main jet, and main choke bore, in conjunction with the right adjustment or setting of the jet needle and the pilot jet.

The volume of mixture, and therefore the power, is controlled from the handlebar twist grip which causes the throttle valve in the carburetter to be raised or lowered, and the correct setting of the carburetter provides the right mixture at all positions of the throttle valve.

The opening of the throttle brings into action first the mixture supply from the pilot system, for idling at slow speed, through the pilot outlet (M). The further progressive opening of the throttle admits air via the main intake and reduces the depression on the pilot outlet (M), but in turn a greater depression is created on the pilot by pass (N) causing the mixture to flow from this opening as well as from the pilot outlet. At about $\frac{1}{8}$th of the throttle opening more air is admitted and the mixture is augmented from the main jet (P). The throttle valve cut-away governs the mixture strength from this position of the throttle to about $\frac{1}{4}$ open. Proceeding up the throttle range the mixture strength is controlled from about $\frac{1}{4}$ to $\frac{3}{4}$ open by the position of the needle (C) working within the needle jet (O). The main jet does not spray directly into the mixing chamber, but discharges through the needle jet into the primary air chamber, and the discharge goes from there as a rich fuel-air mixture through the primary air-choke into the main air-choke. This primary air-choke has a compensating action.* After about - throttle opening the main jet is the only regulation. It will be understood from the foregoing that as the main jet only exercises a regulating effect on the mixture strength after the throttle is opened $\frac{3}{4}$ of its travel or over, the fitting of a smaller main jet for economy purposes is useless, and can only cause overheating due to excessively lean mixtures at high speeds. As the mixture strength over the greater portion of the throttle range is controlled by the setting of the needle within the needle

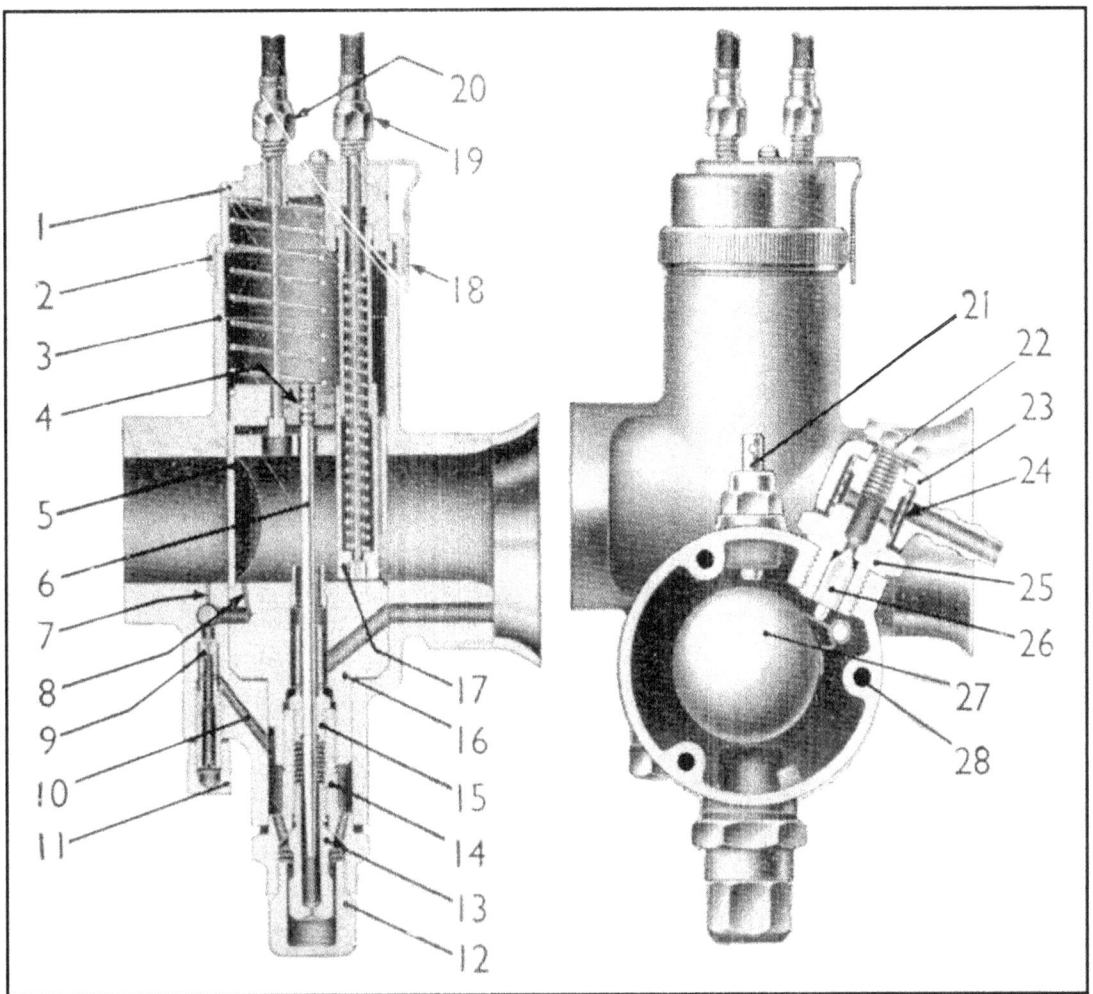

FIG. 27. Section through mixing chamber showing air valve and throttle closed.

FIG. 28. Section through float chamber

jet, cases of excessive fuel consumption are usually capable of improvement by adjustment of the needle setting (referred to later) or by replacement of the needle jet and/or needle because of wear on these components.

A separately operated mixture control is also provided by the air valve, operated from the handlebar, for use when starting from cold, and until the engine is warm enough to accept the full air supply. This air control partially restricts the passage of air through the main choke

THE CARBURETTER (MONOBLOC TYPES).
Petrol Feed (verification).

Later models are fitted with a filter gauze at the inlet to the float chamber. To remove the filter gauze unscrew the banjo bolt (22), the banjo can then be removed and the filter gauze withdrawn from the needle seating. Ensure that the filter gauze is undamaged and free from all foreign matter. Before replacing banjo turn on petrol tap momentarily and see that fuel gushes out.

* On Monobloc types there are bleed holes in the needle jet which serve the double purpose of air compensating the mixture from the needle jet and allowing the fuel to provide a well outside and around the jet which is available for snap acceleration.

Flooding may be due to a worn needle or a leaky float, but nearly all flooding with new machines is due to impurities (grit, fluff, etc.) in the tank —so clean out the float chamber periodically till the trouble ceases. If the trouble persists, the tank might be drained, swilled out, etc.

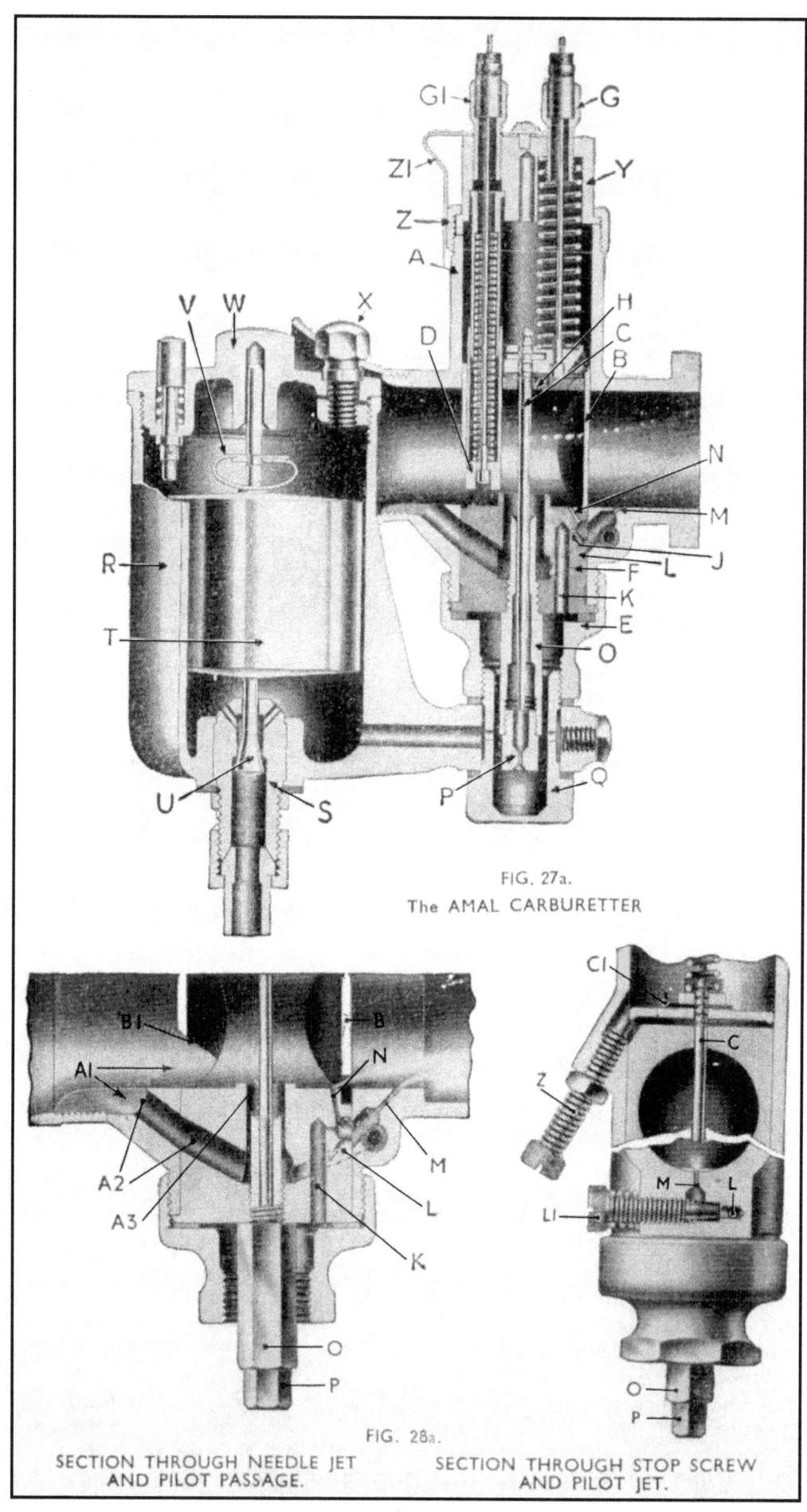

FIG. 27a.
The AMAL CARBURETTER

FIG. 28a.
SECTION THROUGH NEEDLE JET AND PILOT PASSAGE.   SECTION THROUGH STOP SCREW AND PILOT JET.

THE CARBURETTERS *continued*

Re-assembling (after dismantling)

See that the washer on the bottom of the jet block is in good condition, otherwise fuel will leak across its face causing rich erratic running, if the washer is faulty it should be replaced by a new one. When replacing the throttle see that the jet needle goes into the centre hole in the jet block and once in, note the throttle works freely when the mixing chamber cap (2) is screwed down firmly and held by spring (18).

When re-assembling the float see that the narrow leg portion of its hinge is uppermost, as this operates the needle. Care should be taken to see that the joint faces of the side cover and body are not damaged or bruised and that the joint washer is in good condition, otherwise difficulty will be experienced in making a petrol tight joint.

Cable Controls.

See that there is a minimum of backlash when the controls are set back and that any movement of the handlebar does not cause the throttle to open. The adjusters are on the top of the carburetter. See that the throttle shuts down freely.

Adjustment.

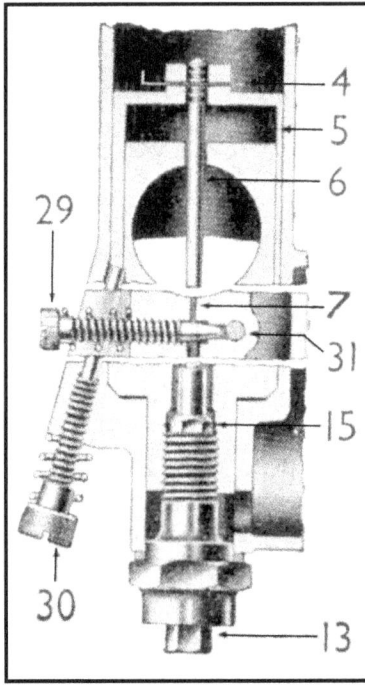

(a) *This figure is three diagrammatic sections of the carburetter to show the throttle adjusting screw (30), and the pilot air adjusting screw (29).*

(b) **Throttle Adjusting Screw.**

Set this screw to hold the throttle open sufficiently to keep the engine running when the twist grip is shut off.

(c) **Pilot Air Adjusting Screw.**

This screw regulates the strength of the mixture for "idling" and for the initial opening of the throttle. The screw controls the depression on the pilot jet by metering the mount of air that mixes with the petrol.

(d) **Main Jet.**

The main jet controls the petrol supply when the throttle is more than three-quarters open, but at smaller throttle openings although the supply of fuel goes through the main jet, the amount is diminished by the metering effect of the needle in the needle jet.

Each jet is calibrated and numbered so that its exact discharge is known and two jets of the same number are alike. *Never reamer a jet out, get another of the right size.* The bigger the number the bigger the jet.

To remove the main jet unscrew the main jet cover, the exposed main jet can then be unscrewed from the jet holder.

(e) **Needle and Needle Jet.**

The needle is attached to the throttle valve and being taper—either allows more or less petrol to pass through the needle jet as the throttle is opened or closed throughout the range, except when idling or nearly full throttle.

The taper needle position in relation to the throttle opening can be set according to the mixture required by fixing it to the throttle valve with the jet needle clip in a certain groove (see Fig. 4 above), thus either raising or lowering it. Raising the needle richens the mixture and lowering it weakens the mixture at throttle openings from quarter to three-quarters open (see Fig. 29 below). The needles are marked with the letters B, C, or D. B types are fitted in the 375 Carburetter, C type in the 376 Carburetter, and D type in the 389 Carburetter. The needles in some cases are marked with a number in addition to a letter.

(f) **Throttle Valve Cut-away.**

The atmospheric side of the throttle is cut away to influence the depression on the main fuel supply and thus gives a means of tuning between the pilot and needle jet range of throttle opening. The amount of cut-away is recorded by a number marked on the throttle valve, viz., 376/3 means throttle valve type 376 with No. 3 cut-away; larger cut-aways, say 4 and 5 give weaker mixtures and 2 a richer mixture.

(g) **Air Valve** is used only for starting and running when cold, and for experimenting with, otherwise run with it wide open.

(h) **Tickler.**

A small plunger spring loaded, in the float chamber wall. When pressed down on the float, the needle valve is allowed to open and so "flooding" is achieved. Flooding temporarily enriches the mixture until the level of the petrol subsides to normal.

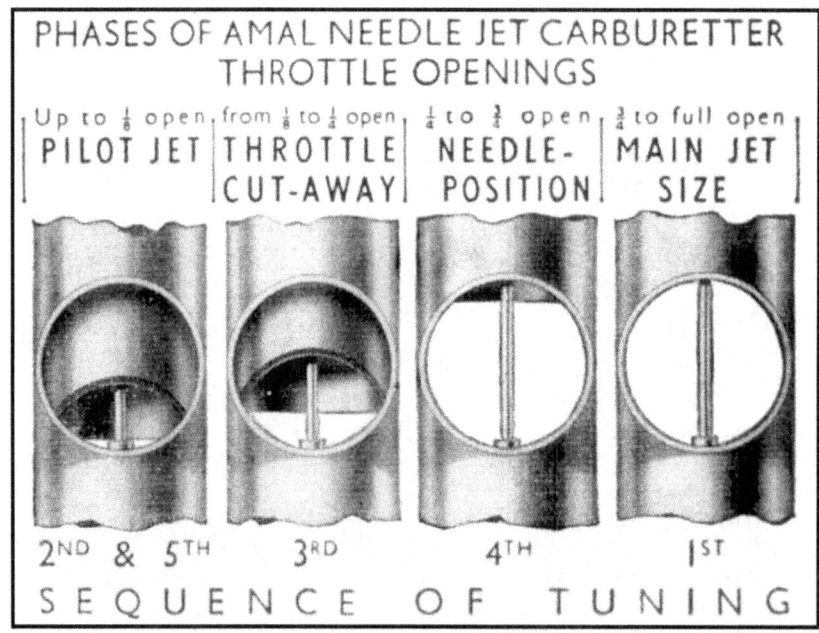

FIG. 29

Adjust in the following order.

Note. The carburetter is automatic throughout the throttle range—the air valve should always be wide open except when used for starting or until the engine has warmed up. We assume normal petrols are used.

Read remarks on pages 65 and 66 for each tuning device and get the motor going perfectly on a quiet road with a slight up gradient so that on test the engine is pulling.

1st Main Jet with throttle in position 1 (Fig. 29).

If at full throttle the engine runs "heavily" the main jet is too large.

If at full throttle by slightly closing the throttle or air valve the engine seems to have better power, the main jet is too small.

With a correct sized main jet the engine at full throttle should run evenly and regularly with maximum power.

If testing for speed work ensure that the main jet size is sufficient for the mixture to be rich enough to keep the engine cool, and to verify this examine the sparking plug after taking a fast run, de-clutching and stopping the engine quickly. If the plug body at its end has a cool appearance the mixture is correct: if sooty, the mixture is rich: if however there are signs of intense heat, the mixture is too weak and a larger main jet is necessary.

2nd. Pilot Jet (Fig. 5). with throttle in positions 2 and 5.

With engine idling too fast with the twist grip shut off and the throttle shut down on to the throttle adjusting screw, and ignition set for best slow running: (1) Screw out throttle adjusting screw until the engine runs slower and begins to falter, then screw pilot air adjusting screw in or out, to make engine run regularly and faster. (2) Now gently lower the throttle adjusting screw until the engine runs slower and just begins to falter, adjust the pilot air adjusting screw to get best slow running; if this 2nd adjustment makes engine run too fast, go over the job again a third time.

3rd. Throttle Cut-away with throttle in position 3 (Fig. 5).

If, as you take off from the idling position, there is objectionable spitting from the carburetter, slightly richen the pilot mixture by screwing in the air screw sufficiently, but if this is not effective, screw it back again, and fit a throttle with a smaller cut-away. If the engine jerks under load at this throttle position and there is no spitting, either the jet needle is much too high or a larger throttle cut-away is required to cure richness.

4th. Needle with throttle in postion 4 (Fig. 5).

The needle controls a wide range of throttle opening and also the acceleration. Try the needle in as low a position as possible, viz., with the clip in a groove as near the top as possible; if acceleration is poor and with air valve partially closed the results are better, raise the needle by two grooves; if very much better try lowering needle by one groove and leave it where it is best. If mixture is still too rich with clip in groove No. 1 nearest the top—the **needle jet** probably wants replacement because of wear. If the needle itself has had several years' use replace it also.

5th. Finally go over the idling again for final touches.

Do not adjust the carburetter to get a very slow tick over, since such a setting will involve the throttle valve having to be opened much further to start from cold, and the consequent reduction of the depression on the pilot system will weaken the mixture and starting will become difficult.

In cases where difficulty is encountered set the throttle stop screw to give a reasonably fast idling speed by screwing the adjuster a little further in. Set the pilot air-bleed screw to give a slightly rich mixture by also screwing it inwards (clockwise) a trifle.

Tracing Faults.

There are only two possible faults in carburation, either richness or weakness of mixture.

Indications of:

Richness.	*Weakness.*
Black smoke in exhaust.	Spitting back in carburetter.
Petrol spraying out of carburetter.	Erratic slow running.
Four strokes, eight-stroking.	Overheating.
Two strokes, four-stroking.	Acceleration poor.
Heavy, lumpy running.	Engine goes better if :—
Sparking plug sooty.	Throttle is not wide open or
	Air Valve is partially closed.

If richness or weakness is present, check if caused by :—

(1) Petrol feed.   Check that jets and passages are clear, that filter gauze in float chamber banjo connection is not choked with foreign matter, and that there is ample flow of fuel.
Check there is no flooding.

(2) Air leaks.   At the connection to the engine or due to leaky inlet valve stems.

(3) Defective or worn parts.   As a loose fitting throttle valve, worn needle jet, loose jets.

(4) Air cleaner being choked up.

(5) An air cleaner having been removed.

Removing the silencer or running with a straight through pipe requires a richer setting.

Having verified the correctness of fuel feed and that there are no air leaks, check over ignition, valve operation and timing. Now at throttle position shown on page 66, fig. 29, test to see if mixtures are rich or weak. This is done by partially closing the air valve, and if engine runs better weakness is indicated, but if engine runs worse richness is indicated.

To remedy, proceed as follows :—

	To cure richness.	*To cure weakness.*
Position 1.	Fit smaller main jet.	Fit larger main jet.
Position 2.	Screw out pilot air adjusting screw.	Screw pilot air adjusting screw in.
Position 3.	Fit a throttle with larger cutaway (para. F, page 66).	Fit a throttle with smaller cutaway (para. F, page 66).
Position 4.	Lower needle one or two grooves (para. E, page 66).	Raise needle one or two grooves (para. E, page 66).

Note. It is not correct to cure a rich mixture at half throttle by fitting a smaller main jet because the main jet may be correct for power at full throttle: the proper thing to do is to lower the needle.

Fixing Carburetter.

Erratic slow running is often caused by air leaks, so verify there are none at the point of attachment to the cylinder or inlet pipe—check by means of an oilcan and eliminate by new washers and the equal tightening up of the flange nuts. On later models a sealing ring is fitted into the attachment flange of the carburetter. Also in old machines look out for air leaks caused by a worn throttle or worn inlet valve guides.

Banging in Exhaust may be caused by too weak a pilot mixture when the throttle is closed or nearly closed—also it may be caused by too rich a pilot mixture and an air leak in the exhaust system; the reason in either case is that the mixture has not fired in the cylinder and has fired in the hot silencer. If the banging happens when the throttle is fairly wide open open the trouble will be ignition—not carburation.

Bad Petrol Consumption of a new machine may be due to flooding, caused by impurities from the petrol tank lodging on the float needle seat and so prevent its valve from closing. Flooding may be caused by a worn float needle valve. Also bad petrol consumption will be apparent if the needle jet (15) (see Fig. 27) has worn; it may be remedied or improved by lowering the needle in the throttle, but if it cannot be—then the only remedy is to get a new needle jet.

Air Filters.

These may affect the jet setting, so if one is fitted afterwards to the carburetter the main jet may have to be smaller. If a carburetter is set with an air filter and the engine is run without it, take care not to overheat the engine due to too weak a mixture; testing with air valve (page 66), will indicate if a larger main jet and higher needle position are required.

Effect of Altitude on Carburetter.

Increased altitude tends to produce a rich mixture. The greater the altitude, the smaller the main jet required. Carburetters ex-works are set suitable for altitudes up to 3,000 feet approximately. Carburetters used constantly at altitudes 3,000 to 6,000 feet should have a reduction in main jet size of 5 per cent, and thereafter for every 3,000 feet in excess of 6,000 feet altitude further reductions of 4 per cent should be made.

THE AMAL MONOBLOC CARBURETTER (External View)

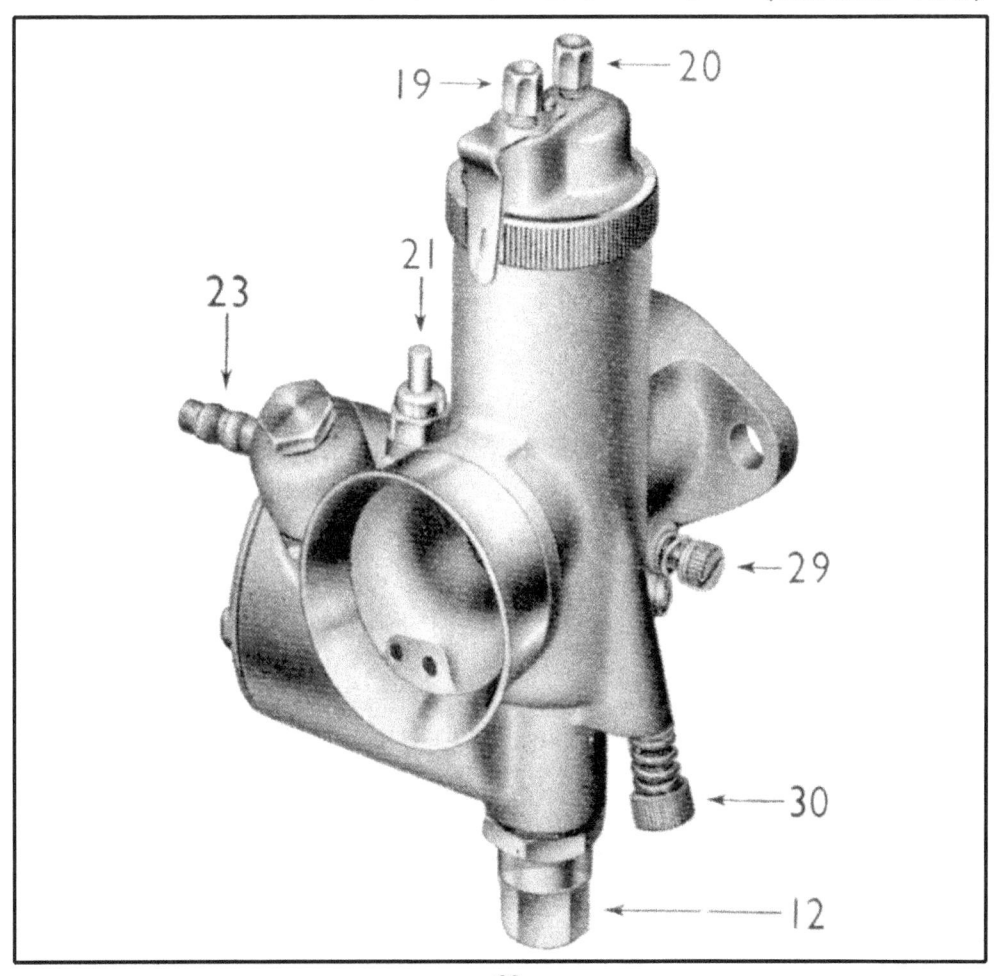

T.T. CARBURETTER.

Note.—The method of adjusting the T.T. Carburetters fitted to Scrambler and Clubman models is similar to that detailed for the standard Monobloc instruments, except that the pilot adjuster is turned **clockwise** to weaken the mixture. The procedure for dismantling also differs. For full details see Amal List No. 374 obtainable from the Carburetter makers.

THE CONCENTRIC CARBURETTER

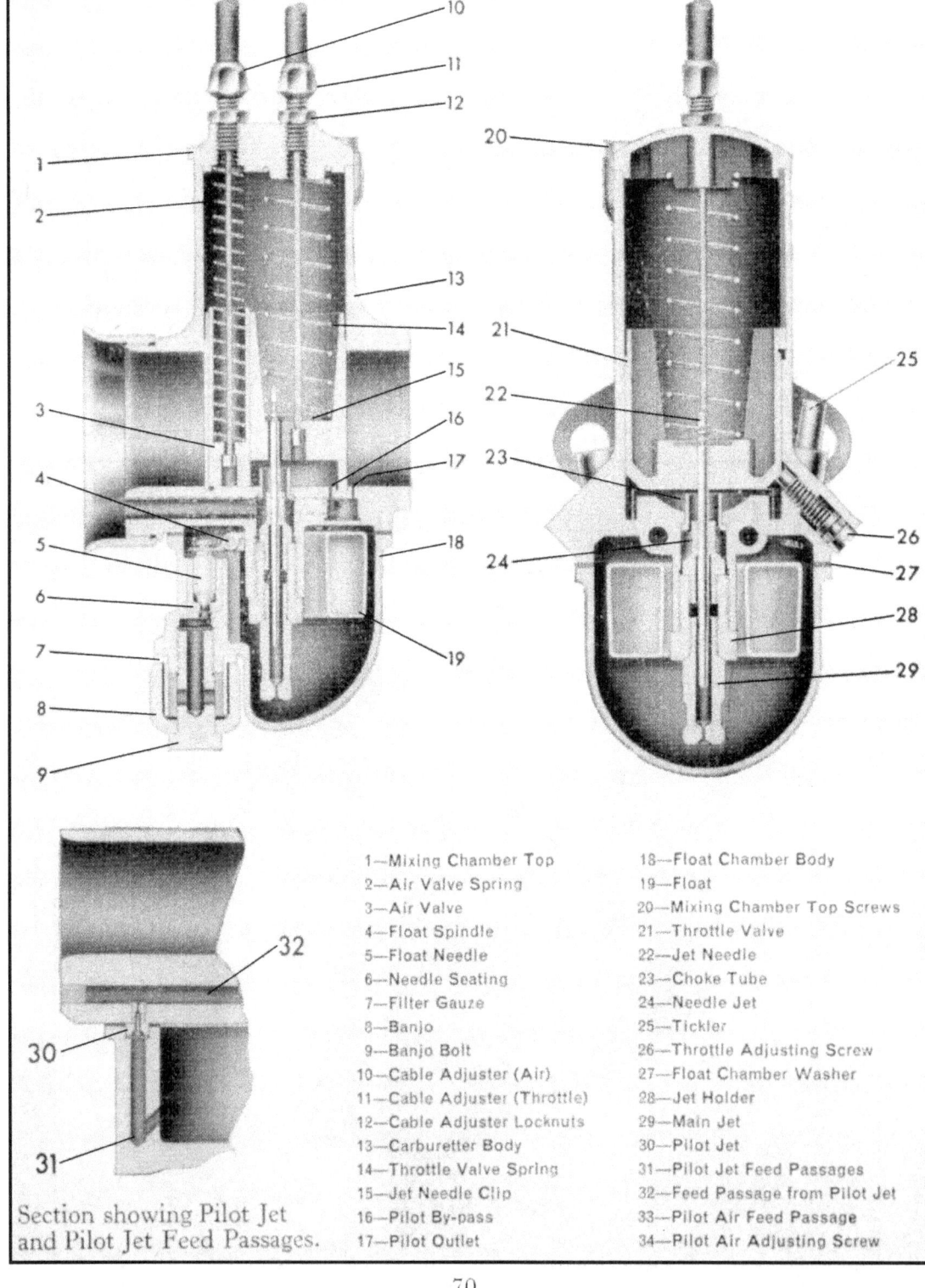

1—Mixing Chamber Top
2—Air Valve Spring
3—Air Valve
4—Float Spindle
5—Float Needle
6—Needle Seating
7—Filter Gauze
8—Banjo
9—Banjo Bolt
10—Cable Adjuster (Air)
11—Cable Adjuster (Throttle)
12—Cable Adjuster Locknuts
13—Carburetter Body
14—Throttle Valve Spring
15—Jet Needle Clip
16—Pilot By-pass
17—Pilot Outlet
18—Float Chamber Body
19—Float
20—Mixing Chamber Top Screws
21—Throttle Valve
22—Jet Needle
23—Choke Tube
24—Needle Jet
25—Tickler
26—Throttle Adjusting Screw
27—Float Chamber Washer
28—Jet Holder
29—Main Jet
30—Pilot Jet
31—Pilot Jet Feed Passages
32—Feed Passage from Pilot Jet
33—Pilot Air Feed Passage
34—Pilot Air Adjusting Screw

Section showing Pilot Jet and Pilot Jet Feed Passages.

How the Carburetter works

The carburetter proportions and atomises the right amount of petrol with the air that is drawn in by the engine because of the correct proportions of jet sizes and the main choke bore. The float chamber maintains a constant level of fuel at the jets and cuts off the supply when the engine stops.

The throttle control from the handlebar controls the volume of mixture and therefore the power and at all positions of the throttle the mixture is automatically correct. The opening of the throttle brings first into action the mixture supply from the pilot jet system for idling, then as it progressively opens, via the pilot by-pass the mixture is augmented from the main jet, the earlier stages of which action is controlled by the needle in the needle jet. The pilot jet system is supplied by the pilot jet (30) which is detachable on removal of the float chamber. On certain other models no pilot jet is fitted but a pilot bush is inserted in the continuation of the pilot air adjusting screw passage. The main jet does not spray directly into the mixing chamber, but discharges through the needle jet into the primary air chamber and goes from there as a rich petrol-air mixture through the primary air choke into the main air choke.

The carburetters usually have a separately operated mixture control called an air valve, for use when starting from cold and until the engine is warm; this control partially blocks the passage of air through the main choke.

This design of carburetter offers perfectly simple and effective tuning facilities.

For full details see Amal List No. 117/3.

THE AIR CLEANER. (Not fitted as standard.)
Maintenance.

After every 5,000 miles running (approximately) the air cleaner should be removed for cleaning and re-oiling. It should not be dismantled, as if it is taken apart and the wire element is unwound it may not be possible to replace this satisfactorily, so as to get an even flow of air through it all round.

The entire filter should be washed in clean petrol until all accumulated dirt has been removed and should afterwards be allowed to dry thoroughly inside and out. Before refitting immerse the filter in clean engine oil (Grade SAE50) and after draining off surplus oil and wiping clean externally refit it to the machine. No other attention is needed.

THE SPARKING PLUG.
Suitable Types.

The type of sparking plug fitted as initial equipment has been selected after exhaustive tests and has the characteristics most suited for general purposes in this type of engine. Sparking plugs are obtainable from several manufacturers who each produce a range of plugs of varying diameters, threads, and reaches (lengths of thread) and each size is usually offered in a range of different heat resistances. At the one extreme, plugs are capable of withstanding very high working temperatures without overheating, and at the other extreme of being able to continue firing in very oily conditions. The first will usually be found to oil up readily, and the second will not work long in a high performance engine before overheating sets in and causes pre-ignition of the charge in the cylinder.

Thus, if a plug of the same make and type as that originally fitted by us is unobtainable, the replacement must be the same diameter and reach and must have similar characteristics. This is very important as, whilst a plug of too high internal heat resistance will usually only cause difficult starting, and misfiring, serious harm can be caused to the engine by the use of a "soft" plug, that is one which becomes overheated easily.

Our recommendations for the MSS are KLG type FE80, Lodge type HLN, and Champion type NA8 and for Venom and Viper models KLG FE100, Champion NA10 or Lodge 3HLN.

The thread diameter is 14 mm. and the reach 18 mm. (extra long). In no circumstances whatever must plugs of different reach be fitted.

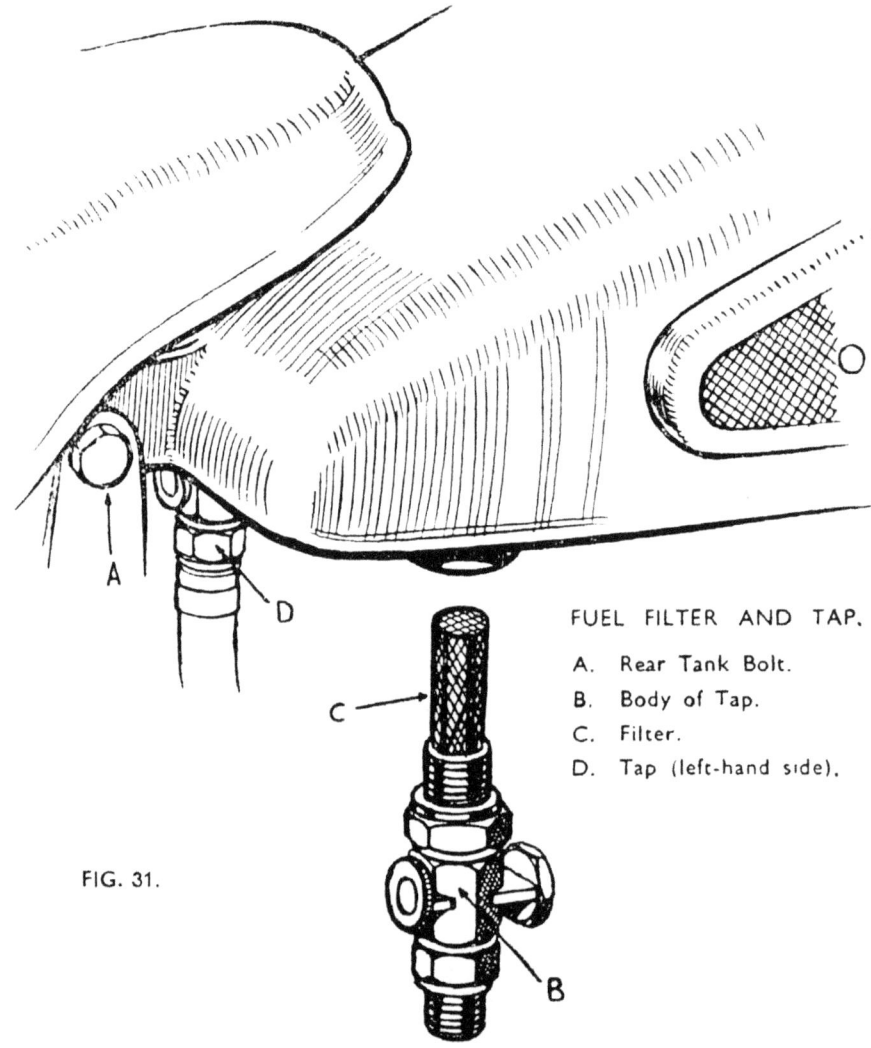

FIG. 31.

FUEL FILTER AND TAP.

A. Rear Tank Bolt.
B. Body of Tap.
C. Filter.
D. Tap (left-hand side).

FUEL TAP AND STRAINER.

Sparking Plugs for Extra Hard Duty and Racing.

The types of sparking plugs recommended above are those suitable for normal road running.

Many Viper and Venom models are driven exceptionally hard and are also being used to an increasing extent for racing. For such purposes plugs having higher heat resistance are often necessary.

For really hard sustained high speed driving on the road with silencer fitted the K.L.G. type FE220 is desirable.

For racing on short circuits where, although speeds are high, the engine is frequently throttled back, the K.L.G. type FE250 is often suitable.

On longer circuits for Clubman racing where there is the opportunity to use full throttle for long periods the K.L.G. type FE280 will be required.

These recommendations must necessarily be in the nature of a guide only. The correct type for any given set of conditions, apart from normal use, must be decided finally on the course after taking plug readings during practice runs before the race.

Maintenance

The plug will require cleaning from time to time and the method used will depend upon whether the plug is constructed so that it may be taken apart for cleaning or is of the " non-detachable " type.

The " non-detachable " type must be cleaned by brushing the electrodes and the insides of the gas space as far as possible with a wire brush, or by " sand-blasting " on one of the special sparking plug cleaning machines. In either case the plug must afterwards be scrupulously cleaned out by washing in petrol to eliminate all risk of dirt, and more particularly, the sand used in cleaning, from working into the combustion chamber during subsequent service. Do not in any circumstances refit a sparking plug immediately after cleaning on a Plug Service Cleaner employing a sand-blast, but wash it well in petrol, and blow out with a compressed air jet.

To clean a " detachable " type plug, take it apart by holding the gland nut firmly, but not so tightly as to cause damage by crushing, in a vice—the jaws of which have been covered to prevent marking the nut. The plug body is then unscrewed off the gland nut. On removing the central portion take care of the sealing washer which must be refitted on reassembly

Scrape the electrode, insulator, and the inside of the body clean of carbon with a penknife or clean with a wire-brush. Rinse in petrol before reassembling, make sure that the copper washer is in good conditions and smear lightly with thin oil. Refit carefully and put the centre into the plug body, tightening the gland nut fully.

Adjusting the Plug Points.

After cleaning, the firing points will require adjusting to a gap of .018-in. to .023-in. Never adjust by bending the centre electrode as this will crack the insulator and render the sparking plug useless. All adjustments must be made by setting the side electrode.

Refitting to the Engine.

Make certain that the threads are quite clean and, if the sparking plug has been cleaned on a " Sand-blast " cleaner, that there is no sand left inside the plug—this is most important.

Lightly smear the threads of the plug with graphite paste or " Oil Dag," and screw in to the head, being most careful to avoid cross threading.

Do not overtighten.

THE DYNAMO AND LIGHTING SET.

Lamps and Bulbs.

The headlamp is fitted with one Bifocal bulb and one parking (Pilot) bulb. The types used are :

Headlamp Bulb : 6-volt 30/24 watt. Double filament. Bifocal Pre-focussed type.

Pilot Bulb : 6-volt. 3 watt. Single filament. M.E.S. Cap.

To remove the lamp front to change a bulb or for other attention, free the clip below the lamp rim and pull the rim away from the lamp from the bottom first. Note that if it is proposed to do any work to the switch involving any connections, always detach the cables from the positive terminal of the battery.

The bulbs are detachable from the back of the reflector after removing the bayonet-fixed contact assembly to which the leads are attached.

To replace lamp glass and reflector unit release the four—or more—fixing clips from under the lip of the head lamp rim. The unit will now come out of the rim.

Do not touch the highly polished inside optical surface of the reflector as this will leave finger marks which it will be most difficult to remove without damaging the surface permanently.

When replacing the reflector see that it is fitted correctly with the opening for the pilot bulb uppermost. Refit the lamp front at the top first—push it over the lower edge, engage the fixing clip.

On Viper and Venom models the rear lamp and stop lamp are combined in one body and the bulb used is a 6-volt $18 \times 6W$ offset pin Stoplight bulb.

To reach the bulb take out two screws from the plastic " light " and remove.

The Dynamo. Maintenance.

The commutator and brushes should be inspected occasionally and should any blackening of the commutator segments be noticed the commutator should be thoroughly cleaned, and all brush dust blown out of the end casing. If the charge rate is satisfactory it is best to leave the dynamo and regulator alone and normally no major attention should be required within the first 10,000 miles running.

Before doing any work at all to the dynamo disconnect the leads from the positive terminal (+) of the battery.

The commutator and brushes are exposed by removing the commutator cover (Fig. 35) which is held to the end casting by a single central screw, after pulling out the single pin plug connecting the positive lead to the dynamo.

See that the brushes move freely in their holders. If stiff remove the brush concerned and clean the sides with a cloth moistened in petrol, or rub lightly with fine glasspaper. Always replace brushes in their original positions.

Brushes which have worn so that they do not bear firmly on the commutator, or which expose the embedded end of the flexible lead on the running face must be replaced at once.

The commutator must be clean, true, and free from all traces of oil or dirt. If dirty or blackened it can be cleaned by pressing a cloth against it and turning it round by the kickstart. If very dirty moisten the cloth in petrol, or hold against it a piece of fine glasspaper whilst turning.

Clean away all traces of dust or carbon before refitting the brushes.

Testing. (Fig. 34.)

The dynamo can be checked quickly and with very little trouble by removing the driving belt, and the commutator cover, and pressing the cut-out points together. If the dynamo does not begin to run as a motor from the battery current there is a fault in it.

This is not a 100% check, as in some circumstances a dynamo with a faulty winding may ' motor,' but by testing in this way a lot of time can be saved.

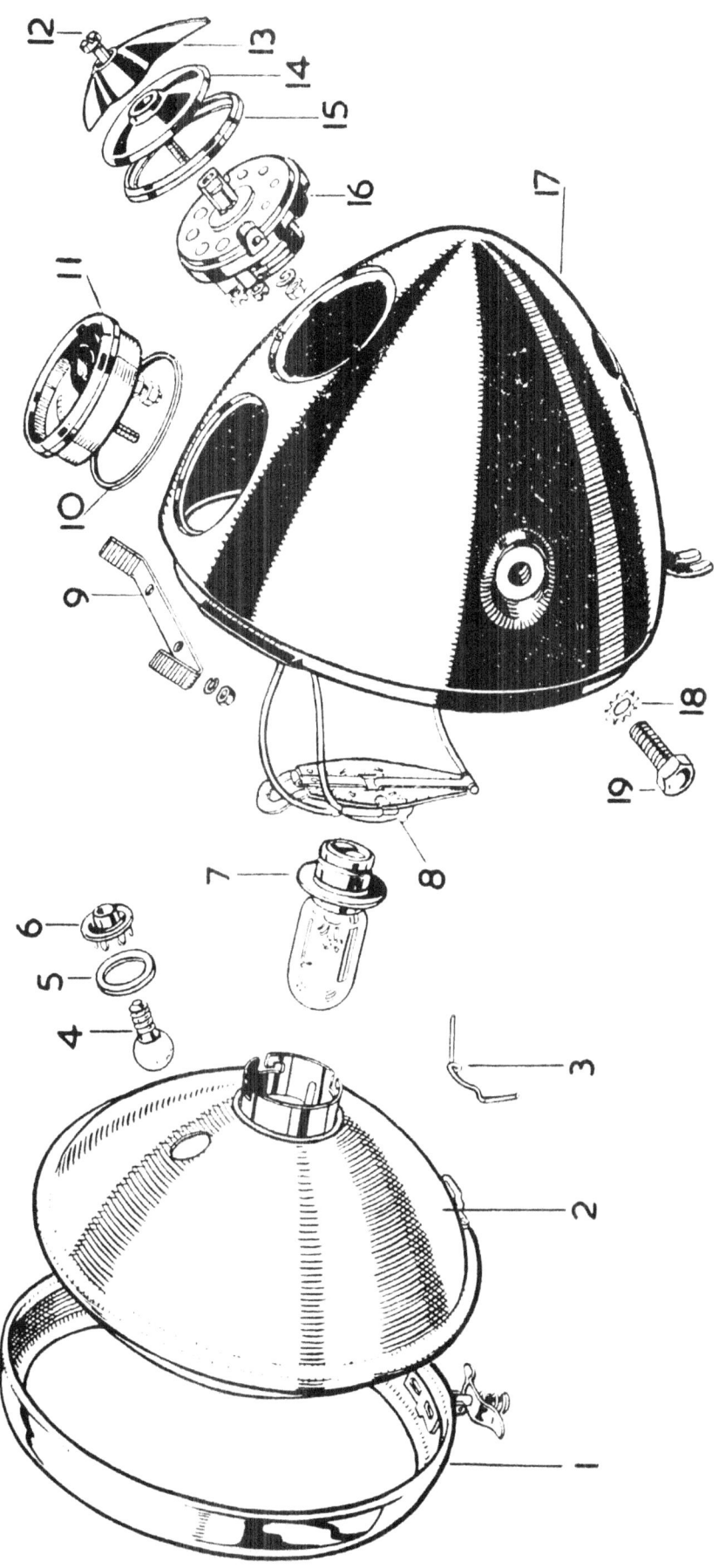

MILLER HEADLAMP 179C.V.   FIG. 32.

The Dynamo (*continued*).

The work about to be described should not be undertaken unless the necessary equipment is available and is best entrusted to a Miller Service Agent.

Remove the commutator cover screw, then remove the cover, exposing the commutator and end bracket. Disconnect the three outside leads (Regulator and headlamp) from terminals D. B. and S. Clip the negative lead of a good quality moving coil voltmeter, reading from 0 to 10-volts to a clean earthing point on the dynamo, and clip the voltmeter positive lead to terminal B.

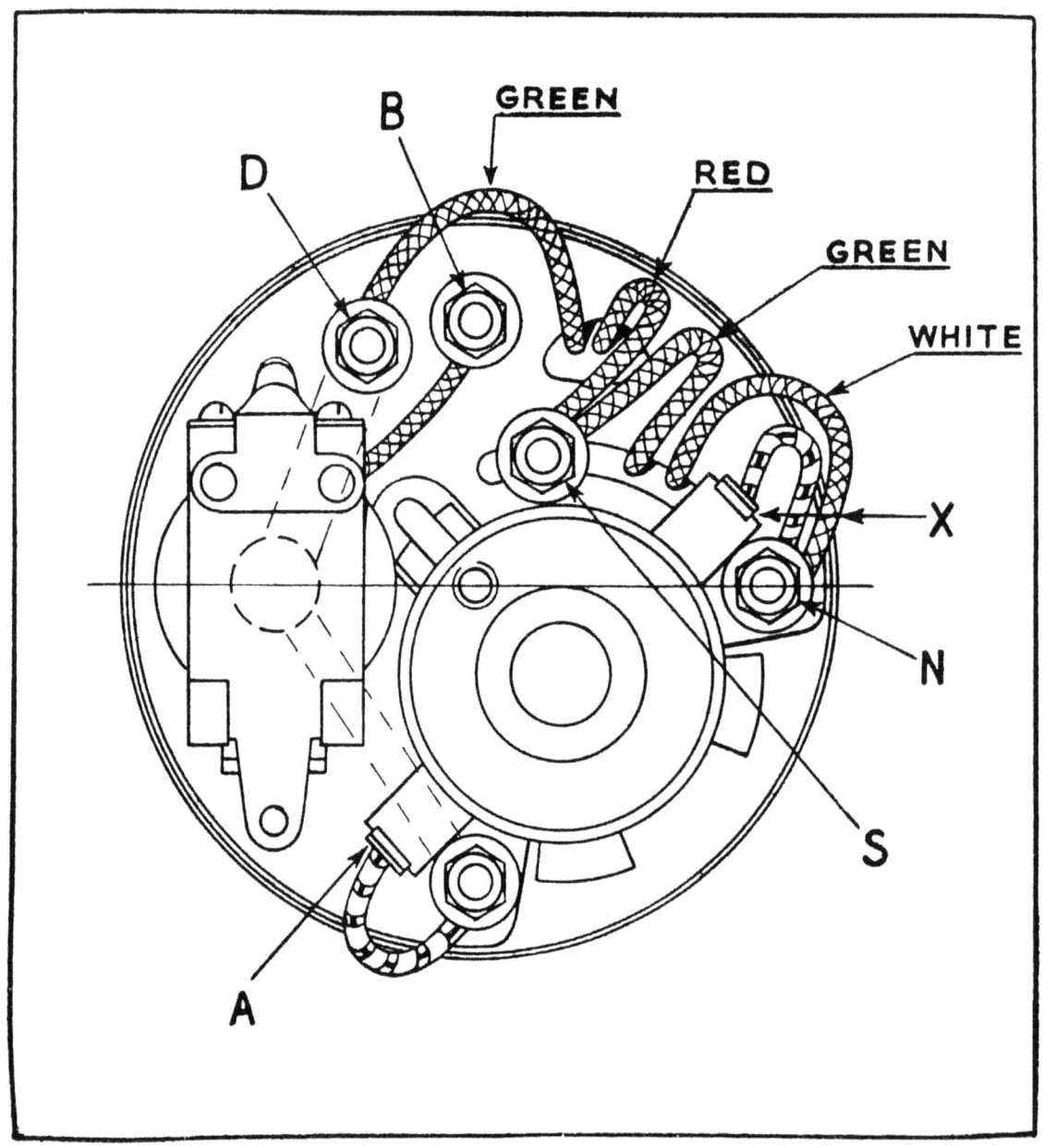

FIG. 34.

Start the engine and slowly increase its speed. If no reading is shown on the Voltmeter transfer the positive lead of the voltmeter to terminal D. If a reading is now shown the cut out is at fault and should be adjusted (see page 83). If no reading the fault is in the dynamo.

On no account must the engine speed be increased to such an extent that a reading 8 volts is exceeded during these tests.

The Dynamo (*continued*).

If dynamo and cut-out are in order, re-connect the three leads to terminals D. B. & S., and test voltage regulator. (See paragraph on Regulator page 80.)

Removal.

Electrical breakdown of the dynamo is most unusual, and the unit should be tested as described above before assuming that removal is necessary.

The removal of the dynamo is described on page 33.

Dismantling. (Figs. 34 and 35.)

Take off the armature shaft nut and washer, and draw the pulley off the tapered end of the armature shaft with a " Claw " extractor, being most careful when using the extractor not to break the thin flange of the pulley.

Remove brushes A and X (Fig. 34) from their holders. Unscrew and remove the two long through bolts (H37, Fig. 35) securing both end castings of the dynamo yoke. The countersunk heads of these screws can be seen at the driving end.

With a $\frac{3}{8}$-in. diameter metal punch and hammer, tap the armature shaft at the commutator end. As soon as the ballrace at the commutator end is clear of the casting, the armature with the driving end casing can be withdrawn.

If it is necessary to remove the driving end casting from the armature shaft, first take out the pulley key (if fitted) from the shaft, and then unscrew and remove the bearing lockring (H38, Fig. 35) which is screwed on the armature shaft just behind the tapered portion.

Do not in any circumstances attempt the removal of the lockring by knocking it round with a punch. Always use a special pin spanner as shown (Fig. 37). This spanner is quite easily made from the details given in the illustration.

Support the bearing retaining plate firmly and press out the armature shaft. Take care not to damage the threads or bend the shaft when removing it.

To remove the commutator end casting from the yoke, first disconnect the four insulated leads at D, N & S (one each white and red, and two green) which pass through the end casting to the field coil (Fig. 34).

The end casing can then be pulled away from the yoke, drawing the four leads carefully through the accommodation slots in the casting and being very careful to avoid damaging them.

Commutator and Brushes.

Check the brushes for cleanliness, condition, and freedom in their holders. If either are stiff, free off as described previously. Inspect the commutator and if not badly worn clean up by polishing with fine glasspaper. To do this whilst the armature is out of the dynamo, it is advisable to rotate the armature in a lathe and hold the glasspaper against the revolving commutator; in this way ensuring that it is true. If required, the commutator micas separating the segments must be undercut afterwards to a depth of approximately .025-in. They must not stand level with the rubbing surfaces of the segments. Clean up carefully afterwards when the armature is ready for refitting.

If new brushes are fitted they must be properly bedded to ensure that they make good contact with the commutator. To do this it is necessary to postpone the fitting until the armature is once more assembled into the dynamo.

To bed the brushes pass a thin strip of superfine glasspaper between the commutator and the brushes with the smooth side of the paper against the commutator. Press each brush in turn lightly on to the glass side of the

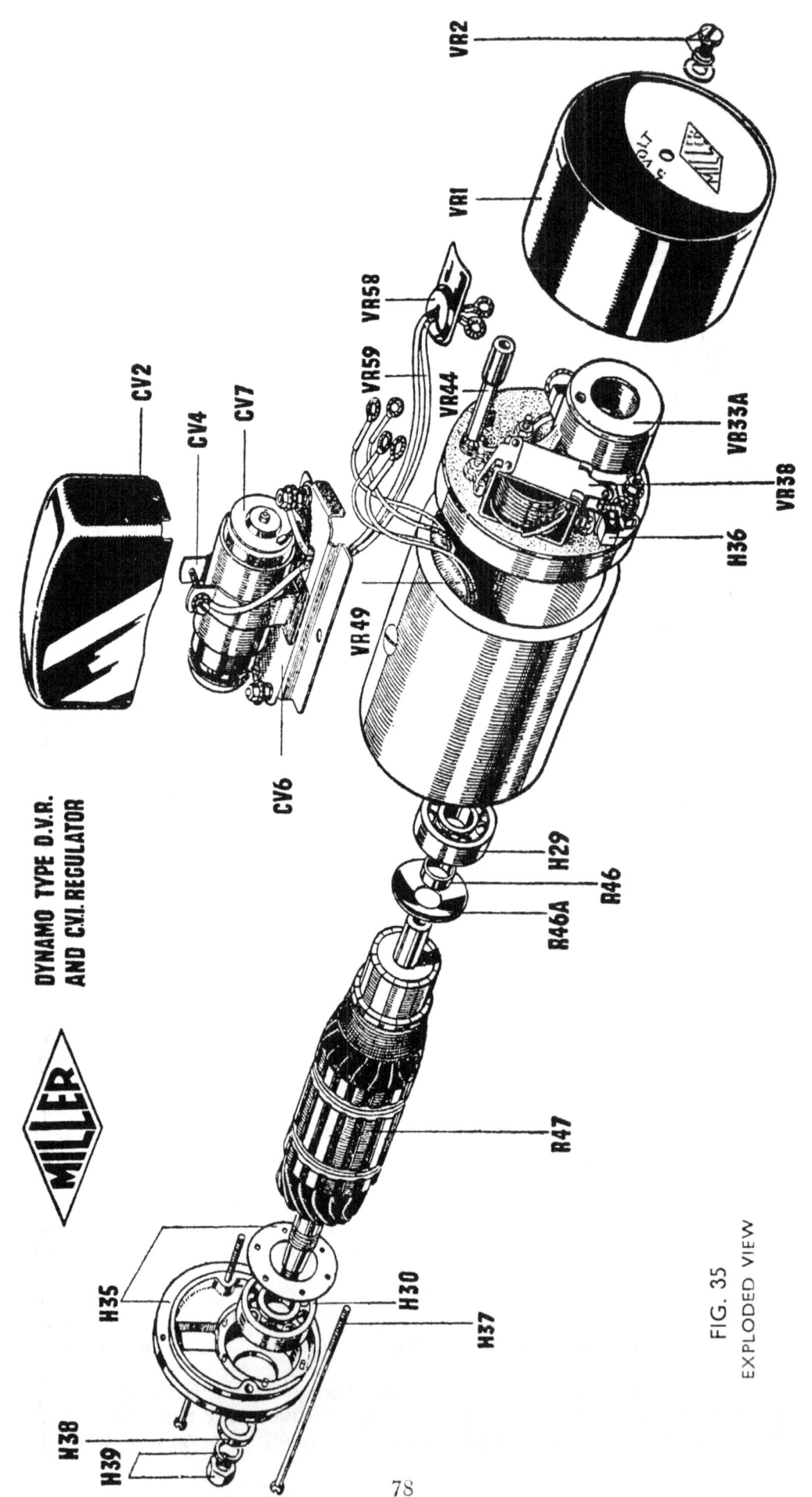

FIG. 35
EXPLODED VIEW

The Dynamo (*continued*).

paper and then pull the paper backwards and forwards several times. This will form the working ends of the brushes to suit the commutator.

Remove the glasspaper and clean out all glass and brush dust—preferably by means of a jet of compressed air.

Dynamo Bearings. (Replacement and Lubrication.)

It is very seldom that the bearings have to be replaced and they should not be removed unless absolutely necessary.

The drive end bearing is retained by a plate rivetted to the end casing (Fig. 35, H35). Only three of the projecting rivets are peened over and these must be filed off flush with the plate to remove it. On refitting the other three projections are used and are peened over to hold the retaining plate.

A small extractor will be needed to draw the commutator end ballrace off the shaft—it is not very tight.

On reassembly the bearings must be carefully packed with a high-melting point grease. Soft grease must not be used. Subsequent lubrication in service can be given by oiling sparingly through the commutator cover fixing screw hole, and to the drive end bearing through the grub screw hole in the top of the bearing housing.

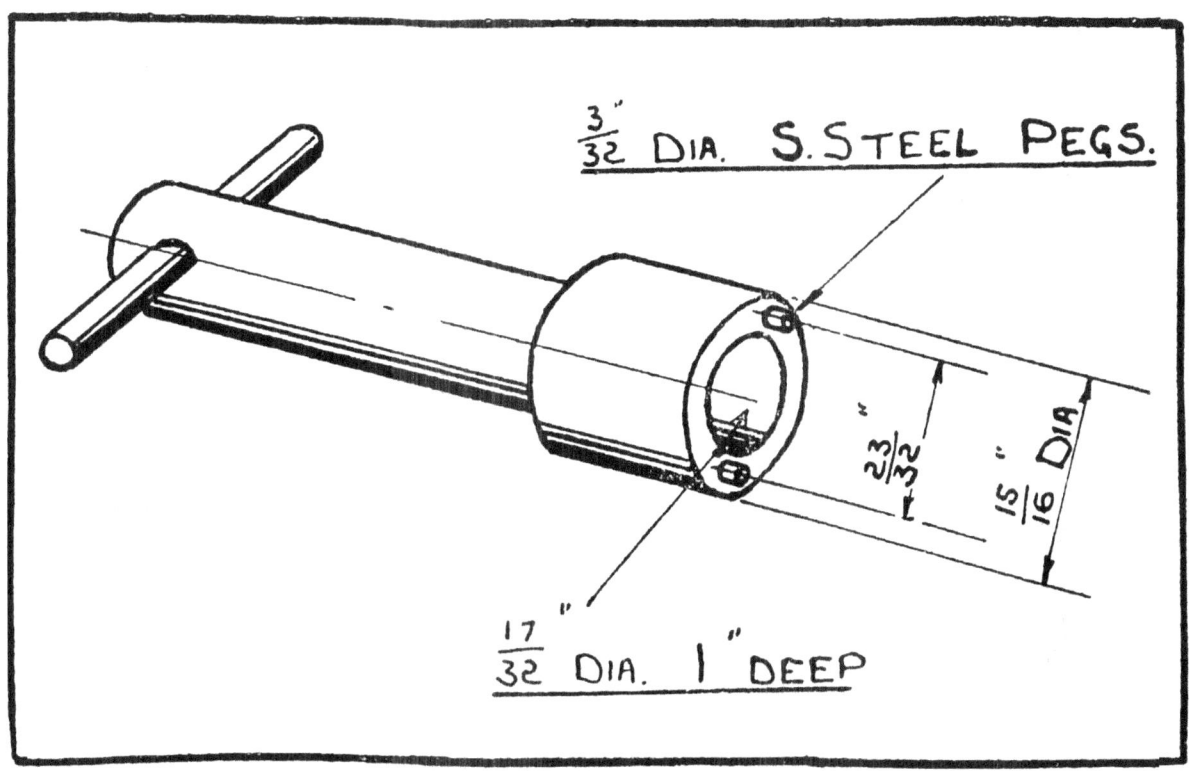

FIG. 36.

Dynamo Armature. (Testing.)

The resistance of the armature coils measured between two adjacent commutator segments should be .2 ohms $\pm$ .01 ohms. Megger test to earth should not be less than 100,000 ohms.

Dynamo Field Coils. (Testing and Fitting.)

The resistance of the field winding (red and white leads) should be 4 ohms $\pm$ .25 ohm., and of the resistance winding (green leads) 7 ohms. $\pm$ .25 ohms. Megger test to earth and megger test between field and resistance windings should not be less than 100,000 ohms.

The Dynamo (*continued*).

When fitting a new field coil, force the yoke and pole on to a mandrel about 8-in. long, the diameter tapering from 1.773-in. to 1.767-in.

Grip the exposed end of the mandrel in a vice, and by using a robust screwdriver tighten the countersunk pole screw (Fig. 36) dead tight to hold the pole shoe firmly to the yoke.

It is most important that there shall be no air gap between the pole shoe and the inner face of the yoke.

Voltage Regulator.

As it is very seldom that the regulator gives trouble it is advisable, if it is suspected that it is at fault, to check the dynamo driving belt adjustment before doing anything else. For instance should it be found that the battery becomes discharged, although there is the normal charge reading of about 2 amperes only, it may be assumed incorrectly that the regulator is failing to increase the charge to compensate for the low state of the battery.

All these symptoms are however, also compatible with a slipping belt, which will drive sufficiently at low speeds to provide a 2 ampere charge but will not drive at higher speeds to provide the higher charge rate that the dynamo would give if driven properly.

The result is that the battery, although requiring a temporarily high charge rate to bring it back to a fully charged condition, does not receive it and gradually becomes discharged.

Normally the regulator provides complete automatic control of the charging so that the dynamo output varies according to the calls upon the battery or its state of charge. In the daytime with no lights in use, and with a battery in good condition the dynamo gives only a trickle charge, so that the ammeter readings will seldom exceed 1 or 2 amperes.

Should the lights be left switched on for only a few minutes, with the engine stationary, it will be found that on the engine being started and its speed increased the charge rate will be increased considerably until the battery is brought up to full charge again. Subsequently the charge rate will drop if there are no further calls on the battery.

The Voltage Regulator. (Testing.)

To test accurately special apparatus is necessary so that the work should be entrusted to a main Miller Service Agent who will have the necessary equipment.

If in normal running conditions, it is found that the battery is continually in a low state of charge, and it is established that this is not due to belt slip, or to a defective battery, and if the dynamo has been tested and found satisfactory, and the cut-out in order, the regulator should be tested by substitution if a replacement is handy.

To test whether the regulator is at fault if no replacement is available, disconnect the battery positive (+) lead, and connect a moving coil voltmeter to the two regulator base terminals (positive and negative), start the engine, and run it at a speed equivalent to about 20 m.p.h. road speed in top gear (approximately 1450 r.p.m.). If the regulator is in correct adjustment the voltmeter reading should be from 7.5 to 8.2 volts.

The Voltage Regulator. (Adjusting.)

If the voltmeter reading is below 7.5 volts, over regulation is taking place, causing the battery to be continually in a low state of charge. In the absence of a replacement, a purely temporary adjustment can be made by screwing out the negative (—) contact screw (which is visible at the conical end of the regulator cartridge), two complete turns.

Should the voltmeter indicate over 8.2 volts, which would cause overcharging, a temporary adjustment can be made by screwing out the positive contact screw at the other end not more than a quarter of a turn.

Note that these adjustments will not give the correct voltage readings, but will enable the machine to be run with improved results until a replacement regulator can be fitted. Note also that it is quite safe to run temporarily without the regulator cartridge in place. With the cartridge removed and the dynamo leads left in place, that is with the red collared lead connected to the base plate and the green collared lead to the clip bolt, the dynamo will give a reduced output with a maximum of about

MILLER CUT-OUT. (DVR TYPE DYNAMO).

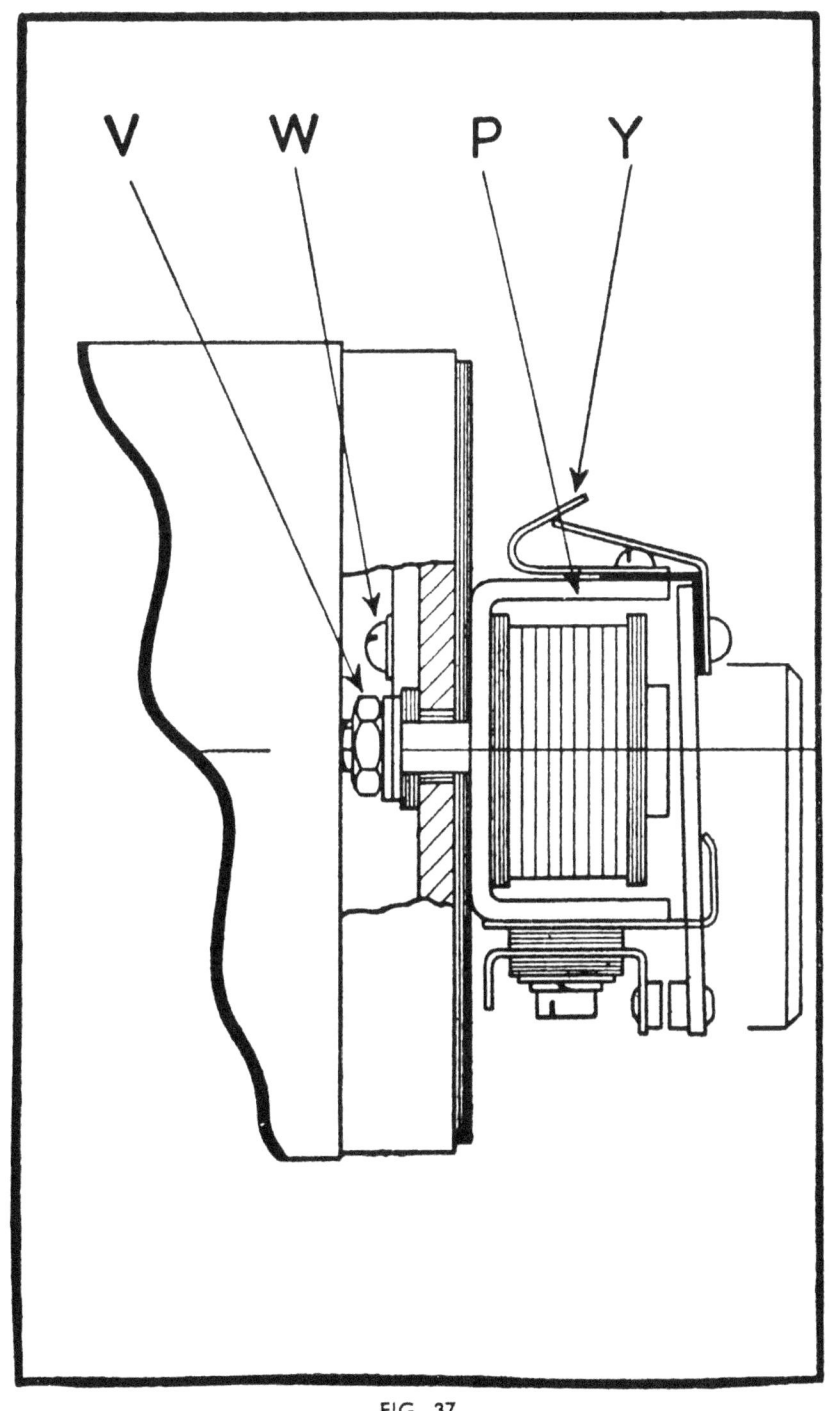

FIG. 37.

THEORETICAL DIAGRAM: MILLER DYNAMO (DVR) and REGULATOR

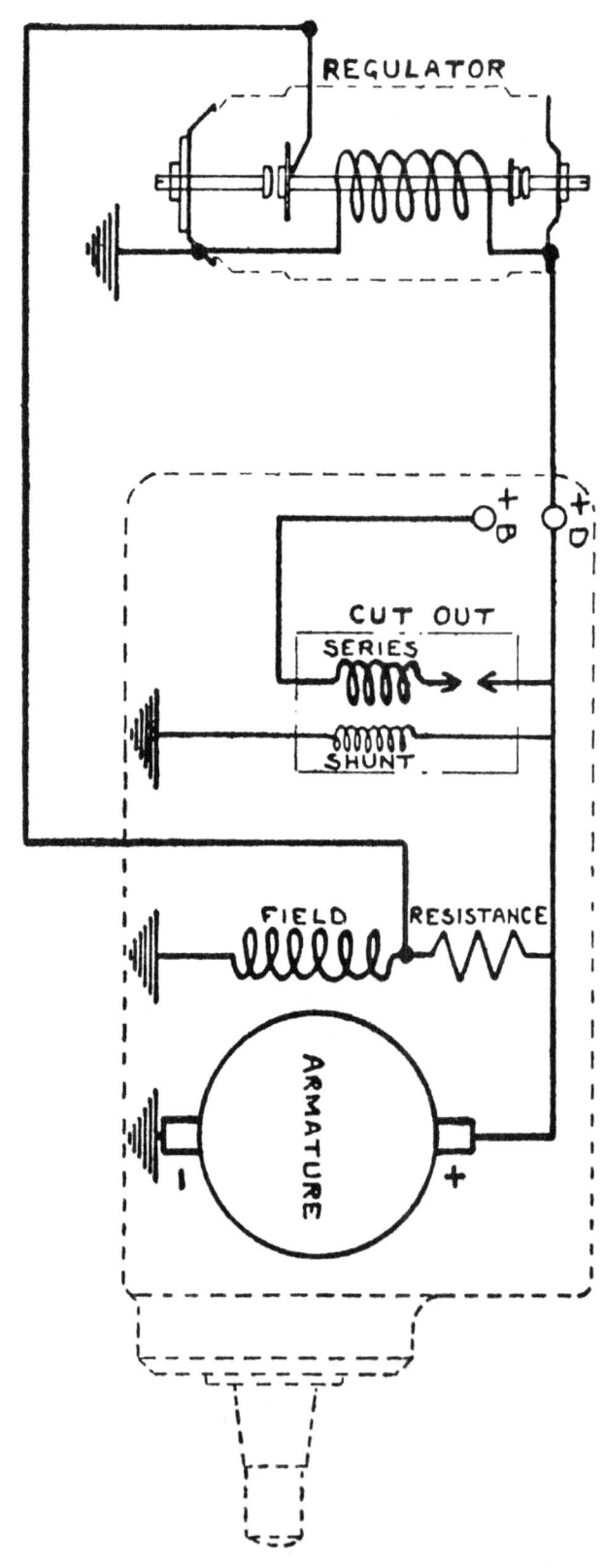

FIG. 39

3.5 amperes. It is advisable to fit a small block of wood or metal 1-in. long by 1¼-in. dia. into the clip temporarily, to allow the clip to be tightened and the lead held firm. Replacement as soon as possible is essential.

The Cut-out (Type VR38). (Fig. 37.)

The cut-out (P) is attached to the dynamo commutator end casing by a nut (V) and is removable after taking off the commutator cover, the nut (V) and disconnecting the earth lead which is attached to the end cover by the screw and washer (W) and the lead to the centre one of the three terminals (B), Fig. 35.

The resistance of the series winding is .09 to .1 ohm. Resistance of shunt winding 55 to 56 ohms. The contact clearance is $\frac{1}{32}$-in. (.031-in.). The contacts should close at approximately 6 volts, when a current of from 0. to ¼ ampere is being generated, and open when the current falls from 0 to ½ ampere discharge. The " off " and " on " tension can be adjusted by bending the brass tensioning bracket (Y).

The Ammeter. (Testing.)

With the engine stationary, switch on the lights. With the head-lamp, main bulb, tail lamp bulb, and speedometer bulb the discharge will be 5.3 amperes. On switching off, the needle should swing back freely to zero. If at fault replace as soon as possible.

The Dynamo (Type DVR) Reassembling.

This is broadly a reversal of the process of dismantling already described but the following should be noted.

Attach the commutator end casting to the yoke first. Pass the red lead and the adjacent lead through the triangular slot and connect to terminals S and D respectively (Fig. 34). Pass the white lead and adjacent green lead through the long curved slot and connect to N and S respectively.

Fit the drive end ballrace to the end casting, refit the retaining plate and screws to the end casting. Place the assembly over the tapered end of the armature shaft. Screw on the lockring tightly. With the commutator end bearing already on the shaft push the armature through the yoke, entering the ballrace in the commutator end casting and press gently home. Refit the two through bolts securing the ends to the yoke and tighten.

Replace the back half of the belt cover on the dynamo and fit the pulley washer, and nut, finally tightening the nut.

Fit the rubber bush protecting the leads into the commutator cover and connect up the leads : Red collared lead from voltage regulator to " D," the plain lead from regulator to terminal " S " and the blue collared lead from ammeter (in headlamp) to " B."

Replace the brushes, fit the dynamo to the machine, afterwards fitting the commutator end cover.

A theoretical diagram of the Miller Dynamo and Regulator is shown in Fig. 39.

THE BATTERY.

Batteries filled with acid must be given their initial charge within one year.

First Charge Instructions for Filled, Uncharged, Varley Batteries.

The Varley is a lead-acid battery having the same general, although greatly improved, characteristics as all lead-acid batteries; the main difference lies in its construction. The plates and separators are assembled and compressed together forming a solid porous block. The acid which is required for the working of the battery is held by absorption in the block of plates and separators and no gravity readings are therefore necessary, or can be taken.

To make ready for service a filled but uncharged battery, the following instructions should be carried out.

(1) Remove sealing tape, unscrew vent stoppers, and if fitted, break away sealing discs in the vents.
(2) Put on charge. Refer to chart below for rates and length of charge.
(3) During the whole of the first charge period the electrolyte level should be maintained ¼-in. above plate/separator block. For this, use distilled water only. Keep vent stoppers in—do not screw down.
(4) The first charge period should be continuous. If for any major reason the current is cut, the open circuit standing time should be allowed for.
(5) The charge is complete when all cells are gassing freely and cell voltages remain constant for five consecutive half-hourly readings.
(6) After charge, allow battery to stand to complete absorption, then, after a period of 30 minutes any electrolyte should be removed. Dry top of battery, screw down vent stoppers and coat terminals and connector bars slightly with Vaseline before putting into service.
(7) A fully charged battery should read at least 6.3 volts on open circuit.

Type MC.7/12.

First Charge	1¼ amperes for 60 hours.
Re-charge	¾ amperes for 24 hours.
Freshening Charge	1½ amperes for 6 hours.

The use of an A.H. meter is strongly recommended.

The makers will be pleased to give any technical advice on any point arising from the charging and servicing of Varley Accumulators and Batteries.

Maintenance and Re-charging Instructions for Fully Charged Batteries.

When not in Use.

To keep the battery in good condition until it is put into service or during any time that it is not in use it should be given a 'freshening' charge once every month. For charge rate and length of 'freshening' charge refer above.

When in use the Motor Cycle dynamo will maintain the battery in a charged condition. Once a month the battery needs topping up with a small quantity of distilled water in order to maintain the plates and separators in a moist condition. Normally a teaspoonful of distilled water per vent is sufficient. *After standing for 15 minutes all surplus liquid should then be removed by siphoning or shaking out if necessary.* Topping up should be carried out after and not before a journey.

The state of charge of a Varley may be checked at any time, by using a moving coil voltmeter.

The following voltages will indicate the approximate state of charge:—

Fully discharged	5.7 volts or under.
Partially discharged	6.15 ,, ,,
Open circuit fully charged	6.3 volts or over.
On charge, fully charged	7.8 ,, ,,

Recharging on the Bench.

If the battery is allowed to get abnormally dry it should be topped up with distilled water before and during charge. After charge all surplus liquid should be removed.

In the event of the battery falling off in capacity after it has been in constant use for some considerable time, it should be topped up with weak acid instead of distilled water for one or two charges.

For charging rate and length of charge see the instruction chart.

THE MAGNETO AND AUTOMATIC TIMING UNIT.
(LUCAS).

Description.

The magneto is of rotating armature pattern, and is fitted with an automatic timing control. The latter employs a driving gear carrying a plate fitted with two pins; a weight is pivoted on each pin and the movement of the weight is controlled by a spring connected between the pivot of the weight and a toggle lever pivoted at approximately the centre of the weight. (Fig. 16).

Holes are provided in each toggle lever, which locate with pegs on the underside of a driving plate secured to the magneto spindle. This plate is also provided with stops that limit the range of control.

When the magneto is stationary, the weights are in the closed position and the magneto retarded for starting. When the engine is started and the speed is increased, centrifugal force acting on the weights overcomes the restraint of the springs and the weights move outwards, causing relative movement between the driving gear and the magneto spindle, so advancing the ignition timing.

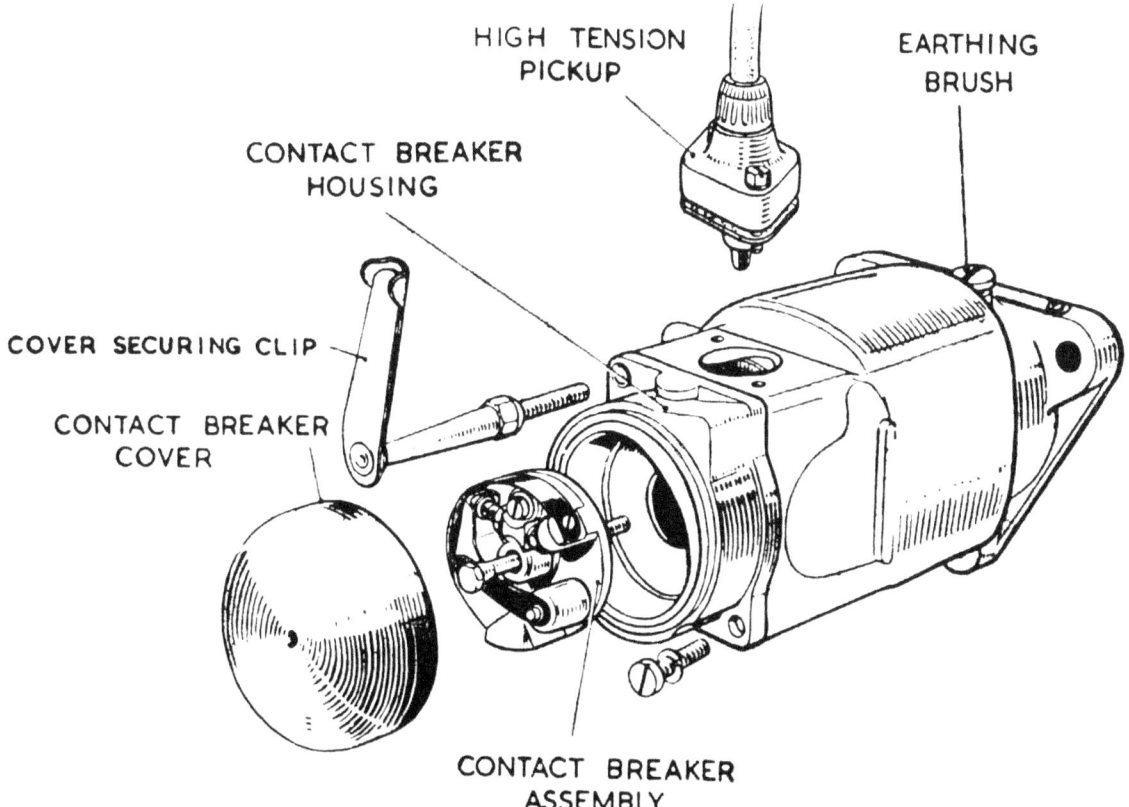

FIG. 40
LUCAS TYPE KIF MAGNETO.
Showing H.T. Brush and Contact Breaker Mechanism, dismantled.

The characteristics of the control are arranged to conform closely with the engine requirements.

Features of the magneto include a ring cam operated contact breaker, and a high energy magnet cast integral with the magneto body.

The armature ball bearings which are packed with grease during assembly, will not need attention until the motor cycle is dismantled for a general overhaul, when it is advisable to have the magneto inspected at a Lucas Service Depot, or by a Lucas Agent.

Maintenance : Lubrication.

Every 3,000 miles take out the hexagon-headed screw from the centre of the contact breaker (Fig. 40) and pull the mechanism off the tapered shaft to which it is fitted. Push aside the rocker arm retaining spring, loosen the two small screws to free the spring—prise the rocker arm off its pivot and smear the bearing lightly with clean engine oil.

The cam is lubricated from a felt pad contained in a pocket in the contact breaker housing. A small hole in the cam is fitted with a wick that enables the oil to reach the surface of the cam. Add a few drops of thin oil (SAE10) to the wick. **Do not allow any oil to get on the contacts.**

When refitting the contact breaker, be sure that the projecting key on the tapered part of the contact breaker base engages with the keyway cut in the magneto spindle, otherwise the timing will be upset.

Tighten the hexagon headed screw carefully. It must not be slack, but no undue force must be used. Check the contact point gap : see below.

Maintenance. Adjustment.

Every 3,000 miles check the contact point gap, after turning the engine until the contacts are fully opened. The correct gap is .012-in. If the setting is correct, the .012-in. gauge will be a sliding fit between the contacts, but if too tight or too loose the gap must be adjusted.

Contact Breaker Adjustment.

To adjust, keep the contact breaker in the position giving the maximum opening of the contacts. The fixed contact plate is secured by a single screw passing through a slotted hole in the plate. To adjust the contact breaker gap, turn the engine until a position of maximum contact separation is reached, slacken the screw and, using a screwdriver, adjust the gap to 0.012"—0.015" (0.305—0.381 mm.) Tighten the screw and check the setting. A flat steel gauge of appropriate thickness should be a sliding fit between the contacts.

Maintenance. Cleaning.

Every 6,000 miles examine the contacts for signs of burning or blackening. Clean them with a fine carborundum stone, or with superfine emery cloth. Wipe away all dust and dirt afterwards with a petrol-moistened cloth.

It is easier to attend to the contacts if the contact breaker is removed.

Remove the high tension pick-up—held to the magneto body by two screws—wipe it clean and polish with a fine dry cloth. The pick up brush must move freely in the holder. If it is dirty, clean with a petrol-moistened cloth. Should the brush be worn to within ⅛-in. of the shoulder it must be renewed.

While the pickup is removed, clean the slip ring track and flanges by holding a soft cloth against the ring with a wedge of wood suitably shaped to conform to the included angle of the slip ring flanges, and turn the engine slowly. Remove the rag, and repeat the cleaning with another piece until all dirt is cleaned from the slip ring.

Testing the Magneto for Causes of Misfiring, or Failure of Ignition.

Disconnect the high tension cable from the sparking plug and hold it so that the terminal end is about ⅛-in. from some metal part of the engine, such as the edge of one of the fins on cylinder or head.

(1) Rotate the engine smartly by means of the kick-start and note the spark that jumps from the terminal to the engine. If the spark is strong and regular the fault lies with the sparking plug which should be removed for inspection and attention.

(2) Examine the high-tension cable. After long service or if oil has been allowed to get on to and remain on it, the insulation may have become perished or cracked. If so fit a new one.

(3) If the magneto has been replaced recently or removed and refitted it may be incorrectly timed. Refer to page 46 for timing instructions.

(4) If the performance of the magneto is still unsatisfactory the contacts may need cleaning and adjustment, or the rocker arm may be sticking and working sluggishly. Badly worn or burned contacts should be replaced by a new Lucas contact set. Should the contact breaker be in good order check the pick-up and high tension pick-up brush. Failing this being responsible there may be an internal fault in the magneto. If this is suspected the advice of a Lucas Service Agent should be sought.

Removal of Magneto.

Remove the timing cover, and engage first gear to hold the crankshaft stationary. Unscrew the hexagon headed centre screw in the automatic timing unit. The screw will loosen and then, almost at once, tighten again. This tightening is caused by the extraction thread coming into operation, and another turn will free the timing unit from the magneto spindle, enabling it to be taken out.

Take off the three nuts and washers holding the triangular flange of the magneto to the crankcase. If the cylinder is in position a waisted $\frac{3}{16}$-in. box spanner will be needed to reach the upper nut nearest the crankcase. The standard spanner LE479 may be modified quite easily to suit.

Refitting the Magneto.

Place the automatic timing unit in position meshing the gear with the intermediate gear, and with the hexagon head screw held against the unit, and the magneto flange gasket in place, push the magneto over the studs, entering the magneto shaft in the centre of the timing unit.

Screw the hexagon headed centre screw on to the magneto shaft holding the head firmly against the mechanism, and allowing the magneto to locate itself under the influence of the screw.

Fit the three flange washers and nuts and tighten fully. See remarks in preceding section *re* spanner.

Re-time the magneto—see page 49, and finally refit the timing cover.

MAGNETO.
B.T.H. Hand Control Type KC.1.

Contact breaker gap .012-in. fully open. The contact breaker can be removed for cleaning by unscrewing the central hexagon headed screw and withdrawing the breaker. The contact lever will lift off from its bearing bush after first raising and moving to one side the check spring which secures it. Take care not to distort the contact lever control spring. When replacing the contact lever, smear the bearing bush very lightly with thin lubricating oil and wipe off any surplus. In no circumstances must oil or grease be allowed to get on to or remain on the contact points themselves.

Removal of the high tension pick-up brush is dealt with in a similar way to that of the standard magneto.

For other directions, see B.T.H. Instruction Book 1377 Edition " E " available from the Magneto makers.

CHAINS.
Maintenance.

The primary chain case will require the addition of oil from time to time and it is usually convenient to squirt a little over the chain from a force-feed oil can whilst the chain is moved forward by the kickstart. The chain cover small inspection cover (Fig. 7) is removed for lubrication purposes.

It is best to remove the rear chain for attention, including thorough washing in paraffin—several changes being used to ensure removal of all dirt.

After draining and drying off, re-lubrication by soaking the chain in molten grease or tallow, preferably containing graphite, is the best method.

The lubricant must be liquid enough to get into the bearings of the chain, but must in no circumstances be boiling. After being satisfied that the lubricant has penetrated the bearings properly, and allowing it to cool off until it begins to solidify, remove the chain and wipe off surplus lubricant.

Adjustment of Primary Chain. (Fig. 15.)

The correct adjustment of the primary chain is $\frac{1}{2}$-in. free up and down movement on one run of the chain midway between the sprockets. In this case the checking is done through the inspection opening in the cover.

The tension must be checked in several different positions so that there is freedom in the tightest place, and the chain must be moved forward by the kickstart and several checks carried out.

Adjustment is by pivoting the gearbox on its bottom-fixing bolt, after freeing off this bolt and the two top ones. To take up excess slack turn the forward one of the two adjusting nuts (Fig. 15) forward on the adjuster and then turn the rear nut in the same direction thus drawing the adjuster, which is attached to the fixing bolt, through the eye-bolt fixed to the engine plate.

When the correct setting is obtained tighten the three fixing bolts and make certain that the adjuster nuts are tight against the eye-bolt.

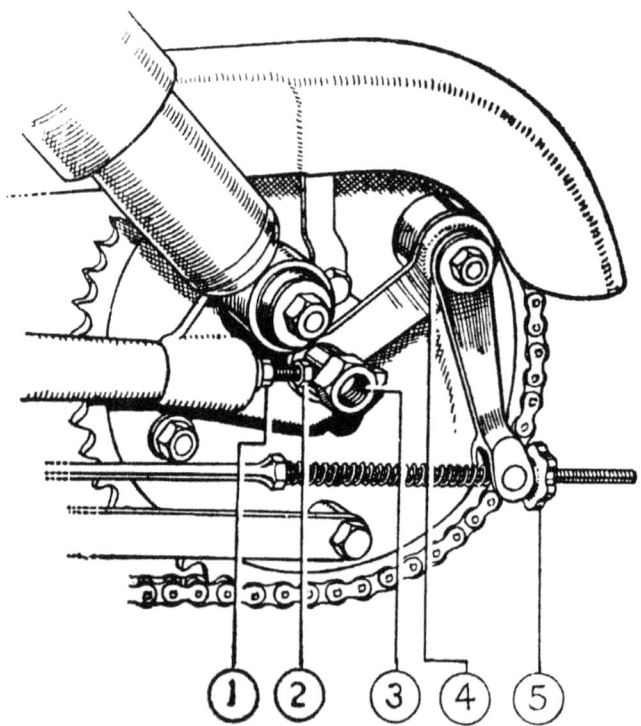

FIG. 41. REAR BRAKE AND REAR CHAIN ADJUSTMENT
    (1) Chain Adjuster Lock Nut
    (2) Chain Adjuster
    (3) Rear Brake Plate Locking Bolt Nut
    (4) Rear Brake Cam Felt Washer
    (5) Rear Brake Adjusting Nut

Adjustment of Rear Chain. (Fig. 41.)

The tension of the rear chain is constantly altering when the springing is working, due to the very slight difference between the actual arc of movement of the rear wheel axis from the theoretical arc, that it would traverse if the rear fork was pivoted on the same axis as the final drive sprocket.

The variation is slight, but the chain is tightest with the fork in mid-position, that is with the struts compressed to $11\frac{1}{2}$-in. centres, and becomes slacker as the fork swings either up on compression or down on extension of the springs. The adjustment must, therefore, be set to give $\frac{1}{2}$-in. free up and down movement on one run of the chain midway between the sprockets with the struts compressed to the distance as shown (Fig. 24).

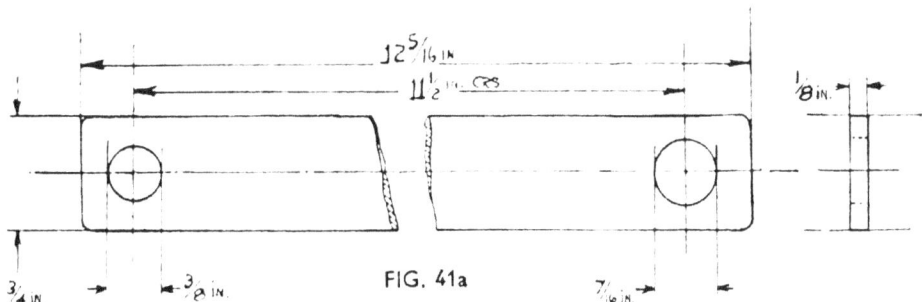

FIG. 41a

To hold the rear springs partly compressed with the swinging fork in the correct position for setting the chain adjustment, a simple strap can be made very easily.

Cut off a piece of mild steel strip $12\frac{5}{16}$-in. long, $\frac{3}{4}$-in. $\times \frac{1}{8}$-in. material is suitable. Mark off the positions for two holes to be drilled at $11\frac{1}{2}$-in. centres. Drill one hole $\frac{3}{8}$-in. dia. and the other $\frac{7}{16}$-in. dia.

To use the strap take off one suspension unit, compress the other to enable the strap to fit over the bottom pivot and to be secured at the top by the pivot bolt being pushed through the slots in the frame lugs and the hole in the strap.

As it would be difficult when working alone to hold the struts compressed without a special tool, the adjustment can be made with the fork at its lowest position, but the setting must allow for the chain becoming tighter when the springing is working. If this alternative method is used support the machine on the centre stand, allowing the tyre to clear the floor—this is important.

Now adjust the chain to give $1\frac{1}{4}$-in. free up and down movement on one run midway between the sprockets.

Whichever method is adopted check the chain in several different positions, turning the rear wheel between checks, to allow the specified freedom in the tightest place.

The alternative method is not so satisfactory as the first one, and if used, the first opportunity should be taken to make a recheck, with the struts held compressed to $11\frac{1}{2}$-in. centres.

FIG. 41b.

INSTRUCTIONS FOR FITTING PANNIERS.

The pannier frames and bags that we can supply as extra equipment are fitted as follows :—

Remove both rear mudguard stay bolts, distance pieces and aluminium inner end caps from the rear suspension brackets on the main frame. The distance pieces are not refitted. Also remove both pillion footrest pivot bolts.

Offer up one pannier frame into place, springing aside the outer aluminium cap to clear the end of the pannier frame tube and push the tube into the end of the suspension bracket. Check the aluminium cap to see if it needs filing to clear the pannier frame tube. Remove the pannier frame and file the aluminium as required. A six inch half-round file is best. Do the same to the other side and also file both inner caps.*

Fit both frames in position bolting them on at the top with the mudguard stay bolts and at the bottom with the pillion footrest pivot bolts. Fit the cross bracing tube to the frames with the bolts provided and finally tighten up all bolts firmly.

A carrier is also available for fitting to the pannier frames.

* The caps on current machines are shaped to clear the pannier tubes.

FIXING TRANSFERS.

The transfers are printed on duplex paper, i.e., one sheet as a guide to place the transfer in position, and the other as a support to the transfer. These two sheets must be separated before transferring. They can be divided by rubbing a corner of the transfer.

Before complete separation is made apply a very thin and even coat of adhesive varnish to the face of the transfer. Keep as closely as possible to the lines of the design so as not to overlap. Allow this varnish to set until it becomes very tacky and then place the transfer in the required position on the article.

Press the transfer down evenly and firmly, and drive out all air bubbles, by rubbing with a soft cloth rolled into a ball, commencing from the centre and working towards the edges. Then with a damp (not wet) sponge or washleather press down again, taking care not to shift the transfer. It is absolutely essential that the transfer should be in **direct contact with the surface in every part.** When this is certain apply water freely by means of a wet sponge, and when the paper support is well soaked, lift it up by one corner and peel or slide it off. Then press the transfer down again to make sure it is fully in contact.

After doing this, sponge with clean water in order to remove the composition remaining on the surface of the transfer. This is an extremely important detail, as unless it is properly done the transfer will crack.

To remove traces of superfluous adhesive varnish around the transfer, use a wet sponge to which has been added a little paraffin. Then quickly wipe it off with a damp washleather, **away from the centre.**

When the transfer is perfectly dry on the article (usually about 24 hours) it can be varnished to add to its lustre. **It must NOT be varnished directly it is transferred.**

TYRE INFLATION RECOMMENDED PRESSURES

The minimum pressures for 3.25 x 19 tyres are 18-lbs. front and 24-lbs. rear, and are sufficient for a solo rider of average weight.

These recommended inflation pressures are based on a rider's weight of 170-lb. If the rider's weight exceeds 170-lb. increase tyre pressure as follows :

Front tyre : Add 1-lb. per sq. in. for every 28-lb. increase in weight above 170-lb.

Rear tyre : Add 1-lb. per sq. in. for every 14-lb. increase in weight above 170-lb.

If additional load is carried in the form of a pillion passenger or luggage the actual load bearing upon each tyre should be determined and the pressure increased in accordance with the Manufacturer's Load and Pressure Schedule.

TYRES.
Maintenance.

Regular checking of tyre pressures is essential for good mileage to be obtained from the tyres. Under inflation, particularly, is very destructive to the casings, and by increasing the rolling resistance tends to increase the fuel consumption.

It should be noted when refitting a cover, or fitting a new one that on some makes the walls are marked to indicate how the cover should fit in relation to the rim. A white spot on the wall must line up with the valve to keep the wheel in balance.

Periodically the tyres should be inspected with the object of removing from the treads any sharp flints or other foreign bodies which may have become embedded in the rubber. Their removal is made easier if the tyre is partly deflated before attempting to prise them out.

Damage to the tyre casing and the tube may often be avoided by the removal of these potential puncture makers.

CLEANING THE MACHINE.
Enamelled and Bare Metal Parts.

Aluminium parts, such as the engine and gearbox, can be cleaned with paraffin and a stiff brush, and afterwards with petrol. These parts are best cleaned before the enamel is tackled.

Accumulated road dirt and mud must never be rubbed or brushed off dry from enamelled parts as the abrasive nature of the dirt will scratch and dull the surface of the enamel.

Always wash off dirt by means of liberal supplies of water, if possible from a hose pipe, but do not employ a high pressure jet.

The water should be set to run at a slow rate so that it does not penetrate where it can do harm, such as into the brakes or items of the electrical equipment and carburetter.

Use a soft cloth or sponge to mop off the dirt when it is properly loosened by the water.

If water is used from a bucket a little household detergent washing powder (such as " Tide ") may be mixed with the water and will help to remove oil or grease.

Dry off with a leather and polish with one of the many polishes now on the market. Chemico " 49 " (Makers : The County Chemical Co., Ltd., 561, Stratford Road, Shirley, Birmingham) will give a high finish which remains waterproof for quite a good time. Proprietary polishes, however, are not a substitute for cleaning and will not give a proper finish unless the surface is properly cleaned first.

Chromium-plated Parts.

All plating is porous, and although Nickel and Chromium are rustless, the surfaces of plated ferrous parts will deteriorate if neglected and left exposed to the weather. Eventually the metal rusts underneath the plating.

Whilst still clean, the plated parts on a new machine should have a rust preventative rubbed in. To avoid leaving them unpleasantly greasy, the excess can be wiped off after application. A proportion of it will have penetrated the pores in the plating.

For this we recommend ' Rust Veto Amber X ' and it can be obtained in small tins from the Service Department or Velocette Dealers.

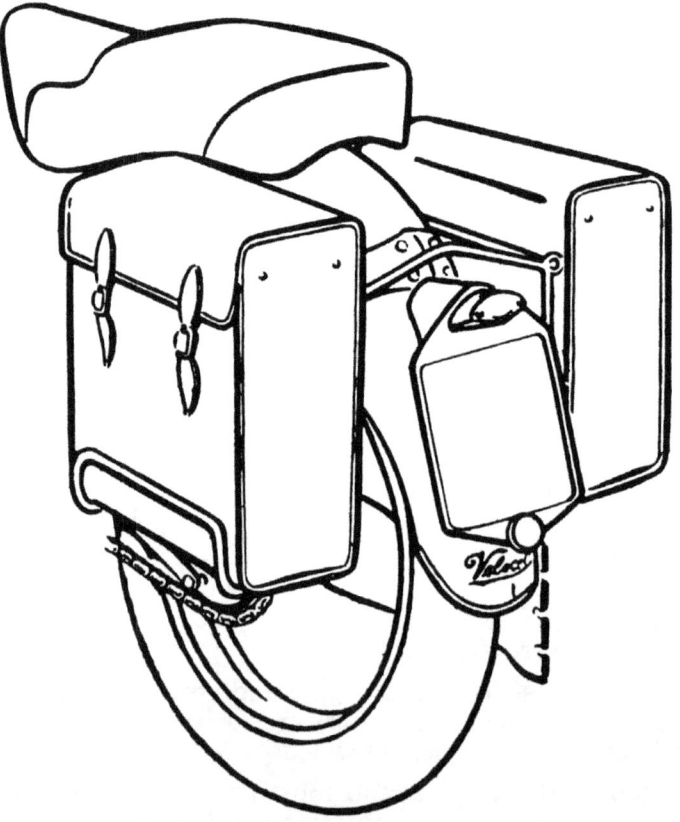

FIG. 42.

To clean the plating wash off dirt and grit with ordinary soap and water. Never rub off dirt that has dried on. Dry off thoroughly after cleaning and polish with a good non-abrasive Chrome Cleaner. We find that 'F.L.P.' supplied by G. H. White, Lowestoft Road, Gorleston, Norfolk, is most satisfactory, and will remove 'pits' and discolouration from neglected plating.

After cleaning rub in 'Rust Veto' and allow it to set before wiping off the excess.

PANNIERS AND LUGGAGE GRID

The panniers that are obtainable from the Service Department have tubular frames specially designed to fit the Velocette frame, and they do not depend for security upon clip fixings. The illustration Fig. 42 shows them fitted.

To fit, remove both rear mudguard stay bolts, distance pieces, and aluminium end caps from the rear suspension brackets. Remove pillion footrests. The distance pieces are discarded.

Offer up one pannier frame into place pushing the tube into the end of the bracket. On early models the aluminium caps will require filing to clear the pannier frame tube and allow it to fit flush against the bracket with the pannier tube in position. Secure the tube by fitting the mudguard stay bolt and attach the bottom of the pannier to the pillion footrest lugs with the footrest pivot bolts, or if pillion footrests are not fitted, by the silencer fixing bolt on the right and an extra similar bolt SL.111/2 on the left. A nut SL.56/27 will also be needed.

Fit the other frame and attach the cross bracing tube with the bolts provided and finally tighten up all bolts securely.

The luggage grid (also obtainable as an extra) fits to the pannier frames and cannot of course be used without them.

SPECIAL INSTRUCTIONS FOR SCRAMBLER MODEL

In most respects the methods of adjustment, and maintenance needed to certain parts of the Scrambler do not differ from those employed for the standard model. The standard instruction literature can be taken to apply therefore unless special reference is made, and other instructions given in this section.

ENGINE STARTING.

Turn on the fuel at both taps, and if the engine is cold, flood the carburetter. (Some machines may need a little flooding even when hot to get a " first-kick " start).

Retard the ignition to approximately half the travel of the lever.

Depress the kick-start crank until compression is felt. Release the crank and allow it to return to the top. Using the exhaust valve lifter control, press down the kick-start crank slowly to the bottom—**not further.**

After bringing the kick-start crank back to the top again the engine is ready to start by using the kick-start without lifting the exhaust valve.

One kick should suffice if the throttle has been set correctly. The throttle valve should not be opened more than approximately $\frac{1}{16}$-in. when starting.

FRONT FORK.

Lubrication.

Each strut carries 120 c.c. of oil. Periodical draining and renewal of the oil is unnecessary. Refilling should be needed only after complete dismantling or in the case of leakage. Oil of S.A.E. 20 viscosity must be used. Grades recommended are :—

Mobiloil Arctic   Duckham's NOL Twenty   B.P. Energol 20.
Wakefield Castolite.   Shell X100 20/20W

Maintenance.

External cleaning only is required.

Dismantling.

Before doing anything else remove the $\frac{3}{8}$-in. dowel screw from the front of the top cross member. This dowel—not fitted to standard models—prevents movement between the cross member and the steering column. All other work is as described in the Service Manual, except that when the adaptors are taken out of the top ends of the fork tubes the damper rods must not be allowed to fall to the bottom of the sliders after the adaptors have been unscrewed from them, as they will bend the ball retaining pins making the ball valves inoperative.

Reassembling.

Assemble as described for standard fork as far as the struts are concerned, but do not fit these until the column and top cross member have been fitted to the steering head, and the dowel screw correctly fitted. Note also that a spring steel washer is fitted between the bearing dust cover and the top cross member. This spring washer takes up play in the head bearings, as adjustment in the normal way is impossible because of the screwed dowel.

After fitting the column and top cross member these must be lined up so that the dowel holes in them register exactly with each other to allow the dowel to be fitted.

If it is difficult to fit, line up the holes again until it will enter readily.

Do not in any circumstances force the dowel or tap out the threads to make it fit.

When the column and cross member are correctly fitted and the dowel is in place and tightened up, fit the struts, pushing them up through the holes in the bottom cross member, setting them so that the vent holes at the top face to the rear.

Pour the correct quantity of oil into each strut and fit the adaptors to the damper rods, tightening the lock nuts. Screw in the adaptors, but tighten them later.

Fit the front wheel, and with the spindle clamp bolt, and bottom cross member clamp bolts just slack, bounce the wheel several times sharply to line up the sliders and to seat the sleeves in the bottom cross member. Finally tighten the three clamp bolts, and tighten adaptors in the fork tubes.

STEERING HEAD BEARINGS.

No adjustment required—see above.

CLUTCH ADJUSTMENT.

Adjust exactly as described on page 29. Note however that the clutch **cable adjuster** is placed accessibly near the carburetter to enable a quick change of cable assembly to be made if necessary. **It is not provided for the adjustment of the clutch**, which is by means of the clutch spring holder as on standard models.

CHAIN ADJUSTMENT.

Primary. See page 88.
Rear.

Adjust when the machine is normally loaded (suspension strut anchor pins at 11½-in. centres) see page 89, with the rider in the saddle. In this position of loading, and with the bottom run of the chain held taut, it must be possible to depress the top run of the chain to within ½-in. of the head of the swinging arm clamp bolt.

TYRES.

Standard Equipment.

Dunlop Sports type : Front, 3 × 21-in.
Rear 4 × 19-in.

Tyre Pressures.

For Scrambles (Moto-Cross) tyre pressures can be adjusted to suit individual requirements and conditions.

GEAR RATIOS.

With standard sprockets (Gearbox, 16 t.; Rear wheel, 60 t.) the overall ratios of the 500 c.c. model are : 1st, 16.65 to 1; 2nd, 11.41 to 1; 3rd, 8.85 to 1. Top, 7.2 to 1. Ratios of 350 c.c. model are : 1st, 17.9 to 1, 2nd, 12.46 to 1, 3rd, 9.5 to 1, Top, 7.85 to 1.

These are the lowest available. Higher ratios are obtainable by using larger gearbox sprockets. These can be supplied in several sizes.

REAR SWINGING FORK.

The left and right hand torque tube assemblies are dowelled to the trunnion shaft, and the dowels have to be removed before the trunnion shaft can be taken out. Otherwise dismantling is as detailed on page 60.

When reassembling the procedure will be as for the standard models except that after having pushed the trunnion shaft through the torque tube end lugs and attached the torque tube clamp tool X2938 it will be necessary to line up the threaded holes in the tops of the lugs with the corresponding holes in the trunnion shaft and fit the dowels before tightening the torque clamp bolts. In no circumstances must the threads be tapped out in order to get the dowels to enter. Perfect alignment of the holes must be achieved.

ENGINE.

Maximum power is developed at 6,200 r.p.m. on 500 c.c. engines and at 7,000 r.p.m. on the 350. Any running at much in excess of these speeds will probably cause the valves to touch one another resulting in loss of compression and power. Over revving must be avoided.

LUBRICATION.

The system is the same as on standard models. Oil of S.A.E. 50 viscosity is recommended. Do not use Castor base oils or additives of any sort in the oil or fuel.

Recommended grades are:—
Shell X100. 50.   Duckham's NOL Fifty   Castrol G.P.
B.P. Energol 50   Mobiloil D

SPARKING PLUGS.

The cylinder head is threaded for 14 mm. ¾-in. (extra long reach) type plug.

Recommended makes and types are :—
Champion NA 8,   or K.L.G. FE 80,   or Lodge HLN, or
Champion NA 10,   or K.L.G. FE 100,   or Lodge 3HLN.

The second row are those having the higher heat resistance (colder).

PISTON.

Gives a compression ratio of 8.75 to one on the 500 c.c. model and 9.3 to one on the 350 for Premium grade (80 Octane) fuel.

Piston Ring Gaps.

The end gaps of new rings (checked just inside the mouth of the cylinder at the bottom of the bore) must not be less than :—
500 c.c. .020-in. on the compression rings, and .020 on the scraper ring.
350 c.c. .015-in.   ,,   ,,   ,,   ,,   .012   ,,   ,,   ,,

IGNITION TIMING.

Contact points to be open to .0015-in. at 38 degrees before top dead centre on full advance. Always check, and if necessary adjust the point gap to .012-in. before checking or resetting the timing. Take all slack out of the timing gears when checking.

TAPPET CLEARANCES.

Tappet clearances cannot be set accurately unless the bottom rocker of the valve that is being adjusted is set midway along the neutral of the cam. See diagram, page 25.

Clearances for checking valve timing—.053-inlet .052 exhaust.
Running clearances—Inlet, .006-in.; Exhaust, .008-in.

It has beenfound that new cylinder base and rocker box gaskets compress during the first forty-eight hours after being fitted, and the shrinkage is enough to reduce the tappet clearances sufficiently to make readjustment necessary.

The shrinkage is due more to the time factor than to heat. In all cases therefore recheck and if necessary reset the clearances after time has been allowed for the gaskets to settle if new ones have been fitted to either or both of these joints.

VALVE TIMING.

Cam No. M17-8. Timing when checked with inlet tappet clearance at .053-in. and exhaust tappet clearance at .052-in.
Inlet opens 45° before T.D.C. Closes 55° after B.D.C.
Exhaust opens 65° before B.D.C. Closes 35° after T.D.C.

Always have the exhaust push rod removed when checking inlet timing, and the Inlet push rod removed when checking the exhaust timing.

The tappet clearances must be reset to the running clearances before starting engine.

CARBURETTERS.

Amal type 10TT9. $1\frac{1}{8}$-in. choke bore.
Main jet, 420. Needle jet, 109. Needle position, 4th from top.
Throttle valve No. 7. Pilot adjusting screw $1\frac{1}{2}$ turns open.
Amal type 10TT9. $1\frac{3}{16}$-in. choke bore.
Main jet, 390. Needle jet, 109. Needle position, 3. Throttle valve No. 7.
Amal type TT9. $1\frac{1}{16}$-in. choke bore.
Main jet, 360. Needle jet, 109. Needle position, 4. Throttle valve No. 7.

These settings are general and alterations may be necessary to suit different course, weather, or barometric conditions to get the best results.

DISMANTLING ENGINE.

See page 38 onwards.

REASSEMBLING ENGINE.

As described page 44 onwards, except that when refitting cylinder head the four cylinder studs must be screwed as far as they will go, without forcing them, into the crankcase studs. Use a screwdriver in the slots in the tops of the studs.

With the head in place and head nuts fitted the studs must not protrude more than $\frac{5}{8}$-in. above the nut faces on any account. On the other hand, the Nylon oil seals in the tops of the special Nylock nuts must engage the top thread of the studs.

THE SPECIAL PREPARATION OF THE VIPER AND VENOM SPORTS AND CLUBMAN MODELS.

As turned out from the factory these give really high performance after careful running in, but it is to assist riders who want to do a little better that these instructions are issued.

There is no short cut to obtaining superlative performance. It is invariably the result of a lot of painstaking work and careful attention to detail with little account of the time taken.

For the standard Viper and Venom models racing carburetters, and racing hand controlled magnetos are obtainable and can be supplied fitted before delivery or bought and fitted later. A Tachometer (Revolution Meter) is also available, but it should be noted that it can not be driven off the automatic timing unit, and a hand controlled magneto and special driving gear are necessary. The full list can be obtained from the Service Department on request.

It is however possible to improve performance or to restore the power of a machine that is "off colour" by careful work alone. This will be dealt with first.

Bear in mind that work expended only upon the engine will be wasted if power is lost in the transmission to the rear wheel. It is essential to start by checking over the entire machine, paying special attention to the elimination of unnecessary frictional losses.

Check both wheels for freedom, including verification that the brake shoes clear the drums when the pedal and lever are released. Test by applying and releasing several times in case there is sluggish working of cam spindles, etc.

Driving chains must be in good condition properly lubricated, correctly adjusted and *in alignment*. To prevent any deflection of the primary chain line under very heavy loading, the Venom, Clubman and Scrambler models have the driving side rear engine plate reinforced. This plate can be supplied for fitting to Vipers or earlier models that did not have it.

The gearbox will absorb some power, but the loss can be reduced by the use of the correct grade of oil and by not over-filling.

Tyre pressures must be as recommended by the makers, otherwise power will be lost, not to mention the detrimental effect on steering, road holding and the tyres themselves.

The clutch adjustment is particularly important. The slightest amount of slip when running on full throttle will reduce the maximum speed several miles per hour. The slip may be so slight as to not be noticeable in normal conditions. Always allow sufficient freedom in the thrust bearing for the full spring pressure to be exerted on the friction linings.

Do this by carrying out the following "Drill" in the strict order given:-

(1) Fully slacken off the mid-way clutch cable adjuster, and slip the cable nipple out of the handlebar lever.

(2) Open throttle and air controls fully. With gears in neutral depress the kick start against compression. If the clutch slips omit operation (3) and carry on with operation (4).

(3) With the clutch adjusting tool engaged in the spring holder, pull the rear wheel backward a little at a time, checking for clutch slip after each movement, being sure to remove the peg from engagement with the spring holder before checking. As soon as any slip can be detected proceed with operation (4). Only the slightest perceptible slip is needed.

(4) Refit the cable nipple to the lever. Re-adjust the mid-way cable adjuster to take up all play in the cable. Take up play and no more. Do not force the adjuster. Tighten lock-nut. Refit the adjuster tool to engage the spring holder and pull the wheel forward a little at a time until the cable pulls freely for $\frac{1}{8}$-in. to $\frac{3}{16}$-in. from the casing without operating the clutch mechanism. (See page 29 for further details.)

Do not overfill the chain cover. For actual racing conditions the primary chain case drain plug can be left out, if a separate continuous drip feed to the inner side of the chain just ahead of the clutch sprocket is provided. The best method is to provide a separate small auxiliary tank leading the oil by means of a double outlet to the ends of the rollers and controlling the flow by a needle valve or a carburetter jet of from 65 to 70 c.c. (6 to 8 drops per minute from each pipe).

Work on the engine must all be directed to the object of reducing frictional losses, starting with the flywheel assembly, check it for freedom in the main bearings when the crank case is hot. Correct the shimming if necessary noting that there is a slight preload (.004-in.) with the crankcase cold. If a new big end or new big end parts such as rollers are fitted, check the bearing with the crank pin fitted into one flywheel so that the cage is accessible. With the connecting rod assembly on the crank pin it should be possible to turn the connecting rod round whilst holding the cage and rollers stationary. There will be slight perceptible up and down play in the bearing when dry.

Check connecting rod alignment as although distortion is unlikely the slightest misalignment will cause heavy drag and loss of power.

Piston Rings must bear evenly on the working faces, and also all round the lands. Factory replacements are correctly gapped. If necessary rings can be lapped into the grooves with metal polish. Be careful to clear it all away before final assembly. Clean out the metal polish with the rings in the grooves to avoid the risk of giving them a permanent 'set' during removal or replacement. For prolonged racing with the Venom model it is advisable to use Clubman oil control ring, part number SL.3/68. On inspection the piston crown after running should present a dry appearance, and no traces of burnt oil. Oil passing the rings or down the valve guides contaminates the fuel mixture and severely reduces power.

There should be ample clearance between the flywheels and crankcase, and there is nothing to be gained by polishing the internal parts. The flywheels of engines previous to Viper No. VR.1144 and Venom No. VM.1114 were larger in diameter with less side clearance from the crankcase. Flywheels from such engines can be modified by us and re-balanced. Otherwise do not modify the flywheels or alter the balance in any way.

The inlet and exhaust ports are ground to a smooth finish after the valve seats have been fitted. Correct shape is more important than a high degree of surface finish. In dealing with the valve seats the inlet can be narrowed and the inner edge blended into the port without reducing the diameter of the base of the seat. This work must be carefully done. Do not reduce the width of the exhaust seating however. Nimonic '80' exhaust valves are now standard equipment on Viper and Venom engines, but can be obtained for earlier models. When grinding in the valves aim at a smooth matt finish on the seats. Do not attempt to polish them.

Valve springs should be replaced if they have had considerable service. If new springs or any new valve parts such as valves, collars, etc., are fitted or if the valve seats have been trued up or new ones fitted, the installed length of the springs must be checked. The measurement between the top face of the valve spring bottom fixing collar and the underside of the loop of the spring where it rests beneath the top collar must not be greater than .562-in., and should lie between .542-in. and .562in. Required correction can be made by fitting shims or washers between the bottom spring mounting and the cylinder head over the valve guides. A reduction in spring poundage either through weakened springs or incorrect installation will allow valve bounce to set in at engine speeds very much lower than the potential maximum, and will of course reduce power output considerably, apart from the risk of bent valves.

Compression plates are fitted in production to get the required ratios for premium grade fuels of approximately 80/100 Octane rating. The standard compression space volumes are :

    Viper ' Clubman '—42 c.c. to 43 c.c.   Viper—47 to 48 c.c.
    Venom ' Clubman '—64 to 65 c.c.   Venom—68 to 69 c.c.

Compression plates are obtainable in 2 thicknesses, .010-in. and .031-in. The differences in volume made are :

    .010-in. Plate on Viper =1.04 c.c.
    .031-in. Plate on Viper =3.24 c.c.
    .010-in. Plate on Venom =1.48 c.c.
    .031-in. Plate on Venom =4.6 c.c.

The compression ratio can be raised slightly if desired, but if the bore is worn the small ridge must be removed from the top edge. For prolonged racing the standard split skirt piston can be replaced with the full skirt Clubman type which having greater clearance will reduce drag. Note, however, that there will be an increase in mechanical noise.

Valve timing is checked with clearances differing from those used for running—See page 26. It is not possible to check timing accurately with both push-rods in place. Remove the inlet push rod whilst checking the exhaust timing and vice-versa. Greater accuracy of reading is obtainable by using .052-in. exhaust clearance, and .053-in. inlet clearance for checking, when the following diagram is obtained :

    Inlet opens 45 degrees B.T.D.C.
    Inlet closes 55 degrees A.B.D.C.
    Exhaust opens 65 degrees B.B.D.C.
    Exhaust closes 35 degrees A.T.D.C.

Do not forget to reset to running clearances after checking. These can be increased to .006-in. inlet and .008-in. exhaust for prolonged speed work.

Check and set contact breaker point gap before timing the ignition. When checking see that all backlash is taken out of the gears. Correct setting is 38 degrees before T.D.C. fully advanced.

Although some owners carry out extensive work on reciprocating parts to reduce weight we are unable to recommend it unless the operator has had a very great deal of experience. It is all too easy to remove material from places where a change in shape or section will make all the difference between the continued reliability of the component and its fracture under load.

As silencers are usually obligatory for Clubman type events a special silencer and complementary exhaust pipe are obtainable for them. The pipe is bent, and silencer fixing modified to give more ground clearance. Apart from this they do not differ from the standard parts. They can not be fitted in conjunction with the standard footrests and pedals.

Do not in any circumstances alter the silencer by modifying the baffle or shroud tubes. The design is carefully worked out to give the best power output consistent with reasonable silencing. From experience we know that any alterations *always* reduce the power and speed—we have never known the contrary to result.

For races where open exhausts can be used the choice lies between a constant diameter pipe or a megaphone. The former is better for standing start events, and sprints, but the megaphone will give a better top end power output at the expense of the output at the lower end.

The length of pipe is important and the measurements quoted in the appended tables of carburetter settings are all as measured down the centre line of the pipe. Changes in the exhaust system make resetting of the carburetter essential.

Whilst settings are quoted these must be considered as a guide only. Final setting must be done to suit the course, the altitude, and the prevailing weather conditions. Always err on the slightly rich side, even at the expense of ultimate maximum speed, to avoid risk of overheating, particularly in lengthy races where heat ' builds up ' and may not become excessive until the major part of the distance has been covered.

Sparking plug recommendations appear on page 72.

PERIODICAL MAINTENANCE

The crankcase and gearbox fairing must be removed to top up the battery, or re-adjust the dynamo belt, clutch, or primary chain. It is fixed by large-headed screws. These can be turned by using a coin in the slots.

A new machine should be checked over after 500 miles use by the dealer from whom it was purchased. See preceding section dealing with the "First 500 mile Free Service Check," (Page 20 Owners Handbook).

Subsequent maintenance work is detailed below and the recommendations are based on an assumed weekly mileage of five hundred. It is, however, impossible to apply rigid limits to maintenance and the intervals quoted are not necessarily the minimum. In some conditions of use more frequent attention may be desirable or even essential.

As a general thing the rule should be a little and often. The effects of neglect are usually expensive in the long run.

The oils and greases suitable for the machine are specified on page 6.

Every 500 miles. Check control cables for freedom and condition, and oil the exposed sections. Oil pivot bolts and nipples. Remove, free off, lubricate and replace any found to be tight or deteriorated.

Check levers and pivots for security of fixings and pivot bolts, etc.
Check level of oil in oil tank and gearbox and top up if needed.
Oil brake cam felt and brake rod trunnions.
Oil stand pivots and folding kickstart footpiece pivot.
Oil chains.
Check tyre pressures.

Every 1,000 miles. (Additional to above). Remove battery vent plugs check filling and top up with distilled water until acid level is $\frac{1}{8}$-in. above separators.

For Batteries. See page 83.

Test battery terminals for security and clean and grease if needed, being sure to remove any corrosion that may have formed.

Check clutch adjustment and re-set if needed.
Grease trunnion shaft bearing nipples—one each side.
Check primary chain and re-adjust if needed.
Top up primary chain case if needed.
Examine rear chain. If dirty, remove, clean, re-lubricate and re-fit.

Every 2,000 miles. (Additonal to above). Drain engine oil tank, re-fit drain plug. **Do not disturb any oil pipes.** Remove, clean and re-fit crankcase suction filter (page 21). Re-fill oil tank.

Check dynamo belt adjustment and re-adjust if needed. To adjust, slacken the dynamo clamp bolt (illustration page 22) and rotate the dynamo in the strap until the belt is reasonably tight. Do not overtighten and do not move the dynamo endwise and put the pulleys out of line. Tighten the clamp bolt when the adjustment has been completed.

Grease speedometer reduction gearbox on **rear** hub.
Grease rear brake pedal bearing. *Oil on Clubman models.*

Every 3,000 miles. Smear contact breaker cam ring inside and out with Mobilgrease No. 2. Apply a spot of clean engine oil to the tip of the pivot post. No oil must be allowed on or near the contacts.

Every 5,000 miles. (Additional to above). Drain gearbox, re-fit drain plug and re-fill.

Check, clean and re-adjust contact breaker.
Remove magneto high tension pick-up (see page 86). Inspect brush, clean brush, brush holder and slip ring. Re-place.
Remove, clean, and re-adjust sparking plug.

Every 10,000 miles. (Additional to above). Remove fabric oil filter element. Fit new element. **Do not attempt to clean the dirty element.**

Drain and re-fill front fork struts. (This is optional).
Check condition of commutator and brushes. Clean commutator if blackened, re-place brushes if necessary. (This work is best entrusted to an Electrical Service Agent).

Remove speedometer flexible drive, pull out inner cable, coat with grease and re-fit.

CARBURETTER SETTINGS.

Venom Model. Normal Settings in Great Britain.

Type of Exhaust System	$1\frac{3}{16}''$ 10TT9 Carburetter		$1\frac{3}{16}''$/389/15 Monobloc	
'A' Exhaust Pipe and silencer (Clubman type pipe 3' 5" down centre line)	Mian Jet Needl Jet Needle Position Throttle Valve	370 109 3 4	Main Jet Needle Jet Needle Position Throttle Valve	330 106 4 $3\frac{1}{2}$
'B' Megaphone Exhaust length of pipe and megaphone 4' 2" down centre line.	Main Jet Needle Jet Needle Position Throttle Valve	390 109 3 5	Main Jet Needle Jet Needle Position Throttle Vale	370 106 4 $3\frac{1}{2}$
'C' Open Exhaust Pipe length 4' 0" to 4' 4" down centre line.	Main Jet Needle Jet Needle Position Throttle Valve	390 109 3 7	Main Jet Needle Jet Needle Position Throttle	370 106 4 $4\frac{1}{2}$

Suggested Alternative Settings (Venom only).

Exhaust System 'A'.	Main Jet 330 to 370 Needle Jet .. 109 Needle Position 3 Throttle Valve 3, 4, or 5	Main Jet 330 to 370 Needle Jet .. 106 Needle Position 4 Throttle Valve $2\frac{1}{2}$, $3\frac{1}{2}$ or $4\frac{1}{2}$
Exhaust System 'B'.	Main Jet 370 to 410 Needle Jet .. 109 Needle Position 3 Throttle Valve 4, 5 or 6	Main Jet 350 to 390 Needle Jet .. 106 Needle Position 4 Throttle Valve $2\frac{1}{2}$, $3\frac{1}{2}$ or $4\frac{1}{2}$
Exhaust System 'C'.	Main Jet 370 to 410 Needle Jet .. 109 Needle Position 3 Throttle Valve 6, 7 or 8	Main Jet 350 to 390 Needle Jet .. 106 Needle Position 4 Throttle Valve $3\frac{1}{2}$, $4\frac{1}{2}$ or $5\frac{1}{2}$

Viper Model. Normal Settings in Great Britain.

	$1\frac{1}{16}''$ TT9 Carburetter.	$1\frac{1}{16}''$ 371/61 Monobloc.
Exhaust System 'A'.	Main Jet .. 340 Needle Jet .. 109 Needle Position 3 Throttle Valve 4	Main Jet .. 270 Needle Jet .. 106 Needle Position 3 Throttle Valve $3\frac{1}{2}$
Exhaust System 'B'.	Main Jet .. 360 Needle Jet .. 109 Needle Position 4 Throttle Valve 7	Main Jet 310 to 330 Needle Jet .. 106 Needle Position 2 Throttle Valve $3\frac{1}{2}$ or $4\frac{1}{2}$
Exhaust System 'C'.	Main Jet .. 360 Needle Jet .. 109 Needle Position 3 Throttle Valve 7	Main Jet 310 to 330 Needle Jet .. 106 Needle Position 3 Throttle Valve $3\frac{1}{2}$ or $4\frac{1}{2}$

Supplement

VENOM THRUXTON 500

This Supplement to the Viper/Venom Service Manual deals exclusively with the Venom Thruxton 500 and the variations affecting the specification, running instructions and maintenance.

The general instructions given for the Venom Clubman in the Viper/Venom Service Manual can be applied as far as practical to the Thruxton 500 with the exceptions given in this supplement.

TECHNICAL DATA

Identification Markings
   The engine number prefix letters are V.M.T.

Tappet Clearances
   Running clearance : Inlet .006". Exhaust .008"

Compression Ratio. 9 to 1.

Carburetter
   AMAL T5GP2.
   Size $1\frac{3}{8}$". Main Jet 280. Needle Jet 109
   Pilot Jet 25. Air Jet ·125. Slide No.3.
   Needle position 5 (counting from top).

Magneto. Lucas Type K.I.F.C. with hand control.

Coil Ignition.   Lucas type

Lighting Equipment.   Lucas Headlamp Type No. M.C.N. 60 fitted with Sealed Beam Unit 700 H. Later models fitted with Headlamp type SS700P.

Gear Ratios.   With 20T Gearbox Sprocket.
   First 10.1 :   Second 6.97 :   Third 5.3 :   Top 4.4 to one.
   T.T. Close Ratios : First 8.4 : Second 6.3 : Third 4.83 : Top 4.4 to one.

Oil capacity. Front Fork. Each strut carries 120cc of oil.

Unladen Weight. 375-lbs. 170 kilograms.

Wheels and Tyres.   Front Tyre 19" × 3.00" Ribbed.
   Rear Tyre 19" × 3.25" or 3.50" Studded.

THE FRONT HUB

FIG. 44. FRONT HUB AND BRAKE ASSEMBLY
1. Brake Torque Bolt
2. Brake Cable Adjuster
3. Brake Adjuster Lock Nut
4. Front Fork Oil Drain Bolt
5. Fork Damper Tube Adaptor Nut
6. Air Scoop
7. Shoe Setting Control Rod
8. Greasers for Top and Bottom Operating Cams (where fitted)

Note.—The brake cable adjuster and lock nut is positioned on the brake plate and is concealed behind the triangular steel plate attached to the mudguard stay.

ADJUSTMENT OF BRAKES

Front Brake Adjustment (see illustration). A twin leading shoe front brake is fitted on the Thruxton with a 7.5" drum diameter and the hub incorporating an air scoop is drilled for cooling. Adjustment is carried out by the cable adjuster as detailed in the Venom Manual.

The Front Hub is supported on a hollow spindle by two non-adjustable journal ball bearings and the process of dismantling and re-assembling the bearings detailed in the Venom Manual is equally applicable. The instructions on re-fitting the brake plate and shoe assembly also apply with the exception that the brake plate has two operating cams.

Re-Setting the Brake Shoes

The brake shoes are set when the brake is assembled at the factory, but renewal of the brake shoes will necessitate re-setting.

To do this, remove the split pin and withdraw the clevis pin from the yoke end at the top of the adjuster rod. Operate the front brake handlebar lever which will bring one brake shoe in firm contact with the drum and retain the pressure on the lever by securing it to the handlebars by the use of a strong rubber band or other means. Slacken off the two lock nuts on the adjuster rod and apply firm pressure to the top cam operating lever which will bring the second brake shoe in contact with the drum. Hold the cam lever in this position and turn the adjuster rod to a position where the clevis pin can be inserted through the cam lever and yoke end of the adjuster rod. Then re-fit the clevis split pin, tighten up the lock nuts on the adjuster rod and release the pressure on the handlebar lever. Finally, check the brake control cable and carry out any adjustment which may be necessary.

THE FRONT FORKS

The telescopic front forks are Scrambler type with two-way damping and fitted with rubber gaiters. The instructions given in the Venom Manual for the Scrambler fork will apply to the Thruxton but it should be noted the ⅜" dowel screw is no longer fitted and that adjustable clip-on handlebars are positioned on top fork tubes.

Speedometer and Rev. Counter

These instruments are mounted independently on brackets attached to the top fork yoke. The speedometer which is illuminated when any of the lights are switched on is on the left-hand side of the machine and the Rev. Counter, which is not illuminated, is on the right-hand side.

Engine Lubrication System

The lubrication system has been improved and made more efficient by the incorporation of a crankcase breather.

DECARBONISING THE ENGINE

Removal of Fuel Tank

It will be noted the rear end of the fuel tank on the Thruxton is now mounted on a thick rubber pad positioned on the top frame tube, eliminating the use of a rear fixing strap.

Rocker Box Assembly

It will be noted the cups at the top end of the push rods are now fixed, being pressed into the rods.

Re-adjustment of Tappet Clearances

The running clearances should be Inlet .006". Exhaust .008". The adjustment procedure is identical to that described in the Venom Service Manual under the heading "Re-adjustment of Tappet Clearances" except that the clearance has in this instance to be checked between the cam and the bottom rocker. It is of course necessary to remove the timing case cover to carry out the check. It is also important to see if the bottom rockers are removed for any purpose they are replaced correctly. They are not inter-changeable, the inlet rocker being marked "In" and the exhaust rocker marked "Ex".

To avoid discrepancies in the tappet settings when checking and re-adjusting (this also applies to the checking of the valve timing) we suggest that the engine is rotated until the bearing face of the exhaust cam follower is located on the base of the exhaust cam (see page 27, para 3, 4). Then carefully remove the timing gear steady plate by removing the four securing bolts and camwheel spindle. (The camwheel oil jet can be left in the plate). DO NOT ROTATE ENGINE UNLESS STEADY PLATE IS REFITTED. UNLESS INTENDING TO REMOVE THE TIMING GEARS, CARE SHOULD BE TAKEN NOT TO DISTURB THESE.

Check exhaust clearance between base of cam and follower. This should read .008-in. for the running clearance. Adjust if necessary. (For checking valve timing see page 100.) Replace timing gear steady plate, etc., and follow similar procedure for checking inlet clearance which should be .006-in. These readings, of course, are taken between the inlet cam and cam follower.

MAXIMUM SPEEDS

All Thruxton models are equipped with a Revolution Counter and IT IS MOST IMPORTANT THAT AT NO TIME MUST A MAXIMUM OF 6,200 R.P.M. BE EXCEEDED. Obviously greater reliability and a much longer engine life will be obtained if the r.p.m. is kept down as much as conveniently possible below the maximum stated.

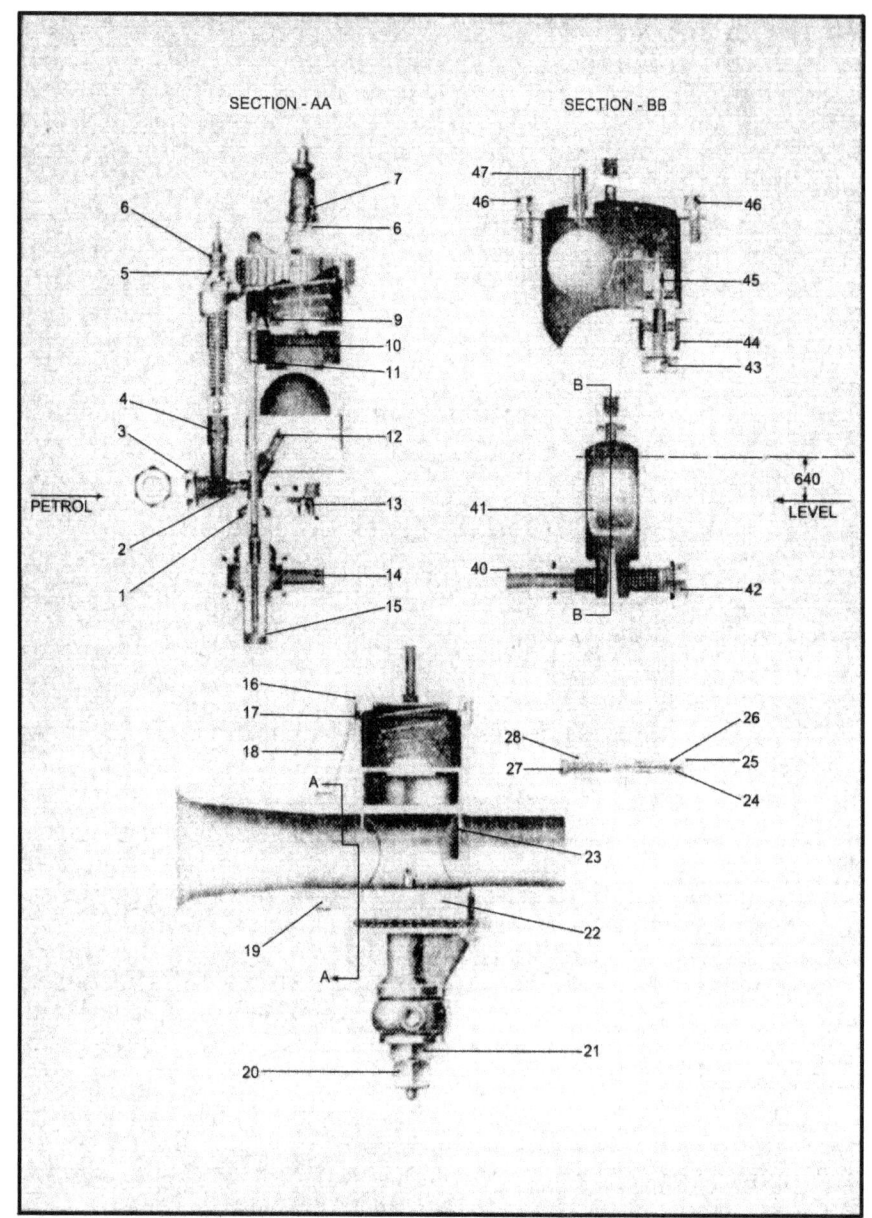

The AMAL Racing Type T5GP2 Carburetter with remotely mounted Float Chamber

FIG. 43

KEY TO SECTIONED ILLUSTRATION
Mixing Chamber

1. Needle Jet
2. Air Jet
3. Air Jet Plug
4. Primary Air Slot
5. Air Valve Cable Adjuster Locknut
6. Air Valve Cable Adjuster
7. Throttle Cable Adjuster
8. Throttle Cable Adjuster Locknut
9. Needle Clip
10. Needle Clip Retaining Screw
11. Metering Needle
12. Spray Tube
13. Choke Adaptor Retaining Screws
14. Petrol Inlet Banjo
15. Main Jet
16. Mixing Chamber Cap
17. Throttle Valve Return Spring
18. Mixing Chamber Cap Lock Spring
19. Air Tube Lock Ring
20. Jet Plug
21. Jet Holder
22. Choke Adaptor
23. Throttle Valve
24. Pilot Jet
25. Pilot Jet Cover Nut
26. Pilot Jet Cover Nut Washer
27. Pilot Air Adjusting Screw
28. Pilot Air Adjuster Locknut

FLOAT CHAMBER

40. Petrol Outlet Connection
41. Float and Hinge
42. Plug Screw
43. Petrol Inlet Banjo Bolt
44. Petrol Inlet Banjo
45. Float Needle
46. Float Chamber Cover Screws
47. Tickler

DRIVING ON MOTORWAYS

It will be appreciated driving on the long and fast stretches of the new motorways demands a different driving technique. The natural tendency is to travel at a constant abnormally high speed and if this is done it is advisable to momentarily close the throttle at periods during the run.

THE CARBURETTER

This is an Amal Racing-type 5GP2 with remotely mounted float chamber and detailed maintenance instructions can be obtained upon application to the carburetter manufacturers : Messrs. Amal Ltd., Holford Drive, Witton, Birmingham 6.

In the GP2 carburetter the pilot adjuster screw controls the volume of air and the petrol is metered through a detachable pilot jet giving much more flexible tuning over the pilot range and at the same time this arrangement has been so designed that the carburetter can be used at an increased downdraught angle.

It is inadvisable to tamper with the carburetter but occasional adjustment of the control cables and cleaning out may be required.

For your guidance we are including in this supplement an illustrated and numbered sectional view of the carburetter and separate float chamber and give below some general details of settings and operation which we hope you will find helpful.

Amal T5GP2	$1\frac{3}{8}$" choke bore
Main Jet	280
Needle Jet	·109
Pilot Jet	25
Needle Position No. (*counting from the top*)	5
Air Jet	·125
Slide No.	3

Design Features

The GP2 carburetter has been designed with a view to obtaining the maximum possible power from the engine, at the same time maintaining a progressive and consistent acceleration throughout the throttle range.

Float Chamber

Remotely mounted with bottom feed and incorporating a lever-type operated float. It is mounted on rubber and is adjustable for position.

Petrol Level

After removing the toolbox, the petrol level in the float chamber can be checked by the use of a small length of clear plastic tubing. Turn off both petrol taps and remove the rubber pipe from the float chamber to the carburetter. Re-place this on the float chamber with an 8" length of $\frac{3}{8}$" bore clear plastic piping. Hold the piping upright on the nearside of the carburetter. Turn on one or both of the petrol taps when the petrol will flow into the float chamber and up the plastic piping. The level of the petrol in the piping should correspond with the lowest point of the circular scribe mark on the air jet plug (3) and to achieve this the float chamber can be raised or lowered by means of the adjusters provided. When the correct level is obtained turn off the petrol taps, remove the plastic piping and re-fit the rubber pipe, being careful not to alter the position of the float chamber in the process.

Locking Devices

A spring blade locking device (18) held in place by the air tube lock ring (19) engages with serrations on the mixing chamber cap (16), which positively prevents the unscrewing of same due to vibration. The jet plug (20), banjo bolt (43), plug screw (42), jet block holding screws (13), float chamber cover screws (46) and the float/hinge spindle head (not illustrated) are drilled to enable them to be lockwired up.

Tuning, General

The tuning sequence of the GP2 carburetter follows the well-established Amal principles, in as much as there is a main jet (15) controlling the fuel supply at full throttle, a needle jet (1), the emission from which is controlled by the position of a taper needle (11) in the same and at the lower throttle openings by the cut-away of the throttle valve (23), a detachable pilot jet (24) and a pilot air adjusting screw (27) controlling the mixture strength for idling; an air jet (2) controls the amount of air which primarily atomises the fuel as it comes out of the needle jet (1) before going into the spray tube (12) and thence to the heart of the choke.

The Needle

The needle control covers a range of the throttle opening from about one-third throttle up to seven-eights throttle opening. The needle grooves in the GP needle will be found to number five instead of seven as previously on the TT instruments, due to the fact that the needle control of the GP carburetter is rather more sensitive than on other types. Two types of needle (11) are available, what we call a standard taper needle and a much weaker taper needle. The standard taper is known as Type 5GP and the weaker taper needle is designated Type 5GP6.

MAIN JET

Always bear in mind, however, that whatever the type of needle used, or the position in which it is fitted, there will be no affectation of the main jet (15).

The main jet (15) can be very readily removed by taking off the hexagon cap (20) at the base of the Carburetter Mixing Chamber. The jet size is marked on the side of these jets and represents the flow in c.c. per minute on the Amal Calibrating Machines at the Works. These jets are made in 10 c.c. increments, that is, for instance—250, 260, 270, etc.

The **Throttle Valve** (23) which surrounds the choke adaptor (22) in the carburetter, controls with its leading edge the velocity of air entering the throttle bore and consequently the depression on the spray tube at the lower throttle opening with a diminishing effect up to a point where the cut-away disappears from the cross bore.

The trailing edge of the throttle valve, of course, controls the volume of mixture passing to the engine.

The **Needle Jet** (1), which is of stainless steel to prevent wear, has been found for the best all round usage on petrol or petrol benzole to require a diameter of .109". For alchohol fuel, of course, larger needle jets are necessary.

Pilot System

This gives a supply of metered fuel through a detachable pilot jet (24) which mixes with air regulated by the pilot air adjusting screw (27) and passes into the mixing chamber through a small hole on the engine side of the throttle slide.

Compensation on this GP2 carburetter is obtained through the medium of the primary air which passes through a slot (4) in the mixing chamber and then, via the air jet (2) previously mentioned, atomises the liquid fuel passing from the needle jet (1).

As the engine supply increases or decreases at a given throttle opening with a varying load, so compensation will take place.

LIGHTING EQUIPMENT—LUCAS

A Lucas lighting set is fitted to the Thruxton and a wiring diagram is included in this supplement. Other constructional details:

Headlamp and Parking Light

The headlamp incorporates the Lucas Light Unit, which consists of a combined reflector and front lens assembly. A "prefocus" bulb is used, ensuring that when the bulb is fitted, the filament is correctly positioned in relation to the reflector and no focussing is necessary. The parking light bulb holder is a push fit in the rear of the Light Unit reflector. The headlamp main bulb is 6-volt 30×24 watt, double filament bifocal and the parking light bulb 6-volt, 3-watt single filament MSS cap.

Setting

Set the headlamp so that when the motor cycle carries its normal load the main or driving beam is projected straight ahead and parallel with the road surface.

Removing Headlamp Front

Slacken the rim securing screw located on top of the headlamp shell.

It will then be possible to detach the front rim complete with Light Unit assembly. To re-place, locate the Light Unit assembly in the lamp body, press the front on at the lower edge first, then at the top and secure in position by tightening the securing screw.

LUCAS LIGHTING SET with Miller Dynamo

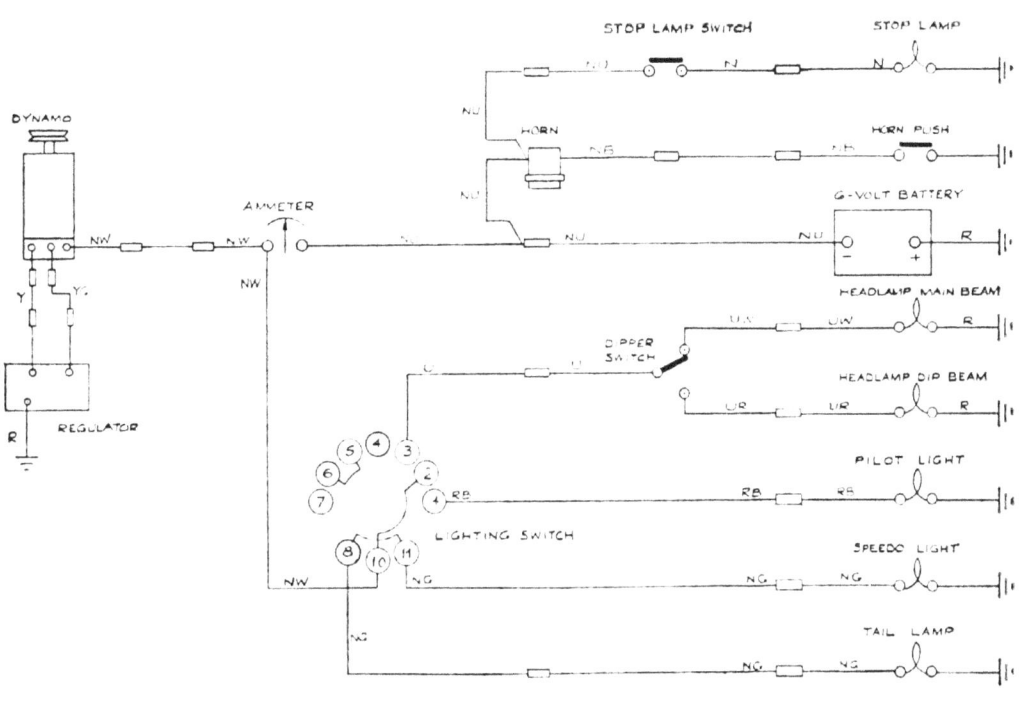

Wiring Diagram for Lamps and Dynamo with A.V. regulator

FIG. 45

Colour Code

B	Black	P	Purple	D	Dark
U	Blue	R	Red	L	Light
N	Brown	S	Slate	M	Medium
G	Green	W	White		
K	Pink	Y	Yellow		

109

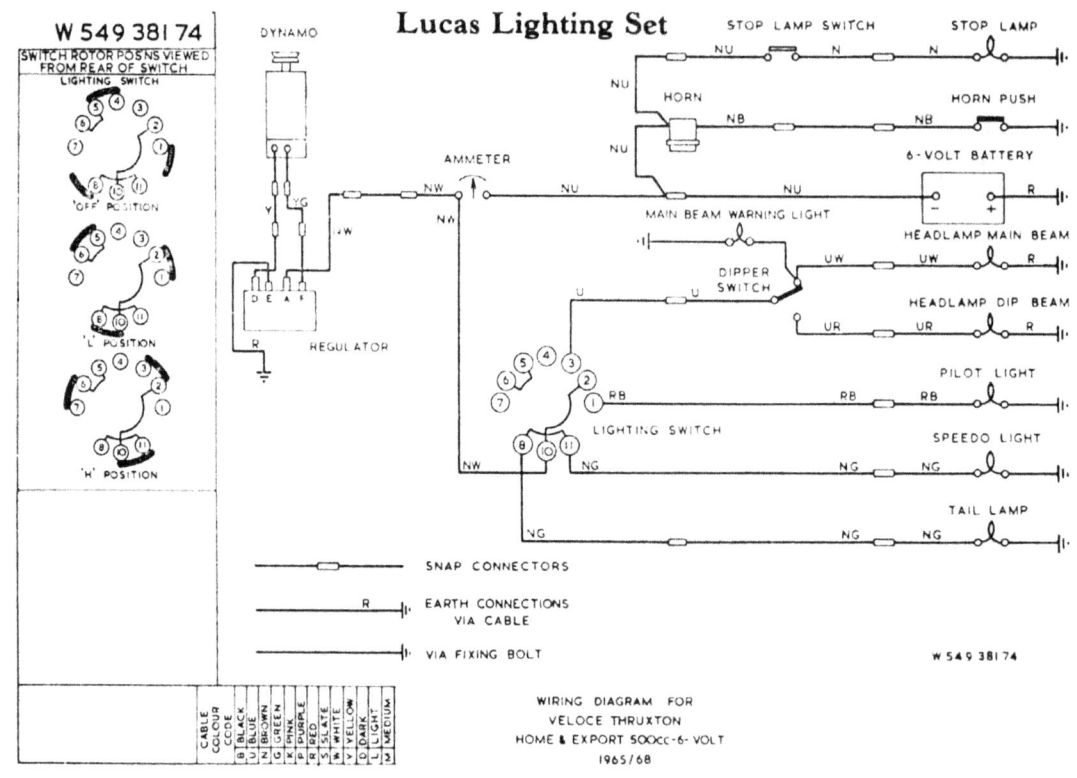

Lucas Lighting Set

WIRING DIAGRAM FOR VELOCE THRUXTON HOME & EXPORT 500cc-6-VOLT 1965/68

Wiring Diagram for Machines fitted with Coil Ignition

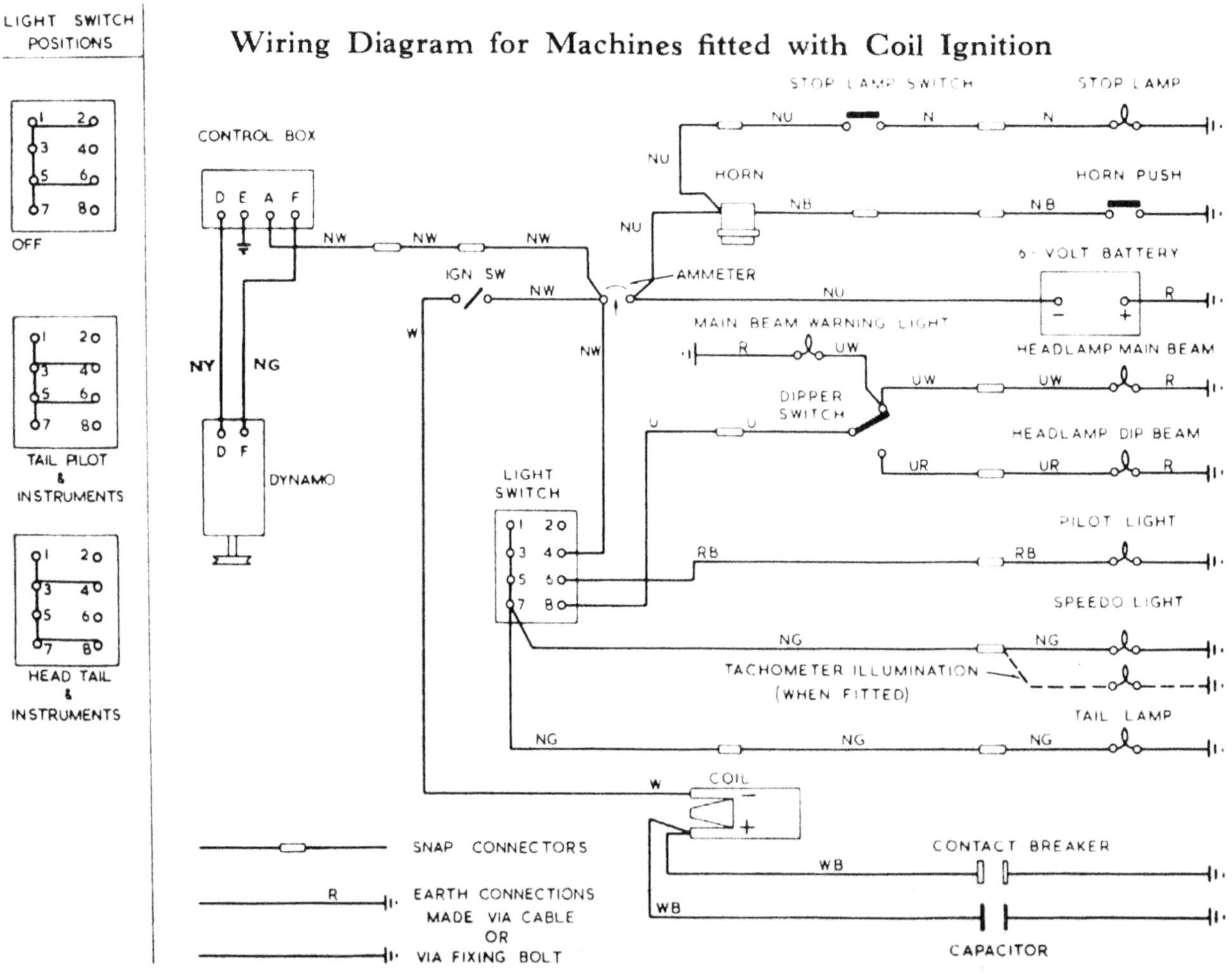

Protection to wiring circuits can be made by adding fuse to earth lead. (Lucas No. 54938986).

Re-placement of Bulbs

When re-placement of a bulb is necessary, it is important not only that the same size bulb is fitted, but also that it has a high efficiency and will focus in the reflector. Cheap inferior re-placement bulbs often have the filament of such a shape that corrrect focussing is not possible for example, the filament may be to one side of the axis of the bulb, resulting in loss of range and light efficiency.

Lucas Bulbs are specially tested to check that the filament is in the correct position to give the best results. To assist in identification, Lucas bulbs are marked on the metal cap with a number. When fitting a re-placement, see that it has the same number as the original bulb.

To gain access to the headlamp bulb remove the front rim and Light Unit assembly as previously described. Push on the adaptor and twist it in an anti-clockwise direction to take it off. The bulb can now be removed from the rear of the reflector. Place the correct re-placement bulb in the holder, engage the projections on the inside of the adapter, press on and secure by twisting to the right.

To gain access to the parking light bulb, remove the front rim and Light Unit assembly and withdraw the bulb holder from the reflector in which it is a push-fit.

Rear Lamp

The rear lamp and stoplight are combined in one body and the bulb bulb used is a 6-volt 18×6 watt off-set pin stoplight or 6-volt 6-watt S.C.C. for rear light only when stoplight is not fitted.

Miller Dynamo

The instructions given in the Venom Service Manual for the dynamo and automatic voltage regulator apply equally to the Thruxton equipped with a Miller dynamo.

MAGNETO — LUCAS

A Lucas Competition Magneto Type KIFC with manual control is fitted on the Thruxton and the general maintenance instructions given in the Venom Manual can be applied.

To clarify the previous instructions we give the following additional information.

Lubrication

The cam ring is supplied with lubricant from a felt strip contained in a recess in the contact breaker housing. Oil reaches the inner surface of the cam ring by way of a small circular wick passing through the thickness of the cam ring.

Remove the contact breaker cover. Take out the central hexagon-headed securing screw and carefully withdraw the contact breaker from the tapered magneto spindle.

Withdraw the cam ring. It is a sliding fit in the contact breaker housing.

Note.—Withdrawal and re-fitting of the cam ring will be made easier if the handlebar control lever is moved to the half-retard position, thus taking the cam ring from its stop peg.

Clean the cam and lightly smear the inside and outside surfaces with light grease.

Add a few drops of thin machine oil to the felt strip and to the circular wick.

Remove the contact breaker lever and smear the pivot with light grease, applying sufficient grease to fill the annular groove. The method of removing the contact breaker will be apparent from Fig. 8. Since the push-on retaining ring may need renewal after removal, an alternative form of lubrication for this pivot post is to apply a spot of clean engine oil to the tip of the post.

While this will obviate the necessity of removing the lever great care must be taken to prevent oil getting on or near the contacts.

Re-fit the contact breaker lever.

Re-fit the cam ring, taking care that the stop peg in the contact breaker housing and the spring loaded plunger engage with their respective slots.

If an earthing brush is fitted at the back of the contact breaker base plate, see that it is clean and can move freely in its holder before re-fitting the contact breaker assembly in the cam ring.

Re-fit the contact breaker assembly, ensuring that the projecting key on the tapered portion of the contact breaker base plate engages correctly with the spindle keyway

Every 3,000 miles

Checking Contact Breaker Gap

To check the contact breaker gap, remove the contact breaker cover and turn the engine over slowly until the contacts are fully open. A flat steel guide of thickness 0.012" to 0.015" (0.3-0.38 mm.) should be a sliding fit between the contacts.

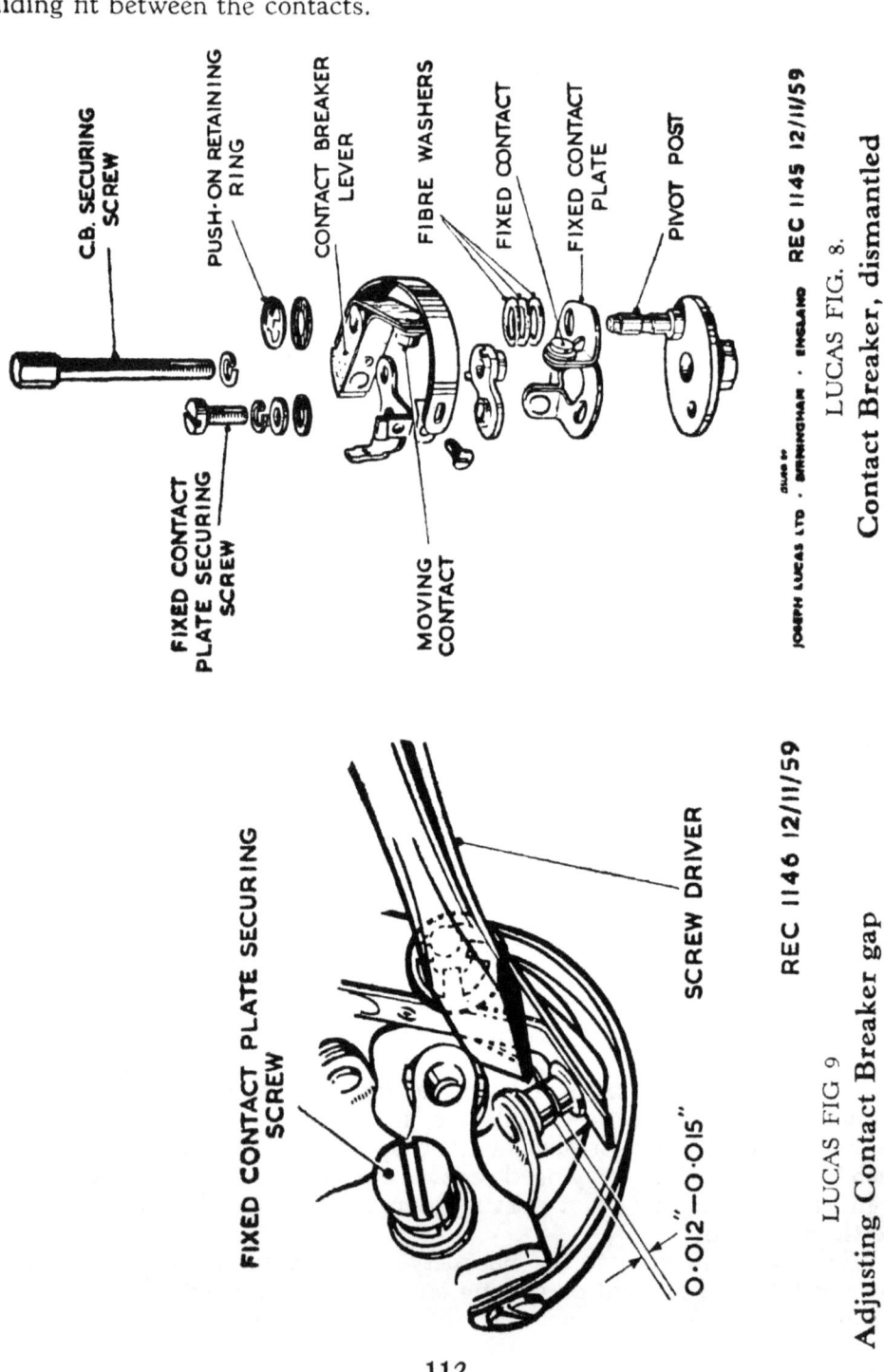

The contact breaker unit is shown in Figs. 8 and 9. It has a fixed contact plate secured by a single screw passing through a slotted hole in the base. To adjust the gap, slacken this screw and, using a screw-driver in the manner shown in Fig. 9, move the fixed contact plate until the correct gap is obtained. Tighten the screw and re-check the gap.

Every 6,000 miles
Cleaning

Remove the contact breaker cover and high tension pick-up mouldings. Thoroughly clean the inside and outside of the magneto using a clean dry fluffless cloth, if necessary moistening it with petrol to remove any grease from the high tension pick-up mouldings and contact breaker contacts. Ensure that the pick-up brush moves freely in its holder. Renew the brush if it is worn to $\frac{1}{8}"$ above the shoulder. Clean the slip ring track and flanges by pressing the cloth on them while the engine is cranked by hand.

Ensure that the gasket between the pick-up mouldings and the magneto body is in good condition before re-assenbliimg.

Examine the contacts when the contact breaker is removed for lubrication. If the contacts are pitted or piled, they should be trimmed with a carborundum stone, silicon carbide paper, or very fine emery cloth.

Contacts do not retain a polished appearance when in use and, if operating correctly, will have a dull grey appearance.

Every Two Years

About every two years, or when the engine is given general overhaul, the magneto should be examined at a Lucas Service Depot.

Renewing High Tension Cables

When the high tension cable shows signs of perishing or cracking it must be renewed.

To re-place the high tension cable on machines fitted with 7 mm. p.v.c. or neoprene covered cable, proceed as follows :—

Remove the metal washer and moulded terminal nut from the defective cable. Thread the new cable through the moulded terminal nut and cut back the insulation for about $\frac{1}{4}"$.

Pass the exposed strands through the metal washer and bend them back radially.

Screw the moulded terminal into the pick-up moulding.

LOCATION AND REMEDY OF FAULTS
Engine will not start or difficult to start

(a) See that the controls are correctly set for starting, petrol turned on, etc.

(b) Turn off the petrol tap. Remove the sparking plug and place on the cylinder head. If a spark occurs regularly at the plug points when the engine is slowly hand-cranked, the magneto is in order. Look for engine defects and check ignition timing.

(c) If a spark does not occur in (b), disconnect the high tension cable from the plug and hold the cable end about $\frac{1}{8}"$ from a metal part of the engine. If a spark occurs regularly when the engine is cranked, the plug is faulty. If there is no spark, disconnect the high tension cable at the magneto, re-place with a new length of cable and test again as before.

Coil Ignition

Check for a fault in the low tension wiring, i.e' from battery to switch, coil and contact breaker. If the wiring proves to be in order, examine the contact breaker; if necessary, clean the contacts and adjust the gap setting. Check capacitor by substitution. If, after carrying out these checks, the ignition system is still inoperative, have it examined by a Lucas Service Depot or Agent.

(d) Should there still be no spark, possible causes of trouble are : contact breaker gap out of adjustment or contacts dirty; contact breaker rocker arm sticking; or pick-up brush worn or broken, or slip ring track dirty. Remedy as described.

Engine Mis-fires

(a) Check as in *para.* (b) and (c) above, to eliminate engine defects, faulty high tension cables and sparking plug.

(b) Check magneto as in *para.* (d) above.

(c) If the fault persists, have the magneto examined by a Lucas Service Depot or Agent.

Coil Ignition

(a) Examine the contact breaker; if necessary, clean the contacts and adjust the gap.

(b) Check capacitor by substitution.

(c) Remove the sparking plug, rest it on the cylinder head and observe if a spark occurs at the plug points when the engine is turned. Irregular sparking may be due to dirty plugs, which may be cleaned and adjusted, or to defective high tension cables. Any cable on which the insulation shows signs of deterioration or cracking should be renewed.

(d) If sparking is regular at the plug when tested as described in (b) the trouble is probably due to engine defects and the carburetter, petrol supply, etc., must be examined.

Charging Circuit

Battery in Low State of Charge

(a) This state will be shown by poor or no light from the lamps when the engine is stationary, with a varying light intensity when the motor cycle is running.

(b) Have the condition of the battery checked and re-charge it if necessary,

(c) Check wiring from battery to switch, rectifier and dynamo, tightening any loose connections or re-placing broken cables.

(d) If the cause of the trouble is still not apparent, have the equipment examined by a Lucas Service Depot or Agent.

Excess Circuit Voltage

(a) This will be indicated by burnt-out or blackened bulbs and possibly poor engine performance due to burned ignition contacts.

(b) Examine all wiring for loose or broken connections.

(c) Check the earthing of battery and rectifier.

(d) Examine the battery, checking electrolyte level and removing any traces of corrosion.

(e) If the ignition is affected, clean the contact breaker contacts, or, if necessary, renew them.

(f) If the fault persists, have the equipment examined by a Lucas Service Depot or Agent.
The Battery Positive (+*ve*) Terminal is Earthed to the Machine. **Under no circumstances must the Negative (—*ve*) Terminal be earthed.**

Lighting Circuits

Failure of lights (machine stationary)

(a) If only one bulb fails to light, re-place with new bulb.

(b) If all lamps fail to light have the condition of the battery checked, re-charging it if necessary either by a long period of daytime running or by connecting it to a suitable battery charger.

(c) Examine the wiring for a broken or loose connection and remedy.

Lamps light, when switched on, but gradually fade
Have the condition of the battery checked, re-charging if necessary.

Brilliance varies with speed of motor cycle
Have the condition of the battery checked, re-charging if necessary.

Lights flicker
Examine the wiring for loose connections, or short circuits caused by faulty cable insulation. Have the condition of the battery checked.

Headlamp illumination insufficient
(a) If the bulb is discoloured or filaments have sagged as a result of long service a new bulb of the same type should be fitted.

(b) Check the setting of the lamp.

THE BATTERY
On a number of Thruxton models, a Lucas Battery—Model PUZ7E/11 is fitted.

Topping-up
During charging, water is lost by gassing and evaporation and each week the electrolyte level of each battery cell should be checked and, if necessary, topped-up.

Remove the battery lid, unscrew the filler plugs and, if necessary, add distilled water carefully to each cell to bring the elctrolyte just level with the line on the container denoting maximum filling level, or, if there is no such line, level with the separator guide.

Maintenance
Occasionally wipe away all dirt and moisture from the top of the battery and ensure that the terminals are clean and tight.

Never leave the battery in a discharged condition. If the motor cycle is to be out of use for a considerable period have the battery fully charged and each fortnight give it a short freshening charge to prevent any tendency for the plates to become permanently sulphated.

Battery Earth
The equipment is designed for use with positive ($+ve$) earth systems. If battery connections are reversed, the equipment will be damaged.

COIL IGNITION SYSTEM
The coil ignition system comprises an MA6 ignition coil and a 6CA contact breaker fitted in the timing cover and driven by the exhaust camshaft. The ignition coil is mounted underneath the petrol tank. Apart from cleaning the coil in between the terminals and checking the low tension and high tension connections, the coil will not require any other attention. The capacitor is no longer part of the contact breaker but is housed separately on the frame of the machine

The best method of approach to a faulty ignition system, is to first check the low tension circuit for continuity as shown below.

Checking Low Tension Circuit
(a) Connect DC voltmeter (black lead) to CB terminal of the contact breaker and (red) lead to earth.

(b) Ensure contact points are open.

(c) Switch on ignition, voltmeter should indicate battery volts.

(d) Ignition still on, close contact points, voltmeter reading should fall to zero.

Conclusions:

No reading for test (c) may indicate faulty ignition switch, open circuit primary winding, broken lead, short circuit to earth on CB lead or faulty capacitor. Low reading indicates high resistance in the primary circuit or across ignition switch contacts.

A reading for test (d) indicates volt drop across the contact points (dirty points.)

Failure to locate a fault in the low tension circuit indicates that the capacitor high tension circuit or sparking plug is faulty and the procedure for testing the high tension must be followed. Before commencing any of the following tests, however, the contact breaker and sparking plug must be cleaned and adjusted to eliminate this possible source of fault.

Ignition Coils

The ignition coil consists of a primary and secondary windings wound concentrically about a laminated soft iron core, the secondary winding being next to the core. The primary winding usually consists of some 300 turns of enamel covered wire and the secondary some 17,000 turns of much finer wire—also enamel covered. Each layer is paper insulated from the next in both primary and secondary windings.

To test the ignition coil on the machine, first ensure that the low tension circuit is in order as described above then disconnect the high tension lead from the sparking plug. Turn the ignition switch to the 'on' position and crank the engine until the contacts are closed. Flick the contact breaker lever open a number of times whilst the high tension lead from the ignition coil is held about $\frac{3}{16}''$ away from the cylinder head. If the ignition coil is in good condition a strong spark should be obtained. If no spark occurs this indicates the ignition coil to be faulty.

Before a fault can be attributed to an ignition coil it must be ascertained that the high tension cables are not cracked or showing signs of deterioration as this may often be the cause of mis-firing, etc. It should also be checked that the ignition points are actually making good electrical contact when closed and that the moving contact is insulated from earth (ground) when open. It is advisable to remove the ignition coil and test it by the method described below.

BENCH TESTING AN IGNITION COIL

Connect the ignition coil into the circuit and set the adjustable gap to 8 mm. With the contact breaker running at 600 r.p.m. and the coil in good condition, not more than 5% missing should occur at the spark gap over a period of fifteen seconds. The primary winding can be checked for short-circuit coils by connecting an ohmeter across the low tension terminals. The reading obtained should be within the figures quoted below (at 20°C.).

Coil	Primary Resistance	
	Minimum	Maximum
MA6	1.8 ohms.	2.4 ohms.

MODEL 6CA CONTACT BREAKER

Introduction

The model 6CA contact breaker incorporates two new design features. One is the provision of an eccentric screw for adjustment of spark timing. This screw, when rotated, allows the timing to be set with great accuracy while at the same time the operation is simple to carry out.

The second is the provision of a similar eccentric screw for adjustment of the contact breaker gap. Again accurate but simple setting is possible which further increases the efficiency of the system.

Fig. 1. Model 6CA Contact Breaker and Automatic Advance Unit

(A Twin Lever type is shown for General reference only)

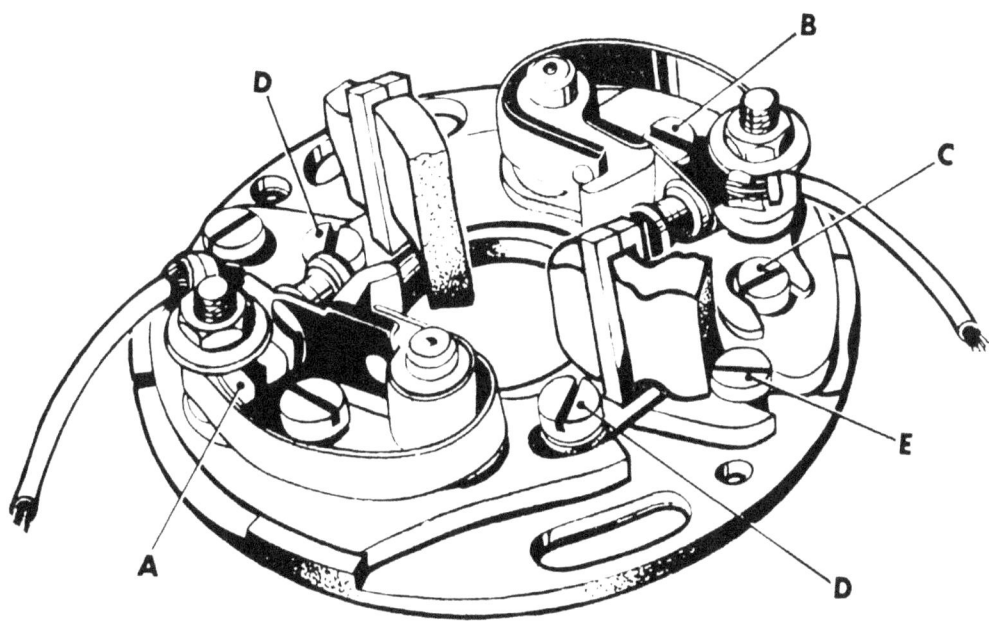

The bearing surface of the shaft and action plate has been treated with a special dry lubricant. **Liquid lubrication (oil, etc.) must not be applied at this point,** or a glutinous paste will be formed resulting in the eventual seizure of the mechanism.

Periodically the weight pivot and the cam foot pivot should be lubricated with one drop of clean engine oil. Any surplus must be wiped away to avoid contamination.

As access to the pivot points entails removal of the contact breaker plate, lubrication should be carried out when the contact breaker points are serviced, *i.e.* every 6,000 miles, 9.600 km.

The illustration shows a twin lever arrangement, but both single and twin lever types are of similar construction. In this case a single lever type is fitted and one contact breaker is deleted. The contact breaker has an improved lightweight heel and it is used with a conventional automatic advance unit. Some units will incorporate a slot in the drive taper for location onto the driving member.

The absence of capacitors will be noted. These are provided as a separate item mounted remote from the contact breaker.

Specification

Contact breaker gap 0.014″ to 0.016″ (0.35 mm to 0.4 mm)
Contact breaker spring load 20-oz.F to 27-oz.F.
(*measured at contacts*)
Extractor thread $\frac{5}{16}$ UNF.

Dismantling

(i) Unscrew and remove the nut securing the c.b. spring to the anchor post
(ii) Lift off the spring and heel together with the insulated bush and c.b. lead termination (A).
(iii) Unscrew and remove the fixed contact (angle plate) securing screw (B) and lift off the fixed contact.

RE-ASSEMBLY

Contacts

When connecting the C.B. and capacitor leads to the anchor post, ensure that the eyelet has its tag (A) inside the curve of the spring but not touching it, otherwise the lead may foul the moving contact.

Maintenance

1. After 500 miles (800 km)—check the contact point gap. Limits 0.014″ to 0.016″ (0.35 mm to 0.40 mm). Re-adjust as necessary.
2. Every 3,000 miles (4,800 km)—add two drops of clean, light engine oil to the rear end of the cam lubricating wick.
3. Every 6,000 miles (9,600 km)—check the contact point gap. Inspect condition of contact surfaces. If burned or blackened they should be cleaned with fine emery cloth or carborundum stone.

Automatic Advance Unit

The correct manner of assembly will be apparent on inspection. However, two points should be carefully noted.

(*a*) Each spring has a tapered loop at one end. This end should be attached to the cam pin.

(*b*) The cam has two weight location pins and the longest of these pins is designed to fit into the radiused range slot.

Precaution

The bearing surface between the cam inner face and the sleeve of the action plate assembly is pre-lubricated at the factory and **must not be oiled.**

GENERATOR MODEL EL3

Part No. 20036 (positive earth)

General

The generator is a shunt-connected two-brush machine, arranged to work in conjunction with Lucas voltage regulator unit model RB 108.

Routine Maintenance

The generator should be dismantled and serviced as required at times of major engine overhaul. Routine maintenance is not necessary although the brushgear and commutator should be inspected at two-yearly intervals.

Performance Data

Cutting-in Speed 1050-1200 rev/min @ 7.0 generator volts
Maximum Output 8.5. amp @ 1850-2000 rev/min @ 7. generator volts

THE ELECTRICAL SETTINGS OF THE CONTROL BOX
Model RB 108 (6-volt) Serial No. 37221

General
All settings are accurately adjusted before control boxes leave the factory and must not be disturbed. Any subsequent attention that may be required after the period of guarantee has expired should only be carried out by a qualified automobile electrician. The control box is a sealed unit but the cover is pierced with two $\frac{1}{2}$" dia. holes for permitting screwdriver access to the voltage regulator and cut-out relay adjusting screws. The holes are plugged with a pair of linked rubber blanks which can be withdrawn when making voltage measurements and adjustments.

The control box frame is at generator potential and so, also, are the adjusting screws, since these pass through tapped holes in the frame It is therefore advisable before making an adjustment to select a small screwdriver having an adequately insulated blade and thus obviate short-circuiting of the generator in the event of the control box cover becoming earthed. If necessary, a piece of insulating tubing of suitable length and bore can be sleeved on to an otherwise uninsulated screwdriver blade.

Preliminary Checking of Charging Circuit
Before disturbing any electrical adjustments, examine as follows to ensure that the fault does not lie outside the control box : —

(i) Check the battery by substitution or with an hydrometer and a heavy discharge tester.

(ii) Check the generator by substitution, or by disconnecting the generator cables and linking large terminal to small terminal and connecting a 0-20 first-grade moving coil voltmeter between this link and earth, and then running the generator up to about 1000 r.p.m.. when a rising voltage should be shown. If satisfactory, restore the generator connections.

(iii) Inspect the wiring of the charging circuit and carry out continuity tests.

(iv) Check earth connections, particularly of the control box.

(v) In the event of reported undercharging, ascertain that this is not due to low mileage.

Checking and Adjusting Voltage Regulator Electrical Setting
Checking and adjusting of the open-circuit voltage setting should be completed as rapidly as possible so as to avoid errors resulting from heating of the voltage regulator shunt coil.

(i) Disconnect the cable from control box terminal

Warning—Do not allow the end of the cable removed to contact any earthed parts of the machine.

(ii) Disengage the linked rubber blanks from the control box cover taking care not to mislay them.

(iii) Start the engine and drive the generator at about 3,000 r.p.m.

(iv) Using test prods, measure the voltage between the exposed head of one of the adjusting screws and a good earth. This should be between the following limits, according to the ambient temperature :—

Ambient Temperature	Open-Circuit Generator Voltage
10°c. (50°f.)	7.85-8.25
20°c. (68°f.)	7.8-8.2
30°c. (86°f.)	7.75-8.15
40°c. (104°f.)	7.70-8.10

An unsteady reading may be due to the voltage regulator contacts requiring cleaning, in which event, remove the cover and clean the contacts, preferably using silicon carbide paper, followed by methylated spirits (de-natured alchohol). If the reading is steady but occurs outside the appropriate limits, the voltage regulator must be re-adjusted. In this event, proceed as in (v) below, otherwise, stop the engine, restore the original connections and re-fit the rubber blanks.

Note—When viewed from the domed embossed end of the cover with rubber blanks uppermost, the left-hand hole gives access to the voltage regulator adjusting screw and the right-hand hole to the cut-out relay adjusting screw.

(v) Clip one of the voltmeter leads (of appropriate polarity) to a good earthing point.

(vi) Using a test prod, contact the other voltmeter lead against the exposed head of the cut-out relay adjusting screw.

(vii) Turn the voltage regulator adjusting screw (clockwise to raise the setting or anti-clockwise to lower it) until the correct open-circuit is obtained.

(viii) Check the setting by stopping the engine and then again raising the generator speed to 3,000 r.p.m.

(ix) Stop the engine, restore the original connections and re-fit the rubber blanks.

IGNITION SWITCH

The Model 45SA Ignition switch incorporates a "barrel" type lock. This type of lock uses an individual "Yale" type key and renders the ignition circuit inoperative when the switch is turned off and the key removed. It is advisable for the owner to note the number stamped on the key to ensure a correct replacement in the event of the key being lost.

Three Lucar connectors are incorporated in the switch and these should be checked from time to time to ensure good electrical contact. The switch body can be released from the tool box panel by removing the large nut retaining the switch in the panel and the switch pushed out. The battery leads should be removed before attempting to remove the switch to avoid a short circuit.

The lock is retained in the body of the switch by a spring loaded plunger. This can be depressed with a pointed instrument through a small hole in the side of the switch body and the lock assembly withdrawn after the lock and switch have been detached from the machine.

ELECTRIC HORN

The 6H Horn is pre-set to give the best performance and, in general no further adjustment is necessary.

If the horn becomes uncertain in its action, giving only a choking sound, or does not vibrate, it does not follow that the horn has broken down—the trouble may be due to a discharged battery, a loose connection, or short-circuit in the wiring of the horn. In particular, ascertain that the horn push bracket is in good electrical contact with the handelbars.

It is also possible that the performance of a horn may be upset by its mounting becoming loose.

Adjustment

The following adjustment will not alter the note of the horn. It will take up any wear of the moving parts, which, if not corrected, may result in roughness and loss of performance.

Operate the horn push and slowly turn the adjustment screw (located at the back of the horn body) until the horn just fails to sound. Release the horn push and turn the adjustment screw clockwise, one notch at a time, until the original performance of the horn is restored. This usually entails a clockwise motion of one quarter to three-quarters of a turn.

On no account must the centre core and locking nut be disturbed. If the original performance cannot be restored by adjustment, do not attempt to dismantle the horn, but return it to a Lucas Service Depot for examination.

HEADLAMP

Description

The SS700P Headlamp is of the sealed beam unit type and access is gained to the bulb holder by withdrawing the rim and beam unit assembly. Slacken the screw at the top of the headlamp and prise off the rim and beam unit assembly.

The bulb can be removed by first pressing the cylindrical cap inwards and turning it anti-clockwise. The cap can then be withdrawn and the bulb is free to be removed.

When fitting a new bulb, note that it locates by means of a cutaway and projection arrangement. Also note that the cap can only be re-placed one way, the tabs being staggered to prevent incorrect re-assembly. Check the replacement bulb voltage and wattage specification and type before fitting. Focussing with this type of beam is unnecessary and there is no provision for such.

Beam Adjustments

The beam must in all cases be adjusted as specified by local lighting regulations. In the United Kingdom the Transport Lighting Regulations reads as follows :—

A lighting system must be arranged so that it can give a light which is incapable of dazzling any person standing on the same horizontal plane as the vehicle at a greater distance than twenty five feet from the lamp, whose eye level is not less than three feet six inches above that plane.

The headlamp must therefore be set so that the main beam is directed straight ahead and parallel with the road when the motorcycle is fully loaded. To achieve this, place the machine on a level road pointing towards a wall at a distance of 25 feet away, with a rider and passenger on the machine, slacken the two pivot bolts at either side of the headlamp and tilt the headlamp until the beam is focussed at approximately two feet six inches from the base of the wall. Do not forget that the headlamp should be on "full beam" lighting during this operation.

Removing and Re-Fitting the Headlamp

Disconnect the leads from the battery terminals then slacken the light unit securing screw at the top of the headlamp. Prise the top of the light unit free.

Detach the pilot bulbholder from the light unit and disconnect the main bulbholder leads at the snap connector. Disconnect the four spade terminals from the lighting switch and the terminals from the ammeter. The lead for the warning light should be parted at the snap connector and then the harness complete can be withdrawn with the grommet from the back of the headlamp shell. Finally remove the pivot bolts to release the shell and collect the spacers.

Re-fitting is the reversal of the above instruction but reference should be made to the appropriate wiring diagram on page 109 and 110. Finally, set the headlamp main beam as instructed previously

Do not tighten the headlamp pivot bolts over the torque setting of 10LB/FT (1.4 kgm) — $\frac{5}{16}$ 26 Whit. S. Med. B.S.84.

TAIL AND STOP LAMP UNIT

Access to the bulbs in the Model 564 and 679 tail and stop lamp unit is achieved by unscrewing the two slotted screws which secure the lens (see illustration). The bulb of the double filament offset pin type and when a replacement is carried out, ensure that the bulb is fitted correctly.

Check that the two supply leads are connected correctly and check the earth (ground) lead to the bulb holder is in satisfactory condition.

When re-fitting the lens, do not overtighten the fixing screws or the lens may fracture as a result.

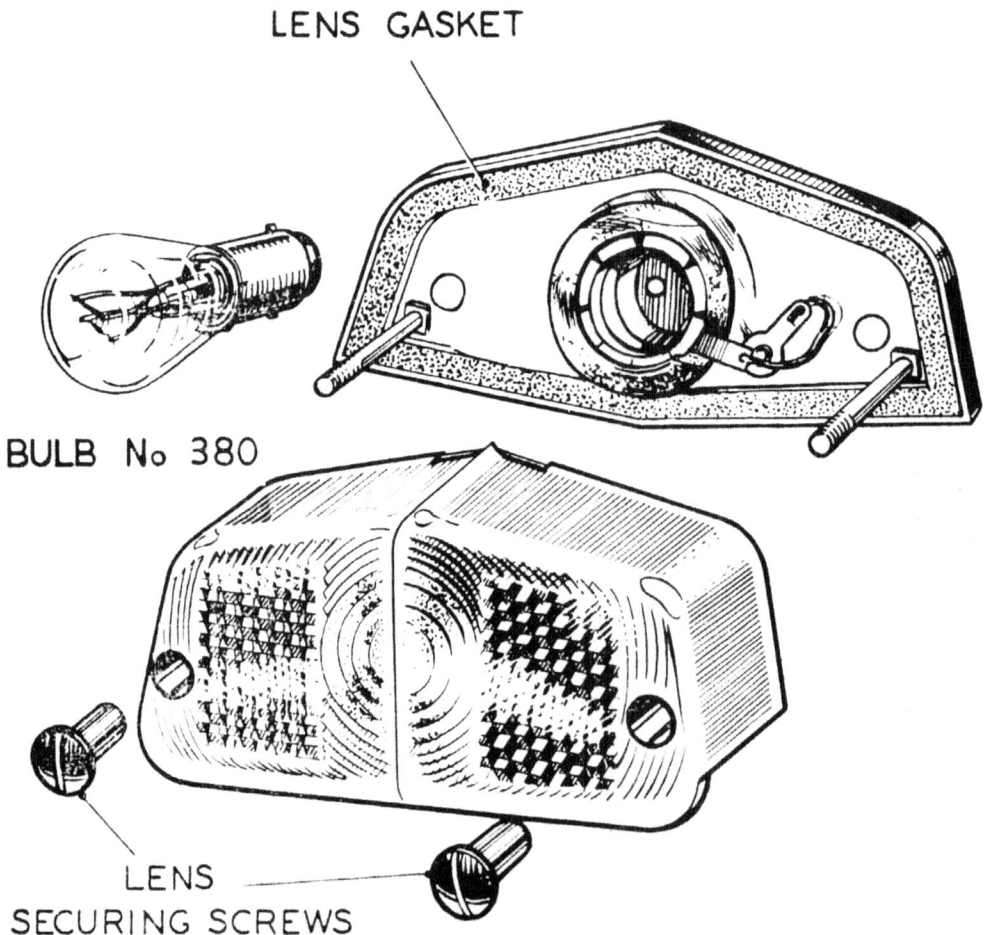

LUCAS STOP-TAIL LAMP
MODEL 564

LENS GASKET

BULB No 380

LENS SECURING SCREWS

REC 1198   4/7/60

ISSUED BY

JOSEPH LUCAS LTD · BIRMINGHAM · ENGLAND

WARNING LAMP

A green warning lamp has been incorporated in the electrical system mounted in the headlamp shell.

LIGHTING SWITCH

Model 57SA Lighting Switch is fitted to all machines with the exception of the following engine numbers :—

VMT775C to VMT814C

VM6488C/89C, VM6491C/92C/93C

MSS13251C/252C

These machines are fitted with an 88SA type switch (for wiring diagram apply Works). For all other application refer to wiring diagram page 110.

LOCATION AND REMEDY OF FAULTS

Although every precaution is taken to eliminate all possible causes of trouble, failure may occasionally develop through lack of attention to the equipment, or damage to the wiring. The following information sets out the recommended procedure for a systematic examination to locate and remedy the causes of some of the more probable faults. The sources of many troubles are by no means obvious and in some cases a considerable amount of deduction from the symptoms is needed before the cause of the trouble is disclosed.

When checking the continuity of circuits, a flashlamp battery and bulb should be used. On no account must the end of a live cable be flicked to earth against the motor cycle frame. If a separate motor cycle battery is used, a low wattage test lamp must be included in the circuit.

If, after carrying out the examination, the cause of the trouble is not found, the owner is advised to get in touch with the nearest Lucas Service Depot or Agent.

Engine will not start

(a) Check battery and associated wiring.

(b) Remove the H.T. cable from the sparking plug terminal and hold the cable end about $\frac{1}{8}''$ away from some metal part of the engine while the latter is slowly turned over. If sparks jump the gap regularly the ignition equipment is functioning correctly. Check for engine defects or examine sparking plug.

(c) Check for a fault in the L.T. wiring, *i.e.* from battery to switch, coil and contact breaker; If the wiring proves to be in order, examine the contact breaker; if necessary clean the contacts and adjust the gap setting. Check capacitor by substitution.

(d) If, after carrying out these checks, the ignition system is still inoperative have it examined by a Lucas Service Depot or Agent.

Engine Misfires

(a) Examine the contact breaker; if necessary, clean the contacts and adjust the gap.

(b) Check capacitor by substitution.

(c) Remove the sparking plug, rest it on the cylinder head and observe if a spark occurs at the plug points when the engine is turned. Irregular sparking may be due to dirty plugs. which may be cleaned and adjusted. or to defective high tension cables. Any cable on which the insulation shows signs of deterioration or cracking should be renewed.

(d) If sparking is regular at the plug when tested as described in (b), the trouble is probably due to engine defects and the carburetter, petrol supply, etc., must be examined.

LIGHTING CIRCUITS

Failure of Lights (machine stationary)

(a) If only one bulb fails to light, replace with new bulb.

(b) If all lamps fail to light have the condition of the battery checked, re-charging it if necessary either by a long period of daytime running or by connecting to a suitable battery charger.

(c) Examine the wiring for a broken or loose connection and remedy.

SPARE PARTS LIST

FOR

500 c.c. MODELS
MSS., VENOM, CLUBMAN (Mk. I & II)
SCRAMBLER, THRUXTON and ENDURANCE

350 c.c. MODELS
VIPER, CLUBMAN (Mk. I & II) and SCRAMBLER

VELOCETTE MOTOR CYCLE CO.
558 BROMFORD LANE, BIRMINGHAM B8 2DT
021-783 3893

Always quote the complete engine number *(including **all** the letters in it. The machine cannot be identified from the numerals only).* If the machine is finished in colour, state colour of parts required.

Illustrations

The illustrations included are not necessarily exact reproductions of the parts they represent and in the case of gears and chain sprockets do not always show the correct number of teeth.

Where standard nuts and bolts are used sizes are given. The bolt length is always taken from underneath the bolt head.

The Models are shown under column headings as follows:

Model		*Column*
MSS		A
VIPER		B
VENOM		C
CLUBMAN	350 cc (Mk. I and Mk. II)	D
SCRAMBLER	350 cc	E
CLUBMAN	500 cc (Mk. I and Mk. II)	F
SCRAMBLER	500 cc	G
THRUXTON		H
ENDURANCE		J

From page 56 onwards the List deals with components peculiar only to Clubman (Mk. I and Mk. II), Scrambler Endurance and Thruxton Models.

PROPRIETARY ARTICLES

Customers are requested to deal direct with the manufacturers of Proprietary Articles for any technical information or claims under guarantee. Overseas owners should obtain the above information either from the Velocette Agent or the Proprietary Manufacturer's Representative in their Territory

---

For our Customers' convenience we give the addresses of our suppliers below:

CARBURETTER EQUIPMENT
Amal Ltd., Holford Road, Witton, Birmingham 6

LIGHTING & IGNITION EQUIPMENT
H. Miller & Co. Ltd., Aston Brook Street, Birmingham 6
J. Lucas Ltd., Great King Street, Birmingham 19
B.T.H. Co., Alma Street, Coventry

SPARKING PLUGS
K.L.G. Sparking Plugs Ltd.
    Robinhood Engineering Works, Putney Vale, London SW15
Lodge Plugs Ltd., Rugby
Champion Sparking Plugs, Feltham, Middlesex

ELECTRIC HORNS
Clear Hooters Ltd., Hampton Street, Birmingham 19

TYRES
Dunlop Rubber Co. Ltd., Fort Dunlop, Birmingham 24
Goodyear Tyre Co., Bushbury, Wolverhampton

BATTERIES
Chloride Electrical Storage Co., Dale End, Birmingham 4
Varley Dry Accumulators Ltd., By-Pass Road, Barking, Essex
J. Lucas Ltd., Great King Street, Birmingham 19

SPEEDOMETERS
S. Smith & Sons (M.A.) Ltd.
    Cricklewood Works, Cricklewood, London NW12

SUSPENSION UNITS
Jonas-Woodhead & Sons Ltd., Kirkstall Road, Leeds 4
Girling Ltd., Kings Road, Birmingham 11

ILLUSTRATION A

FOR PART NUMBERS AND DESCRIPTION OF ITEMS
- 1 to 22 see page 4
- 23 to 46 " " 5
- 47 to 64 " " 6
- 65 to 71 " " 7
- 72 to 85 " " 8

ORDER BY PART NUMBERS—DO NOT QUOTE ILLUSTRATION REFERENCES

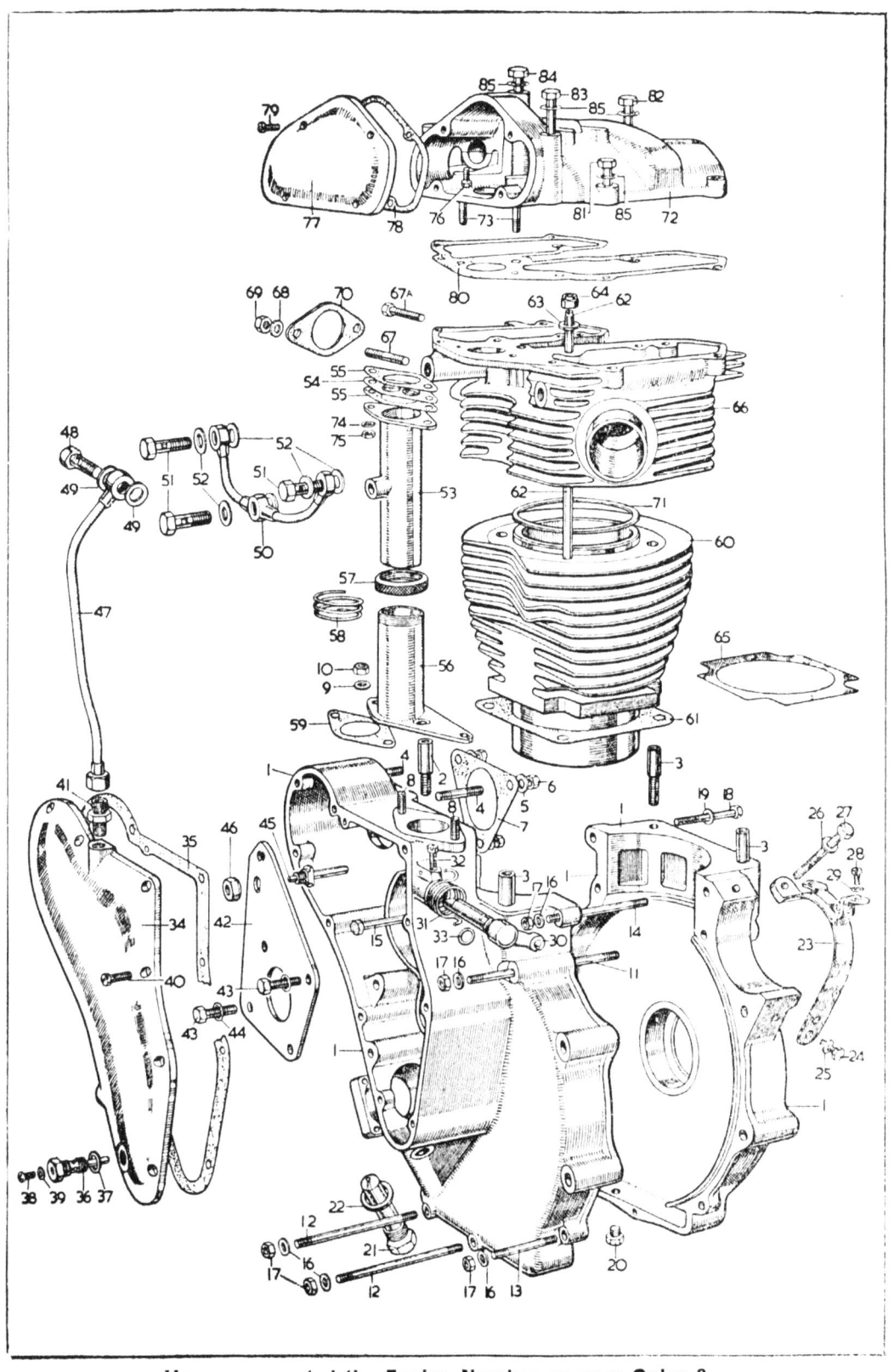

Have you quoted the Engine Number on your Order?

ENGINE SECTION   See Illustration "A" page Three

Crankcase, Crankcase Bolt and Stud Group

Note—Quote Part Numbers when ordering   NOT Illustration References
Always quote complete engine number and letters
Before ordering also see respective sections on pages 56 to 74 inclusive

Illus. Ref.	Part No.	Description	A	B	C	D	E	F	G	H	J
1	MAS29/5	Crankcase assembly. Includes items marked *	1	1	1	1	1	1	1	—	1	1
	MAS29/6		1	1	1	1	1	1	1	—	1	1
2	M56/2	* $\frac{5}{16}$" Crankcase stud. Cylinder base, rear timing side	1	1	—	—	—	—	—	1	1	1
	M56/6	$\frac{3}{8}$" Crankcase stud. Cylinder base, rear timing side	1	—	1	1	1	1	1	—	—	—
3	M56/4	* $\frac{5}{16}$" Crankcase stud. Cylinder base, front timing side and front and rear driving side	3	3	—	—	—	—	—	3	3	3
	M56/7	$\frac{3}{8}$" Crankcase stud. Cylinder base, front timing side and front and rear driving side	3	—	3	3	3	3	3	—	—	3
4	SL31/3	Crankcase stud. Magneto fixing $\frac{5}{16}$" 18×18T.×$1\frac{11}{32}$"	3	3	3	3	3	3	3	3	3	3
5	SL6/40	Crankcase stud washer. Magneto fixing	3	3	3	3	3	3	3	3	3	3
6	SL56/13	Crankcase stud nut. Magneto fixing $\frac{5}{16}$" 18T. .447" hex.	3	3	3	3	3	3	3	3	3	3
7	M260	Magneto flange gasket	1	1	1	1	1	1	1	1	1	1
8	SL30/21	* Crankcase stud. Push rod cover fixing, $\frac{1}{4}$" B.S.F.×$\frac{13}{16}$"	2	2	2	2	2	2	2	2	2	2
9	SL6/32	Crankcase stud washer. Push rod cover fixing, $\frac{1}{4}$" B.S.F.	2	2	2	2	2	2	2	2	2	2
10	SL56/4	Crankcase stud nut. Push rod cover fixing, $\frac{1}{4}$" B.S.F.	2	2	2	2	2	2	2	2	2	2
11	SL30/1	* Crankcase stud. Through crankcase. $\frac{1}{4}$" B.S.F.×$4\frac{1}{4}$"	1	1	1	1	1	1	1	1	1	1
12	SL30/2	* Crankcase stud. Through crankcase. $\frac{1}{4}$" B.S.F.×$3\frac{1}{2}$"	2	2	2	2	2	2	2	2	2	2
13	SL30/14	Crankcase stud. Through crankcase. $\frac{1}{4}$" B.S.F.×$1\frac{3}{4}$"	2	2	2	2	2	2	2	2	2	2
14	SL30/23	Crankcase stud. Through crankcase. $\frac{1}{4}$" B.S.F.×$2\frac{5}{8}$"	1	1	1	1	1	1	1	1	1	1
15	SL30/24	Crankcase stud. Through crankcase. $\frac{1}{4}$" B.S.F.×$4\frac{1}{16}$"	1	1	1	1	1	1	1	1	1	1
16	SL6/32	* Crankcase stud washer. $\frac{1}{4}$"	11	11	11	11	11	11	11	11	11	11
17	SL56/4	Crankcase stud nut. $\frac{1}{4}$" 20T.×$1\frac{1}{2}$"	12	12	12	12	12	12	12	12	12	12
18	SL8/11	Crankcase bolt. $\frac{1}{4}$" 20T.×$1\frac{1}{2}$"	1	1	1	1	1	1	1	1	1	1
19	SL6/32	Crankcase bolt washer. $\frac{1}{4}$"	1	1	1	1	1	1	1	1	1	1
20	B38	Crankcase drain plug. $\frac{1}{8}$" B.S.P.	1	1	1	1	1	1	1	1	1	1
21	K246/5	Crankcase filter plug	1	1	1	1	1	1	1	—	—	—
22	KA115/2	Crankcase filter plug gasket	1	1	1	1	1	1	1	—	—	—
Not shown	M275	Crankcase breather adaptor	1	1	1	1	1	1	1	1	1	1

* Included in Crankcase Assembly MAS29/5 and MAS29/6

Engine Section—continued See Illustration "A" page Three

Note—Quote Part Numbers when ordering NOT Illustration References
Always quote complete engine number and letters
Before ordering also see respective sections on pages 56 to 74 inclusive

Illus. Ref.	Part No.	Description	A	B	C	D	E	F	G	H	J
Dynamo and Voltage Regulator Group											
23	MAS44/2	Dynamo strap assembly	1	1	1	1	—	—	1	1	1
Not shown											
24	SL8/15	Dynamo strap bolt. Strap to crankcase. $\frac{1}{4}"$ 20T. × .437"	1	1	1	1	—	—	1	1	1
25	SL6/32	Dynamo strap bolt washer. $\frac{1}{4}"$	1	1	1	1	—	—	1	1	1
26	SL6/40	Dynamo strap clamping bolt washer. $\frac{5}{16}"$	1	1	1	1	—	—	1	1	1
27	SL9/22	Dynamo strap clamping bolt. $\frac{5}{16}"$ B.S.F. × $1\frac{1}{2}"$	1	1	1	1	—	—	1	1	1
28	SL80/21	Voltage control box screw. 2BA × $\frac{1}{4}"$	2	2	2	2	—	—	2	2	2
29	LE366	Voltage control box lockwasher. $\frac{3}{16}"$	2	2	2	2	—	—	2	2	2
Not shown	SL56/2	Voltage control box screw nut. Mudguard fixing	2	2	2	2	—	2	—	2	2
Exhaust Valve Lifter Group											
30	M11	Exhaust valve lifter lever	1	1	1	1	1	1	1	1	1
31	M155/2	Exhaust valve lifter lever spring	1	1	1	1	1	1	1	1	1
32	K76	Exhaust valve lifter lever screw	1	1	1	1	1	1	1	1	1
33	M261	Exhaust valve lifter lever oil seal	1	1	1	1	1	1	1	1	1
Timing Cover and Steady Plate Group											
34	M45/7	Timing Cover	1	1	1	1	1	1	—	1	1
34	M45/8	Timing Cover. With provision for Tachometer drive. To special order only	—	—	—	—	—	—	1	—	—
35	M68	Timing cover gasket	1	1	1	1	1	1	1	1	1
36	M212	Timing cover oil jet	1	1	1	1	1	1	1	1	1
37	A37/2	Timing cover oil jet gasket	1	1	1	1	1	1	1	1	1
38	SL80/22	Timing cover oil jet screw. 2BA × $\frac{3}{8}"$	10	10	10	10	10	10	10	10	10
39	A37/6	Timing cover oil jet screw gasket	1	1	1	1	1	1	1	1	1
40	K55	Timing cover fixing screw	1	1	1	1	1	1	1	1	1
41	K119	Timing cover oil union. Rocker oil feed. $\frac{1}{8}" \times \frac{1}{4}"$ B.S.P.	2	2	2	2	2	2	2	2	2
42	M199/2	Timing gear steady plate	2	2	2	2	2	2	2	2	2
43	M211	Steady plate bolt. Plate to crankcase, $\frac{5}{16}"$	2	2	2	2	2	2	2	2	2
44	LE368	Steady plate bolt lockwasher, $\frac{5}{16}"$	2	2	2	2	2	2	2	2	2
45	M259	Steady plate oil jet—Cam feed	1	1	1	1	1	1	1	1	1
46	M244	Steady plate oil jet nut	1	1	1	1	1	1	1	1	1

Engine Section—continued   See Illustration "A", page Three

Note—Quote Part Numbers when ordering   NOT Illustration References
Always quote complete engine number and letters
Before ordering also see respective sections on pages 56 to 74 inclusive

Illus. Ref.	Part No.	Description	A	B	C	D	E	F	G	H	J
Rocker Oil Feed and Return Pipe Group											
47	MAS18/2	Oil pipe assembly. Rocker oil feed	1	1	1	1	1	1	1	1	1
48	M214	Oil pipe hollow bolt	1	1	1	1	1	1	1	1	1
49	A37/7	Oil pipe hollow bolt gasket	2	2	2	2	2	2	2	2	2
50	MAS101	Oil return pipe assembly	1	1	1	1	1	1	1	1	1
51	M214	Oil return pipe hollow bolt	3	3	3	3	3	3	3	3	3
52	A37/7	Oil return pipe hollow bolt gasket	6	6	6	6	6	6	6	6	6
Push Rod Cover Group											
53	MAS102	Push rod cover assembly—top	1	1	1	1	1	1	1	1	1
54	M234	Push rod guide plate	1	1	1	1	1	1	1	1	1
55	M120	Push rod cover flange gasket—top	2	2	2	2	2	2	2	2	2
56	M50/2AS	Push rod cover assembly—bottom	1	1	1	1	1	1	1	1	1
57	M52	Push rod cover gland nut	1	1	1	1	1	1	1	1	1
58	K53	Push rod cover gland nut packing	1	1	1	1	1	1	1	1	1
59	M120/2	Push rod cover flange gasket—bottom	1	1	1	1	1	1	1	1	1
Cylinder Barrel, Cylinder Stud, Compression Plate and Gasket Group											
60	M22/17	Cylinder barrel. Cast Iron	1	1	1	1	1	1	1	—	1
60	M22/16	Cylinder barrel. Cast Iron	—	—	—	—	—	—	—	1	—
60	M22/18	Cylinder barrel. Cast Iron	—	—	—	—	—	—	—	1	—
Not shown	M271	Cylinder base ring (Viper alloy barrel only)	—	—	—	—	1	1	1	1	—
61	M70/3	Cylinder barrel gasket	1	1	1	1	1	1	1	1	1
61	M70	Cylinder barrel gasket (Viper alloy barrel only)	—	—	—	—	1	1	1	—	—
62	M249/2	Cylinder holding down stud. 5/16″ to MSS. 11786 only	4	4	4	4	4	4	4	4	4
62	M249/4	Cylinder holding down stud 3/8″. To MSS. 11786 only	4	4	4	4	4	4	4	4	4
	SL6/40	Cylinder stud washer, 5/16″	4	4	4	4	4	4	4	4	4
	SL6/50	Cylinder stud washer, 3/8″	4	4	4	4	4	4	4	4	4
	M262	Cylinder stud nut. 5/16″ Special Nylock. To MSS. 11786 only	4	4	4	4	4	4	4	4	4
64	M266	Cylinder stud nut. 3/8″ Special Nylock	4	4	4	4	4	4	4	4	4
Not shown	M261	Cylinder stud oil seal	4	4	4	4	4	4	4	4	4

Engine Section—*continued* See Illustration "A" page Three

Note—Quote Part Numbers when ordering NOT Illustration References
Always quote complete engine number and letters
Before ordering also see respective sections on pages 56 to 74 inclusive

Cylinder Barrel, Cylinder Stud, Compression Plate and Gasket Group—*continued*

Illus. Ref.	Part No.	Description	A	B	C	D	E	F	G	H	J
	M203/5	Compression Plate .010" thick	\} *as required all Models*								
	M203/6	Compression Plate .031" thick									
65	M203/7	Compression Plate .031" thick. Alfin cylinder barrel	\} *as required Viper and 350 cc. Scrambler*								
	M203/8	Compression Plate .010" thick. Alfin cylinder barrel									
	M203/5	Compression Plate .010" thick. Cast iron barrel	1	—	—	—	—	—	—	—	—
	M203/6	Compression Plate .031" thick. Cast iron barrel	2	—	—	—	—	—	—	—	—

Cylinder Head Assembly Group

Illus. Ref.	Part No.	Description	A	B	C	D	E	F	G	H	J
66	MAS32/2	Cylinder head assembly. Includes valve guides	1	—	—	—	—	—	—	—	—
	MAS32/3	Cylinder head assembly. Includes valve guides	—	1	1	—	1	1	1	—	—
	MAS32/4	Cylinder head assembly. Includes valve guides	2	—	—	—	—	—	—	—	2
67	SL103/2	Cylinder head stud. Carburetter fixing. $\tfrac{5}{16}$" B.S.F. $\times 1\tfrac{3}{16}$"	2	2	2	—	2	2	2	—	—
67a	SL109/2	Cylinder head bolt—carburetter fixing. $\tfrac{5}{16}$" B.S.F. $\times \tfrac{7}{8}$" Replaces SL103/2 and SL56/38	2	2	2	—	2	2	2	—	2
68	SL6/40	Cylinder head stud washer. Carburetter fixing $\tfrac{5}{16}$" B.S.F.	2	2	2	1	2	2	2	—	—
69	SL56/38	Cylinder head stud nut. $\tfrac{5}{16}$" B.S.F.	1	1	1	1	1	1	1	1	1
70	M180/2	Carburetter flange gasket. (Heating insulating)	1	1	1	—	1	1	1	—	1
71	M220/3	Cylinder head gasket	4	4	4	—	4	4	4	4	—
33	K220	Cylinder head gasket	—	—	—	—	—	—	—	1	—
66	MAS32/6	Cylinder head. Includes valve guides	—	—	—	1	—	—	—	—	1
—	M274	Induction manifold	1	—	—	—	—	—	—	—	—

Engine Section—continued See Illustration "A" page Three

Note—Quote Part Numbers when ordering NOT Illustration References
Always quote complete engine number and letters
Before ordering also see respective sections on pages 56 to 74 inclusive

Illus. Ref.	Part. No.	Description	A	B	C	D	E	F	G	H	J
Rocker Box and Cover Group											
72	MAS99	Rocker box assembly. Includes items idicated thus †	1	1	1	1	1	1	1	1	1
73	† SL30/7	Rocker box stud. Push rod cover fixing. $\frac{1}{4}''$ B.S.F. $\times 1\frac{1}{8}''$	2	2	2	2	2	2	2	2	2
74	SL6/32	Rocker box stud washer. Push rod cover fixing. $\frac{1}{4}''$ B.S.F.	2	2	2	2	2	2	2	2	2
75	SL56/4	Rocker box stud nut. Push rod cover fixing. $\frac{1}{4}''$ B.S.F.	2	2	2	2	2	2	2	2	2
76	K95	† Rocker bearing cap screw	8	8	8	8	8	8	8	8	8
77	M198/3	Rocker box cover	1	1	1	1	1	1	1	1	1
78	M256/2	Rocker box cover gasket	1	1	1	1	1	1	1	1	1
79	K95	Rocker box cover screw	4	4	4	4	4	4	4	4	4
80	M263	Rocker box gasket	1	1	1	1	1	1	1	1	1
81	SL109/10	Rocker box bolt. $\frac{5}{16}''$ B.S.F. $\times 1\frac{1}{4}''$	4	4	4	4	4	4	4	4	4
82	SL109/11	Rocker box bolt. $\frac{5}{16}''$ B.S.F. $\times 1\frac{5}{8}''$	2	2	2	2	2	2	2	2	2
83	SL109/12	Rocker box bolt. $\frac{5}{16}''$ B.S.F. $\times 2\frac{3}{4}''$	2	2	2	2	2	2	2	2	2
84	SL109/13	Rocker box bolt. $\frac{5}{16}''$ B.S.F. $\times 3\frac{5}{8}''$	1	1	1	1	1	1	1	1	1
85	LE368	Rocker box bolt lockwasher $\frac{5}{16}''$	9	9	9	9	9	9	9	9	9
Not shown	MAS144/2	Set of decoking gaskets	1	—	1	—	1	1	1	1	1
Not shown	MAS144/3	Set of decoking gaskets	—	1	—	1	—	—	—	—	—

8

ILLUSTRATION B

FOR PART NUMBERS AND DESCRIPTION OF ITEMS
{ 1 to 11 ,, ,, 10
12 to 26 ,, ,, 11
26 to 30 ,, ,, 12
31 to 54 ,, ,, 13
55 to 75 ,, ,, 14 }

ORDER BY PART NUMBERS—DO NOT QUOTE ILLUSTRATION REFERENCES

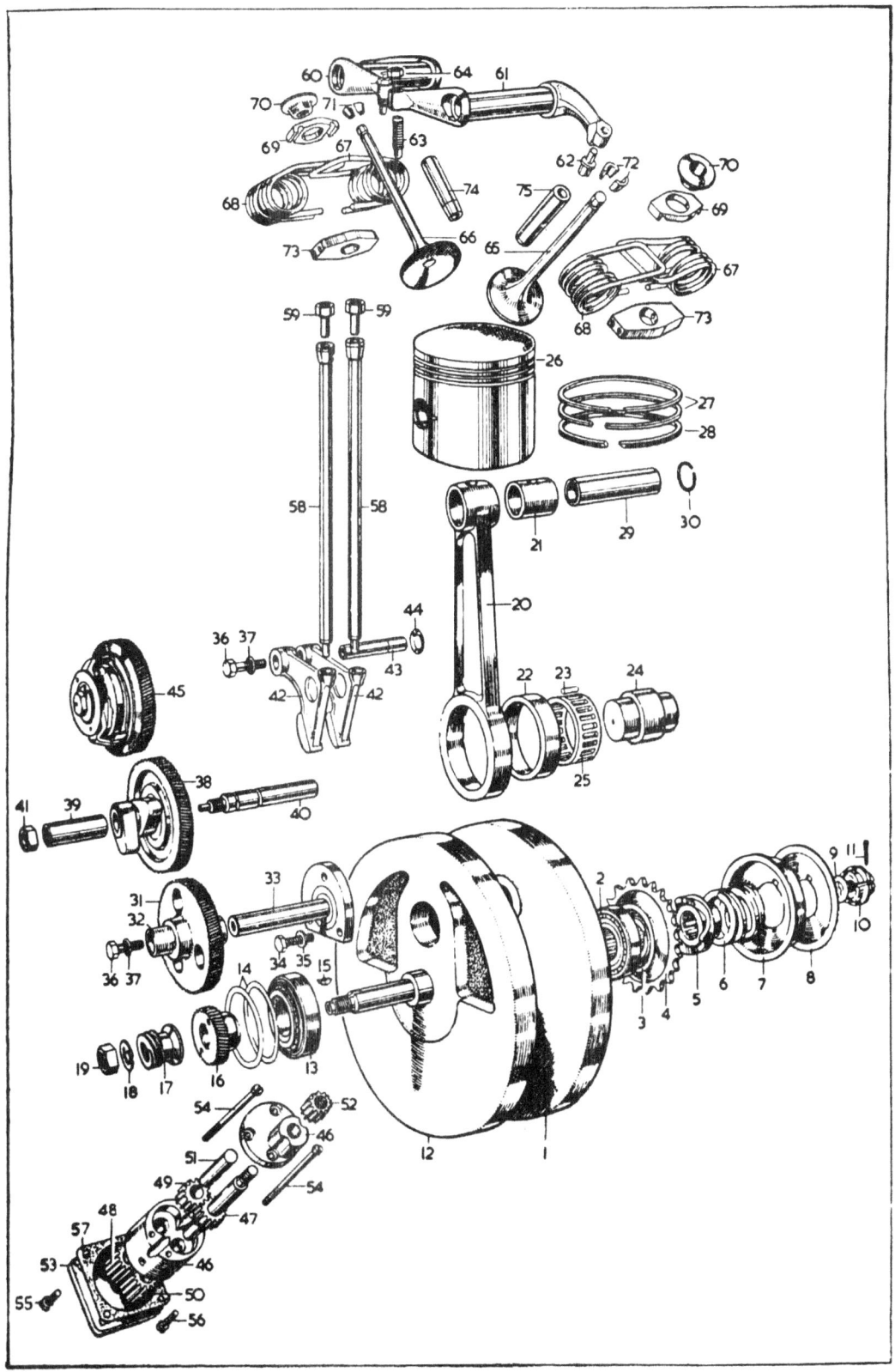

The Engine Number Prefix Letters identify the type   Are they on your Order ?

Engine Section—continued See Illustration "B" page Nine

Note—Quote Part Numbers when ordering   NOT Illustration References
Always quote complete engine number and letters
Before ordering also see respective sections on pages 56 to 74 inclusive

Driving Side Flywheel, Bearing and Shock Absorber Group

Illus. Ref.	Part No.	Description	A	B	C	D	E	F	G	H	J
1	MAS22/4	Flywheel and shaft assembly. Driving side. From MSS12304	1	1	1	1	1	1	1	1	1
2	M87/3	Driving shaft roller bearing	1	1	1	1	1	1	1	1	1
	M245	Driving shaft shim. .003″ thick	as required								
	M245/2	Driving shaft shim. .005″ thick	as required								
	M245/3	Driving shaft shim. .008″ thick	as required								
3	M245/4	Driving shaft shim. .002″ thick	as required								
4	M89/8	Engine sprocket. ½″ P. × .305″ 23 teeth	1	—	1	1	1	—	1	—	1
	M89/9	Engine sprocket. ½″ P. × .305″ 21 teeth	—	1	—	—	—	1	—	1	—
5	M91/4	Shock absorber clutch	1	1	1	1	1	1	1	1	1
6	M90/2	Shock absorber spring	1	1	1	1	1	1	1	1	1
7	E19/6	Dynamo driving pulley	1	1	1	—	1	1	1	—	1
	E19/8	‡ Dynamo driving pulley. 'V' type	1	1	1	1	1	1	—	1	1
8	E19/7	Dynamo driving pulley flange	1	1	1	—	1	1	1	—	1
	E19/9	‡ Dynamo driving pulley flange. 'V' type	1	1	1	1	1	1	—	1	1
Not shown	E12/4	Dynamo pulley. For 'V' belt	1	1	1	1	—	1	—	—	1
Not shown	E12/5	* Dynamo pulley. For 'V' belt	1	1	1	1	—	1	—	—	1
		‡ Used from Engine No. MSS11970 to MSS 12914									
		‡* Used from Engine No. MSS 12915 onwards									
		* Used from Engine No. VR 3605 onwards									
		* Used from engine No. VM 5049 onwards									
9	SL6/67	Shock absorber washer	1	1	1	1	1	1	1	1	1
10	M93/2	Shock absober spring collar	1	1	1	1	1	1	1	1	1
11	SL71/1	Split cotter. 3⁄16″ × 1″	1	1	1	1	1	1	1	1	1

Engine Section—continued   See Illustration "B" page Nine

Note—Quote Part Numbers when ordering   NOT Illustration References

Always quote complete engine number and letters

Before ordering also see respective sections on pages 56 to 74 inclusive

Illus. Ref.	Part No.	Description	A	B	C	D	E	F	G	H	J
Timing Side Flywheel, Bearing, Timing Pinion and Pump Worm Group
12	{ MAS21/4	* Flywheel and shaft assembly—Timing side (Replaced by MAS21/5)	1	1	1	1	1	1	1	–	1
	MAS21/5	Flywheel and shaft assembly—Timing side	1	1	1	1	1	1	1	1	1
13	M87/3	Flywheel shaft roller bearing	1	1	1	1	1	1	1	1	1
	{ M245	Timing shaft shim. .003" thick	as required
	M245/2	Timing shaft shim. .005" thick	as required
14	M245/3	Timing shaft shim. .008" thick	as required
	M245/4	Timing shaft shim. .002" thick	as required
15	K36/2	Timing shaft key	1	1	1	1	1	1	1	1	1
16	M32/4	Timing pinion	1	1	1	1	1	1	1	1	1
17	M206/2	Oil pump driving worm	1	1	1	1	1	1	1	1	1
18	K127	Timing shaft washer	1	1	1	1	1	1	1	1	1
19	SL56/32	Timing shaft nut. ½" 20. L.H.T.	1	1	1	1	1	1	1	1	1
		* Use with Crankpin M192/6
Connecting Rod, Big End and Piston Group
20	MAS96	Connecting rod assembly. Includes bush M29/3	1	1	1	1	1	1	1	1	1
22	M29/3	Connecting rod small end bush. Included in assembly MAS96	1	1	1	1	1	1	1	1	1
21	M190/2	Connecting rod outer race	1	1	1	1	1	1	1	1	1
	{ K191	Connecting rod roller	18	18	18	18	18	18	18	18	18
23	K191/3	Connecting rod roller. .0004" oversize diameter	18	18	18	18	18	18	18	18	18
	K191/4	Connecting rod roller. .0002" oversize diameter	18	18	18	18	18	18	18	18	18
24	M192/6	Crankpin	1	1	1	1	1	1	1	1	1
25	M193/2	Connecting rod roller cage	1	1	1	1	1	1	1	1	1
	{ MAS97	Piston assembly. Standard. c/w rings and gudgeon pin	1	1	1	1	1	1	1	–	–
26	MAS97/2	Piston assembly. .020" oversize. c/w rings and gudgeon pin	1	1	1	1	1	1	1	–	–
	MAS97/3	Piston assembly. .040" oversize. c/w rings and gudgeon pin	1	1	1	1	1	1	1	–	–

The above for use with 'Alfin' cylinder barrel

Engine Section—continued   **See Illustration "B" page Nine**

Note—Quote Part Numbers when ordering   NOT Illustration References
Always quote complete engine number and letters
Before ordering also see respective sections on pages 56 to 74 inclusive

Illus. Ref.	Part No.	Description		A	B	C	D	E	F	G	H	J
Connecting Rod, Big End and Piston Group—continued												
26	MAS97/22	Piston assembly. Standard.	c/w rings and gudgeon pin	1	—	—	—	—	—	—	—	—
	MAS97/23	Piston assembly. .020" oversize.	c/w rings and gudgeon pin	1	—	—	—	—	—	—	—	—
	MAS97/24	Piston assembly. .040" oversize.	c/w rings and gudgeon pin	1	—	—	—	—	—	—	—	—
	MAS97/19	Piston assembly. Standard.	c/w rings and gudgeon pin	—	—	1	1	—	—	—	—	—
	MAS97/20	Piston assembly. .020" oversize.	c/w rings and gudgeon pin	—	—	1	1	—	—	—	—	—
	MAS97/21	Piston assembly. .040" oversize.	c/w rings and gudgeon pin	—	—	1	1	—	—	—	—	—
	MAS97/25	Piston assembly. Standard.	c/w rings and gudgeon pin	—	—	—	—	—	1	1	1	1
	MAS97/26	Piston assembly. .020" oversize.	c/w rings and gudgeon pin	—	—	—	—	—	1	1	1	1
	MAS97/27	Piston assembly. .040" oversize.	c/w rings and gudgeon pin	—	—	—	—	—	1	1	1	1

The above for use with cast iron cylinder barrel

Illus. Ref.	Part No.	Description	A	B	C	D	E	F	G	H	J
27	SL3/67	Piston ring—compression. Standard diameter	2	—	—	—	—	—	—	—	—
	SL3/76	Piston ring—compression. .020" oversize diameter	2	—	—	—	—	—	—	—	—
	SL3/78	Piston ring—compression. .040" oversize diameter	2	—	—	—	—	—	—	—	—
	SL3/70	Piston ring—compression. Standard diameter	—	—	2	2	2	—	—	—	—
	SL3/72	Piston ring—compression. .020" oversize	—	—	2	2	2	—	—	—	—
	SL3/74	Piston ring—copmression. .040" oversize	—	—	2	2	2	—	—	—	—
28	SL3/68	Piston ring—scraper. Standard diameter	1	—	—	—	—	1	1	1	1
	SL3/77	Piston ring—scraper. .020" oversize diameter	1	—	—	—	—	1	1	1	1
	SL3/79	Piston ring—scraper. .040" oversize diameter	1	—	—	—	—	1	1	1	1
	SL3/71	Piston ring—scraper. Standard diameter	—	—	1	1	1	—	—	—	—
	SL3/73	Piston ring—scraper. .020" oversize	—	—	1	1	1	—	—	—	—
	SL3/75	Piston ring—scraper. .040" oversize	—	—	1	1	1	—	—	—	—
29	M31/3	Gudgeon pin	1	—	—	—	—	—	—	—	—
	M31/4	Gudgeon pin	—	—	1	1	1	1	1	1	1
30	K149/2	Gudgeon pin circlip	2	—	2	2	2	2	2	2	2

Engine Section—continued   See illustration "B" page Nine

Note—Quote Part Numbers when ordering.   NOT Illustration References
Always quote complete engine number and letters
Before ordering also see respective sections on pages 56 to 74 inclusive

Illus Ref.	Part No.	Description	A	B	C	D	E	F	G	H	J
Timing Gear, Timing Spindle, Bottom Rocker and Timing Unit Group											
31	MAS1/2	Intermediate gear assembly. Includes bush M202/4	1	1	1	1	1	1	1	1	1
32	M202/4	Intermediate gear bush. Included in assemblies MAS1 and MAS1/2	1	1	1	1	1	1	1	1	1
33	M200/4	Intermediate gear spindle	3	3	3	3	3	3	3	3	3
34	SL8/5	Intermediate gear spindle bolt. $\frac{1}{4}''$ B.S.F. $\times \frac{3}{4}''$	3	3	3	3	3	3	3	3	3
35	SL6/32	Intermediate gear spindle bolt washer $\frac{1}{4}''$	2	2	2	2	2	2	2	2	2
36	M210	Steady plate bolt. Steady plate to spindles	2	2	2	2	2	2	2	2	2
37	LE367	Steady plate bolt lockwasher $\frac{1}{4}''$	2	2	2	2	2	2	2	2	2
38	{MAS19/4	Camwheel assembly. Includes bush M12/2	1	1	1	1	1	1	—	—	—
	MAS19/5	Camwheel assembly. Includes bush M12/2	—	—	—	—	—	—	1	1	1
39	M12/2	Camwheel bush. Included in assembly MAS19/4 and MAS19/5	1	1	1	1	1	1	1	1	1
40	M15/2	Camwheel spindle	1	1	1	1	1	1	1	1	1
41	M244	Camwheel spindle nut	1	1	1	1	1	1	1	1	1
42	MAS118	Bottom rocker. Inlet and exhaust	2	2	2	2	2	2	—	—	2
42	MAS118/2	Bottom rocker. Exhaust	—	—	—	—	—	—	1	1	—
42	MAS118/3	Bottom rocker. Inlet	—	—	—	—	—	—	1	1	—
43	M10	Bottom rocker spindle	1	1	1	1	1	1	1	1	1
44	M216	Bottom rocker thrust washer	1	1	1	1	1	1	1	1	1
45	{MAS40	Magneto gear assembly	1	1	1	1	1	1	—	—	1
	MAS40/2	Magneto gear assembly	—	—	—	—	—	—	1	1	—
	M72/9	Magneto gear. Replaces MAS40 and MAS40/2 when hand control is fitted to special order	—	—	—	—	—	—	—	—	—
Oil Pump Assembly Group ‡											
46	MAS98	Oil pump body and cover assembly	1	1	1	1	1	1	1	1	1
47	{M80/2	Oil pump spindle. For use with M83 gear	1	1	1	1	1	1	1	1	1
	M80/5	Oil pump spindle. For use with M83/2 gear	1	1	1	1	1	1	1	1	1
48	M81	Oil pump return gear—loose	1	1	1	1	1	1	1	1	1
49	M82	Oil pump feed gear—loose	1	1	1	1	1	1	1	1	1
50	{M83	Pump fixed gear. 'Central spline'	1	1	1	1	1	1	1	1	1
	M83/2	Pump fixed gear. 'End spline'	1	1	1	1	1	1	1	1	1
51	M98	Oil pump fixed spindle	1	1	1	1	1	1	1	1	1
52	M217/2	Oil pump driven gear	1	1	1	1	1	1	1	1	1
53	M207	Oil pump base plate	1	1	1	1	1	1	1	1	1
54	M97/2	Oil pump fixing screw	4	4	4	4	4	4	4	4	4

Engine Section—continued See Illustration "B" page Nine NOT Illustration References

Note—Quote Part Numbers when ordering
Always quote complete engine number and letters
Before ordering also see respective sections on pages 56 to 74 inclusive

Illus. Ref.	Part No.	Description	A	B	C	D	E	F	G	H	J
Oil Pump Assembly Group—continued											
Not shown	MAS47/2	Oil pump assembly	1	1	1	1	1	1	1	1	1
55	K55	Oil pump assembly fixing screw—short	3	3	3	3	3	3	3	3	3
56	K95	Oil pump assembly fixing screw—long. Inner front	1	1	1	1	1	1	1	1	1
57	M226	Oil pump base plate gasket	1	1	1	1	1	1	1	1	1
Push Rod, Rocker, Tappet, Valve Guide, Valve Spring Group											
58	MAS100	Push rod assembly	2	2	2	2	2	2	2	—	2
58	MAS100/2	Push rod assembly	—	—	—	—	—	—	—	2	—
59	M194/3	Push rod end—loose	2	2	2	2	2	2	2	2	2
60	M9/9	Rocker—inlet. Also replaces MAS103	1	1	1	1	1	1	1	1	1
61	M9/8	Rocker—exhaust. Also replaces MAS104	1	1	1	1	1	1	1	1	1
62	M41/2	Rocker end. Included in assemblies MAS103, and MAS104									
		Not used with M9/8 and M9/9	2	—	2	—	2	2	2	2	2
63	M39/2	Rocker tappet	2	2	2	2	2	2	2	2	2
64	SL56/33	Rocker tappet lock nut. 5/16" .447" hexagon	2	2	2	2	2	2	2	2	2
65	M2/6	Valve exhaust	1	—	1	—	1	1	—	—	—
65	M2/16	Valve exhaust. Inlet and exhaust	—	1	—	1	—	—	1	—	—
65	M2/17	Valve exhaust. Inlet and exhaust	—	—	—	—	—	—	—	1	1
66	M2/7	Valve—inlet	1	—	1	—	1	1	—	—	—
66	M2/12	Valve—inlet	—	—	—	—	—	—	—	—	—
67	M6/4	Valve spring. Inlet and exhaust	2	2	2	2	2	2	2	2	2
68	M6/5	Valve spring. Inlet and exhaust	2	2	2	2	2	2	2	2	2
69	K4/6	Valve spring collar—outer	2	2	2	2	2	2	2	2	2
70	K4/4	Valve spring collar—inner, loose	2	2	2	2	2	2	2	2	2
71	K5/6	Valve cotter—inlet	1	1	1	1	1	1	1	1	1
72	K5/7	Valve cotter—exhaust	1	1	1	1	1	1	1	1	1
73	M38/4	Valve spring bottom washer	2	2	2	2	2	2	2	2	2
74	M3/6	Valve guide—inlet									
		(included in cylinder head assemblies MAS32/2, MAS32/3, MAS32/4 and MAS32/5)	1	1	1	1	1	1	1	1	1
75	M3/5	Valve guide—exhaust									
		(included in cylinder head assemblies MAS32/2, MAS32/3, MAS32/4 and MAS32/5)	1	1	1	1	1	1	1	1	1

ILLUSTRATION C

FOR PART NUMBERS AND DESCRIPTION OF ITEMS
{ 1 to 30 see page 16
 31 to 47 ,, ,, 17
 48 to 72 ,, ,, 18
 73 to 93 ,, ,, 19 }

ORDER BY PART NUMBERS—DO NOT QUOTE ILLUSTRATION REFERENCES

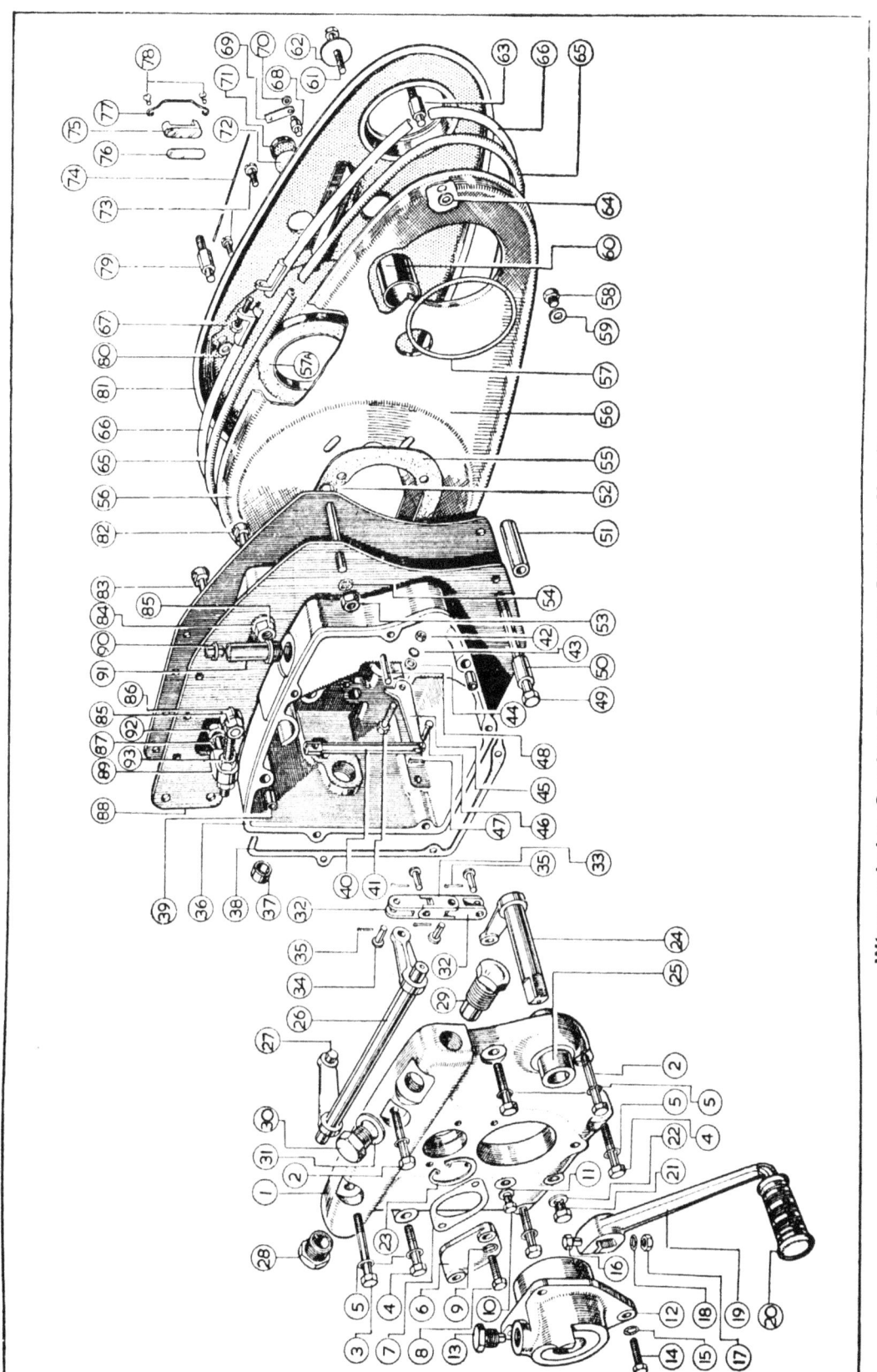

When ordering Gearbox Parts quote Gearbox Number

GEARBOX AND CLUTCH SECTION See Illustration "C" page Fifteen

Gearbox Housing, End Cover, Kickstart Bearing and Gear Lever Group

Note—Quote Part Numbers when ordering   NOT Illustration Reference Numbers
Always quote complete engine number and letters
Before ordering also see respective sections on pages 56 to 74 inclusive

Illus. Ref.	Part No.	Description	A	B	C	D	E	F	G	H	J
1	MAS55	Gearbox end cover assembly	1	1	1	1	1	1	1	1	1
2	SL108/3	Gearbox end cover bolt, $\frac{1}{4}''$ B.S.F. $\times 1\frac{3}{8}''$	2	2	2	2	2	2	2	2	2
3	SL108/4	Gearbox end cover bolt, $\frac{1}{4}''$ B.S.F. $\times 1\frac{1}{8}''$	1	1	1	1	1	1	1	1	1
4	SL108/5	Gearbox end cover bolt, $\frac{1}{4}''$ B.S.F. $\times 1\frac{1}{2}''$	4	4	4	4	4	4	4	4	4
5	LE367	Gearbox end cover bolt lockwasher, $\frac{1}{4}''$	7	7	7	7	7	7	7	7	7
6	B97	Gearbox end cover plate	1	1	1	1	1	1	1	1	1
7	B98	Gearbox end cover plate gasket	1	1	1	1	1	1	1	1	1
8	SL108/2	Gearbox end cover plate bolt, $\frac{1}{4}''$ B.S.F. $\times \frac{5}{8}''$	2	2	2	2	2	2	2	2	2
9	LE367	Gearbox end cover plate bolt lockwasher, $\frac{1}{4}''$	2	2	2	2	2	2	2	2	2
10	SL8/1	Gearbox oil level plug, $\frac{1}{4}''$ B.S.F. $\times \frac{3}{8}''$	1	1	1	1	1	1	1	1	1
11	A37/5	Gearbox oil level plug gasket	1	1	1	1	1	1	1	1	1
12	BK4	Kickstart bearing	1	1	1	1	1	1	1	1	1
13	BK73/2	Kickstart return spring anchor peg	1	1	1	1	1	1	1	1	1
14	SL108/2	Kickstart bearing fixing bolt, $\frac{1}{4}''$ B.S.F. $\times \frac{5}{8}''$	3	3	3	3	3	3	3	3	3
15	LE367	Kickstart bearing fixing bolt lockwasher, $\frac{1}{4}''$	3	3	3	3	3	3	3	3	3
16	SL108/3	Foot lever clamp bolt, $\frac{1}{4}''$ B.S.F. $\times 1\frac{3}{8}''$	1	1	1	1	1	1	1	1	1
17	SL56/4	Foot lever clamp bolt nut, $\frac{1}{4}''$ B.S.F.	1	1	1	1	1	1	1	1	1
18	LE367	Foot lever clamp bolt lockwasher, $\frac{1}{4}''$	1	1	1	1	1	1	1	1	1
19	GC4/21	Gear change foot lever	1	1	1	1	1	1	1	1	1
20	B60/4	Gear change foot lever rubber	1	1	1	1	1	1	1	1	1
21	B38	Gearbox oil drain plug, $\frac{1}{8}''$ B.S.P.	1	1	1	1	1	1	1	1	1
22	A37/7	Gearbox oil drain plug gasket	1	1	1	1	1	1	1	1	1
23	B100	Gearbox end cover circlip	1	1	1	1	1	1	1	1	1
24	GC55	Gearchange foot lever shaft	1	1	1	1	1	1	1	1	1
25	GC42/3†	Gearchange foot lever shaft bush	1	1	1	1	1	1	1	1	1
26	MAS46/3	Gearchange rocker shaft assembly. Replaces MAS46/2	1	1	1	1	1	1	1	1	1
27	GC60	Gearchange rocker shaft pin. (included in MAS46/2 assembly)	1	1	1	1	1	1	1	1	1
28	GC53	Rocker shaft bush—rear, short	1	1	1	1	1	1	1	1	1
29	GC54	Rocker shaft bush—front, long	1	1	1	1	1	1	1	1	1
30	BK40	Gearbox oil filler	1	1	1	1	1	1	1	1	1

† Included in MAS55 End Cover Assembly

Gearbox and Clutch Section—*continued*   See Illustration "C" page Fifteen

Note—Quote Part Numbers when ordering   NOT Illustration References

Always quote complete engine number and letters

Before ordering also see respective sections on pages 56 to 74 inclusive

Illus. Ref.	Part No.	Description	A	B	C	D	E	F	G	H	J
\multicolumn{12}{l}{**Gearbox Housing, End Cover, Kickstart Bearing and Gear Lever Group**—*continued*}
31	LE75	Gearbox oil filler plug gasket	1	1	1	1	1	1	1	1	1
32	GC56	Gear change yoke end	2	2	2	2	2	2	2	–	2
33	GC58	Gear change connecting link	1	1	1	1	1	1	1	–	–
Not shown	GC58/2	Gear change connecting link				1*	1*	1*	1*	1	2
34	GC59	Gear change clevis pin	4	4	4	4	4	4	4	–	4
Not shown	GC59/2	Gear change clevis pin				2*	2*	2*	2*	2	2
not shown	MAS149	Gear change shafts assembly (Comprising MAS46/3, GC58/2, GC59/2(2), and GC55)	1*	1*	1*	1*	1*	1*	1*	1	1
35	SL71/2	Gear change clevis pin split cotter, $\frac{1}{16}'' \times \frac{1}{2}''$. Includes BK36/2 Bush	4	4	4	4	4	4	4	–	4
36	MAS53/2	Gearbox housing (bushed). Included in MAS53/2 assembly	1	1	1	1	1	1	1	1	1
37	BK36/2	Gearbox housing bush	1	1	1	1	1	1	1	1	1
38	B43/2	Gearbox end cover gasket	1	1	1	1	1	1	1	1	1
39	LE333	Gearbox housing dowel	2	2	2	2	2	2	2	2	2
		* Used from gearbox No. 14/4916 on MSS									
		* Used from gearbox No. 12/7081 on Viper and Venom									
\multicolumn{12}{l}{**Clutch Operation, Chain Case and Rear Engine Plate Group**}
40	CK34/4	Clutch operating plunger	1	1	1	1	1	1	1	1	1
41	SL8/13	Clutch operating lever bolt, $\frac{1}{4}''$ B.S.F. $\times 1\frac{1}{16}''$	1	1	1	1	1	1	1	1	1
42	SL56/4	Clutch operating lever bolt nut, $\frac{1}{4}''$ B.S.F.	1	1	1	1	1	1	1	1	1
43	LE367	Clutch operating lever bolt lockwasher, $\frac{1}{4}''$	1	1	1	1	1	1	1	1	1
44	SL6/32	Clutch operating lever bolt washer, $\frac{1}{4}''$	1	1	1	1	1	1	1	1	1
45	C31/3	Clutch operating lever	1	1	1	1	1	1	1	1	1
46	S32	Clutch operating plunger clevis pin	1	1	1	1	1	1	1	1	1
47	SL71/2	Clutch operating plunger split cotter, $\frac{1}{16}'' \times \frac{1}{2}''$	1	1	1	1	1	1	1	1	1

Gearbox and Clutch Section—continued   See Illustration "C" page Fifteen

Note—Quote Part Numbers when ordering.   NOT Illustration References
Always quote complete engine number and letters
Before ordering also see respective sections on pages 56 to 74 inclusive

Clutch Operation, Chain Case and Rear Engine Plate Group—continued

Illus. Ref.	Part No.	Description	A	B	C	D	E	F	G	H	J
48	C30	Clutch operating thrust pin, 1.328" long	*	*	*	*	*	*	*	*	*
	C30/2	Clutch operating thrust pin, 1.343" long	*	*	*	*	*	*	*	*	*
		* One off used per gearbox—the length being determined by selective assembly									
49	SL11/2	Rear engine plate fixing bolt (long) $\frac{3}{8}$" 26 T.P.I.$\times 3\frac{7}{8}$"	1	1	1	1	1	1	1	1	1
50	FK221/3	Rear engine plate distance piece. (Outside right-hand plate)	1	1	1	1	1	1	1	1	1
51	F305	Rear engine plate distance piece (between plates)	1	1	1	1	1	1	1	1	1
52	SL11/1	Rear engine plate and bottom gearbox bolt, $\frac{3}{8}$" 26 T.P.I.$\times 2\frac{3}{4}$"	4	4	4	4	4	—	4	4	4
53	SL56/8	Rear engine plate and bottom gearbox bolt nut, $\frac{3}{8}$" 26 T.P.I.	4	4	4	4	4	—	4	4	4
54	LE369	Rear engine plate and bottom gearbox bolt lockwasher, $\frac{3}{8}$"	4	4	4	4	4	—	4	4	4
55	A179/6	Chaincase packing	1	1	1	1	1	1	—	—	—
56	F45/6	Chaincase rear half. Strap joint type only	1‡	1	1	1	1	1	—	—	—
	F45/7	Chaincase rear half. Strap joint type only	1	—	—	—	—	—	1	1	1
57	F285	Chaincase oil seal	1‡	1	1	1	1	1	—	—	—
	F285/2	Chaincase oil seal	1	—	—	—	—	—	1	1	1
		‡ From MSS 12079 onwards									
57A	F309	Chaincase felt ring	1	1	1	1	1	1	1	1	1
58	B38	Chain case drain plug, $\frac{1}{8}$" B.S.P.	1	1	1	1	1	1	1	1	1
59	A37/7	Chaincase drain plug gasket	1	1	1	1	1	1	1	1	1
60	FK205	Chaincase distance piece	1	1	1	1	1	1	1	1	1
	F310	Chaincase distance piece (inner). Fits on bolt inside FK205	1	1	1	1	1	1	1	1	1
61	SL109/3	Chaincase bolt, $\frac{5}{16}$" B.S.F.$\times 1\frac{3}{16}$"	1	1	1	1	1	1	1	1	1
62	SL6/42	Chaincase bolt washer, $\frac{5}{16}$"$\times 1\frac{3}{16}$" O/D	1	1	1	1	1	1	1	1	1
63	FK207/2	Chaincase stud. (Dynamo cover)	1	1	1	1	1	1	1	1	1
64	SL6/32	Chaincase stud washer	1	1	1	1	1	1	1	1	1
65	F284/2	Chaincase joint moulding. Strap joint type only	1	1	1	1	1	1	—	—	—
66	MAS16/2	Chaincase strap assembly. Strap joint type only	1	1	1	1	1	1	—	—	—
67	SL107/4	Chaincase strap fixing pin, 2BA$\times 1$". Strap joint type only	1	1	1	1	1	1	—	—	—
68	T95/2	Chaincase stud. (Inspection cap)	1	1	1	1	1	1	1	1	1
69	T72/19	Chaincase inspection cap clip	1	1	1	1	1	1	1	1	1
70	SL6/8	Chaincase stud washer, $\frac{3}{32}$"$\times \frac{9}{32}$" O/D	1	1	1	1	1	1	1	1	1
71	T71/19K	Chaincase inspection cap	1	1	1	1	1	1	1	1	1
72	KA244	Chaincase inspection cap pad	1	1	1	1	1	1	1	1	1

Gearbox and Clutch Section—continued   See Illustration "C" page Fifteen

Note—Quote Part Numbers when ordering   NOT Illustration References
Always quote complete engine number and letters
Before ordering also see respective sections on pages 56 to 74 inclusive

Illus. Ref.	Part No.	Description	A	B	C	D	E	F	G	H	J
Clutch Operation, Chain Case and Rear Engine Plate Group—*continued*											
73	F201/2	Chaincase fixing pin	4	4	4	4	4	4	4	4	4
74	FK264	Chaincase fixing pin locking plate	2	2	2	2	2	2	2	2	2
75	BK70	Clutch operating thrust pad	1	1	1	1	1	1	1	1	1
76	BK97	Clutch operating thrust pad shim	*as required*							
77	BK52	Clutch operating thrust cup wire clip	1	1	1	1	1	1	1	1	1
78	B34	Clutch operating thrust cup screw, 1/8" (Whit.) 40 T.P.I. c/s head	2	2	2	2	2	2	2	2	2
79	FK207/2	* Chaincase stud (Rear chain cover)	2	2	2	2	2	2	2	2	2
80	SL6/32	* Chaincase stud washer—inside 1/4"	1	1	1	1	1	1	1	–	1
81	MAS50/2	Chaincase front half assembly. (Includes items marked *). Strap joint	1	1	1	1	1	1	1	–	1
		* Items included in MAS50/2 and MAS50/4 assemblies									
Not shown	MAS50/4	Chaincase front half assembly. (Includes items marked *). Pin joint type	1	1	1	–	–	1	–	1	1
Not shown	MAS148/2	Chaincase rear half assembly. Pin joint type	1	1	1	1	1	1	1	1	1
Not shown	A179/5	Chaincase gasket. Pin joint type	1	1	1	1	1	1	1	1	1
Not shown	SL80/22	Chaincase joint screw. Pin joint type	14	14	14	14	14	14	14	14	14
82	FK81/2	Gearbox fixing bolt top. (Short)	1	1	1	1	1	1	1	1	1
83	FK81	Gearbox fixing bolt top (long)	1	1	1	1	1	1	1	1	1
84	SL6/48	Gearbox fixing bolt washer (top) 3/8"	2	2	2	2	2	2	2	2	2
85	SL56/8	Gearbox fixing bolt nut, 3/8", 26 T.P.I.	2	2	2	2	2	2	2	2	2
86	FK19/2	Gearbox adjuster	1	1	1	1	1	1	1	1	1
87	LE369	Rear engine plate	1	1	1	1	1	1	1	1	1
88	FK27/9	Gearbox adjuster stop lock washer 3/8"	2	2	2	2	2	2	2	–	2
89	FK228	Gearbox adjuster stop	1	1	1	1	1	1	1	1	1
90	CK14/2	Clutch cable stop	1	1	1	1	1	1	1	1	1
91	CK21/2	Clutch cable stop holder	1	1	1	1	1	1	1	1	1
92	SL56/8	Gearbox adjuster stop nut, 3/8", 26 T.P.I.	1	1	1	1	1	1	1	1	1
93	SL56/13	Gearbox adjuster nut, 5/16", 18 T.P.I.	2	2	2	2	2	2	2	2	2
Not shown	FK27/10	Rear engine plate strengthener	–	–	–	–	1	1	1	–	1

19

ILLUSTRATION D

FOR PART NUMBERS AND DESCRIPTION OF ITEMS
{ 1 to 20 see page 21
21 to 47 ,, ,, 22
48 to 75 ,, ,, 23
76 to 86 ,, ,, 24 }

ORDER BY PART NUMBERS—DO NOT QUOTE ILLUSTRATION REFERENCES

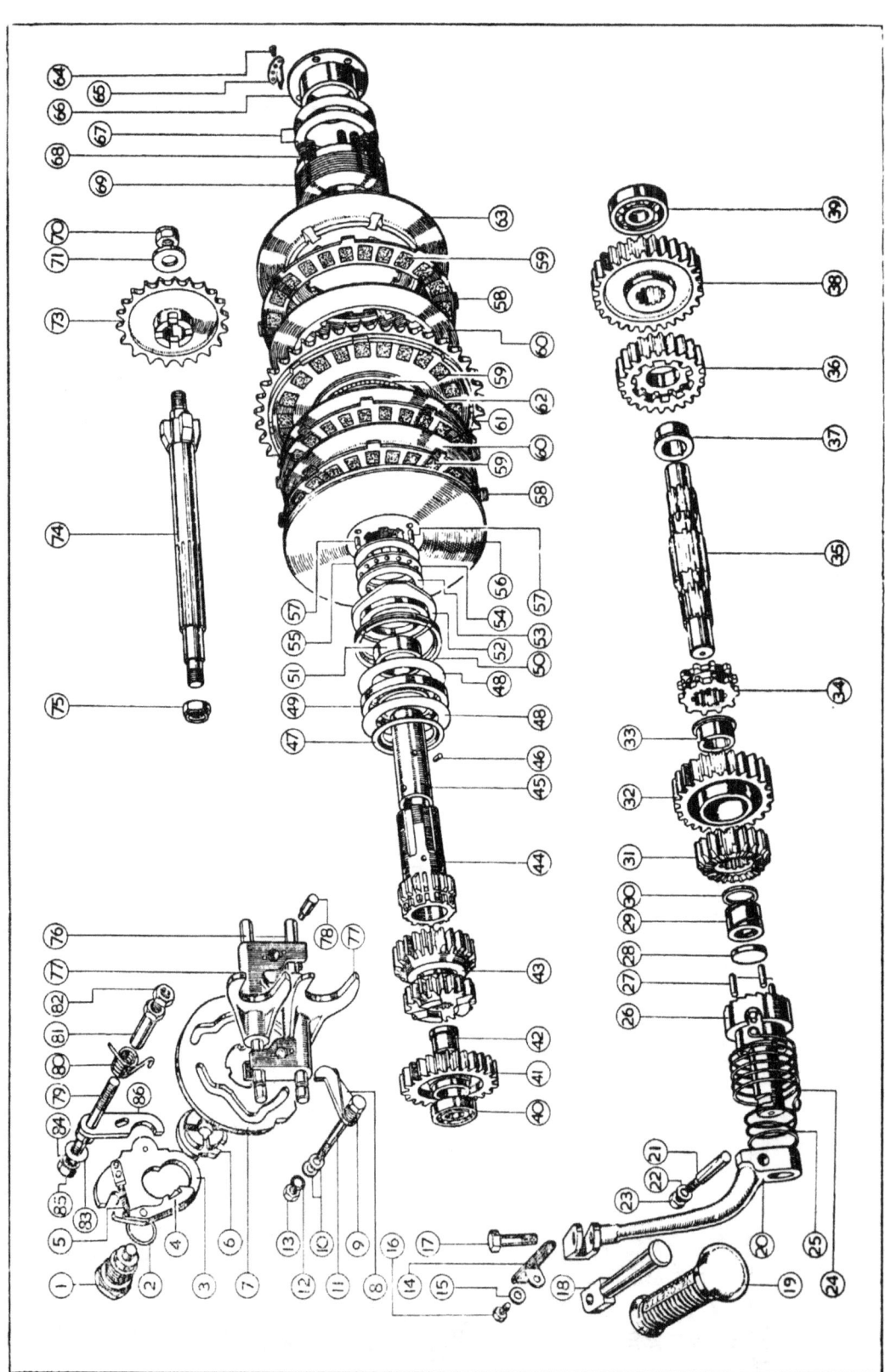

Have you quoted the Gearbox Number and Prefix on your Order?

Gearbox and Clutch Section—continued See Illustration "D" page Twenty

Camplate, Striking Plate and Indexing Mechanism Group

Note—Quote Part Numbers when ordering   NOT Illustration References
Always quote complete engine number and letters
Before ordering also see respective sections on pages 56 to 74 inclusive

Illus. Ref.	Part No.	Description	A	B	C	D	E	F	G	H	J
1	BK64/3	Camplate pivot	1	1	1	1	1	1	1	1	1
2	BK96	Camplate pivot shim				as required					
3	MAS45	Striking plate assembly	1	1	1	1	1	1	1	1	1
4	GC23/2	Striking pawl	1	1	1	1	1	1	1	1	1
5	GC24/2	Striking pawl spring	1	1	1	1	1	1	1	1	1
6	BK98/2	Camplate ratchet plate	1	1	1	1	1	1	1	1	1
7	BK80/5	Camplate	1	1	1	1	1	1	1	1	1
8	BK66	Indexing pawl	1	1	1	1	1	1	1	1	1
9	BK68	Indexing pawl spring	1	1	1	1	1	1	1	1	1
10	SL6/32	Indexing pawl washer, 1/4"	2	2	2	2	2	2	2	2	2
11	BK83/2	Indexing pawl pivot	1	1	1	1	1	1	1	1	1
12	LE367	Indexing pawl pivot lockwasher 1/4" B.S.F.	1	1	1	1	1	1	1	1	1
13	SL56/4	Indexing pawl pivot nut 1/4" B.S.F.	1	1	1	1	1	1	1	1	1

Kickstart Ratchet, Spring, and Crank Group

Illus. Ref.	Part No.	Description	A	B	C	D	E	F	G	H	J
14	A254/3	Kickstart footpiece retaining spring. Spring blade type	1	1	1	1	1	1	1	1	1
15	SL6/32	Kickstart retaining spring plain washer, 1/4" dia. Spring blade type	1	1	1	1	1	1	1	1	1
16	SL8/1	Kickstart retaining spring bolt, 1/4" B.S.F. × 3/8". Spring blade type	1	1	1	1	1	1	1	1	1
17	SL11/15	Kickstart footpiece bolt, 3/8", 26 T.P.I. × 1 1/16". Both types	1	1	1	1	1	1	1	1	1
18	BK18	Kickstart footpiece. Spring blade type	1	1	1	1	1	1	1	1	1
Not shown	BK18/3	Kickstart footpiece. Spring plunger type	1	1	1	1	1	—	—	—	—
19	B60/5	Kickstart rubber. Both types	1	1	1	1	1	1	1	1	1
20	BK12/6	Kickstart crank*. Spring blade type	1	1	1	1	1	—	—	—	—
Not shown	BK12/7	Kickstart crank. Spring plunger type	1	1	1	1	1	—	—	—	1
Not shown	LE353	Kickstart crank plunger. Spring plunger type	1	1	1	1	1	—	—	—	1
Not shown	LE118	Kickstart crank plunger spring. Spring plunger type	1	1	1	1	1	—	—	—	1

* Obsolete replaced by Part Nos. BK12/7, BK18/3, LE353 and LE118

Gearbox and Clutch Section—continued   See Illustration "D" page Twenty

Note—Quote Part Numbers when ordering.   NOT Illustration References
Always quote complete engine number and letters
Before ordering also see respective sections on pages 56 to 74 inclusive

Illus Ref.	Part No.	Description	A	B	C	D	E	F	G	H	J
Kickstart Ratchet, Spring and Crank Group—continued										
21	LE242	Kickstart crank cotter pin	1	1	1	1	1	1	1	1	1
22	SL6/32	Kickstart crank cotter pin washer ¼"	1	1	1	1	1	1	1	1	1
23	SL56/4	Kickstart crank cotter pin nut ¼" B.S.F.	1	1	1	1	1	1	1	1	1
24	BK19	Kickstart return spring	1	1	1	1	1	1	1	1	1
25	BK19/2	Kickstart spring (engaging)	1	1	1	1	1	1	1	1	1
26	BK14	Kickstart ratchet	1	1	1	1	1	1	1	1	1
27	K191	Kickstart bearing thrust pin (3/16" × 9/16") Bearing roller	3	3	3	3	3	3	3	3	3
28	BK82	Kickstart layshaft thrust washer	1	1	1	1	1	1	1	1	1
29	BK85/2	Kickstart bearing bush	1	1	1	1	1	1	1	1	1
Shafts, Gears, Clutch Plate and Bearing Group										
30	BK95	Layshaft washer	1	1	1	1	1	1	1	1	1
31	BK87	Layshaft first gear wheel	1	1	1	1	1	1	1	1	1
32	BK89AS	Layshaft third gear wheel assembly. (Includes BK91 Bush)	1	1	1	1	1	1	1	1	1
33	BK91	Layshaft third gear wheel bush. (Included in BK89AS assembly)	1	1	1	1	1	1	1	1	1
34	BK77	Layshaft sliding dog	1	1	1	1	1	1	1	1	1
35	BK11/2	Layshaft	1	1	1	1	1	1	1	1	1
36	BK88AS	Layshaft second gear wheel assembly. (Includes BK91 Bush)	1	1	1	1	1	1	1	1	1
37	BK91	Layshaft second gear wheel bush. (Included in BK88AS assembly)	1	1	1	1	1	1	1	1	1
38	BK86	Layshaft driving gear, 28T ratio	1	—	1	—	1	—	1	—	1
38	BK86/2	Layshaft driving gear, 27T ratio	—	1	—	1	—	1	—	1	—
39	B22/2	Gearbox housing ball bearing (for layshaft)	1	1	1	1	1	1	1	1	1
40	B23	Gearbox end cover ball bearing	1	1	1	1	1	1	1	1	1
41	MAS122	Gearshaft first gear wheel assembly. (Includes Bush BK75/5)	2	2	2	2	2	2	2	2	2
42	BK75/5	Gearshaft first gear wheel bush. (Included in MAS122 assembly)	2	2	2	2	2	2	2	2	2
43	BK78	Gearshaft sliding gear	1	1	1	1	1	1	1	1	1
44	BK8/2AS	Sleeve gear assembly, 16T ratio	1	1	1	1	1	1	1	1	1
44	BK8/3AS	Sleeve gear assembly, 17T ratio	—	—	—	—	—	—	—	—	—
		These two assemblies included BK7/2 Bush and B101 Peg.									
45	BK7/2	Sleeve gear bush	1	1	1	1	1	1	1	1	1
46	B101	Sleeve gear peg	1	1	1	1	1	1	1	1	1
47	BK33	Sleeve gear oil thrower	1	1	1	1	1	1	1	1	1

Gearbox and Clutch Section—continued

See Illustration "D" page Twenty

Note—Quote Part Numbers when ordering. NOT Illustration References. Always quote complete engine number and letters. Before ordering also see respective sections on pages 56 to 74 inclusive

Shafts, Gears, Clutch Plate and Bearing Group—continued

Illus. Ref.	Part No.	Description	A	B	C	D	E	F	G	H	J
48	B31/2	Gearbox housing oil retaining shim	2	2	2	2	2	2	2	2	2
49	B22	Gearbox housing ball bearing	1	1	1	1	1	1	1	1	1
50	B39/26	Gearbox bearing retaining ring	1	1	1	1	1	1	1	1	1
51	B35/3	Sleeve gear distance piece	1	1	1	1	1	1	1	1	1
52	C29/26	Clutch operating thrust cup	1	1	1	1	1	1	1	1	1
53	C28	Clutch spherical thrust ring	1	1	1	1	1	1	1	1	1
54	MAS57	Clutch thrust bearing assembly	1	1	1	1	1	1	1	1	1
55	C7/26	Clutch thrust ring	1	1	1	1	1	1	1	1	1
56	KC1/2	Clutch back plate	3	3	3	3	3	3	3	3	3
57	C6/3	Clutch back plate thrust pin	3	3	3	3	3	3	3	3	3
58	MAS106	Clutch plate assembly. (Includes C25/2 insert—22 off)	3	3	3	3	3	3	3	3	3
59	C25/2	Clutch plate insert. (Included in MAS106 and MAS105 assemblies)	88	88	88	88	88	88	88	88	88
60	C24/2	Clutch spacing plate	3	3	3	3	3	3	3	3	3
61	MAS105	Clutch chain wheel assembly. (Includes C25/2 insert—22 off)	1	1	1	1	1	1	1	1	1
62	C26AS	Clutch ballrace assembly	1	1	1	1	1	1	1	1	1
63	KC2/25	Clutch front plate	1	1	1	1	1	1	1	1	1
64	B34	Sleeve gear locking plate screw, $\frac{1}{8}''$ Whit. c/s head	2	2	2	2	2	2	2	2	2
65	C32/2	Sleeve gear nut locking plate	16	16	16	16	16	16	16	20	16
66	C5/2	Sleeve gear nut	1	1	1	1	1	1	1	–	1
67	C8	Sleeve gear shim	–	–	–	–	–	–	–	–	–
68	C12/4	Clutch spring	2	2	2	2	2	2	2	–	2
69	KC40/2AS	Clutch spring holder assembly	1	1	1	1	1	1	1	1	1
70	BK106	Gearshaft nut (sprocket end) $\frac{1}{2}'' \times 20$ T.P.I. Nylock	1	1	1	1	1	1	1	1	1
Not shown	(SL56/21)	Gearshaft nut. (Sprocket end), $\frac{1}{2}''$ 20 T.P.I.	1	1	1	1	1	1	1	–	1
71	BK106/2	Gearshaft nut. (Sprocket end), $\frac{1}{2}''$ B.S.F. Nylock	1	1	1	1	1	1	1	1	1
73	SL6/65	Gearshaft washer, $\frac{1}{2}'' \times 1\frac{1}{8}''$ O/D	1	1	1	1	1	1	1	1	1
73	SL94/1	Gearbox sprocket 21 teeth $\frac{1}{2}''$ pitch	–	–	–	–	–	–	–	–	–
73	SL95/5	Gearbox sprocket 18 teeth .625 pitch	1	1	1	1	1	1	1	–	1
73	SL95/7	Gearbox sprocket 20 teeth .625 pitch	–	–	–	–	–	–	–	–	–
74	BK5/6	Gearshaft, $\frac{1}{2}''$ B.S.F. threads	1	1	1	1	1	1	1	1	1
75	BK106	Gearshaft nut (Cover end), $\frac{1}{2}'' \times 20$ T.P.I. Nylock	1	1	1	1	1	1	1	–	1
Not shown	(SL56/21)	Gearshaft nut (cover end), $\frac{1}{2}''$ 20 T.P.I.	2	2	2	2	2	2	2	–	2
Not shown	BK106/2	Gearshaft nut. (Cover end), $\frac{1}{2}''$ B.S.F. Nylock	1	1	1	1	1	1	1	1	1

23

Gearbox and Clutch Section—*continued*   **See Illustration "D" page Twenty**

Note—Quote Part Numbers when ordering   NOT Illustration References

Always quote complete engine number and letters
Before ordering also see respective sections on pages 56 to 74 inclusive

Illus. Ref.	Part No.	Description	A	B	C	D	E	F	G	H	J
Selector Fork and Centralising Mechanism Group											
76	BK90/2	Selector fork rod	2	2	2	2	2	2	2	2	2
77	MAS43	Selector fork assembly. (Includes BK32 Selector fork pin)	2	2	2	2	2	2	2	2	2
78	BK32	Selector fork pin	2	2	2	2	2	2	2	2	2
79	BK100/3	Centralising lever pivot	1	1	1	1	1	1	1	1	1
80	BK101/2	Centralising lever spring	1	1	1	1	1	1	1	1	1
81	BK102	Centralising lever pivot sleeve	1	1	1	1	1	1	1	1	1
82	SL56/17	Centralising lever pivot lock nut, $\frac{3}{8}'' \times 26$ T.P.I., $\frac{1}{4}''$ thick	1	1	1	1	1	1	1	1	1
83	BK103	Centralising lever pivot shim	*as required*								
84	LE369	Centralising lever pivot lock washer, $\frac{3}{8}''$	1	1	1	1	1	1	1	1	1
85	SL56/8	Centralising lever pivot nut, $\frac{3}{8}''$ 26 P.T.I.	1	1	1	1	1	1	1	1	1
86	BK99/2	Centralising lever	1	1	1	1	1	1	1	1	1

ILLUSTRATION E

FOR PART NUMBERS AND DESCRIPTION OF ITEMS
{ 1 to 26 see page 26
27 to 53 ,, ,, 27
54 to 82 ,, ,, 28
83 to 10 ,, ,, 29 }

ORDER BY PART NUMBERS—DO NOT QUOTE ILLUSTRATION REFERENCES

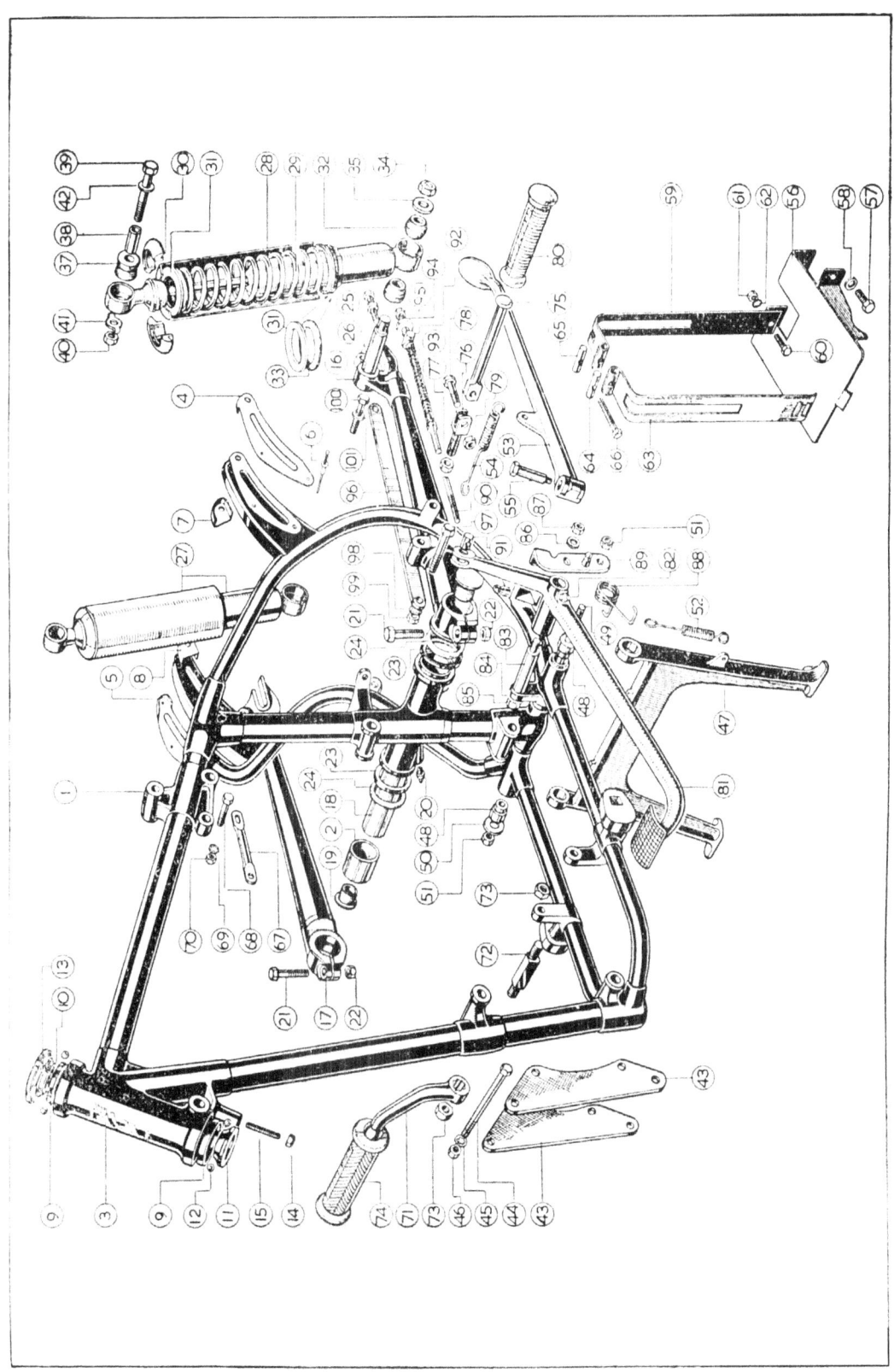

Is the Forwarding Address on your Order quite clear ?

FRAME SECTION   See Illustration "E" page Twenty-five
Main Frame, Torque Tube, Trunnion Bearing, Head Bearing and Chain Adjuster Group

Note—Quote Part Numbers when ordering   NOT Illustration References
Always quote complete engine number and letters
Before ordering also see respective sections on pages 56 to 74 inclusive

Illus. Ref.	Part No.	Description	A	B	C	D	E	F	G	H	J
1	MAS31/2	Frame assembly (L.H. sidecar), top dualseat fixing ⎫	2	2	2	2	2	2	2	2	2
	MAS31/7	Frame assembly (L.H. sidecar), bottom dualseat fixing ⎬ up to 1961	1	1	1	1	1	1	1	1	1
	MAS31/3	Frame assembly (R.H. sidecar), top dualseat fixing ⎪	1	1	1	1	1	1	1	1	1
	MAS31/8	Frame assembly (R.H. sidecar), bottom dualseat fixing ⎭	4	4	4	4	4	4	4	4	4
2	FA3/5	* Trunnion shaft bush	1	1	1	1	1	1	1	1	1
3	A133	** Steering head transfer	2	2	2	2	2	2	2	2	2
4	FA104	** Rear suspension bracket end cap—Outer left hand-	1	1	1	1	1	1	1	1	1
5	FA105	** Rear suspension bracket end cap—Outer right-hand	1	1	1	1	1	1	1	1	1
6	LE380/4	* Rear suspension bracket end cap rivet	38	38	38	38	38	38	38	38	38
7	FA106	Rear suspension bracket end cap—Inner left-hand	1	1	1	1	1	1	1	1	1
8	FA107	Rear suspension bracket end cap—Inner right-hand	1	1	1	1	1	1	1	1	1
9	LE532	* Steering head cup	2	2	2	2	2	2	2	2	2
10	F32/3	Steering head cone—top	1	1	1	1	1	1	1	1	1
11	F32/4	Steering head cone—bottom	1	1	1	1	1	1	1	1	1
12	K100	Steering head ball $\frac{1}{4}"$	38	38	38	38	38	38	38	38	38
13	F165	Steering head dust cap	1	1	1	1	1	1	1	1	1
14	SL56/6	Steering damper stud nut, $\frac{5}{16}"$ 26 T.P.I.	1	1	1	1	1	1	1	1	1
15	FK239	Steering damper stud	1	1	1	1	1	1	1	1	1
16	MAS35	Torque tube assembly—left-hand	1	1	1	1	1	1	1	1	1
17	MAS36	Torque tube assembly—right-hand	1	1	1	1	1	1	1	1	1
18	FA1/3	Trunnion shaft	1	1	1	1	1	1	1	1	1
19	F302	Trunnion shaft end plug	2	2	2	2	2	2	2	2	2
20	KA46	Trunnion shaft lug grease nipple. Screw-in type ⎱	2	2	2	2	2	2	2	2	2
	KA46/3	Trunnion shaft lug grease nipple. Drive-in type ⎰	2	2	2	2	2	2	2	2	2
21	SL111/1	Trunnion lug clamp bolt, $\frac{7}{16}"$ B.S.F. × $1\frac{3}{8}"$	2	2	2	2	2	2	2	2	2
22	SL56/27	Trunnion lug clamp bolt nut, $\frac{7}{16}"$ B.S.F.	2	2	2	2	2	2	2	2	2
23	F300	Trunnion lug felt washer housing	2	2	2	2	2	2	2	2	2
	F301	Trunnion lug felt washer	2	2	2	2	2	2	2	2	2
25	FA47	Rear chain adjuster	2	2	2	2	2	2	2	2	2
26	SL56/4	Rear chain adjuster locknut, $\frac{1}{4}"$ B.S.F.	2	2	2	2	2	2	2	2	2

* Included in assemblies Nos. MAS31/2, MAS31/3, MAS31/7 and MAS31/8

Frame Section—continued   See Illustration "E" page Twenty-five

Note—Quote Part Numbers when ordering.   NOT Illustration References
Always quote complete engine number and letters
Before ordering also see respective sections on pages 56 to 74 inclusive

Illus. Ref.	Part No.	Description	A	B	C	D	E	F	G	H	J
Rear Suspension Unit and Mounting Group											
27	MAS33/2	Rear suspension unit. Woodhead Monroe. Obsolete	2	2	2	2	—	—	—	—	—
Not shown	MAS33/4	Rear suspension unit. Woodhead Monroe. Replaces MAS33/2	2	2	2	2	2	2	—	—	2
Not shown	MAS33/6	Rear suspension unit. Girling	2	2	2	2	2	2	—	—	2
28	A314/3	Rear suspension unit dust cover. Woodhead Monroe	2	2	2	2	2	2	—	—	2
29	A315	Rear suspension unit spring. Woodhead Monroe	2	2	2	2	2	2	—	—	2
30	A323	Rear suspension unit dust cover retainer. Woodhead Monroe	4	4	4	4	4	4	—	—	4
31	A320	Rear suspension unit dust cover washer. Woodhead Monroe	4	4	4	4	4	4	—	—	4
32	A316	Rear suspension unit grommet. Woodhead Monroe	4	4	4	4	4	4	—	—	4
33	A319	Rear suspension unit felt washer. Woodhead Monroe	4	4	4	4	4	4	4	4	4
34	SL56/27	Rear suspension pivot pin nut $\frac{7}{16}$" B.S.F.	2	2	2	2	2	2	2	2	2
35	SL6/60	Rear suspension pivot pin washer $\frac{7}{16}$"	2	2	2	2	2	2	2	2	2
37	F295	Rear suspension unit fixing sleeve	2	2	2	2	2	2	2	2	2
38	F296	Rear suspension unit fixing distance piece	2	2	2	2	2	2	2	2	2
39	SL110/3	Rear suspension unit fixing bolt, $\frac{3}{8}$" B.S.F. $\times 1\frac{5}{8}$"	2	2	2	2	2	2	2	2	2
40	SL56/7	Rear suspension unit fixing bolt $\frac{3}{8}$"	2	2	2	2	2	2	2	2	2
41	F297	Rear suspension unit fixing bolt tab washer	2	2	2	2	2	2	2	2	2
42	SL6/50	Rear suspension unit fixing bolt washer $\frac{3}{8}$	2	2	2	2	2	2	2	2	2
Front Engine Plate, Stand and Battery Mounting Group											
43	FK26/11	Front engine plate	2	2	2	2	2	2	2	2	2
44	SL11/2	Front engine plate bolt, $\frac{3}{8}$" 26 T.P.I., $3\frac{7}{8}$"	4	4	4	4	4	4	3	4	4
45	LE369	Front engine plate bolt lockwasher $\frac{3}{8}$"	4	4	4	4	4	4	4	4	4
46	SL56/8	Front engine plate bolt nut, $\frac{3}{8}$" 26 T.P.I.	4	4	4	4	4	4	4	4	4
47	F293	Centre stand	1	1	1	1	1	1	—	1	1
48	F292	Centre stand pivot	2	2	2	—	—	—	2	—	2
49	SL31/17	Centre stand stud, $\frac{5}{16}$" B.S.F. $\times 10\frac{1}{8}$" long	1	1	1	1	1	1	1	1	1
50	SL6/39	Centre stand stud washer, $\frac{5}{16}$" $\times$ 1" O/D	1	1	1	1	1	1	1	1	1
51	SL56/38	Centre stand stud nut, $\frac{5}{16}$" B.S.F.	2	2	2	2	2	2	2	2	2
52	F69/5	Centre stand spring	1	1	1	1	1	1	—	—	1
53	FK29/11	Prop. stand	1	1	1	1	1	1	1	1	1

Frame Section—continued   See Illustration "E" page Twenty-five

Note—Quote Part Numbers when ordering. NOT Illustration References
Always quote complete engine number and letters
Before ordering also see respective sections on pages 56 to 74 inclusive

Illus. Ref.	Part No.	Description	A	B	C	D	E	F	G	H	J
Front Engine Plate, Stand and Battery Mounting Group—continued										
54	F69/5	Prop. stand spring	1	1	1	1	1	1	—	1	1
55	F4/10	Prop. stand pivot pin	1	1	1	1	1	1	—	1	1
56	E8/8	Battery platform	1	1	1	1	1	1	—	1	1
57	SL9/3	Battery platform bolt, $\frac{5}{16}''$ T.P.I. $\times \frac{1}{2}''$	3	3	3	3	3	3	—	3	3
58	SL6/40	Battery platform bolt washer $\frac{5}{16}''$	3	3	3	3	3	3	—	3	3
59	E9/6	Battery strap—rear	1	1	1	1	1	1	—	1	1
60	SL8/3	Battery strap bolt, $\frac{1}{4}''$ B.S.F. $\times \frac{9}{16}''$	1	1	1	1	1	1	—	1	1
61	SL56/4	Battery strap bolt nut, $\frac{1}{4}''$ B.S.F.	1	1	1	1	1	1	—	1	1
62	LE367	Battery strap bolt lockwasher, $\frac{1}{4}''$	1	1	1	1	1	1	—	1	1
63	E9/5	Battery strap front	1	1	1	1	1	1	—	1	1
64	E51	Battery strap trunnion—plain hole	1	1	1	1	1	1	—	—	—
65	E51/2	Battery strap trunnion—threaded hole	1	1	1	1	1	1	—	—	—
66	E53	Battery strap clamp bolt, 2BA	1	1	1	1	1	1	—	1	1
Engine Steady, Footrest, Brake Pedal, Brake Rod and Torque Arm Group										
67	FK75/14	Engine steady	1	1	1	1	1	1	—	1	1
68	SL109/3	Engine steady bolt, $\frac{5}{16}''$ B.S.F. $\times 1\frac{3}{16}''$	2	2	2	2	2	2	—	2	2
69	LE368	Engine steady bolt lockwasher, $\frac{5}{16}''$	2	2	2	2	2	2	—	2	2
70	SL56/38	Engine steady bolt nut, $\frac{5}{16}''$ B.S.F.	2	2	2	2	2	2	—	2	2
71	F126/6	Footrest hanger	2	2	2	2	2	2	—	2	2
72	FK23/14	Footrest rod	4	4	4	4	4	4	—	4	4
73	SL56/27	Footrest nut, $\frac{7}{16}''$ B.S.F.	2	2	2	2	2	2	—	2	2
74	KA76/2	Footrest rubber	2	2	2	2	2	2	—	2	2
75	BK18	Pillion footrest footpiece	2	2	2	2	2	2	—	2	2
76	F298	Pillion footrest eyebolt	2	2	2	2	2	2	—	2	2
77	SL56/27	Pillion footrest eye bolt nut, $\frac{7}{16}''$ B.S.F.	2	2	2	2	2	2	—	2	2
78	SL110/2	Pillion footrest bolt (Pivot) $\frac{3}{8}''$ B.S.F. $\times 1\frac{1}{4}''$	2	2	2	2	2	2	—	2	2
79	SL56/7	Pillion footrest bolt nut, $\frac{3}{8}''$ B.S.F.	2	2	2	2	2	2	—	2	2
80	B60/5	Pillion footrest rubber	2	2	2	2	2	2	—	2	2
81	F39/11	Brake pedal	1	1	1	1	1	1	1	1	1
82	{KA46	Brake pedal grease nipple. Screw-in type	1	1	1	1	1	1	1	1	1
	{KA46/3	Brake pedal grease nipple. Drive-in type	1	1	1	1	1	1	1	1	1

Frame Section—continued   See Illustration "E" page Twenty-five

Note—Quote Part Numbers when ordering   NOT Illustration References
Always quote complete engine number and letters
Before ordering also see respective sections on pages 56 to 74 inclusive

Engine Steady, Footrest, Brake Pedal, Brake Rod and Torque Arm Group—continued

Illus. Ref.	Part No.	Description	A	B	C	D	E	F	G	H	J
83	F130/14	Brake pedal support	1	1	1	1	1	1	1	1	1
84	SL6/57	Brake pedal support washer $\frac{7}{16}$"	1	1	1	1	1	1	1	1	1
85	SL56/27	Brake pedal support nut $\frac{7}{16}$" B.S.F.—Inner	1	1	1	1	1	1	1	1	1
86	SL6/40	Brake pedal support washer $\frac{5}{16}$"—Outer	1	1	1	1	1	1	1	1	1
87	SL56/38	Brake pedal support nut $\frac{5}{16}$" B.S.F.—Outer	1	1	1	1	1	1	1	1	1
88	F233/5	Brake pedal return spring	1	1	1	1	1	1	1	1	1
89	MAS38	Brake pedal stop	1	1	1	1	1	1	1	1	1
90	MAS41	Rear brake rod assembly	1	1	1	1	1	1	1	1	1
91	FK43	Rear brake rod trunnion—threaded hole	1	1	1	1	1	1	1	1	1
92	FK43/2	Rear brake rod trunnion—plain hole	1	1	1	1	1	1	1	1	1
93	KS43/2	Rear brake rod spring	1	1	1	1	1	1	1	1	1
94	KS44	Rear brake rod adjusting nut	1	1	1	1	1	1	1	1	1
95	SL56/4	Rear brake rod locknut $\frac{1}{4}$" B.S.F.	1	1	1	1	1	1	1	1	1
96	S55/3	Rear brake torque stay	1	1	1	1	1	1	1	1	1
97	SL110/3	Rear brake torque stay bolt—front $\frac{3}{8}$" B.S.F. × $1\frac{5}{8}$'''	1	1	1	1	1	1	1	1	1
98	LE369	Rear brake torque stay lockwasher $\frac{3}{8}$"	1	1	1	1	1	1	1	1	1
99	SL56/7	Rear brake torque stay nut $\frac{3}{8}$" B.S.F.	1	1	1	1	1	1	1	1	1
100	SL110/2	Rear brake torque stay bolt—rear $\frac{3}{8}$" B.S.F. × $1\frac{1}{4}$"	1	1	1	1	1	1	1	1	1
101	SL6/50	Rear brake torque stay bolt washer $\frac{3}{8}$"	1	1	1	1	1	1	1	1	1
Not shown	KA326	Fairing—Left-hand	1	1	1	—	—	—	—	—	—
Not shown	MAS147	Fairing assembly—Right-hand	1	1	1	—	—	—	—	—	—
Not shown	FK260	Fairing mounting pillar. Driving side	1	1	1	—	—	—	—	—	—
Not shown	FK261	Fairing mounting pillar. Timing side	1	1	1	—	—	—	—	—	—
Not shown	MAS141	Battery strap assembly	1	1	1	—	—	—	—	—	—
Not shown	MAS146	Fairing attachment strap assembly	2	2	2	—	—	—	—	—	—
Not shown	FK262	Fairing mounting pin	6	6	6	—	—	—	—	—	—

ILLUSTRATION F

FOR PART NUMBERS AND DESCRIPTION OF ITEMS { 1 to 22 see page 31
23 to 50 " " 32
51 to 63 " " 33 }

ORDER BY PART NUMBERS—DO NOT QUOTE ILLUSTRATION REFERENCES

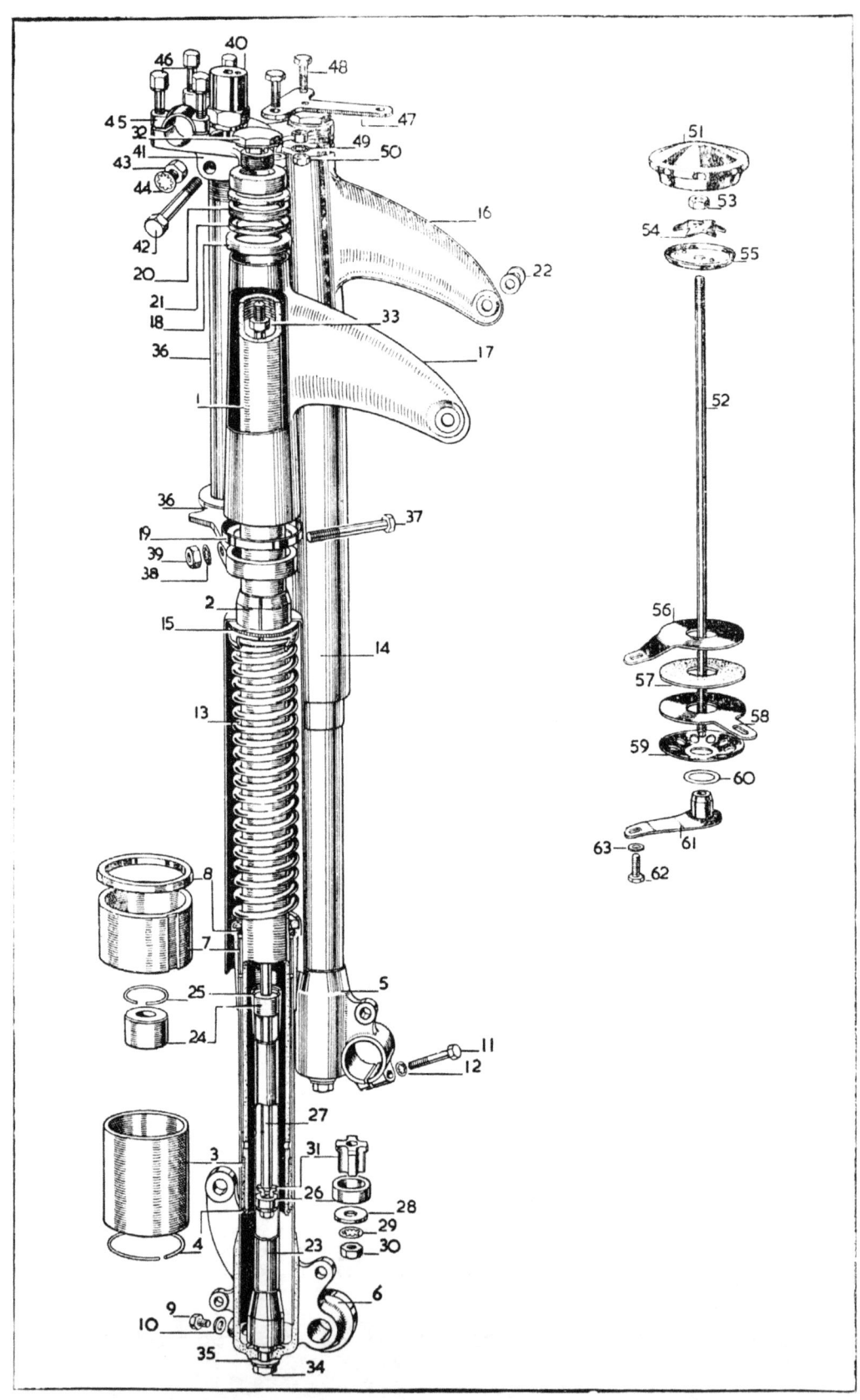

Have you quoted the Engine Number and Prefix Letters of your Order?

FRONT FORK SECTION   See Illustration "F" page Thirty

Note—Quote Part Numbers when ordering   NOT Illustration References

Always quote complete engine number and letters
Before ordering also see respective sections on pages 56 to 74 inclusive

Fork, Tube, Slider, Spring and Lamp Bracket Group

Illus. Ref.	Part No.	Description	A	B	C	D	E	F	G	H	J
1	F246	Front fork tube	2	2	2	2	2	–	2	2	2
2	F262	Front fork tube sleeve	2	2	2	2	2	2	2	2	2
3	LE216	Front fork tube bush	2	2	2	2	2	2	2	2	2
4	LE191	Front fork tube circlip	2	2	2	2	2	2	2	2	2
5	MAS3	Fork slider tube assembly. Left-hand	1	1	1	1	1	1	1	1	1
6	MAS4	Fork slider tube assembly. Right-hand	1	1	1	1	1	1	1	1	1
7	LE215	Fork slider tube bush	2	2	2	2	2	2	2	2	2
8	LE335/2	Fork slider tube oil seal	2	2	2	2	2	2	2	2	2
9	SL8/1	Fork oil drain bolt. $\tfrac{1}{4}''$ B.S.F.× $\tfrac{3}{8}''$	2	2	2	2	2	2	2	2	2
10	A37/5	Fork oil drain bolt gasket	2	2	2	2	2	2	2	2	2
11	SL109/3	Front wheel spindle clamp bolt. $\tfrac{5}{16}''$ B.S.F.× $1\tfrac{3}{16}''$	1	1	1	1	1	1	1	1	1
12	LE368	Front wheel spindle clamp bolt lockwasher	1	1	1	1	1	1	1	1	1
13	F252	Front fork spring. Solo type	2	2	2	–	2	–	2	–	2
13	F252/2	Front fork spring. Sidecar type. Alternative to special order	–	–	–	2	–	2	–	2	–
14	F245	Front fork spring dust cover	2	2	2	2	2	2	2	2	2
15	F282	Front fork dust cover washer—Rubber	2	2	2	2	2	2	2	2	2
16	MAS8	Headlamp bracket assembly. Left-hand	1	1	1	1	1	1	1	–	–
16	MAS8/2	‡ Headlamp cowl bracket. Left-hand side	–	–	–	–	–	–	–	1	1
17	MAS9	Headlamp bracket assembly. Right-hand	1	1	1	1	1	1	1	–	–
17	MAS9/2	‡ Headlamp cowl bracket. Right-hand side	–	–	–	–	–	–	–	1	1
Not shown	MAS134	‡ Headlamp cowl	1	1	1	1	1	1	1	–	–
Not shown 18	LE598/4	‡ Headlamp cowl beading	1	1	1	1	1	1	1	–	–
19	F271	Headlamp bracket locating cup—Top	2	2	2	2	2	2	2	2	2
20	F257	Headlamp bracket locating cup—Bottom	2	2	2	2	2	2	2	2	2
21	F278	Headlamp bracket rubber buffer	4	4	4	4	4	4	4	4	4
22	F274	Headlamp bracket rubber buffer housing	2	–	–	–	–	–	–	–	–
		Headlamp washer. Licence holder fixing									

‡ Used on MSS from Engine MSS12239 onwards

Front Fork Section—continued See Illustration "F" page Thirty

Note—Quote Part Numbers when ordering NOT Illustration References
Always quote complete engine number and letters
Before ordering also see respective sections on pages 56 to 74 inclusive

Illus. Ref.	Part No.	Description	A	B	C	D	E	F	G	H	J
Fork Damper Assembly Group											
23	MAS5	*Fork damper tube assembly	2	2	2	2	—	—	—	—	2
24	F260	Fork damper bush	2	2	2	2	2	2	2	2	2
25	F267	Fork damper bush circlip	2	2	2	2	2	2	2	2	2
26	F265	Fork damper piston	2	2	2	2	2	2	2	2	2
27	F259	*Fork damper piston rod	2	2	2	2	—	—	—	—	2
28	F266	*Fork damper piston rod washer	2	2	2	2	—	—	—	—	2
29	LE366	Fork damper piston rod lockwasher 3/16"	2	2	2	2	2	2	2	2	2
30	SL56/2	Fork damper piston rod nut. 2BA	2	2	2	2	2	2	2	2	2
31	F251	*Fork damper valve	2	2	2	2	—	—	—	—	2
32	F253	Fork damper piston rod adaptor	2	2	2	2	2	2	2	2	2
33	SL56/38	Fork damper piston rod locknut, 5/16" B.S.F.	2	2	2	2	2	2	2	2	2
34	SL56/7	Fork damper tube adaptor nut, 3/8" B.S.F.	2	2	2	2	2	2	2	2	2
35	SL6/50	Fork damper tube adaptor washer, 3/8"	2	2	2	2	2	2	2	2	2
		*Used also on Clubman and Thruxton Models from 1967 onwards									
Cross Member, Column and Speedometer Bracket Group											
36	MAS7/2	Steering column assembly	1	1	1	1	1	1	1	1	1
37	SL109/6	Fork cross member clamp bolt, 5/16" B.S.F.×1 3/32"	2	2	2	2	2	2	2	2	2
38	LE368	Fork cross member lockwasher	2	2	2	2	2	2	2	2	2
39	SL56/38	Fork cross member nut, 5/16" B.S.F.	2	2	2	2	2	2	2	2	2
40	F270/2	Steering head locknut. For steering damper if fitted	1	1	1	1	1	1	1	1	1
	MAS6	Steering head locknut assembly. Used when no steering damper is fitted	1	1	1	1	1	1	1	1	1
41	F249/2	Fork cross member—top	1	1	1	1	1	1	1	1	1
42	SL110/8	Fork cross member clamp bolt 3/8" B.S.F.×1 29/32"	2	2	2	2	2	2	2	2	2
43	SL56/7	Fork cross member nut 3/8" B.S.F.	2	2	2	2	2	2	2	2	2
44	LE369	Fork cross member lockwasher 3/8"	2	2	2	2	2	2	2	2	2
45	F268	Handlebar clip	2	2	2	2	2	2	2	2	2
46	F269	Handlebar clip bolt	4	4	4	4	4	4	4	4	4
47	KA269/3	Speedometer bracket	1	1	1	1	1	1	1	1	1
48	SL109/2	Speedometer bracket or headlamp cowl bolt 5/16" B.S.F.×7/8"	2	2	2	2	2	2	2	2	2
49	LE368	Speedometer bracket or headlamp cowl bolt lockwasher 5/16"	2	2	2	2	2	2	2	2	2
50	SL56/38	Speedometer bracket or headlamp cowl bolt nut 5/16"	2	2	2	2	2	2	2	2	2
Not shown	SL6/40	Headlamp cowl fixing bolt washer, 5/16"	2	2	2	2	2	—	—	—	2

Front Fork Section—*continued* See Illustration "F" page Thirty

Note—Quote Part Numbers when ordering   NOT Illustration References

Always quote complete engine number and letters
Before ordering also see respective sections on pages 56 to 74 inclusive

Illus. Ref.	Part No.	Description	A	B	C	D	E	F	G	H	J
Steering Damper Group—*(if fitted)*											
51	MAS159	Steering damper wing nut	1	1	1	1	1	1	1	—	—
52	F263	Steering damper rod	1	1	1	1	1	1	1	—	—
53	SL56/6	Steering damper rod locknut $\frac{5}{16}$" 26T	1	1	1	1	1	1	1	—	—
54	FK248	Steering damper star spring	1	1	1	1	1	1	1	—	—
55	FK247	Steering damper location plate	1	1	1	1	1	1	1	—	—
56	FK243	Steering damper backplate	1	1	1	1	1	1	1	1	1
57	FK249	Steering damper friction disc	1	1	1	1	1	1	1	1	1
58	FK242	Steering damper plate	1	1	1	1	1	1	1	1	1
59	FK246	Steering damper pressure disc	1	1	1	1	1	1	1	1	1
60	FK244	Steering damper washer	1	1	1	1	1	1	1	1	1
61	MAS39	Steering damper sleeve assembly	1	1	1	1	1	1	1	1	1
62	SL8/3	Steering damper bolt, $\frac{1}{4}$" B.S.F. $\times \frac{7}{16}$"	1	1	1	1	1	1	1	1	1
63	SL6/32	Steering damper bolt washer $\frac{1}{4}$"	1	1	1	1	1	1	1	1	1

ILLUSTRATION G

FOR PART NUMBERS AND DESCRIPTION OF ITEMS { 1 to 20 see page 35
21 to 32 " " 36 }

ORDER BY PART NUMBERS—DO NOT QUOTE ILLUSTRATION REFERENCES

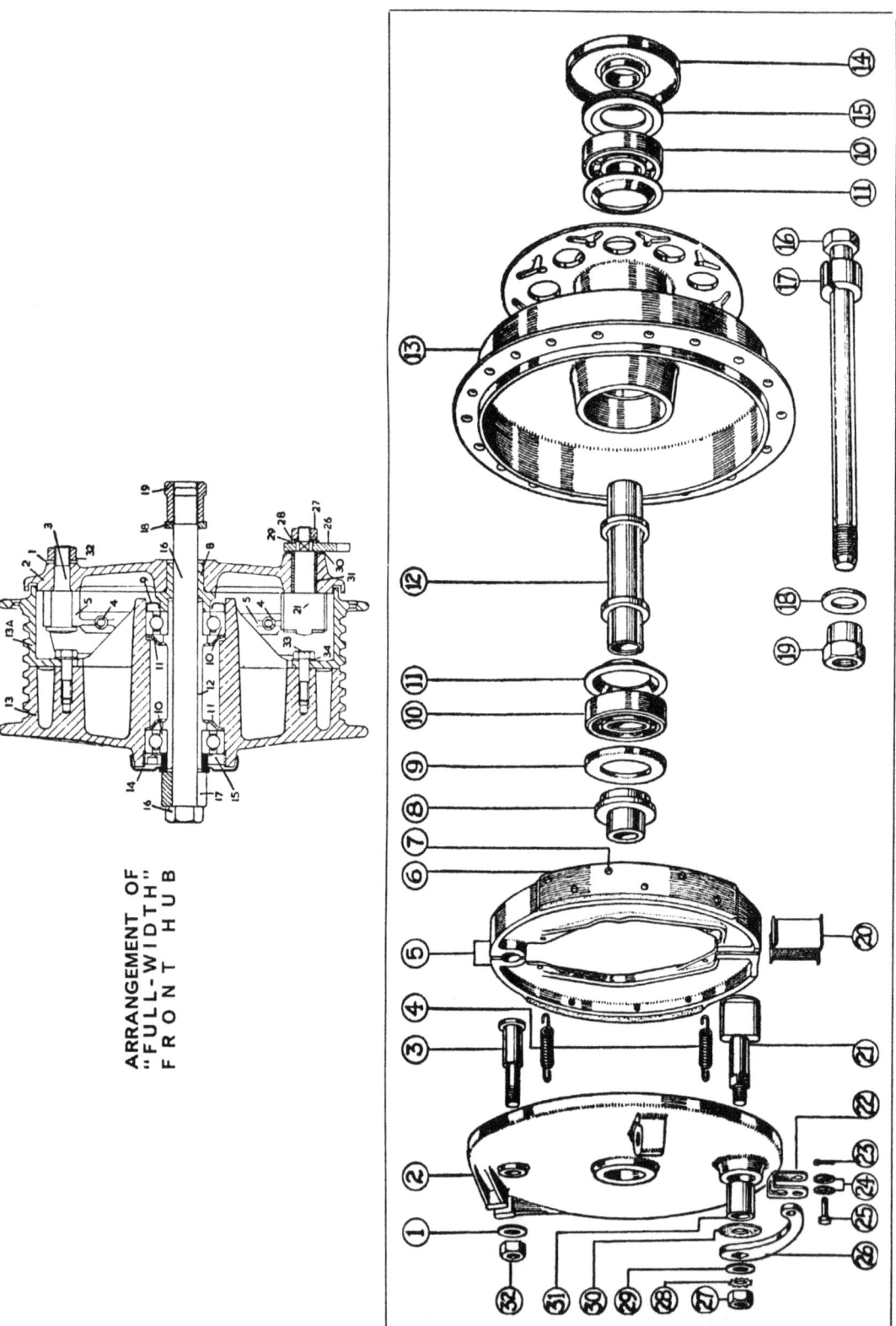

ARRANGEMENT OF "FULL-WIDTH" FRONT HUB

FRONT WHEEL AND BRAKE SECTION   See Illustration "G" page Thirty-four

Note—Quote Part Numbers when ordering   NOT Illustration References
Always quote complete engine number and letters
Before ordering also see respective sections on pages 56 to 74 inclusive

Illus. Ref.	Part No.		Description	A	B	C	D	E	F	G	H	J
1	SL6/50	‡	Front brake shoe fulcrum pin washer 3/8"	1	1	1	1	1	1	1	1	1
2	MAS72		Front brake plate assembly. (Includes W71 bush)	—	—	—	—	—	—	—	—	—
	MAS72/2		Front brake plate assembly. (Includes W71 bush)	1	1	1	1	1	1	1	1	1
3	W10/4	‡	Front brake shoe fulcrum pin	1	1	1	1	1	1	1	1	1
4	S27/2		Brake shoe spring	2	2	2	2	2	2	2	2	2
5	MAS74/75		Brake shoe assembly. Left and right-hand. Includes lining and rivets. Pair	1	1	1	1	1	1	1	1	1
	MAS74/2/75/2		Brake shoe assembly. Left and right-hand. Includes lining and rivets. Pair	—	—	—	—	—	—	—	—	—
6	KS19/2		Brake shoe lining. (Included in assemblies MAS74 and MAS 75)	2	2	2	2	2	2	2	2	2
	KS19/5		Brake shoe lining. (Included in MAS72/2/75/2)	—	—	—	—	—	—	—	—	—
7	KS31		Brake shoe lining rivet. (Included in assemblies MAS74 and MAS 75)	12	14	14	14	12	14	12	—	14
	KS31		Brake shoe lining rivet. (Included in MAS74/2/75/2)	—	—	—	—	—	—	—	—	—
8	W52/3	‡	Front brake plate distance piece	1	1	1	1	1	1	1	1	1
9	KS11/4	*	Front hub inner dust cap	2	2	2	2	2	2	2	2	2
10	KS18/3	*	Front hub ball bearing	2	2	2	2	2	2	2	2	2
11	KS57/3	*	Front hub grease retainer	2	2	2	2	2	2	2	2	2
12	W62/2		Front hub hollow spindle	1	1	1	1	1	1	1	1	1
13	MAS70		Front hub shell assembly	—	—	—	—	—	—	—	—	—
13	W1/13		Front hub shell	1	1	1	1	1	1	1	1	1
	W2/4		Front brake drum	1	1	1	1	1	1	1	1	1
Not shown	SL8/14		Front brake drum bolt. Drum to hub. 1/4" B.S.F.×1"	—	6	6	6	—	6	—	6	6
Not shown	LE367		Front brake drum bolt lockwasher 1/4"	—	6	6	6	—	6	—	6	6
14	MAS73	*	Front hub outer dust cover assembly	1	1	1	1	1	1	1	1	1
15	KS61	*	Front hub lockring	1	1	1	1	1	1	1	1	1
16	W21/6		Front wheel spindle	1	1	1	1	1	1	1	1	1
17	W64/2		Front wheel spindle distance piece	1	1	1	1	1	1	1	1	1
18	W51/2		Front wheel spindle washer	1	1	1	1	1	1	1	1	1
19	W65/2		Front wheel spindle nut	1	1	1	1	1	1	1	—	1
20	KS16/2		Brake shoe slipper (Included in assemblies MAS74, MAS75, MAS74/2 and MAS 75/2)	2	2	2	2	2	2	2	2	2

See page 36 under Assemblies Available for key to ‡ and *

Front Wheel and Brake Section—*continued*   See Illustration "G" page Thirty-four

Note—Quote Part Numbers when ordering   NOT Illustration References

Always quote complete engine number and letters

Before ordering also see respective sections on pages 56 to 74 inclusive

Illus. Ref.	Part No.	Description	A	B	C	D	E	F	G	H	J
21	MAS76	‡ Front brake cam assembly	1	1	1	1	1	1	1	1	1
22	FB54	‡ Front brake cable shackle	1	1	1	1	1	1	1	1	1
23	SL71/2	‡ Clevis pin split cotter, $\frac{1}{16}'' \times \frac{1}{2}''$	2	2	2	2	2	2	2	2	2
24	FB61	‡ Cable shackle felt washer	1	1	1	1	1	1	1	1	1
25	S32	‡ Cable shackle clevis pin	1	1	1	1	1	1	1	1	1
26	FB11/5	‡ Front brake cam lever	1	1	1	1	1	1	1	1	1
27	SL56/6	‡ Front brake cam nut, $\frac{5}{16}''$ 26 T.P.I.	1	1	1	1	1	1	1	1	1
28	LE368	‡ Front brake cam lock washer, $\frac{5}{16}''$	1	1	1	1	1	1	1	1	1
29	FB60	‡ Front brake cam lever washer	1	1	1	1	1	1	1	1	1
30	W12/2	‡ Front brake cam bush. Included in assembly MAS72 and MAS72/2	1	1	1	1	1	1	1	1	1
31	W71	‡ Front brake cam felt washer	1	1	1	1	1	1	1	1	1
32	SL56/8	‡ Brake shoe fulcrum pin nut	1	1	1	1	1	1	1	1	1

Parts not illustrated—

	Part No.	Description	A	B	C	D	E	F	G	H	J
	A17/8	Front wheel rim. WM2×19". 36 holes	1	–	–	–	–	–	–	–	–
	A17/9	Front wheel rim. WM2×19". 40 holes	–	1	1	–	–	–	–	–	1
	KA18/15	Front wheel spoke. 10 S.W.G. × 6⅝"	18	–	–	–	–	–	–	–	–
	KA18/26	Front wheel spoke. 10 S.W.G. × 7¼"	18	–	–	–	–	–	–	–	–
	KA18/30	Front wheel spoke (long). 8/10 S.W.G. × 6 7/16". Outside flange	–	20	20	–	20	20	–	20	20
	KA18/31	Front wheel spoke (short). 8/10 S.W.G. × 6 5/16". Inside flange	–	20	20	–	20	20	–	20	20
	KA19	Front wheel spoke nipple	36	40	40	36	40	40	–	40	40

Assemblies available—

	Part No.	Description	A	B	C	D	E	F	G	H	J
	MAS69	Front hub assembly. Comprises MAS70 and items marked *	1	–	–	1	–	–	1	–	–
	MAS69/2	Front hub assembly. Comprises W1/13, W2/4, SL8/14, KA18/5, LE367 and items marked *	–	1	1	–	1	1	–	1	1
	MAS67	Front wheel assembly. Comprises MAS69, A17/8, KA18/8, KA18/26 and KA19	1	–	–	–	–	–	–	–	–
	MAS67/3	Front wheel assembly. Comprises MAS69/2, A17/9, KA18/30 and KA19	–	1	1	–	–	–	–	–	1
	MAS71	Brake plate and shoes assembly. Comprises MAS72, MAS 74/75 and items marked ‡	1	1	1	1	1	1	1	1	1
	MAS71/2	Brake plate and shoes assembly. Comprises MAS72/2, MAS74/2/75/2 and items marked ‡	–	1	1	–	1	1	–	1	1

ILLUSTRATION H

FOR PART NUMBERS AND DESCRIPTION OF ITEMS
- 1 to 23 see page 38
- 24 to 37 " " 39
- 38 to 61 " " 40
- 62 to 71 " " 41

ORDER BY PART NUMBERS—DO NOT QUOTE ILLUSTRATION REFERENCES

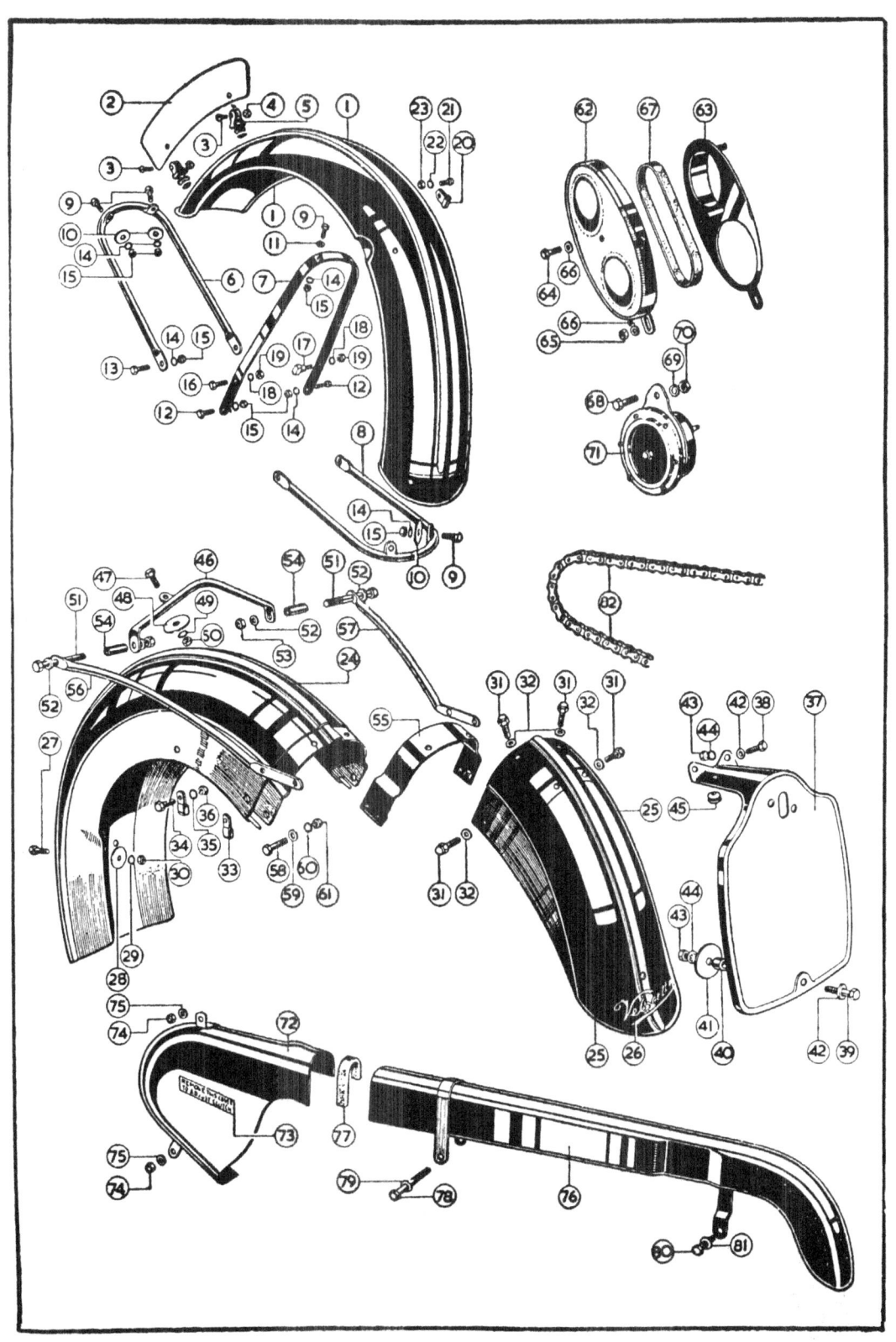

Have you stated Colour of Machine on your Order?

MUDGUARD, DYNAMO DRIVE COVER, CHAIN GUARD, CHAIN AND HORN SECTION

See Illustration "H" page Thirty-seven

Note—Quote Part Numbers when ordering NOT Illustration References
Always quote complete engine number and letters
Before ordering also see respective sections on pages 56 to 74 inclusive

Illus. Ref.	*Part No.*	*Description*	A	B	C	D	E	F	G	H	J
Front	**Mudguard Group**										
1	KA16/9	Front mudguard. Includes A283 (2 *off*)	1	–	–	–	–	–	–	–	–
	KA16/13	Front mudguard	–	1	1	1	–	1	–	–	–
2	A23/4	Front number plate	1	1	1	1	–	1	–	1	–
	MAS137	Front number plate assembly *obsolete.*									
	LE598/3	Front number plate beading *if fitted.*	–	1	1	1	–	1	–	–	–
Not shown	SL56/4	Front number plate fixing nut, $\frac{1}{4}''$ B.S.F.	2	2	2	2	–	2	–	2	–
Not shown	SL6/32	Front number plate fixing washer, $\frac{1}{4}''$	2	2	2	2	–	2	–	2	–
3	SL80/22	Front number plate screw, 2BA $\times \frac{3}{8}''$	2	2	2	2	–	2	–	2	–
4	SL56/2	Front number plate screw nut, 2BA	2	2	2	2	–	2	–	2	–
5	A283	Front number plate clip assembly. (Included in KA16/9)	2	2	2	2	2	2	2	2	2
6	FK157/14AS	Front mudguard stay—front	1	–	–	–	–	–	–	–	–
	FK157/19	Front mudguard stay—front	–	2	2	2	–	2	–	–	–
7	FK157/15	Front mudguard stay—centre	1	1	1	1	–	1	–	–	–
8	FK157/16AS	Front mudguard stay—rear	1	–	–	–	–	–	–	–	–
	FK157/20	Front mudguard stay—rear	–	2	2	2	–	2	–	–	–
9	SL8/3	Front mudguard stay fixing bolt, $\frac{1}{4}''$ B.S.F. $\times \frac{9}{16}''$. (Stays to mudguard)	6	6	6	6	–	6	–	6	–
10	KA145/2	Front mudguard stay strengthening washer	4	4	4	4	–	4	–	2	–
11	SL6/32	Front mudguard stay washer, $\frac{1}{4}''$	2	2	2	2	–	2	–	4	–
12	SL8/14	Front mudguard stay fixing bolt, $\frac{1}{4}''$ B.S.F. $\times 1''$. (Centre and rear stays to fork end)	2	2	2	2	–	2	–	2	–
13	SL8/29	Front mudguard stay fixing bolt, $\frac{1}{4}''$ B.S.F. $\times \frac{3}{4}''$. (Front stay to fork end)	2	2	2	2	–	2	–	1	–
14	LE367	Front mudguard stay lock washer $\frac{1}{4}''$	10	10	10	10	–	10	–	10	–
15	SL56/4	Front mudguard stay nut, $\frac{1}{4}''$ B.S.F.	10	10	10	10	–	10	–	10	–
16	SL9/6	Front mudguard stay fixing bolt, $\frac{5}{16}''$ 26 T.P.I. $\times \frac{13}{16}''$ (Centre stay to fork end)	1	1	1	1	–	1	–	–	–
17	FK50/2	Brake torque bolt. (Centre stay to fork end—Right-hand)	1	1	1	1	1	1	1	1	1
18	LE368	Front mudguard stay lock washer $\frac{5}{16}''$	2	2	2	2	2	2	2	2	2
19	SL56/6	Front mudguard stay nut $\frac{5}{16}''$ 26 T.P.I.	2	2	2	2	2	2	2	2	2
20	LE201/2	Front brake cable clip. Cable assembly to mudguard	1	1	1	1	–	1	–	1	–
21	SL8/26	Front brake cable clip bolt, $\frac{1}{4}''$ B.S.F. $\times \frac{7}{16}''$	1	1	1	1	–	1	–	1	–
22	LE367	Front brake cable clip lock washer $\frac{1}{4}''$	1	1	1	1	–	1	–	1	–
23	SL56/4	Front brake cable clip nut, $\frac{1}{4}''$ B.S.F.	1	1	1	1	–	1	–	1	–

Mudguard, Dynamo Drive Cover, Chain Guard, Chain and Horn Section—*continued* See Illustration "H" page Thirty-seven

Note—Quote Part Numbers when Ordering   NOT Illustration References
Always quote complete engine number and letters
Before ordering also see respective sections on pages 56 to 74 inclusive

Rear Mudguard Section. Mudguard Extension and Number Plate Group

Illus. Ref.	Part No.	Description	A	B	C	D	E	F	G	H	J
24	A15/19	Rear mudguard	1	–	–	–	–	–	–	–	–
	MAS84/5	Rear mudguard assembly	–	1	1	1	1	–	–	–	–
25	MAS85	Rear mudguard extension assembly. Includes A15/12	–	1	1	1	1	–	–	–	–
26	A131	Rear mudguard transfer. Included in A15/12	1	1	1	1	1	–	–	–	–
		These two items may be ordered together as :									
	MAS84/8	Rear mudguard assembly	1	–	–	–	–	–	–	–	–
27	SL8/3	Rear mudguard bolt, $\frac{1}{4}$" B.S.F. × $\frac{9}{16}$". (Guard to seat tube lug)	2	2	2	2	2	–	2	2	–
	SL8/26	Rear mudguard and toolbox fixing bolt. Right-hand side $\frac{1}{4}$" B.S.F. × $\frac{7}{16}$"	1	1	1	1	1	–	1	1	–
28	KA145/2	Rear mudguard bolt washer	2	2	2	2	2	–	2	2	–
29	LE367	Rear mudguard bolt lockwasher $\frac{1}{4}$"	2	2	2	2	2	–	2	2	–
30	SL56/4	Rear mudguard bolt nut $\frac{1}{4}$" B.S.F.	4	–	–	–	–	–	–	–	–
31	KA303	Rear mudguard extension bolt. (Extension to mudguard)	4	2	2	2	2	–	2	2	–
32	SL6/32	Rear mudguard extension bolt washer $\frac{1}{4}$"	4	2	2	2	2	–	2	2	–
33	F306	Rear mudguard clip. Tail lamp cable fixing	1	1	1	1	1	–	1	1	–
34	SL8/26	Rear mudguard clip bolt $\frac{1}{4}$" B.S.F. × $\frac{7}{16}$"	2	1	1	1	1	–	1	1	–
35	LE367	Rear mudguard clip lock washer $\frac{1}{4}$"	1	1	1	1	1	–	1	1	–
36	SL56/4	Rear mudguard clip nut $\frac{1}{4}$" B.S.F.	1	–	–	–	–	–	–	–	–
37	A22/20	Rear number plate. *Obsolete*									
	LE319/2	Rear number plate for use with MAS117/2	1	1	1	1	1	1	1	1	1
Not shown	MAS117/2	Rear number plate bracket assembly	1	1	1	1	1	1	1	1	1
Not shown	SL107/1	Rear number plate bracket and number plate bolt. 2BA × $\frac{27}{64}$"	8	8	8	8	8	8	8	8	–
Not shown	SL56/2	Rear number plate bracket and number plate nut 2BA	8	8	8	8	8	8	8	8	–
Not shown	SL6/25	Rear number plate bracket washer $\frac{3}{16}$"	4	4	4	4	4	4	4	4	–
Not shown	LE366	Rear number plate lockwasher $\frac{3}{16}$"	4	4	4	4	4	4	4	4	–
Not shown	LE598	Rear number plate bracket beading	1	1	1	1	1	1	1	1	–

Rear Mudguard Section, Mudguard, Extension and Number Plate Group—*continued* See Illustration "H" page Thirty-Seven

NOT Illustration References

Note—Quote Part Numbers when ordering
Always quote complete engine number and letters
Before ordering also see respective sections on pages 56 to 74 inclusive

Illus. Ref.	Part No.	Description	A	B	C	D	E	F	G	H	J
Not shown	LAS178	Rear reflector. *Obsolete*	—	—	—	—	—	—	—	—	—
38	SL8/26	Rear number plate bolt—top $\frac{1}{4}"$ B.S.F. $\times \frac{7}{16}"$ For A22/20 only	1	—	4	—	4	—	4	—	4
39	SL8/14	Rear number plate bolt—bottom $\frac{1}{4}"$ B.S.F. $\times 1"$	1	—	—	—	—	—	—	—	—
40	A181	Rear number plate bolt buffer	1	—	4	—	4	—	4	—	4
41	KA145/2	Rear number plate bolt washer $\frac{1}{4}"$	1	—	—	—	—	—	—	—	—
42	SL6/32	Rear number plate bolt washer $\frac{1}{4}"$	3	—	4	—	4	—	4	—	4
43	SL56/4	Rear number plate bolt nut $\frac{1}{4}"$ B.S.F.	3	—	—	—	—	—	—	—	—
44	LE367	Rear number plate bolt lock washer $\frac{1}{4}"$	3	—	—	—	—	—	—	—	—
45	A20	Rear number plate grommet (for Tail lamp cable)	2	2	2	2	2	2	2	2	—

Bridge, Stay and Lifting Handle Group

Illus. Ref.	Part No.	Description	A	B	C	D	E	F	G	H	J
46	MAS60	Rear mudguard stay assembly	1	1	1	1	—	—	—	—	—
47	SL8/3	Rear mudguard stay bolt, $\frac{1}{4}"$ B.S.F. $\times \frac{9}{16}"$ (Sta to guard)	2	2	2	2	—	—	—	—	—
48	KA145/2	Rear mudguard stay washer $\frac{1}{4}"$	2	2	2	2	—	—	—	2	—
49	LE367	Rear mudguard stay lock washer $\frac{1}{4}"$ B.S.F.	2	2	2	2	—	—	—	—	—
50	SL56/4	Rear mudguard stay nut $\frac{1}{4}"$ B.S.F.	2	2	2	2	—	—	—	—	—
51	{ SL109/6 SL9/18	Rear mudguard stay bolt, $\frac{5}{16}"$ B.S.F. $\times 1\frac{3}{32}"$ (Stay to frame) $\frac{5}{16}"$, 26T. $\times 2\frac{11}{16}"$	— 2	— 2	— 2	— 2	2 4	2 4	2 4	2 4	— —
52	SL6/40	Rear mudguard stay bolt washer $\frac{5}{16}"$ B.S.F.	2	2	2	2	4	4	4	4	—
53	{ SL56/38 SL56/6	Rear mudguard stay bolt nut $\frac{5}{16}"$ B.S.F., 26T.	2	2	2	2	2 2	2 2	2 2	2 2	—
54	F303	Rear mudguard stay distance piece	2	2	2	2	2	2	2	2	—

Note—For bolts used to fix front ends of lifting handle stays see "Horn Mounting Group"

Illus. Ref.	Part No.	Description	A	B	C	D	E	F	G	H	J
55	MAS61	Rear mudguard bridge assembly	1	—	1	—	1	—	1	—	—
56	FK58/62	Lifting handle—Left-hand	1	1	1	1	1	1	1	1	—
57	{ MAS125/6 FK58/63 MAS125/3	Lifting handle stay—Left-hand Lifting handle—Right-hand Lifting handle stay—Right-hand	1	1	1	1	1 1 1	1 1 1	1 1 1	1 1 1	—
58	SL8/3	Lifting handle bolt $\frac{1}{4}"$ B.S.F. $\times \frac{9}{16}"$ (Lifting handle to guard)	2	2	2	2	2	2	2	2	—
59	SL6/32	Lifting handle bolt washer $\frac{1}{4}"$	2	2	2	2	2	2	2	2	—
60	LE367	Lifting handle bolt lock washer $\frac{1}{4}"$	2	2	2	2	2	2	2	2	—
61	SL56/4	Lifting handle bolt nut $\frac{1}{4}"$ B.S.F.	2	2	4	4	2	2	4	4	4

Mudguard, Dynamo Drive Cover, Chain Guard, Chain and Horn Section—*continued*   See illustration "H" page Thirty-seven

Note—Quote Part Numbers when ordering   NOT Illustration References
Always quote complete engine number and letters
Before ordering also see respective sections on pages 56 to 74 inclusive

Illus. Ref.	Part No.	Description	A	B	C	D	E	F	G	H	J
Dynamo Belt and Cover Group											
62	KA93/3AS	Dynamo belt cover assembly—front	—	1	1	1	—	—	—	—	—
	KA93/11	‡ Dynamo belt cover—front	—	1	1	1	—	—	—	—	—
63	KA93/8AS	‡ Dynamo belt cover assembly—rear	—	1	1	1	—	—	1	—	—
	MAS120	‡ Dynamo belt cover assembly—rear	—	1	1	1	—	—	1	—	—
Not shown	LE598/2	‡ Dynamo belt cover beading	—	1	1	1	—	—	1	—	—
64	SL8/26	Dynamo belt cover bolt, $\frac{1}{4}"$ B.S.F. $\times \frac{7}{16}"$	—	1	1	1	—	—	1	—	—
65	SL56/4	Dynamo belt cover nut, $\frac{1}{4}"$ B.S.F.	—	2	2	2	—	—	2	—	—
66	SL6/32	Dynamo belt cover washer, $\frac{1}{4}"$	—	—	—	—	—	—	—	—	—
67	E16/2	Dynamo driving belt. 'V' type	1	—	—	—	—	—	—	—	—
	E16/3	Dynamo driving belt. 'V' type	1‡	1	1	1	—	—	1	—	—
	E16/4	Dynamo driving belt. 'V' type	1*	1*	1*	1*	—	—	1*	—	1

‡ Used from Engine No. MSS11970 to MSS12914

* Used from Engine No. MSS12915 onwards

* Used from Engine No. VR3605 onwards

* Used from Engine No. VM5049 onwards

Electric Horn and Mounting Group

			A	B	C	D	E	F	G	H	J
68	SL109/1	Horn fixing bolt $\frac{5}{16}"$ B.S.F. $\times \frac{5}{8}"$	1	—	2	2	—	2	—	—	—
	SL109/2	Horn fixing and lifting handle bolt $\frac{5}{16}"$ B.S.F. $\times \frac{7}{8}"$	—	—	2	2	—	2	—	—	—
69	SL6/40	Fixing bolt washer $\frac{5}{16}"$	1	—	2	2	—	1	—	—	—
	SL6/45	Lifting handle stay distance piece. Used on right-hand side only	—	—	1	1	—	—	—	—	—
70	SL56/38	Fixing bolt nut, $\frac{5}{16}"$ B.S.F.	1	—	2	2	—	2	—	—	—
71	E21/4	Electric horn assembly	1	—	1	1	—	1	—	—	—

41

Mudguard, Dynamo Drive Cover, Chain Guard, Chain and Horn Section—*continued* See Illustration "H" page Thirty-seven

Note—Quote Part Numbers when ordering NOT Illustration References
Always quote complete engine number and letters
Before ordering also see respective sections on pages 56 to 74 inclusive

Illus. Ref.	Part No.	Description	A	B	C	D	E	F	G	H	J
Chain and Chain Guard Group											
72	MAS24	Rear chain cover assembly. Includes A253 transfer. Not used with fairings	1	1	1	1	1	—	1	1	1
73	A253	Rear chain cover transfer. Included in MAS24	1	1	1	1	1	—	1	1	1
74	SL56/4	Chain case fixing nut ¼" B.S.F. To primary chain case	2	2	2	2	2	—	2	2	2
75	SL6/32	Chain case fixing nut washer ¼"	2	2	2	2	2	—	2	2	2
76	MAS95	Rear chain guard and felt assembly. Includes F291 Joint strip	1	1	1	1	1	—	1	1	1
77	F291	Rear chain guard joint strip. Included in MAS95	1	1	1	1	1	—	1	1	1
78	SL108/4	Rear chain guard bolt—front B.S.F.×1½"	1	1	1	1	1	—	1	1	1
79	SL6/32	Rear chain guard bolt washer ¼"	1	1	1	1	1	—	1	1	1
80	SL109/5	Rear chain guard bolt—rear 5⁄16" B.S.F. ×½"	1	1	1	1	1	—	1	1	1
81	SL6/40	Rear chain guard bolt washer 5⁄16"	1	1	1	1	1	—	1	1	1
	⎧ KA27/2	Primary chain .5"×.305"× 68 Pitches	1	1	—	—	—	—	—	1	1
82	⎨ KA28/6	Rear chain .625"×.380"×101 Pitches (Solo)	1	1	—	—	—	1	—	—	—
	KA28/2	Rear chain .625"×.380"×100 Pitches (S/car)	—	—	—	—	—	—	—	—	—
	⎩ KA27/4	Primary chain .5"×.303"× 67 Pitches	—	—	1	1	1	—	1	—	—
	A28/8	Rear chain .5"×.305"×124 Pitches	—	—	1	1	1	—	1	—	—
Not shown	F289/2	Rear chain cover. Used with fairings	1	1	1	1	1	1	—	—	—

ILLUSTRATION I

FOR PART NUMBERS AND DESCRIPTION OF ITEMS
{ 1 to 19 see page 44
20 to 37 ,, ,, 45
38 to 58 ,, ,, 46
59 to 80 ,, ,, 47 }

ORDER BY PART NUMBERS—DO NOT QUOTE ILLUSTRATION REFERENCES

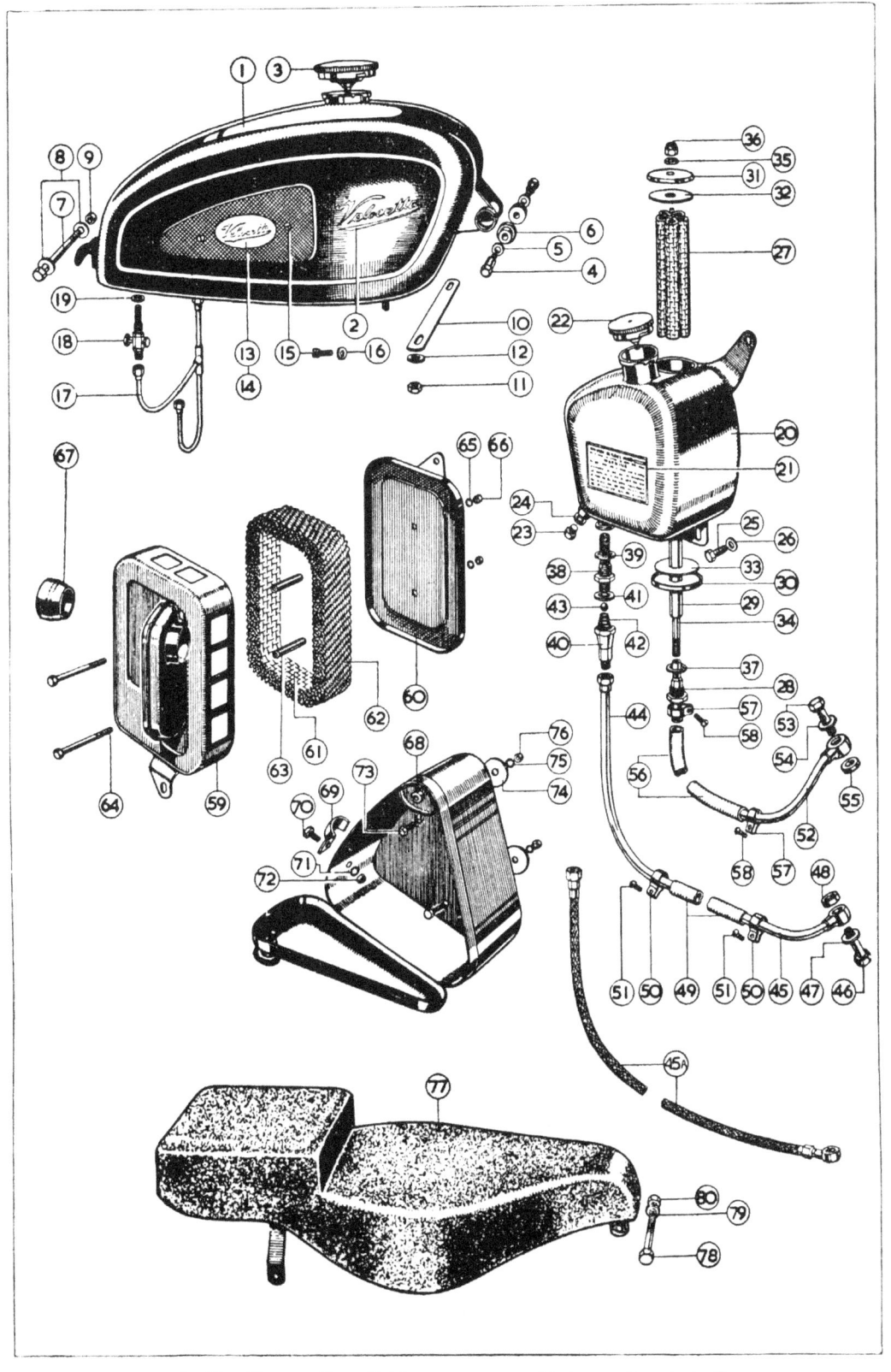

Is the Forwarding Address on your Order quite clear?

PETROL TANK, OIL TANK, OIL FILTER, OIL PIPE, AIR CLEANER, TOOL BOX AND SEAT SECTION

See Illustration "I" page Forty-three   NOT Illustration References

Note—Quote Part Numbers when ordering
Always quote complete engine number and letters
Before ordering also see respective sections on pages 56 to 74 inclusive

Illus. Ref.	Part No.	Description	A	B	C	D	E	F	G	H	J
Petrol Tank Section—Tank and Mounting Group											
1	§ MAS63/4	Petrol tank 3 gallon	1	1	1	1	1	1	–	–	–
	* MAS63/5	Petrol tank 4¼ gallon	1	1	1	1	1	1	–	–	–
		Note—The style of finish and colour required must be specified when ordering									
	A132	Petrol tank transfer	2	–	–	–	–	–	2	–	–
2	KA315	Petrol tank badge—black background	–	2	–	2	–	–	–	–	–
	KA315/2	Petrol tank badge—red background	2	1	2	–	2	–	–	–	–
	* KA315/4	Petrol tank badge—rectangular	2	2	2	2	2	2	–	–	–
Not shown											
	KA328	Petrol tank motif—Left-hand	1	1	1	1	1	1	–	–	–
	KA329	Petrol tank motif—Right-hand	1	1	1	1	1	1	–	–	–
	KA331	Motif connecting strip	1	1	1	1	1	1	–	–	–
	KA314/3	Motif and badge fixing screws	10	10	10	10	10	10	–	–	–
	§ KA314	Petrol tank badge fixing screws	4	4	4	4	4	4	–	–	–
3	KA4/9	Petrol tank cap	1	1	1	1	1	1	1	–	–
4	FK152/2	Petrol tank fixing bolt—front	2	2	2	2	2	2	2	2	2
5	SL6/57	Petrol tank fixing bolt washer $\frac{7}{16}'' \times \frac{7}{8}''$ O/D	2	2	2	2	2	2	2	2	2
6	FK151/4	Petrol tank fixing bolt buffer	2	2	2	2	2	2	2	2	2
7	SL9/18	Petrol tank fixing bolt—rear $\frac{5}{16}''$ 26 T.P.I. $\times 2\frac{11}{16}''$	2	2	2	2	2	2	2	2	2
8	SL6/43	Petrol tank fixing bolt washer $\frac{5}{16}'' \times 1''$ O/D	2	2	2	2	2	2	2	2	2
9	SL56/6	Petrol tank fixing bolt nut $\frac{5}{16}''$ 26 T.P.I.	2	2	2	2	2	2	2	2	2
10	A276/2	Petrol tank strap	1	1	1	1	1	1	–	–	–
11	SL56/4	Petrol tank strap nut ¼" B.S.F.	2	2	2	2	2	2	–	–	–
12	SL6/32	Petrol tank strap washer ¼"	2	2	2	2	2	2	–	–	–
	§ Used up to November 1962 * Used from November 1962										
Petrol Pipe, Tap and Knee Grip Group											
13	KA70/5AS	Petrol tank knee grip—Right-hand side *Obsolete*	1	1	1	1	1	1	–	–	–
14	KA70/6AS	Petrol tank knee grip—Left-hand side *Obsolete*	1	1	1	1	1	1	–	–	–
15	KA287	Petrol tank knee grip screw	4	4	4	4	4	4	–	–	–
16	SL6/32	Petrol tank knee grip washer ¼"	4	4	4	4	4	4	–	–	–
17	MAS27	Petrol pipe assembly	1	1	1	1	1	1	–	–	–
	MAS27/2	Petrol pipe assembly—for Monobloc Carburetter	–	–	–	–	–	–	–	–	–
18	A2/5	Petrol tap	2	2	2	2	2	2	–	–	–
19	KA115	Petrol tap gasket	2	2	2	2	2	2	–	–	–

Petrol Tank, Oil Tank, Oil Filter, Oil Pipe, Air Cleaner, Tool Box and Seat Section—continued

See Illustration "I" page Forty-three

Note—Quote Part Numbers when ordering NOT Illustration References
Always quote complete engine number and letters
Before ordering also see respective sections on pages 56 to 74 inclusive

Illus. Ref.	Part No.	Description	A	B	C	D	E	F	G	H	J
Oil Tank, Oil Filter and Ball Valve Group											
20	MAS13/2	Oil Tank assembly*. Enamelled and transferred. Non-breather type. Obsolete	1	1	1	1	1	1	—	—	—
Not shown	MAS13/4	Oil tank assembly. Enamelled and transferred. Breather type	—	—	—	—	—	—	1	1	1
21	A134/4	Oil tank transfer	1	1	1	1	1	1	1	1	1
22	KA6/6	Oil tank filler cap. Non-breather type tank	1	1	1	1	1	1	—	—	—
Not shown	KA6/4	Oil tank filler cap*. Breather type tank	—	—	—	—	—	—	1	1	1
Not shown	KA221/15	Vent pipe hose. 5/16" bore. 11" long. Breather type tank	—	—	—	—	—	—	1	1	1
Not shown	KA100/18	Vent pipe hose clip* (Mudguard end). Breather type tank	—	—	—	—	—	—	1	1	1
Not shown	KA100	Vent pipe hose Clip* (tank end) Breather type tank	—	—	—	—	—	—	1	1	1
Not shown	LE433	Vent pipe hose clip screw* (tank end) Breather type tank	—	—	—	—	—	—	1	1	1
23	B38	Oil tank drain plug 1/8" B.S.P.	1	1	1	1	1	1	1	1	1
24	A37/7	Oil tank drain plug gasket	1	—	—	—	—	1	1	—	1
25	SL9/3	Oil tank fixing bolt—bottom 5/16" 26 T.P.I. × 1½"	2	2	2	2	2	2	2	2	2
26	SL6/40	Oil tank fixing bolt washer 5/16"	2	2	2	2	2	2	2	2	2
27	A288	Oil tank filter element	1	1	1	1	1	1	1	1	1
28*	LE547	Oil tank filter cap adaptor	1	1	1	1	1	1	1	—	1
29**	A293/2	Oil tank filter centre tube	1	1	1	1	1	1	1	—	1
30	LE543	Oil tank filter cap—bottom	1	1	1	1	1	1	1	1	1
31	LE570	Oil tank filter cap—top	1	1	1	1	1	1	1	1	1
32	LE572	Oil tank filter cap gasket—top	1	1	1	1	1	1	1	1	1
33	A287	Oil tank filter cap gasket—bottom	1	1	1	1	1	1	1	1	1
34	SL102/13	Oil tank stud ¼" B.S.F. × 7¾" long	1	1	1	1	1	1	1	1	1
35	A37/5	Oil tank stud gasket	1	1	1	1	1	1	1	1	1
36	A291	Oil tank stud nut. (Simmonds NP/F.082) ¼" B.S.F.	1	1	1	1	1	1	1	1	1
37	LE573	Oil tank filter cap adaptor gasket	1	1	1	1	1	1	1	1	1

See Page 49 for key to *

Petrol Tank, Oil Tank, Oil Filter, Oil Pipe, Air Cleaner, Tool Box and Seat Section—continued

See Illustration "I" page Forty-three

Note—Quote Part Numbers when ordering NOT Illustration References
Always quote complete engine number and letters
Before ordering also see respective sections on pages 56 to 74 inclusive

Illus. Ref.	Part No.	Description	A	B	C	D	E	F	G	H	J
Oil Tank, Oil Filter, and Ball Valve Group—continued											
38	MAS14	Ball valve union assembly	1	1	1	1	1	1	1	1	1
39	KA115/2	Ball valve union gasket	1	1	1	1	1	1	1	1	1
40	M253	Ball valve body	1	1	1	1	1	1	1	1	1
41	KA115/3	Ball valve body gasket	1	1	1	1	1	1	1	1	1
42	M255	Ball valve spring	1	1	1	1	1	1	1	1	1
43	W15/2	Ball valve ball	1	1	1	1	1	1	1	1	1
		* May be ordered together as MAS94/3 Oil Filter Centre Tube Assembly									
		† Obsolete replace by MAS13/4 and items marked *									
Oil Pipe Group											
44	MAS15/2	Oil feed pipe assembly. Tank end. Obsolete use MAS115/2	1	1	1	1	1	1			
45	MAS26	Oil feed pipe assembly. Engine end. Obsolete use MAS115/2	1	1	1	1	1	1			
45a	MAS115/2	Oil feed pipe assembly							1	1	1
46	M214	Oil feed pipe hollow bolt. For banjo union	1	1	1	1	1	1	1	1	1
47	A37/7	Oil feed pipe banjo gasket. Outer	1	1	1	1	1	1	1	1	1
48	A37/7	Oil feed pipe banjo gasket. Inner. (Between banjo and crankcase)	1	1	1	1	1	1	1	–	1
49	KA264/2	Oil feed pipe hose. 3/8″ bore × 8½″ long	1	1	1	1	1	1	1	1	1
50	KA100/16	Oil feed pipe hose clip — These are supplied together only	2	2	2	2	2	2	2	–	2
51	LE433	Oil feed pipe hose clip screw. Obsolete use MAS152	1	1	1	1	1	1	1	–	1
52	MAS90	Oil return pipe assembly	1	1	1	1	1	1	1	1	1
53	M214	Oil return pipe hollow bolt	1	1	1	1	1	1	1	1	1
54	A37/7	Oil return pipe banjo gasket. Outer	1	1	1	1	1	1	1	1	1
55	A37/7	Oil return pipe banjo gasket inner (between banjo and crankcase)	1	1	1	1	1	1	1	–	1
56	KA221/14	Oil return pipe hose. 5/16″ bore × 19″ long	2	2	2	2	2	2	2	2	2
57	KA100	Oil return pipe hose clip — Supplied together only	2	2	2	2	2	2	2	2	2
58	LE433	Oil return pipe hose clip screw	2	2	2	2	2	2	2	2	2
Not shown	MAS152	Oil return pipe assembly. c/w banjo, union nipple and nut	1	1	1	1	1	1	1	–	1
Not shown	KA100/19	Oil feed pipe clip. Rear. To stand pivot stud	1	1	–	1	–	1	1	–	1
Not shown	KA100/20	Oil feed pipe clip. Front. To footrest rod	1	1	–	1	–	1	1	1	1

Petrol Tank, Oil Tank, Oil Filter, Oil Pipe, Air Cleaner, Tool Box and Seat Section—*continued*

See Illustration "I" page Forty-three   NOT Illustration References

Note—Quote Part Numbers when ordering
Always quote complete engine number and letters
Before ordering also see respective sections on pages 54 to 76 inclusive

Illus. Ref.	Part No.	Description	A	B	C	D	E	F	G	H	J
Air Cleaner Group—(Obtainable as optional extra Equipment)											
59	MAS59/3	* Air cleaner body assembly	1	1	1	1	1	1	1	1	1
60	MAS62/3	* Air cleaner cover assembly	1	1	1	1	1	1	1	1	1
61	A303	* Air cleaner element gauze	1	1	1	1	1	1	1	1	1
62	A304	* Air cleaner element. (Knitted steel wire)	1	1	1	1	1	1	1	1	1
63	A305	* Air cleaner distance piece	1	1	1	1	1	1	1	1	1
64	SL107/6	* Air cleaner pin 2BA × $1\frac{5}{8}''$	1	1	1	1	1	1	1	1	1
65	LE366	* Air cleaner pin lockwasher $\frac{3}{16}''$	1	1	1	1	1	1	1	1	1
66	SL56/2	* Air cleaner pin nut 2BA	1	1	1	1	1	1	1	1	1
67	A297/3	* Air cleaner connecting elbow—to carburetter	1	1	1	1	1	1	1	1	1

* These items may be ordered assembled as MAS51/3 Air Cleaner Assembly (Monbloc Carburetter only)

Toolbox Group

68	{ MAS37	Toolbox with knob assembly	1	—	—	—	—	—	—	—	—
	{ MAS37/2	Toolbox with knob assembly	—	1	1	1	1	1	1	1	1
Not shown	FK257	Toolbox attachment bracket	—	1	1	1	1	1	1	—	1
69	A153/2	Toolbox fixing clip	1	2	2	2	2	2	2	—	2
70	SL8/3	Toolbox fixing clip bolt $\frac{1}{4}''$ B.S.F. × $\frac{9}{16}''$	1	2	2	2	2	2	2	—	2
71	LE367	Toolbox fixing clip bolt lockwasher $\frac{1}{4}''$	1	2	2	2	2	2	2	—	2
72	SL56/4	Toolbox fixing bolt nut $\frac{1}{4}''$ B.S.F.	1	2	2	2	2	2	2	—	2
73	SL8/26	Toolbox fixing bolt $\frac{1}{4}''$ B.S.F. × $\frac{7}{16}''$	2	—	—	—	—	—	—	—	—
	SL8/29	Toolbox attachment bracket bolt—Toolbox to bracket. $\frac{1}{4}''$ B.S.F. × $\frac{3}{4}''$	—	1	1	1	1	1	1	—	1
74	KA145/2	Toolbox fixing bolt washer	2	2	2	2	2	2	1	—	1
75	LE367	Toolbox fixing bolt lockwasher $\frac{1}{4}''$	2	1	1	1	1	1	1	—	1
76	SL56/4	Toolbox fixing bolt nut $\frac{1}{4}''$	2	1	1	1	1	1	1	—	1

Dual Seat Group

77	MAS89/8	Dual seat up to November 1962	1	1	1	1	1	1	1	—	1
	MAS89/9	Dual seat from November 1962 onwards	1	1	1	1	1	1	1	—	1
78	SL109/15	Dual seat fixing bolt $\frac{5}{16}''$ B.S.F. × $3''$	1	1	1	1	1	1	1	—	1
79	SL6/43	Dual seat fixing bolt washer $\frac{5}{16}''$	1	1	1	1	1	1	1	—	1
80	SL56/38	Dual seat fixing bolt nut $\frac{5}{16}''$ B.S.F.	1	1	1	1	1	1	1	—	1

ILLUSTRATION J

FOR PART NUMBERS AND DESCRIPTION OF ITEMS
{ 1 to 17 see page 49
18 to 37 " " 50
38 to 45 " " 51 }

ORDER BY PART NUMBERS—DO NOT QUOTE ILLUSTRATION REFERENCES

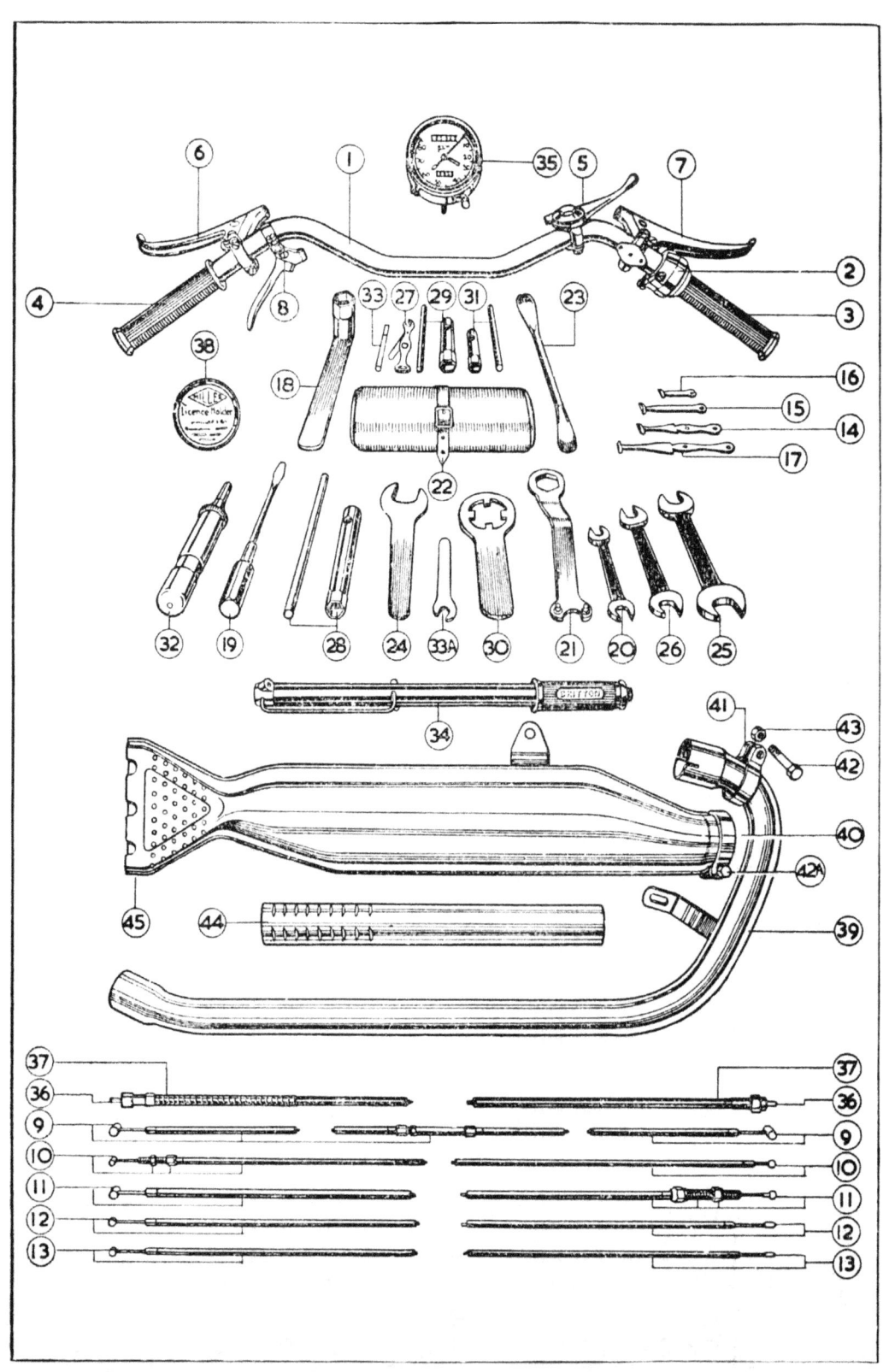

Have you quoted the Engine Number and Prefix Letters on your Order?

48

HANDLEBAR, CONTROLS, CABLES, TOOL KIT, SPEEDOMETER, LICENCE HOLDER AND EXHAUST SYSTEM SECTION   See Illustration "J" page Forty-eight

Note—Quote Part Numbers when ordering   NOT Illustration References
Always quote complete engine number and letters
Before ordering also see respective sections on pages 56 to 74 inclusive

Illus. Ref.	Part No.	Description	A	B	C	D	E	F	G	H	J
Handlebar and Control Section. Handlebar, Twist Grip and Lever Group
1	FK61/8	Handlebar bend. Standard	1	1	1	1	1	1	1	—	—
	F61/5	Handlebar bend. Special American style upswept	—	—	*Optional*	—	—	—	—	—	1
2	A211/2	Twist grip assembly. Includes twist grip rubber A220/2	1	1	1	1	1	1	1	1	1
3	A220/2	Twist grip rubber. Included in assembly A211/2	1	1	1	1	1	1	1	1	1
4	A225/2	Handlebar grip. (Amal No. 16/069)	1	1	1	1	1	1	1	1	1
5	A36/3	Handlebar air control lever (Amal No. 12/120)	1	1	1	1	1	1	1	1	1
Not shown	A36/2	Ignition control lever	1	1	*Optional*	1	1	1	1	—	1
6	KC16/3	Handlebar clutch or brake lever. (Amal No. 18/582)	1	1	1	1	—	—	—	—	1
7	KC16/4	Handlebar brake lever. With platform clip for flange fitting horn push	1	1	1	1	1	1	1	1	1
8	A72/3	Handlebar exhaust lifter. Obsolete use A72/5	1	1	1	1	1	1	1	1	1
	A72/5	Handlebar exhaust lifter	1	1	1	1	1	1	1	1	1
Cable Assembly and Cable Clip Group
9	KC17/9AS	Clutch cable assembly—standard	1	1	1	1	1	1	1	—	1
	KC17/10AS	Clutch cable assembly. Special length for use with American style bar	—	—	*Optional*	—	—	—	—	—	1
10	A125/4AS	Exhaust lifter cable assembly—Standard for use with A72/3	1	1	1	1	1	1	1	1	1
	A125/6AS	Exhaust lifter cable assembly—'American for use with A72/3	1	1	1	1	1	1	1	1	1
	A125/7AS	Exhaust lifter cable assembly—Standard for use with A72/5	1	1	1	1	1	1	1	1	1
	A125/8AS	Exhaust lifter cable assembly—'American' for use with A72/5	1	1	1	1	1	1	1	1	1
11	W33/6AS	Front brake cable assembly—Standard	1	1	1	1	1	1	1	—	1
	W33/8AS	Front brake cable assembly—Special length for use with American style bar	—	—	1	—	—	—	—	—	1
12	A237/3AS	Air cable assembly—Standard	1	1	1	1	1	1	1	1	1
	A237/5AS	Air cable assembly—Special length for use with American style bar	—	—	1	—	—	—	—	—	1
13	A234/10AS	Throttle cable assembly—Standard	1	1	1	1	1	1	1	1	1
	A234/12AS	Throttle cable assembly—Special length for use with American style bar	—	—	1	—	—	—	—	—	1
Not shown	MAS131	Ignition control cable assembly—B.T.H. Magneto Manual Control	1	1	1	1	1	1	1	—	1
15	A256/2	Cable clip—Rubber. John Bull type 'C'	5	5	5	5	5	5	5	—	5

Handlebar, Controls, Cables, Toolkit, Speedometer, Licence Holder and Exhaust System Section—continued

See Illustration "J" page Forty-eight

Note—Quote Part Numbers when ordering   NOT Illustration References

Always quote complete engine number and letters

Before ordering also see respective sections on pages 56 to 74 inclusive

Toolkit and Inflator Group

Illus. Ref.	Part No.	Description	A	B	C	D	E	F	G	H	J
18	A55/4	* Sparking plug and suction filter plug spanner	1	1	1	1	1	1	1	1	1
19	A57	* Screwdriver	1	1	1	1	1	1	1	1	1
20	A58	* Double open-ended spanner $\frac{1}{8}'' \times \frac{3}{16}''$ Whit.	1	1	1	1	1	1	1	1	1
21	A61/2AS	* Peg spanner	1	1	1	1	1	1	1	1	1
22	A63	* Tool roll	1	1	1	1	1	1	1	1	1
23	A64	* Tyre lever	1	1	1	1	1	1	1	1	1
24	A65/2	* Steering head locknut spanner	1	1	1	1	1	1	1	1	1
25	A101	* Double open-ended spanner $\frac{3}{8}'' \times \frac{7}{16}''$ Whit.	1	1	1	1	1	1	1	1	1
26	A102	* Double open-ended spanner $\frac{1}{4}'' \times \frac{5}{16}''$ Whit.	1	1	1	1	1	1	1	1	1
27	A154/2	* Magneto spanner	1	1	1	1	1	1	1	1	1
28	A227	* Tubular spanner $\frac{3}{8}''$ Whit.—and tommy bar	1	1	1	1	1	1	1	1	1
29	A228	* Tubular spanner $\frac{1}{4}''$ Whit.—and tommy bar	1	1	1	1	1	1	1	1	1
30	A229	* Shock absorber nut spanner	1	1	1	1	1	1	1	1	1
31	A248	* Tubular spanner $\frac{3}{16}''$ Whit.—and tommy bar	1	1	1	1	1	1	1	1	1
32	KA51	* Grease gun	1	1	1	1	1	1	1	1	1
33	KA62/2	* Clutch adjusting tool	1	1	1	1	1	1	1	1	1
33A	KA52	* Tappet adjusting spanner	1	1	1	1	1	1	1	1	1
		* **Note**—The sixteen items above may be ordered as :									
—	MAS88/2	Tool kit assembly. (Includes all items in the section marked*)	1	1	1	1	1	1	1	1	1
34	A25/3	Tyre inflator	1	1	1	1	1	1	1	1	1

Speedometer and Drive Group

Illus. Ref.	Part No.	Description	A	B	C	D	E	F	G	H	J
35	KA268/15	Speedometer‡	1	1	1	1	—	—	1	—	1
	KA268/17	Speedometer‡	—	—	—	—	1	1	—	1	—
36	KA270/4	Speedometer drive cable	1	1	1	1	1	1	1	1	1
37	KA271/4	Speedometer drive cable casing } MAS58 Speedo-drive cable assembly	1	1	1	1	1	1	1	1	1
		‡ Speedometers registering kilometres can be supplied to special order									

Handlebar, Controls, Cables, Toolkit, Speedometer, Licence Holder and Exhaust System Section—continued

See Illustration "J" page Forty-eight

Note—Quote Part Numbers when ordering. NOT Illustration References
Always quote complete engine number and letters
Before ordering also see respective sections on pages 56 to 74 inclusive

Illus. Ref.	Part No.	Description	A	B	C	D	E	F	G	H	J
Licence Holder Group											
38	A157	Licence holder. Headlamp bracket fixing	1	1	1	1	1	—	—	—	—
—	A157/2	Licence holder	—	—	—	—	—	1	1	1	—
—	LE458	§Licence holder glass	1	1	1	1	1	1	1	1	—
—	LE459	§Licence holder rubber ring	1	1	1	1	1	1	1	1	—
—	LE460	§Licence holder rim	1	1	1	1	1	1	1	1	—

§ These items, which are included in A157 and A157/2 Licence holders can only be supplied together

Illus. Ref.	Part No.	Description	A	B	C	D	E	F	G	H	J
Exhaust Pipe and Silencer Group											
39	MAS28/12	Exhaust pipe assembly	1	—	—	—	—	—	—	—	—
39	MAS28/11	Exhaust pipe assembly	—	1	1	1	1	1	1	1	1
40	A141/2	Exhaust pipe clip—Silencer end	1	1	1	1	1	1	1	1	1
41	KA141/2	Exhaust pipe clip—Engine end	1	1	1	1	1	1	1	1	1
42A	SL108/3	Exhaust pipe clip bolt $\tfrac{1}{4}''$ B.S.F. $\times 1\tfrac{3}{8}''$ —Silencer end	2	2	2	2	2	2	2	2	2
42	SL8/9	Exhaust pipe clip bolt $\tfrac{1}{4}''$ B.S.F. $\times 1\tfrac{9}{16}''$ —Engine end	1	1	1	1	1	1	1	1	1
43	SL56/4	Exhaust pipe clip nut $\tfrac{1}{4}''$ B.S.F.	2	2	2	2	2	2	2	2	2
44	KA142/2	Silencer baffle	1	1	1	1	1	1	1	1	—
45	MAS30/2	Silencer assembly	1	1	1	1	1	1	1	1	—
Not shown	SL111/2	Silencer fixing bolt $\tfrac{7}{16}''$ B.S.F. $\times 1\tfrac{1}{32}''$	1	1	1	1	1	1	1	1	—

ILLUSTRATION K

FOR PART NUMBERS AND DESCRIPTION OF ITEMS { 1 to 30 see page 53
31 to 38 " " 54

ORDER BY PART NUMBERS—DO NOT QUOTE ILLUSTRATION REFERENCES

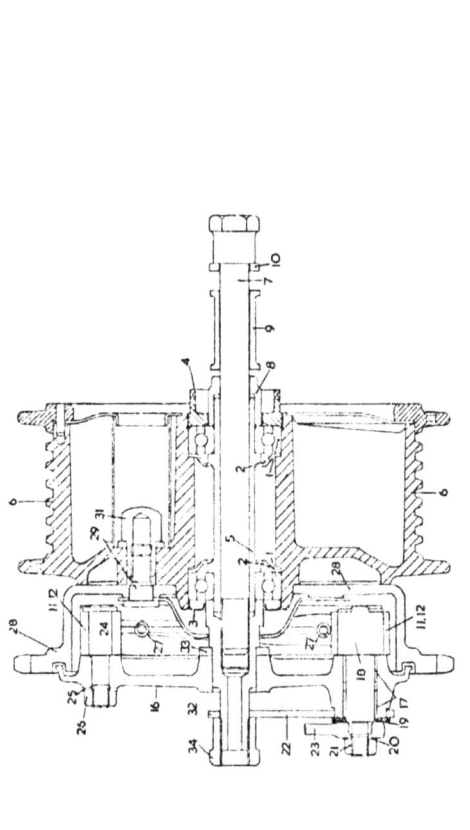

ARRANGEMENT OF "FULL-WIDTH" FRONT HUB

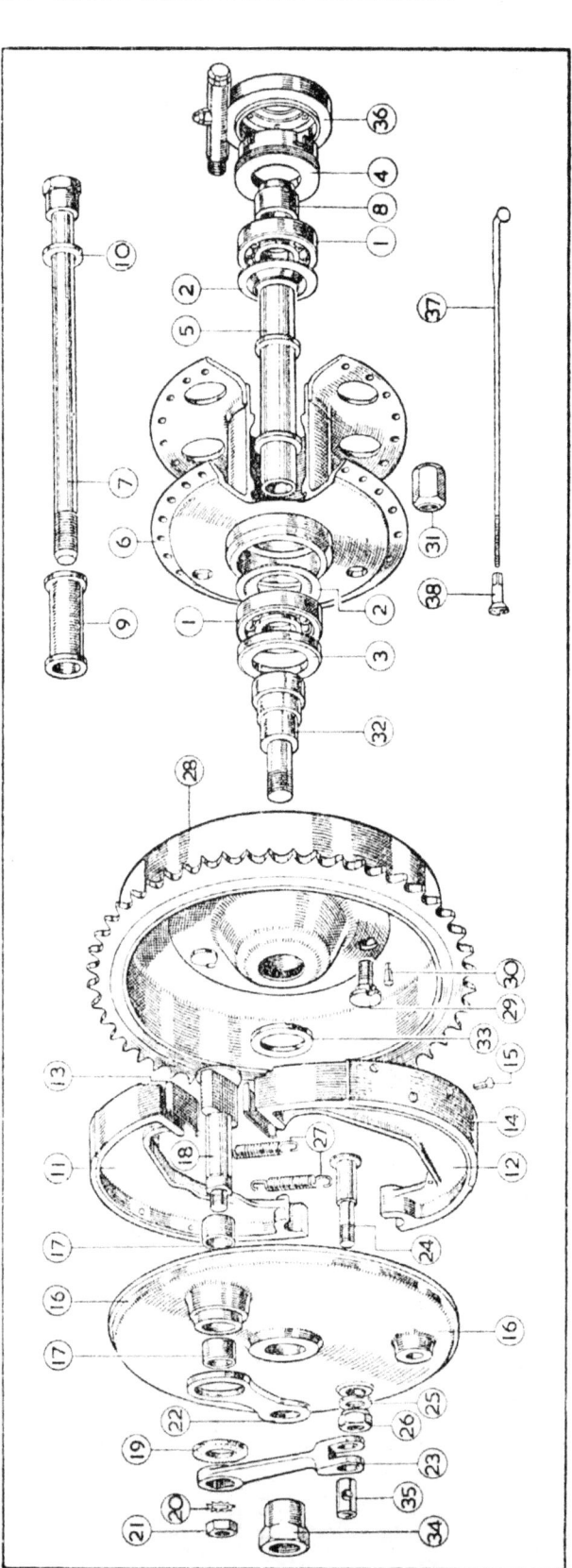

Is the Forwarding Address on your Order quite clear?

52

REAR WHEEL AND BRAKE SECTION

See Illustration "K" page Fifty-two

Note—Quote Part Numbers when ordering   NOT Illustration References
Always quote complete engine number and letters
Before ordering also see respective sections on pages 56 to 74 inclusive

Illus. Ref.	Part No.	Description	A	B	C	D	E	F	G	H	J
1	KS18/3	*Rear hub ball bearing	2	2	2	2	2	2	2	2	2
2	KS57/3	*Rear hub grease retainer	2	2	2	2	2	2	2	2	2
3	KS11/4	*Rear hub inner dust cap	1	1	1	1	1	1	1	1	1
4	KS61/2	*Rear hub retaining ring	1	1	1	1	1	1	1	1	1
5	KS8/9	*Rear hub hollow spindle	1	1	1	1	1	1	1	1	1
6	{ MAS83	Rear hub shell assembly	1	1	—	—	1	1	—	—	—
	MAS83/2	Rear hub shell assembly	—	—	1	1	—	—	1	1	1
7	KS8/10	Rear wheel spindle	1	1	1	1	1	1	1	1	1
8	KS62/3	Rear hub clamping sleeve	1	1	1	1	1	1	1	1	1
9	KS52/4	Rear wheel distance piece	1	1	1	1	1	1	1	1	1
10	KS51/2	Rear wheel spindle washer	1	1	1	1	1	1	1	1	1
11	MAS75	⁓Brake shoe assembly—Right-hand ⎫ Not supplied separately	2	2	2	2	2	2	2	2	2
12	MAS74	⁓Brake shoe assembly—Left-hand ⎭	2	2	2	2	2	2	2	2	2
13	KS16/2	⁓Brake shoe slipper. (Included in assemblies MAS74 and MAS75)	2	2	2	2	2	2	2	2	2
14	KS19/2	⁓Brake shoe lining. (Included in assemblies MAS74 and MAS75)	2	2	2	2	2	2	2	2	2
15	KS31	⁓Brake shoe lining rivet	12	12	12	12	12	12	12	12	12
16	MAS81	Rear brake plate assembly	1	1	1	1	1	1	1	1	1
17	S68	⁓Rear brake plate bush. (Included in assembly MAS81)	2	2	2	2	2	2	2	2	2
18	MAS78	Rear brake cam assembly	1	1	1	1	1	1	1	1	1
19	LE106	Rear brake cam felt washer	1	1	1	1	1	1	1	1	1
20	LE369	Rear brake cam lockwasher 3/8"	1	1	1	1	1	1	1	1	1
21	SL56/8	Rear brake cam nut 3/8" 26 T.P.I.	1	1	1	1	1	1	1	1	1
22	S41/5	Rear brake cam steady	1	1	1	1	1	1	1	1	1
23	S3/5	Rear brake lever	1	1	1	1	1	1	1	1	1
24	W10/4	Brake shoe fulcrum pin	2	2	2	2	2	2	2	2	2
25	SL6/50	Brake shoe fulcrum pin washer 3/8" × 3/4" O/D	1	1	1	1	1	1	1	1	1
26	SL56/8	Brake shoe fulcrum pin nut 3/8" 26 T.P.I.	1	1	1	1	1	1	1	1	1
27	S27/2	Brake shoe spring	2	2	2	2	2	2	2	2	2
28	{ MAS77/2	Rear brake drum assembly.(Includes KS12/4 Stud and KS73 Locking peg)	1	1	—	1	1	1	1	—	1
	MAS77	Rera brake drum assembly. (Includes KS12/4 and KS 73 Locking peg).	—	—	1	—	—	—	—	1	—
29	KS12/4	Rear brake drum driving stud. (Included in assemblies MAS77 and MAS77/2)	3	3	3	3	3	3	3	3	3
30	KS73	Rear brake drum locking peg. (Included in assemblies MAS77 and MAS77/2)	3	3	3	3	3	3	3	3	3

Rear Wheel and Brake Section—continued   See Illustration "K" page Fifty-two

Note—Quote Part Numbers when ordering   NOT Illustration References

Always quote complete engine number and letters
Before ordering also see respective sections on pages 56 to 74 inclusive

Illus. Ref.	Part No.	Description	A	B	C	D	E	F	G	H	J
31	KS60	Rear brake drum stud nut	3	3	3	3	—	—	—	—	3
	KS60/2	Rear brake drum stud nut	3	3	3	3	6	6	6	—	3
32	S66/3	Rear brake plate locking bolt	1	1	1	1	1	3	1	3	1
33	S67	Rear brake plate washer	1	1	1	1	1	1	1	1	1
34	W65/2	Rear wheel spindle nut	1	1	1	1	1	1	1	1	1
35	FK43/2	Rear brake rod trunnion. Plain hole	1	1	1	1	1	1	1	1	1
36	KA272/2	Speedometer drive reduction gearbox	1	—	1	—	1	—	1	—	1
37	KA18/25	Rear wheel spoke, 8/10 S.W.G. × 7⅛" long	40	—	—	—	—	—	—	—	40
	KA18/30	Rear wheel spoke, 8/10 S.W.G. × 6⁷⁄₁₆" long. Outside flange	—	20	20	20	—	20	—	20	—
	KA18/31	Rear wheel spoke, 8/10 S.W.G. × 6⁵⁄₁₆" long. Inside flange	—	20	20	20	—	20	—	20	—
38	KA19	Rear wheel spoke nipple, 10 S.W.G.	40	40	40	40	40	40	40	40	40
—	A17/7	Rear wheel rim, WM2 × 19" (40 holes)	1	—	—	—	1	—	—	—	—
—	A17/9	Rear wheel rim, WM2 × 19" (40 holes)	—	1	1	1	—	1	—	—	—
—	W14/10	Rear wheel rim, WM3 × 19" (40 holes)	—	—	—	—	—	—	1	1	1

Assemblies available—

Part No.	Description
MAS82	Rear hub assembly Comprising MAS83 and items marked *
MAS82/3	Rear hub assembly.. Comprising MAS83/2 and items marked *
MAS79	Rear wheel assembly Comprising MAS82, A17/7, KA18/25 and KA19
MAS79/4	Rear wheel assembly.. Comprising MAS82/3, A17/9, KA18/30, KA18/31 and KA19
MAS80	Brake plate and shoes assembly. Comprising items marked §

SCHEDULE OF PARTS PECULIAR to 350 and 500 c.c. "SPECIAL" MACHINES

Part No.	Description	Quantity off
MAS68/3	Front Hub and Brake Assembly	1
KA18/5	Front Wheel Spoke	36
KA268/14	Speedometer Head	1
MAS134/2	Nacelle	1
MAS63/4	Petrol Tank 3-gall. (blue)	1
KA328/2	Petrol Tank Motif—Left-hand	1
KA329/2	Petrol Tank Motif—Right-hand	1

Note— The following items have the same part numbers as the MSS, but are enamelled in blue :

Front and Rear Wheel Rims

Rear Hub Assembly

The following items have the same part numbers as the Viper and Venom but are enamelled in blue :

Front and Rear Mudguards

Front and Rear Mudguard Stays

Oil Tank

Tool Box

SCHEDULE OF PARTS PECULIAR to CLUBMAN (Mk.1), SCRAMBLER, ENDURANCE and THRUXTON MODELS

Page	Ref.		Description	D	E	F	G	H	J
		Engine Section							
9	26	MAS97/16	Piston assembly. Includes rings, gudgeon pin and circlips	—	1	—	—	—	—
9	26	MAS97/17	Piston assembly, .020" oversize	—	1	—	—	—	—
9	26	MAS97/18	Piston assembly, .040" oversize	—	1	—	—	—	—
9	26	MAS97/28	Piston assembly. Includes rings, gudgeon pin and circlips	1	—	1	1	1	1
9	26	MAS97/29	Piston assembly, .020" oversize	1	—	1	1	1	1
9	26	MAS97/30	Piston assembly, .040" oversize	1	—	1	1	1	1
9	27	SL3/67	Piston ring—compression	2	2	2	2	2	2
9	45	M72/9	Magneto gear (steel)	—	—	—	1	1	1
—	—	M270	Shock absorber distance piece	1	1	1	—	—	—
—	—	M274	Induction manifold	1	1	1	—	2	—
—	—	SL109/4	Induction manifold bolt 5/16" B.S.F. × 1"	—	—	—	—	2	—
—	—	SL6/40	Induction manifold bolt washer 5/16"	1	1	1	—	2	—
—	—	M180/4	Induction manifold gasket (paper)	1	1	1	—	1	—
—	—	M275	Crankcase breather adaptor	—	—	—	1	—	1
—	—	SL103/3	Induction manifold studs 5/16"	2	2	2	—	2	—
—	—	LE368	Induction manifold stud washer 5/16"	1	1	1	—	2	—
—	—	SL56/38	Induction manifold stud nut 5/16" B.S.F.	2	2	2	—	2	—
—	—	M180/3	Induction manifold gasket (Tufnol)	1	1	1	—	1	—
—	—	M2/18	Inlet valve	—	—	—	—	1	—
		Gearbox Section							
15	19	GC4/24	Gear change lever	1	1	1	—	—	—
20	6	BK98	Camplate ratchet plate	1	1	1	—	1	—
20	7	BK80/3	Camplate	1	1	1	—	1	—
20	20	BK12/5	Kickstart crank	1	1	1	—	1	—
20	31	BK87/4*	First gear on layshaft 19T (Ratchet gear)	1	1	1	—	1	—
20	38	BK86/3*	Driving gear on layshaft 26T	1	1	1	—	1	—
20	41	MAS122/2*	First gear assembly on gearshaft 25T	1	1	1	—	1	—
20	44	BK8/4AS*	Sleeve gear assembly 18T	1	1	1	—	1	—
23	73	SL94/2	20T sprocket ⎫ 1/2" × .305" chain	1	1	1	—	—	—
23	73	SL94/3	19T sprocket ⎬	—	—	—	—	—	—
23	73	SL94/7	22T sprocket. Available for "M" models	—	—	—	—	—	—

56

Schedule of Parts Peculiar to Clubman (Mk. I), Scrambler, Endurance and Thruxton Models—continued

Page	Ref.	Part No.	Description	D	E	F	G	H	J
			Gearbox Section—continued						
23	73	SL95/3	16T sprocket	—	—	1	1	—	—
23	73	SL95/4	17T sprocket	—	—	1	1	1	—
23	73	SL95/6	19T sprocket	—	1	1	1	1	—
23	73	SL95/7	20T sprocket ⎫ $\frac{3}{8}'' \times \frac{5}{8}''$ chain	—	1	1	1	1	1
23	73	SL95/8	21T sprocket ⎬	—	1	1	1	1	1
23	73	SL95/9	22T sprocket ⎭	—	1	1	1	1	1
16	19	GC4/22	Footchange lever	—	1	1	1	1	1
42	82	KA28/7	Rearchain, .625″ × .380″ 108 pitches	1	1	1	1	—	1
—	—	MAS167	Clutch spring holder	—	—	—	—	1	—

* T.T. Close Ratios—Fitted to Special Orders Only

Frame Section

Page	Ref.	Part No.	Description	D	E	F	G	H	J
25	1	MAS31/10	Frame assembly—1961 models onwards	1	1	1	—	1	—
		MAS142	Footrest plate assembly—Left-hand side	1	1	1	—	—	—
		FK220/5	Footrest plate—Right-hand side	1	1	1	—	—	—
		SL31/19	Footrest plate stud top $\frac{5}{16}''$ B.S.F. $\times 9\frac{7}{8}''$	1	1	1	—	—	—
		SL31/18	Footrest plate stud bottom $\frac{5}{16}''$ B.S.F. $\times 10\frac{1}{4}''$	1	1	1	—	—	—
		SL62/30	Footrest plate stud distance piece $\frac{1}{2}'' \times 9\frac{3}{32}''$	3	3	3	—	—	—
		SL6/40	Footrest plate stud washer $\frac{5}{16}''$	3	3	3	—	—	—
		SL56/38	Footrest plate stud nut $\frac{5}{16}''$ B.S.F.	2	2	2	—	—	—
		FK167/7	Footrest support strap	2	2	2	—	—	—
		SL12/7	Footrest support bolt $\frac{7}{16}''$ 26T $\times 1\frac{3}{16}''$	1	1	1	—	—	—
		SL6/57	Footrest support bolt washer	1	1	1	—	—	—
		SL56/9	Footrest support bolt nut—Left-hand side $\frac{7}{16}''$ 26 T.P.I.	1	1	1	—	—	—
		SL56/14	Footrest support bolt nut—Right-hand side $\frac{7}{16}''$ 26T.P.I.	1	1	1	—	—	—
25	75	BK18	Footrest footpiece	2	2	2	—	—	—
25	76	F298	Footrest eye bolt	2	2	2	—	—	—
25	77	SL56/27	Footrest eye bolt nut—$\frac{7}{16}''$ B.S.F.	2	2	2	—	—	—
25	78	SL6/55	Footrest eyebolt distance piece $\frac{15}{32}'' \times \frac{7}{8}''$	2	2	2	—	—	—
25	80	SL110/2	Footrest bolt (pivot) $\frac{3}{8}''$ B.S.F. $\times 1\frac{1}{4}''$	2	2	2	—	—	—
25	81	B60/5	Footrest rubber	2	2	2	—	—	—
		F39/4	Brake Pedal	1	1	1	—	—	—
		F292/2	Brake pedal pivot bush	1	1	1	—	—	—
25	79	SL56/7	Footrest bolt nut $\frac{3}{8}''$ B.S.F.	2	2	2	—	—	—

Schedule of Parts Peculiar to Clubman (Mk. 1), Scrambler, Endurance and Thruxton Models—continued

Frame Section—continued

Page	Ref.	Part No.	Description	D	E	F	G	H	J
25	83	SL109/9	Brake pedal pivot bolt $\frac{5}{16}''$ B.S.F. $\times 1\frac{3}{8}''$	–	1	1	–	–	–
25	84	SL6/39	Brake pedal pivot washer—outer $\frac{17}{64}'' \times \frac{1}{2}''$	–	1	1	–	–	–
25	85	SL56/38	Brake pedal pivot nut $\frac{5}{16}''$ B.S.F.	–	1	1	–	–	–
25	86	SL6/40	Brake pedal pivot washer—inner $\frac{5}{16}'' \times \frac{5}{8}''$	–	1	1	–	–	–
25	90	MAS41/2	Rear brake rod assembly	–	1	1	–	–	–
26	1	MAS31/9	Frame assembly	–	–	–	1	1	–
38	71	MAS128/2	Footrest hanger—Right-hand	–	–	–	1	1	–
38	71	MAS129	Footrest hanger—Left-hand	–	–	–	1	1	–
38	72	SL13/3	Footrest hanger bolt	–	2	2	2	1	–
37	27	MAS33/5	Suspension unit	–	2	2	2	2	–
38	81	F39/2	Rear brake pedal	–	1	1	1	1	–
		MAS126	Undershield	–	2	2	–	1	–
		F321	Trunnion shaft location peg	–	1	1	–	–	–
42	76	MAS95/2	Rear chain guard assembly						
	*	MAS13/5	Left-hand oil tank assembly together }	as required
		MAS51/4	with double capacity air filter						

* These two parts are usually fitted in conjunction with one another

Front Fork Section

Page	Ref.	Part No.	Description	D	E	F	G	H	J
30		MAS10/4	Front fork assembly	–	–	–	–	1	–
30		MAS10/7	Front fork assembly	1	1	1	1	–	1
30	23	MAS5/2	Fork damper tube assembly	2	2	2	2	2	2
30	27	MAS133	Damper piston rod assembly	2	2	2	2	2	2
30	28	F266/2	Damper piston rod washer	2	2	2	2	2	2
30	31	F251/3	Damper valve	2	2	2	2	2	2
30	32	F253/2	Damper piston rod adaptor—for use with Tachometer brakcet only	1	1	1	1	1	2
30		F311	Ball valve body	2	2	2	2	2	2
30		K100	Ball valve ball—$\frac{1}{4}''$	2	2	2	2	2	2
30		F312	Ball valve peg	2	2	2	2	2	2
30	47	KA280/2	Tachometer bracket	1	1	1	1	–	1
30	48	SL109/3	Bolt—Tachometer bracket to fork $\frac{5}{16}''$ B.S.F. $\times 1\frac{3}{16}''$	1	1	1	1	–	1
30	48	SL109/5	Bolt—Tachometer bracket to fork $\frac{5}{16}''$ B.S.F. $\times 1\frac{1}{2}''$	1	1	1	1	–	1
30		SL56/38	Tachometer bracket bolt nut $\frac{5}{16}''$ B.S.F.	–	–	–	–	–	–
30	49	SL6/40	Tachometer bracket washer $\frac{5}{16}'' \times .062''$	1	1	1	1	–	1
30		SL6/45	Tachometer bracket washer $\frac{5}{16}'' \times .5''$	1	1	1	1	–	1

Schedule of Parts Peculiar to Clubman (Mk. 1), Scrambler, Endurance and Thruxton Models—continued

Page	Ref.	Part No.	Description	D	E	F	G	H	J
			Front Fork Section—continued						
31	1	F246/2	Front fork tube (plated)	—	2	2	—	2	2
31	13	F252/3	Front fork spring	—	2	2	2	2	2
		KA312	Gaiter	2	2	2	2	2	2
		KA100/17	Gaiter clips	4	4	4	4	4	4
		F245/2	Gaiter shroud	2	2	2	2	2	2

* Double Damping Details fitted as Extras from 1967 onwards

Primary Chain Case Section

Page	Ref.	Part No.	Description	D	E	F	G	H	J
		MAS50/5	Front chain case assembly	—	1	1	1	—	—

Petrol Tank Section

Page	Ref.	Part No.	Description	D	E	F	G	H	J
43	1	MAS63/6	Petrol tank—3 gall. type	1	1	—	—	1	—
43	1	MAS63/5	Petrol tank—4¼ gall. type 1961 and onwards	1	—	1	—	1	—
43	1	MAS63/7	Petrol tank	—	—	—	1	—	1
—	1	KA4/10	Petrol tank filler cap	2	—	2	—	—	—
43	2	KA315/4	Petrol tank medallion	1	—	1	—	1	—
		KA328	Petrol tank motif—Left-hand side	1	—	1	—	—	—
		KA329	Petrol tank motif—Right-hand side	1	—	1	—	—	—
		KA331	Petrol tank motif connecting strip	2	—	2	—	—	—
43	10	A276/3	Petrol Tank Fixing Strap	1	—	1	—	1	—
43	10		Petrol tank fixing strap. Used on 4¼ gall. petrol tanks with only one A276/3 and one LE681. Fitted from Engine Nos. VR4134 and VM5551 onwards.						
43	13	KA70/7	Petrol tank knee grip	10	—	10	—	—	—
43	15	KA314/3	Petrol tank medallion and motif fixing screw	1	—	1	—	1	—
		LE678	Petrol tank strap rubber buffer in rear strap	4	—	4	—	2	—
		SL109/5	Petrol tank strap bolt—strap to tank 5/16" B.S.F. × 1/2"	4	—	4	—	1	—
		SL6/40	Petrol tank strap washer 5/16" × 5/8"	1	—	1	—	1	—
		LE681	Petrol tank mounting rubber—on top frame tube	1	—	1	—	—	—
		FK152/6	Petrol tank location stud—in front strap up to VR4134 and VM5551	1	—	1	—	1	—
		SL56/38	Petrol tank location stud nut—5/16" B.S.F. up to VR4134 and VM5551	1	—	1	—	1	—
		FK151/5	Petrol tank location rubber buffer on location stud up to VR4134 and VM5551	1	—	1	—	1	1
43	17	MAS27/2	Petrol pipe assembly	—	1	—	2	—	2
43	17	MAS63/2	Petrol tank assembly	2	—	2	—	2	2
43	18	KA31/13	Petrol pipe assembly	—	—	—	—	—	—
43		A2/6	Petrol taps	2	—	—	—	—	—

59

Schedule of Parts Peculiar to Clubman (Mk. 1), Scrambler, Endurance and Thruxton Models—continued

Page	Ref.	Part No.	Description	D	E	F	G	H	J
			Dual Seat Section						
47	77	MAS89/9	Clubman Dual Seat	—	—	1	1	—	1
47	77	MAS89/8	Scrambler Dual Seat	1	1	—	—	1	—
			Handlebar Section						
48	1	FK61/9	Handlebars	—	—	1	1	—	—
48	1	MAS153	Handlebar bend—Clubman Veeline models	1	1	—	—	1	—
48	6 & 7	A36/2	Magneto control lever	1	1	1	1	1	—
48	5	KC16/7	Handlebar clutch or brake lever	2	2	2	2	2	—
48	11	A36/3	Air control lever	—	—	1	1	—	—
48	9	W33/8AS	Front brake cable assembly	1	1	1	1	1	—
48		KC17/11	Clutch cable assembly	1	1	1	1	1	—
48		MAS131	Ignition control cable assembly—*B.T.H. Magneto*	1	1	1	1	1	—
48	12	A237/6AS	Air lever cable assembly	—	—	1	1	—	—
48	13	A234/13AS	Throttle cable assembly	1	1	1	1	1	—
48	10	A125/6AS	Exhaust lifter cable assembly	1	1	—	—	1	—
48	3	A211/3AS	Twist grip assembly—*Obsolete*	—	—	—	—	—	—
			Exhaust Pipe and Silencer Section						
48		MAS28/17	Exhaust Pipe assembly	—	—	—	—	—	1
48		MAS28/13	Exhaust pipe assembly	—	—	1	1	—	—
48	39	MAS28/8	Exhaust pipe assembly	—	1	—	—	—	—
48	39	MAS28/9	Exhaust pipe assembly	1	—	—	—	1	—
		SL110/2	Exhaust pipe fixing bolt $\frac{5}{16}''$ B.S.F. $\times \frac{7}{8}''$	1	1	1	1	1	—
		SL6/50	Exhaust pipe fixing bolt washer $\frac{3}{8}'' \times \frac{3}{4}''$	1	1	1	1	1	—
		SL56/7	Exhaust pipe fixing bolt nut $\frac{3}{8}''$ B.S.F.	1	1	1	1	1	—
48	45	MAS30/4	Silencer assembly—does not include Baffle tube KA142/2	1	1	1	1	1	—
			Wheels and Mudguards Section						
		A17/10	Wheel rim (alloy)	2	2	2	2	2	—
		MAS68	Front hub assembly and brake assembly	—	—	1	1	—	—
		MAS69	Front hub with bearings assembly	—	—	1	1	—	—
		MAS66/3	Rear hub assembly and brake assembly	1	1	1	1	1	—
		MAS82/2	Rear hub with bearings assembly	1	1	1	1	1	—

Schedule of Parts Peculiar to Clubman (Mk. I), Scrambler, Endurance and Thruxton Models—continued

Wheels and Mudguards Section—continued

Page Ref.	Part No.	Description	D	E	F	G	H	J
	MAS77/3	Rear brake drum assembly	—	1	—	1	—	—
	KA18/28	Front wheel spokes	—	18	—	18	—	—
	KA18/27	Front wheel spokes	—	18	—	18	—	—
	KS52/4	Rear wheel spindle distance piece	—	1	—	1	—	—
	W13/5	Front rim WM 1×21"	—	1	—	1	—	1
	WM14/10	Rear rim WM 3×19"	—	1	—	1	—	1
	MAS132	Security bolts—front	—	2	—	2	—	1
	MAS132/2	Security bolts—rear	—	2	—	2	—	1
	KA16/11	Front mudguard (alloy)	—	1	—	1	—	1
	MAS84/3	Rear mudguard (alloy)	—	1	—	1	—	1
	FK157/17	Front mudguard stays—Top	—	1	—	1	—	1
	MAS123	Front mudguard stays—Bottom	—	1	—	1	—	1
	FK58/65	Rear mudguard bridge plate	—	1	—	1	—	—
	KS29/4	Rear driving sprocket 60T	—	1	—	1	—	—
	S28/3	Rear wheel sprocket fixing bolts	—	8	—	8	—	—
	LE368	Rear wheel sprocket locking washer	—	8	—	8	—	—
	KS35	Rear wheel sprocket nuts	—	8	—	8	—	—

SCHEDULE OF PARTS PECULIAR to CLUBMAN (Mk.II) and THRUXTON MODELS

Frame Section

Part No.	Description	D	F	H
MAS33/7	Rear suspension units	2	2	2
FK27/11	Rear engine plate	—	—	2
FK27/12	" " "	—	—	2
SL11/23	" " " strengthener	—	—	1
MAS155	" " " bolt 3/8" B.S.F. ×3⅝"	—	—	1
SL107/12	" " " cover assembly	—	—	1
SL6/25	" " " bolt front 3/16"×½"	—	—	2
SL9/3	" " " washer 3/16"	—	—	2
SL6/40	" " " bolt rear 5/16" 26T.P.I.×½"	—	—	1
	" " " washer 5/16"	—	—	1

Schedule of Parts Peculiar to Clubman (Mk. II) and Thruxton Models—continued

Front Fork and Handlebar Section

Part No.		D	F	H
MAS10/7	Front fork assembly	1	1	1
F246/2	Front fork assembly tubes	2	2	2
F270/3	Steering column locknut	1	1	1
F249/3	Front fork cross member	1	1	1
F263/2	Steering damper rod	1	—	1
MAS159	Steering damper rod wingnut	—	—	1
SL56/33	Steering damper rod nut $\frac{5}{16}$" .447" hexagon	—	—	1
FA135	Steering damper rod head lock stop	1	1	1
KA280/4	Speedometer bracket	—	—	1
KA280/3	Rev. counter bracket	1	1	1
SL109/3	Bolts for brackets	1	1	2
SL6/45	Bolts for brackets distance piece	2	2	4
SL6/40	Bolts for brackets washer $\frac{5}{16}$"	1	1	2
SL109/5	Bolts for brackets	1	1	1
SL56/38	Bolts for brackets nut $\frac{5}{16}$" B.S.F.	1	1	1
MAS8/3	Headlamp bracket—Left-hand	1	1	1
MAS9/3	Headlamp bracket—Right-hand	1	1	1
SL108/4	Headlamp bracket clamp bolt	2	2	2
A291	Headlamp bracket clamp bolt nut	2	2	2
E67	Headlamp distance piece	2	2	2

Front Mudguard Section

Part No.		D	F	H
KA16/15	Front mudguard	1	1	1
A283	Front mudguard Number plate clip	2	2	2
FK157/21	Front mudguard stay—Left-hand—front	1	1	1
FK157/22	Front mudguard stay—Right-hand—front	1	1	1
FA122	Front mudguard stay distance piece (centre)	1	1	1
FK157/23	" " " " (rear)	1	1	1
MAS123/2	" " " "	6	6	6
SL8/3	" " bolt $\frac{1}{4}$" B.S.F. × $\frac{9}{16}$"	1	1	1
SL8/29	" " bolt $\frac{1}{4}$" B.S.F. × $\frac{3}{4}$"	1	1	1
SL8/7	" " bolt $\frac{1}{4}$" B.S.F. × $1\frac{1}{4}$"	2	2	2
SL8/14	" " bolt $\frac{1}{4}$" B.S.F. × 1"	4	4	4
SL6/32	" " washer $\frac{1}{4}$"	10	10	10
LE367	" " lock washer $\frac{1}{4}$"	10	10	10

Schedule of Parts Peculiar to Clubman (Mk. II) and Thruxton Models—continued

Front Mudguard Section—continued

Part No.		D	F	H
SL56/4	Front mudguard stay nut $\frac{3}{4}$″ B.S.F.	10	10	10
SL9/1	,, ,, ,, $\frac{5}{16}$″ 26T.P.I.×$\frac{15}{16}$″	1	1	1
LE368	,, ,, ,, lock washer $\frac{5}{16}$″	2	2	2
SL56/6	,, ,, ,, nut $\frac{5}{16}$″ 26 T.P.I.	2	2	2
SL6/30	,, ,, ,, washer $\frac{5}{16}$″	2	2	2
KA145/2	Rear stay fixing bolt washer	2	2	2

Petrol Tank Section

Part No.		D	F	H
KA4/10	Petrol tank filler cap	—	—	1
KA332	Petrol tank filler cap spindle	—	—	1
A353	Petrol tank rubber	—	—	1
KA100/19	Rev. counter cable clip	—	—	1
KA264/4	Rev. counter cable clip sleeve	—	—	1

Float Chamber Fixing Section

Part No.		D	F	H
FA132	Float chamber fixing bracket	—	—	1
SL103/6	,, ,, ,, stud $\frac{5}{16}$″×1$\frac{5}{16}$″	—	—	1
LE368	,, ,, ,, lockwasher $\frac{5}{16}$″	—	—	2
SL56/38	,, ,, ,, nut $\frac{5}{16}$″ B.S.F.	—	—	3
SE43	,, ,, ,, grommet	—	—	1
SL8/1	,, ,, ,, bolt $\frac{1}{4}$″ B.S.F.×$\frac{3}{8}$″	—	—	1
LE367	,, ,, ,, lockwasher $\frac{1}{4}$″	—	—	1
FA133	Float chamber adjustment bracket	—	—	1
SL108/11	,, ,, ,, bolt	—	—	1
SL6/36	,, ,, ,, washer	—	—	2
SL56/4	,, ,, ,, nut $\frac{1}{4}$″ B.S.F.	—	—	3
FA134	Float chamber fixing distance piece	—	—	1
KA264/5	Petrol hose	—	—	1

Schedule of Parts Peculiar to Clubman (Mk. II) and Thruxton Models—*continued*

Part No.			D	F	H
	Rear Mudguard Section				
A15/21	Rear mudguard	..	1	1	1
MAS125/7	Rear mudguard stay assembly	..	1	1	1
SL109/2	,, ,, ,, bolt (front) $\frac{5}{16}''$ B.S.F $\times \frac{7}{8}''$		2	2	2
SL6/40	,, ,, ,, washer $\frac{5}{16}''$ B.S.F.		6	6	6
SL56/38	,, ,, ,, nut $\frac{5}{16}''$ 26 T.P.I.		2	2	2
SL9/18	,, ,, ,, bolt $\frac{5}{16}''$ B.S.F. $\times 2\frac{11}{16}''$		2	2	2
SL6/40	,, ,, ,, washer $\frac{5}{16}''$ B.S.F.		4	4	4
SL56/6	,, ,, ,, nut $\frac{5}{16}''$ 26 T.P.I.		2	2	2
F303	,, ,, ,, distance piece		2	2	2
SL8/3	,, ,, ,, (rear) $\frac{1}{4}''$ B.S.F. $\times \frac{5}{16}''$		2	2	2
LE367	,, ,, ,, lockwasher $\frac{1}{4}''$		2	2	2
SL56/4	,, ,, ,, nut $\frac{1}{4}''$ B.S.F.		2	2	2
LE817	,, ,, ,, rubber sleeve	..	1	1	1
	Electric Horn and Bracket Section				
E21/6	Electric Horn	..	1	1	1
FA139	Horn fixing bracket	..	1	1	1
SL107/12	Horn fixing bracket bolt 2BA $\times \frac{1}{2}''$		2	2	2
LE366	Horn fixing bracket lockwasher $\frac{3}{16}''$		2	2	2
SL56/2	Horn fixing bracket nut $\frac{3}{16}''$		2	2	2
	Exhaust Pipe and Silencer Section				
MAS28/16	Exhaust Pipe	..	1	1	1
MAS28/15	Exhaust pipe .. .. 1967 onwards		—	—	—
SL110/8	Exhaust pipe fixing bolt $\frac{3}{8}''$ B.S.F. $\times 2''$		1	1	1
SL6/48	Exhaust pipe fixing bolt washer—outer $\frac{3}{8}''$		1	1	1
SL6/53	Exhaust pipe fixing bolt washer—inner		1	1	1
SL56/7	Exhaust pipe fixing bolt nut $\frac{3}{8}''$ B.S.F.		1	1	1
FA137	Exhaust pipe fixing bolt distance piece		—	—	1
MAS30/5	Silencer assembly	..	1	1	1
KA142/2	Silencer assembly baffle	..	—	—	1
F298/3	Pillion footrest eyebolt—Right-hand		1	1	1
MAS30/4	Silencer assembly	..	1	1	1

Schedule of Parts Peculiar to Clubman (Mk. II) and Thruxton Models—continued

Handlebar Control Cables and Levers

Part No.		D	F	H
A234/16AS	Throttle control cable assembly	—	—	1
A237/9AS	Air throttle control cable assembly	—	1	1
A125/7AS	Exhaust lifter cable assembly	—	—	1
MAS131/2	Magneto cable assembly	1	1	1
W33/6AS	Front brake cable assembly	1	1	1
A225/3	Handlebar grip	—	—	1
A220/3	Twist grip rubber	—	—	1
KC16/10	Front brake/air control lever	—	—	1
KC16/9	Clutch/Magneto control lever	—	—	1
MAS164	Handlebar assembly—Left-hand	—	—	4
SL108/4	Handlebar assembly clamp bolt $\frac{3}{4}''$ B.S.F. $\times 1\frac{1}{2}''$	—	—	1
MAS165	Handlebar assembly—Right-hand	—	—	4
A291	Handlebar assembly clamp bolt nut	—	2	1
A354	Diplite/Horn switch fixing screw	2	2	2

Speedometer and Rev Counter Section

KA268/17	Speedometer head	1	1	1
KA282/3	Rev counter head	—	—	1
KA285/2	Rev counter gearbox	—	—	1
MAS58/4	Rev counter drive cable assembly	—	—	1

Dual Seat Section

MAS89/10	Dualseat	—	—	1
SL110/12	Dualseat fixing bolt $\frac{3}{8}''$ B.S.F. $\times 1\frac{1}{4}''$	—	—	1
SL6/50	Dualseat fixing bolt washer $\frac{3}{8}''$	—	—	2
SL56/7	Dualseat fixing bolt nut $\frac{3}{8}''$ B.S.F.	—	—	1

Battery Box and Cover Section

MAS162	Battery box and cover assembly	1	1	1
SL108/7	Battery box bolt $\frac{1}{4}''$ B.S.F. $\times 3\frac{3}{8}''$	1	1	1
SL56/4	Battery box bolt nut $\frac{1}{4}''$ B.S.F.	1	1	1
A20	Battery box bolt rubber grommet	1	1	1
LE310/2	Battery fixing bolt strap	1	1	1

Schedule of Parts Peculiar to Clubman (Mk. II) and Thruxton Models—continued

Battery Box and Cover Section—continued

Part No.		D	F	H
SL109/17	Battery box bolt (top) $\frac{5}{16}''$ B.S.F. $\times 3\frac{3}{8}''$	1	1	1
SL6/40	Battery box washer $\frac{5}{16}''$	1	1	1
SL56/38	Battery box nut $\frac{5}{16}''$ B.S.F.	1	1	1
SL9/3	Battery box bolt $\frac{5}{16}''$ 26 T.P.I. $\times \frac{1}{2}''$	2	2	2
SL6/40	Battery box washer $\frac{5}{16}''$	2	2	2
LAS72/3	Battery box cover assembly	1	1	1
LE689	Battery box cover knob	1	1	1
SL6/50	Battery box cover washer	1	1	1
LE669	Battery box cover circlip	1	1	1

Oil Tank and Oil Pipe Group

Part No.		D	F	H
MAS13/6	Oil tank assembly	—	—	1
A20/4	Oil tank fixing grommet	—	—	2
FA121	Oil tank grommet sleeve	—	—	2
FA138	Oil tank breather hose—engine to oil tank (21.375″)	—	—	1
FA141	Oil tank breather—Oil tank to wheel (27.5″)	—	—	1
MAS163	Oil tank fixing link assembly	—	—	1
LE368	Oil tank fixing link washer $\frac{5}{16}''$	—	—	1
SL56/38	Oil tank fixing link nut $\frac{5}{16}''$ B.S.F.	—	—	1
SL6/43	Oil tank fixing link washer $\frac{5}{16}''$	—	—	1
MAS152/2	Oil return pipe assembly	—	—	1
M214	Oil return pipe hollow bolt	—	—	2
A37/7	Oil return pipe hollow bolt gasket	—	—	3
MAS115/5	Oil feed pipe assembly	—	—	1
SL109/2	Oil tank fixing linkage bolt	—	—	1
SL6/40	Oil tank fixing linkage bolt washer	—	—	1
LE369	Oil tank fixing linkage bolt lockwasher	—	—	1
SL56/38	Oil tank fixing linkage bolt nut $\frac{5}{16}''$ B.S.F.	—	—	1
SL6/53	Oil tank fixing washer $\frac{3}{8}''$	—	—	3
A292/2	Adaptor	—	—	1

Schedule of Parts Peculiar to Clubman (Mk. II) and Thruxton Models—*continued*

GEAR CHANGE AND FOOTBRAKE SECTION
See Illustration "L" Page 75

Ref. No.	Part No. Steel Pedal Assembly	Part No. Alloy Pedal Assembly	Description	D	F	H
1	MAS169	GC4/26	Gearchange pedal assembly	1	1	1
2	MAS171	F39/14	Brake pedal assembly	1	1	1
3	GC42/4	—	Bush brake and gearchange pedal	2	2	2
4	KA46/4	KA46/3	Greaser brake and gearchange pedal	2	2	2
5	GC45/3	GC45/4	Gearchange pedal support	1	1	1
6	LE369	SL6/57	Gearchange pedal support lockwasher	1	1	1
7	SL56/7	SL56/27	Gearchange pedal support nut	1	1	1
8	B60/6	B60/7	Gearchange pedal rubber	1	1	1
9	GC41/7	GC41/8	Gearchange lever (gearbox)	1	1	1
10	SL8/7	SL108/4	Gearchange lever bolt	1	1	1
11	A291	A291	Gearchange lever bolt nut	1	1	1
12	SL31/21	SL30/40	Gearchange rod	1	1	1
13	GC9/4	GC9/5	Gearchange rod yoke end	2	2	2
14	SL56/33	—	Gearchange rod nut $\frac{5}{16}''$	2	2	2
	—	SL56/4	Gearchange rod nut $\frac{1}{4}''$	2	2	2
15	S32/2	S32/3	Gearchange yoke clevis pin	2	2	2
16	SL71/4	SL71/2	Gearchange yoke clevis pin cotter	2	2	2
17	F126/7	BK18	Footrest support—Right-hand	1	1	1
18	SL109/4	SL110/2	Footrest support bolt	2	2	2
19	SL56/38	SL56/7	Footrest support bolt nut	2	2	2
20	F126/8	F126/9	Footrest support—Left-hand	1	1	1
21	LE369	SL6/57	Footrest support washer	2	2	2
22	SL56/7	SL56/27	Footrest support nut	2	2	2
Not shown	B60/5	B60/5	Footrest support rubbers	2	2	2
23	FK167/8	FK167/9	Brake pedal support	1	1	1
24	F130/15	F130/16	Brake pedal support washer	2	2	2
25	LE369	SL6/50	Brake pedal support nut	2	2	2
26	SL56/7	SL56/7	Brake pedal stop pin	1	1	1
27	F196/6	F196/7	Brake pedal stop pin nut	1	1	1
28	FK265	A291	Footrest plate—Left-hand	1	1	1
29	FK220/6	FK220/8	Footrest plate—Right-hand	1	1	1
30	FK220/7	FK220/9	Footrest plate stud (top)	1	1	1
31	FK266	FK266/2		1	1	1

Schedule of Parts Peculiar to Clubman (Mk. II) and Thruxton Models—continued

Gear Change and Footbrake Section—continued

Ref. No.	Part No. Steel Pedal Assembly	Part No. Alloy Pedal Assembly	Description	D	F	H
32	F292/3	F292/4	Footrest plate stud pivot	2	2	2
33	SL6/40	SL6/40	Footrest plate stud washer	1	1	1
Not shown	SL56/38	SL56/38	Footrest plate stud nut	1	1	1
Not shown	SL31/22	SL31/18	Footrest plate stud (bottom)	1	1	1
Not shown	SL6/40	SL6/40	Footrest plate stud washer	2	2	2
Not shown	SL56/6	SL56/38	Footrest plate stud nut	2	2	2
Not shown	MAS41/3	MAS41/3	Brake rod	1	1	1
Not shown	—	SL107/12	Brake pedal stop pin (stoplight switch)	1	1	1
Not shown	—	SL107/11	Stoplight switch bolt } extra	2	2	2
Not shown	—	LE366	Stoplight switch bolt lockwasher } fitting	2	2	2
Not shown	—	SL56/2	Stoplight switch bolt nut	2	2	2

Schedule of Parts Peculiar to Clubman (Mk. II) and Thruxton Models—continued

FRONT BRAKE SECTION

Early Type Quote Engine No.	Later Type Quote Engine No.	Description	D	F	H
MAS71/3	MAS71/4	Front brake plate assembly	1	1	1
W38/7	MAS76/2	Front brake cam assembly	2	2	2
SL6/50	FB60	Front brake cam washer	2	2	2
W12/4	W12/2	Front brake cam felt washer	2	2	2
—	LE368	Front brake cam lockwasher	2	2	2
SL56/8	SL56/6	Front brake cam nut	1	1	1
FB11/6	FB11/8	Front brake cam lever (top)	1	1	1
FB11/7	FB11/9	Froht brake cam lever (bottom)	1	1	1
SL31/20	SL30/39	Front brake rod	1	1	1
SL56/33	SL56/4	Front brake rod locknut	2	2	2
GC9/3	GC9/5	Front brake rod yoke end	2	2	2
S32/2	S32/3	Front brake rod yoke clevis pin	2	2	2
SL71/4	SL71/2	Front brake rod yoke split cotter	2	2	2
W12/4	FB61/2	Front brake rod yoke felt washer	2	2	1
MAS72/3	MAS72/4	Front brake plate (bushed)	1	1	1
W71/3	LE377	Front brake plate bush	4	4	4
W52/3	W52/3	Front brake plate distance piece	1	1	1
KS81	—	Front brake plate air duct	1	1	1
—	KS85	Front brake plate air duct	4	4	4
KS82	—	Front brake plate gauze	4	4	4
MAS74/3	KA314/3	Front brake plate gauze rivet	4	4	4
KS16/4	MAS74/4	Front brake plate air duct screw	2	2	2
KS19/6	KS16/2	Front brake shoe	2	2	2
KS31/3	KS19/5	Front brake shoe slipper	2	2	2
—	—	Front brake shoe lining	16	16	16
KS31	KS31	Front brake shoe rivet	14	14	14
KS10/6	W10/7	Front brake shoe fulcrum pin	2	2	2
LE370	SL6/50	Front brake shoe fulcrum washer	2	2	2
SL56/28	SL56/17	Front brake shoe fulcrum nut	2	2	2
S27/3	S27/2	Front brake shoe spring	1	1	1
FB54/2	FB54	Front brake cable shackle	1	1	1
W12/4	—	Front brake cable shackle felt	3	3	3

Schedule of Parts Peculiar to Clubman (Mk. II) and Thruxton Models—*continued*

Front Brake Section—*continued*

Early Type Quote Engine No.	Later Type Quote Engine No.	Description	D	F	H
—	FB61	Front brake cable shackle felt	2	2	2
S32/2	S32	Front brake cable shackle clevis pin	1	1	1
SL71/4	—	Clevis pin split cotter	2	2	2
—	SL71/2	Clevis pin split cotter	1	1	1
KS83	KS83/2	Front brake fulcrum plate	2	2	2
KS84	—	Fulcrum plate socket screw	2	2	2
SL6/27	—	Fulcrum plate socket screw washer	2	2	2

MISCELLANEOUS COMPONENTS NOT ILLUSTRATED BUT FITTED ON LATER MODELS

Note—*Quote Part Numbers when ordering*

Always quote complete engine number and letters

ENGINE AND GEARBOX SECTION

Part No.	Description	A	B	C	D	E	F	G	H	J
MAS29/6	Crankcase assembly	1	1	1	1	1	1	1	1	1
LE333	Crankcase dowel	2	2	2	2	2	2	2	2	2
SL8/21	Crankcase dowel bolt ¼" × 20T 1¾" u/h	1	1	1	1	1	1	1	1	1
B38	Crankcase drain plug	3	3	3	3	3	3	3	3	3
A37-7	Crankcase drain plug gasket	3	3	3	3	3	3	3	3	3
M275	Crankcase vent hose adaptor	1	1	1	1	1	1	1	1	1
M274	Inlet manifold	1	1	1	1	1	1	1	1	1
M180/3	Inlet manifold gasket	—	—	—	—	—	—	—	—	—
M180/4	Carburetter flange gasket	—	—	—	—	—	—	—	1	1
SL103/3	Inlet manifold stud	—	—	—	—	—	—	—	—	—
LE368	Inlet manifold stud washer	—	—	—	—	—	—	—	2	2
SL56/38	Inlet manifold stud nut	—	—	—	—	—	—	—	2	2
SL109/4	Inlet manifold bolt	—	—	—	—	—	—	—	2	2
SL6/40	Inlet manifold bolt washer	—	—	—	—	—	—	—	2	2
M261	Cylinder holding down bolt O ring	4	4	4	4	4	4	4	4	4
SL6/50	Cylinder holding down bolt washer	4	4	4	4	4	4	4	4	4
SL56/7	Cylinder holding down bolt nut	4	4	4	4	4	4	4	4	4
MAS102/2	Push rod cover assembly (non-telescopic)	1	1	1	1	1	1	1	1	1
M209/3	Push rod cover flange	1	1	1	1	1	1	1	1	1
M261/2	Push rod cover O ring	2	2	2	2	2	2	2	2	2
SL102/1	Rocker box stud	2	2	2	2	2	2	2	2	2

MISCELLANEOUS COMPONENTS NOT ILLUSTRATED BUT FITTED TO LATER MODELS

Note—*Quote Part Number when ordering*
Always quote engine number and letters

ENGINE AND GEARBOX SECTION

Part No.	Description	A	B	C	D	E	F	G	H	J
MAS105/2	Clutch chain wheel assembly	1	1	1	1	1	1	1	1	1
KC3/2	Clutch chain wheel	1	1	1	1	1	1	1	1	1
C27/2	Clutch chain wheel ring	1	1	1	1	1	1	1	1	1
C40	Clutch chain wheel bearing	1	1	1	1	1	1	1	1	1
MAS178	Clutch back plate assembly	1	1	1	1	1	1	1	1	1
KC1/2	Clutch back plate	1	1	1	1	1	1	1	1	1
C26/2	Clutch back plate ring	1	1	1	1	1	1	1	1	1

FRAME AND FORK SECTION

Part No.	Description	A	B	C	D	E	F	G	H	J
MAS31/11	Frame assembly	1	1	1	1	1	1	1	1	1
F256-2	*Front fork tube bush	–	–	2	–	–	2	–	2	–
	*Used on Venom Models from Engine No. 6362 and on Thruxton Model from Engine No. 506									
SL110/6	Rear engine plate and bottom gearbox bolt	–	–	–	4	4	4	4	3	4

FRONT WHEEL AND BRAKE SECTION

Part No.	Description	A	B	C	D	E	F	G	H	J
MAS70-3	Front hub shell assembly	1	1	–	–	–	–	–	–	–
A17-11	Front wheel rim	1	1	–	–	–	–	–	–	–
KA18-5	Front wheel spoke—Flange side	18	18	–	–	–	–	–	–	–
KA18-32	Front wheel spoke—Brake side	18	18	–	–	–	–	–	–	–
MAS69-3	Front hub assembly	1	1	–	–	–	–	–	–	–
MAS67-5	Front wheel assembly	1	1	–	–	–	–	–	–	–

MISCELLANEOUS COMPONENTS NOT ILLUSTRATED BUT FITTED TO LATER MODELS

Note—Quote Part Numbers when ordering

Always quote complete engine number and letters

PETROL TANK AND OIL TANK SECTION

Part No.	Description	A	B	C	D	E	F	G	H	J
MAS27-3	Petrol pipe assembly for R930 carburetter	1	1	1	1	–	–	–	–	1
MAS13-7	Oil tank assembly	1	1	1	1	–	–	–	–	1
A296	Oil tank fixing ear plate	1	1	1	1	–	–	–	–	1
FA142	Vent hose pipe—Oil tank to rear wheel	–	1	1	1	–	–	–	–	1
FA138-2	Vent hose pipe—Crankcase to oil tank	1	1	1	1	–	–	–	–	1
KA100-21	Vent hose pipe clip—Rear brake bolt	–	2	2	2	–	–	–	–	1
KA70-7	Petrol tank knee grip	–	–	–	–	–	–	–	–	–

REAR WHEEL AND BRAKE SECTION

Part No.	Description	A	B	C	D	E	F	G	H	J
MAS79-7	Rear wheel assembly—New Speedo drive	1	1	–	–	–	–	–	–	–
MAS79-9	Rear wheel assembly—New speedo drive	–	–	–	–	–	–	1	1	1
MAS79-5	Rear wheel assembly—New speedo drive	–	–	1	1	–	–	–	–	–
MAS79-6	Rear wheel assembly—New speedo drive	–	–	–	–	1	1	–	–	–
MAS82-4	Rear hub assembly	1	1	–	–	–	–	–	–	–
MAS82-5	Rear hub assembly	–	–	1	1	–	–	–	–	–
MAS82-6	Rear hub assembly	–	–	–	–	1	1	1	1	1
MAS83-3	Rear hub shell assembly	1	1	1	1	–	–	–	–	–
MAS83-4	Rear hub shell assembly	–	–	–	–	1	1	1	1	1
KS61-3	Rear hub retaining ring	1	1	1	1	–	–	–	–	–
KS61-4	Rear hub retaining ring	–	–	–	–	1	1	1	1	1
KS62-4	Rear hub clamping sleeve	1	1	1	1	–	–	–	–	–
KS62-5	Rear hub clamping sleeve	–	–	–	–	1	1	1	1	1
KS52-5	Rear wheel distance piece	1	1	1	1	–	–	–	–	–
KS52-6	Rear wheel distance piece	–	–	–	–	1	1	1	1	1
KA272-3	Speedometer gearbox	1	1	1	1	–	–	–	–	–
A17-11	Rear wheel rim	1	1	–	–	–	–	–	–	–
KA18-32	Rear wheel spoke	36	36	–	–	–	–	–	–	–

MISCELLANEOUS COMPONENTS NOT ILLUSTRATED BUT FITTED ON LATER MODELS FOR AMERICAN MARKET

Note—*Quote Part Numbers when Ordering*
Always quote complete Engine Number and letters

Part No.	Description	A	B	C	D	E	F	G	H	J
MAS129/2	Footrest hanger L.H. —Knock-up type	—	—	—	—	1	—	1	1	1
MAS128/3	Footrest hanger R.H. —Knock-up type	—	—	—	—	1	—	1	1	1
FK23/14	Footrest rod	—	—	—	—	2	—	2	2	2
SL56/27	Footrest rod nut	—	—	—	—	4	—	4	4	4
BK18	Footrest footpiece	—	—	—	—	2	—	2	2	2
SL110/2	Footrest footpiece bolt	—	—	—	—	2	—	2	2	2
SL56/7	Footrest footpiece bolt nut	—	—	—	—	2	—	2	2	2
B60/5	Footrest rubber	—	—	—	—	2	—	2	2	1
MAS8/4	Headlamp bracket assembly—L.H pivoting	1	1	—	1	—	—	—	—	1
MAS9/4	Headlamp bracket assembly—R.H. pivoting	1	1	—	1	—	—	—	—	1
F327/2	Headlamp distance piece—Inner	2	2	—	1	—	1	—	—	2
E67	Headlamp distance piece—Outer	2	2	—	1	—	1	—	—	2
SL9/9	Headlamp fixing bolt	2	2	—	1	—	1	—	—	2
MAS173	Rear lamp plate assembly	1	1	—	1	1	1	—	—	1
LE986	Rear lamp plate assembly screw No. 6 Type Z	1	1	—	1	1	1	—	—	1
KA336	Rear lamp attachment casing	3	3	—	3	3	3	—	3	3
SL107/1	Rear lamp attachment casing pin	3	3	—	3	3	3	—	3	3
LE366	Rear lamp attachment casing lock washer	3	3	—	3	3	3	—	3	3
MAS30/6	Megaphone silencer assembly	—	—	—	—	—	—	—	—	1
FK267	Megaphone silencer heat shield	—	—	—	—	—	—	—	—	—
KA287/2	Megaphone silencer heat shield screw	—	—	—	—	—	—	—	—	2
MAS51/5	Air cleaner assembly	—	—	—	—	1	—	1	—	—
MAS59/5	Air cleaner body assembly	—	—	—	—	1	—	1	—	—
MAS182	Air cleaner cover assembly front	—	—	—	—	—	—	—	—	—
KA314/2	Air cleaner cover screw $\frac{1}{8}'' \times 40T \frac{1}{4}''$ u/h	—	—	—	—	3	—	3	—	—
A361	Air cleaner element	—	—	—	—	2	—	2	—	—
A297/3	Air intake sleeve	—	—	—	—	1	—	1	—	—

ILLUSTRATION L

FOR PART NUMBERS AND DESCRIPTION OF ITEMS SEE PAGES 67 & 68
ORDER BY PART NUMBERS—DO NOT QUOTE ILLUSTRATION REFERENCES

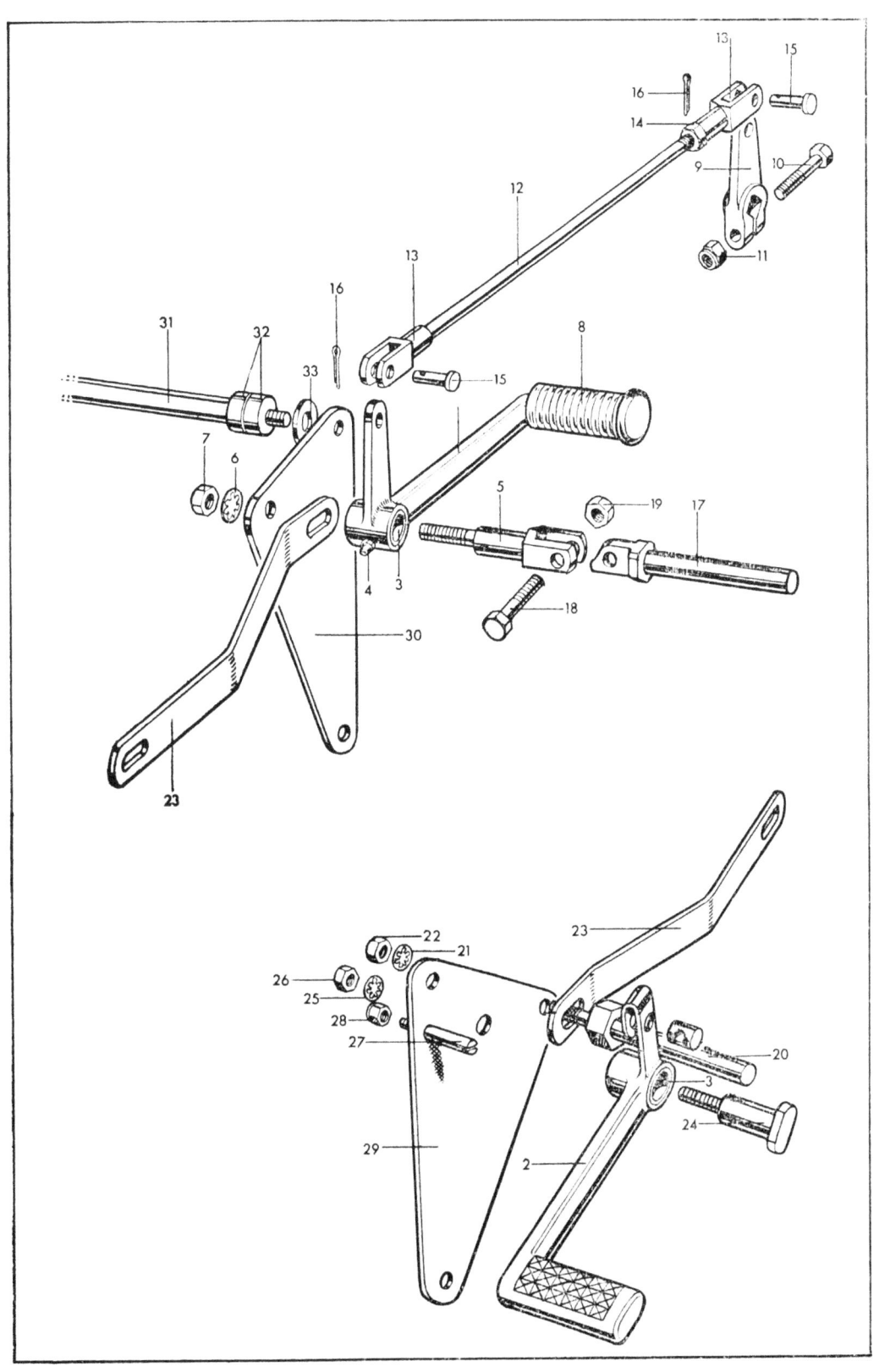

Have you quoted the Engine Number and Prefix Letters on your Order ?

VELOCEPRESS MANUALS – MOTORCYCLE BY MAKE

AJS 1932-1948 SINGLES & TWINS 250cc THRU 1000cc (BOOK OF)
AJS 1945-1960 SINGLES 350cc & 500cc MODELS 16 & 18 (BOOK OF)
AJS 1955-1965 SINGLES 350cc & 500cc (BOOK OF)
AJS 1957-1966 FACTORY WSM - ALL SINGLES & TWINS
ARIEL UP TO 1932 (BOOK OF)
ARIEL 1932-1939 PREWAR MODELS (BOOK OF)
ARIEL 1933-1951 (WORKSHOP MANUAL)
ARIEL 1939-1960 4 STROKE SINGLES (BOOK OF)
ARIEL 1958-1964 LEADER & ARROW (BOOK OF)
BMW R26 R27 (1956-1967) FACTORY WORKSHOP MANUAL
BMW R50 R50S R60 R69S (1955-1969) FACTORY WORKSHOP MANUAL
BRIDGESTONE 90 SERIES FACTORY WSM & PARTS CATALOGUE
BRIDGESTONE 175 SERIES FACTORY WSM & PARTS CATALOGUE
BRIDGESTONE 350 SERIES FACTORY WSM & PARTS CATALOGUES
BSA SERVICE SHEETS MASTER CATALOGUE ALL MODELS 1945-1967
BSA BANTAM D1 TO D7 1948-1966 FACTORY SERVICE SHEETS MANUAL
BSA BANTAM ALL MODELS FROM 1948 ONWARDS (BOOK OF)
BSA DANDY FACTORY WORKSHOP MANUAL (COMPILATION)
BSA SINGLES & V-TWINS UP TO 1927 (BOOK OF)
BSA SINGLES & V-TWINS UP TO 1930 (BOOK OF)
BSA SINGLES & V-TWINS UP TO 1935 (BOOK OF)
BSA SINGLES & V-TWINS 1936-1939 (BOOK OF)
BSA C10, C11 & C12 1945-1958 FACTORY SERVICE SHEETS MANUAL
BSA OHV & SV SINGLES 250-600cc 1945-1959 (BOOK OF)
BSA C15 & B40 1958-1967 FACTORY SERVICE SHEETS MANUAL
BSA OHV & SV SINGLES 250cc (ONLY) 1954-1970 (BOOK OF)
BSA B31, B32, B33 & B34 1945-60 FACTORY SERVICE SHEETS MANUAL
BSA OHV SINGLES 350 & 500cc 1955-1967 (BOOK OF)
BSA M20, M21 & M33 1945-1963 FACTORY SERVICE SHEETS MANUAL
BSA TWINS A7 & A10 1948-1962 FACTORY SERVICE SHEETS MANUAL
BSA TWINS A7 & A10 1948-1962 (BOOK OF)
BSA TWINS A50 & A65 1962-1965 FACTORY WORKSHOP MANUAL
BSA A50 & A65 1962-1969 (SECOND BOOK OF)
DOUGLAS 1929-1939 PREWAR ALL MODELS (BOOK OF)
DOUGLAS 1948-1957 POSTWAR ALL MODELS FACTORY SHOP MANUAL
DUCATI 160cc, 250cc & 350cc OHC MODELS FACTORY SHOP MANUAL
HONDA 50cc ALL MODELS UP TO 1970 INC MONKEY & TRAIL (BOOK OF)
HONDA 90cc ALL MODELS UP TO 1966 (BOOK OF)
HONDA 50-65-70-90cc OHC SINGLES 1959-1983 FACTORY WSM
HONDA 100-125cc SINGLES CB/CD/CL/SL/TL 1970-1984 FACTORY WSM
HONDA 125-150cc TWINS C/CS/CB/CA FACTORY WORKSHOP MANUAL
HONDA 125-160-175-200cc TWINS 1965-1978 WORKSHOP MANUAL
HONDA 250-305cc TWINS C/CS/CB 1959-1967 FACTORY WSM
HOHDA 250-350cc TWINS CB/CL/SL 1968-1973 FACTORY WSM
HONDA 450cc CB/CL 1965-1974 K0 TO K7 WORKSHOP MANUAL
HONDA 750cc SHOC 4 CYL 1969-1978 K0~K8 WORKSHOP MANUAL
HONDA C100 SUPER CUB FACTORY WORKSHOP MANUAL
HONDA C110 SPORT CUB 1962-1969 FACTORY WORKSHOP MANUAL
HONDA TWINS & SINGLES 50cc THRU 305cc 1960-1966 (BOOK OF)
HONDA TWINS ALL MODELS 125cc THRU 450cc UP TO 1968 (BOOK OF)
INDIAN PONYBIKE, BOY RACER & PAPOOSE ILL PARTS LIST & SALES LIT
J.A.P. ENGINES 1927-1952 & MOTORCYCLES 1934-1952 (BOOK OF)
MATCHLESS 1931-1939 ALL MODELS 250cc THRU 990cc (BOOK OF)
MATCHLESS 1945-1956 350 & 500cc SINGLES (BOOK OF)
MATCHLESS 1955-1966 350 & 500cc SINGLES (BOOK OF)
MATCHLESS 1957-1966 FACTORY WSM - ALL SINGLES & TWINS
NEW IMPERIAL ALL SV & OHV FROM 1935 ONWARDS (BOOK OF)
NORTON 1932-1939 PREWAR MODELS (BOOK OF)
NORTON 1932-1947 (BOOK OF)
NORTON 1938-1956 (BOOK OF)
NORTON 1955-1963 MODELS 19, 50 & ES2 (BOOK OF)
NORTON 1955-1965 DOMINATOR TWINS (BOOK OF)
NORTON 1960-1970 TWIN CYLINDER FACTORY WORKSHOP MANUAL
NORTON 1970-1975 COMMANDO 850 & 750cc FACTORY WSM
NORTON 1975-1978 MK 3 COMMANDO 850 cc FACTORY WSM
PANTHER 1932-1958 LIGHTWEIGHT MODELS 250 & 350cc (BOOK OF)
PANTHER 1938-1966 HEAVYWEIGHT MODELS 600 & 650cc (BOOK OF)
RALEIGH MOTORCYCLES 1919-1933 (BOOK OF)
ROYAL ENFIELD 1934-1946 SINGLES & V TWINS (BOOK OF)
ROYAL ENFIELD 1937-1953 SINGLES & V TWINS (BOOK OF)
ROYAL ENFIELD 1946-1962 SINGLES (BOOK OF)
ROYAL ENFIELD 1958-1966 250cc & 350cc SINGLES (SECOND BOOK OF)
ROYAL ENFIELD 1962-1970 INTERCEPTOR WSM'S & PARTS (Compilation)
RUDGE 1933-1939 (BOOK OF)
SUNBEAM 1928-1939 (BOOK OF)
SUNBEAM 1946-1957 S7 & S8 (BOOK OF)
SUZUKI 50cc & 80cc UP TO 1966 (BOOK OF)
SUZUKI T10 1963-1967 FACTORY WORKSHOP MANUAL
SUZUKI T20 & T200 1965-1969 FACTORY WORKSHOP MANUAL
SUZUKI TWINS 1962 ONWARDS 125-500cc WORKSHOP MANUAL
TRIUMPH 1935-1949 SINGLES & TWINS (BOOK OF)
TRIUMPH 1937-1951 (WORKSHOP MANUAL)
TRIUMPH 1945-1955 FACTORY WORKSHOP MANUAL
TRIUMPH 1945-1959 TWINS (BOOK OF)
TRIUMPH 1956-1969 TWINS (BOOK OF)
TRIUMPH 1963-1970 UNIT CONSTRUCTION 650cc FACTORY WSM
TRIUMPH 1963-1974 UNIT CONSTRUCTION 350-500cc FACTORY WSM
TRIUMPH 1968-1974 TRIDENT T150 & T150V FACTORY WSM
VELOCETTE 1925-1970 ALL SINGLES & TWINS (BOOK OF)
VELOCETTE 1954-1971 MSS-VENOM-THRUXTON-VIPER FACTORY WSM
VILLIERS ENGINE UP TO 1959 INC. 3 WHEELERS (BOOK OF)
VILLIERS ENGINE UP TO 1969 (BOOK OF)
VINCENT 1935-1955 (WORKSHOP MANUAL)
YAMAHA 1961-1967 YA5 & YA6 (WORKSHOP MANUAL & ILL PARTS LIST)
YAMAHA 1971-1972 JT1& JT2 (WORKSHOP MANUAL & ILL PARTS LIST)

VELOCEPRESS TECHNICAL BOOKS – MOTORCYCLE

1930'S BRITISH MOTORCYCLE CARBS & ELEC COMPONENTS (BOOK OF)
1930'S BRITISH MOTORCYCLE ENGINES (OVERHAUL & MAINTENANCE)
1930'S BRITISH MOTORCYCLE GEARBOXES & CLUTCHES (BOOK OF)
CATALOG OF BRITISH MOTORCYCLES (1951 MODELS)
LUCAS ELECTRONICS BRITISH M/CYCLES REPAIR & PARTS (1950-1977)
MOTORCYCLE ENGINEERING (P.E. Irving)
MOTORCYCLE ROAD TESTS 1949-1953 (Motor Cycle Magazine UK)
SPEED AND HOW TO OBTAIN IT (Motor Cycle Magazine UK)
TUNING FOR SPEED (P.E. Irving)
WIPAC (COMBO) MANUAL NUMBER 3 + M/CYCLE & SCOOTER MANUAL

VELOCEPRESS MANUALS – SCOOTERS BY MAKE

BSA SUNBEAM SCOOTER WORKSHOP MANUAL 1959-1965
BSA SUNBEAM SCOOTER 1959-1965 (BOOK OF)
LAMBRETTA 1947-1957 ALL 125 & 150cc MODELS (BOOK OF)
LAMBRETTA 1957-1970 LI & TV MODELS (SECOND BOOK OF)
NSU PRIMA 1956-1964 ALL MODELS (BOOK OF)
TRIUMPH TIGRESS SCOOTER WORKSHOP MANUAL 1959-1965
TRIUMPH TIGRESS SCOOTER (BOOK OF)
VESPA 1951-1961 (BOOK OF)
VESPA 1955-1963 125 & 150cc & GS MODELS (SECOND BOOK OF)
VESPA 1955-1968 GS & SS (BOOK OF)
VESPA 1963-1972 90, 125 & 150cc (THIRD BOOK OF)

VELOCEPRESS MANUALS – MOPEDS & MOTORIZED BICYCLES

CYCLEMOTOR (BOOK OF)
NSU QUICKLY 1953-1963 ALL MODELS (BOOK OF)
PUCH MAXI N & S MAINTENANCE & REPAIR (3 MANUAL COMPILATION)
RALEIGH MOPEDS 1960-1969 (BOOK OF)

VELOCEPRESS MANUALS - THREE WHEELER'S

BOND MINICAR THREE WHEELER 1948-1967 (BOOK OF)
BMW ISETTA FACTORY WORKSHOP MANUAL
BSA THREE WHEELER (BOOK OF)
RELIANT REGAL THREE WHEELER 1952-1973 (BOOK OF)
VINTAGE MORGAN THREE WHEELER (BOOK OF)

VELOCEPRESS MANUALS – AUTOMOBILE BY MAKE

ALFA ROMEO GIULIA WORKSHOP MANUAL 1300 TO 2000cc 1962-1975
ALFA ROMEO GIULIA TECH MANUAL CARBURETED CARS FROM 1962
ALFA ROMEO GIULIA TECH MANUAL FUEL INJECTED CARS FROM 1969
ALFA ROMEO GIULIETTA & GIULIA 750 & 101 SERIES 1955-1965 WSM
AUSTIN-HEALEY SPRITE & MG MIDGET WORKSHOP MANUAL 1958-1971
BMW 600 LIMOUSINE FACTORY WORKSHOP MANUAL
BMW 600 LIMOUSINE OWNERS HAND BOOK & SERVICE MANUAL
BMW 2000 & 2002 1966-1976 WORKSHOP MANUAL
CORVAIR 1960-1969 WORKSHOP MANUAL
CORVETTE V8 1955-1962 WORKSHOP MANUAL
FERRARI 250/GT SERVICE & MAINTENANCE MANUAL
FIAT 500 FACTORY WORKSHOP MANUAL 1957-1973
FIAT 600, 600D & MULTIPLA FACTORY WORKSHOP MANUAL 1955-1969
JAGUAR E-TYPE 3.8 & 4.2 SERIES 1 & 2 WORKSHOP MANUAL
JAGUAR MK 7, 8, 9 & XK120, 140, 150 WORKSHOP MANUAL 1948-1961
METROPOLITAN FACTORY WORKSHOP MANUAL
MGA & MGB OWNERS HANDBOOK & WORKSHOP MANUAL
MG MIDGET TC, TD, TF & TF1500 WORKSHOP MANUAL
PORSCHE 356 1948-1965 WORKSHOP MANUAL
PORSCHE 911 2.0, 2.2, 2.4 LITRE 1964-1973 WORKSHOP MANUAL
PORSCHE 911 2.7, 3.0, 3.2 LITRE 1973-1989 WORKSHOP MANUAL
PORSCHE 912 WORKSHOP MANUAL
TRIUMPH TR2, TR3, TR4 1953-1965 WORKSHOP MANUAL
VOLKSWAGEN TRANSPORTER, TRUCKS & WAGONS 1950-1979 WSM
VOLVO 1944-1968 ALL MODELS WORKSHOP MANUAL

VELOCEPRESS TECHNICAL BOOKS - AUTOMOBILE

FERRARI OWNER'S HANDBOOK
HOW TO BUILD A FIBERGLASS CAR
HOW TO BUILD A RACING CAR
HOW TO RESTORE THE MODEL 'A' FORD
MASERATI OWNER'S HANDBOOK
PERFORMANCE TUNING THE SUNBEAM TIGER
SOUPING THE VOLKSWAGEN
SOLEX CARBURETORS (EMPHASIS ON UK & EU AUTOMOBILES)
SU CARBURETORS (EMPHASIS ON UK AUTOMOBILES)
WEBER CARBURETORS (EMPHASIS ON ALFA & FIAT)

VELOCEPRESS BOOKS & GUIDES - AUTOMOBILE

COMPLETE CATALOG OF JAPANESE MOTOR VEHICLES
FERRARI 308 SERIES BUYER'S AND OWNER'S GUIDE
FERRARI BROCHURES AND SALES LITERATURE 1968-1989
FERRARI SERIAL NUMBERS PART I - ODD NUMBERS TO 21399
FERRARI SERIAL NUMBERS PART II - EVEN NUMBERS TO 1050
HENRY'S FABULOUS MODEL "A" FORD
MASERATI BROCHURES AND SALES LITERATURE

VELOCEPRESS BOOKS – RACING

CARRERA PANAMERICANA - MEXICAN ROAD RACE (BOOK OF)
DIALED IN - THE JAN OPPERMAN STORY
VEDA ORR'S NEW REVISED HOT ROD PICTORIAL